Lonely Planet Publications
Melbourne | Oakland | London

D0005759

Brendan Sainsbury

Havana

Sitting pretty near the Castillo de los Tres Santos Reyes Magnos del Morro (p93) at sunset

Habana Cityscapes

Habana is a one-off. Sitting pretty as the Caribbean's largest and most viva-cious city, its romantic atmosphere and infectious energy are the stuff of legend. Where else do you find vintage American cars running off Russian Lada engines, ration shops juxtaposed against gleaming colonial palaces, and revolutionary sloganeering drowned out by all-night parties?

Habaneros (inhabitants of Habana) love their city and it's not difficult to see why. Amid the warm crystalline waters of the sparkling Caribbean, over 500 years of roller-coaster history have conspired to create one of Latin America's most electric and culturally unique societies. The stomp-ing ground for swashbuckling pirates, a heavily fortified slave port for the Spanish and a lucrative gambling capital for the North American Mafia, Habana has survived everything that has been thrown at it and still found time to innovate. At the forefront of modern Latino culture, Habana has spawned salsa and mambo, Havana Club rum and Cohiba cigars, mural painting and Che Guevara iconography… And the list goes on.

But with its crumbling tenements and increasingly traffic-clogged streets, Habana is no conventional beauty. Despite boasting colonial edifices to rival Buenos Aires and a dramatic coastline to match California, the city lacks the jaw-dropping magnificence of Paris or the spectacular physical setting of Rio de Janeiro. Instead, a large part of Habana's attraction lies in the visceral and the abstract. Walk the mildewed neighborhoods of Centro Habana or Vedado and you'll soon pick up the scent – here a mysterious Santería ritual, there a couple of drummers pounding out a rumba beat. The ins and outs are often hard to define and the contradictions endlessly confusing – perhaps this is why Habana's real essence is so difficult to pin down. Plenty of writers have had a try, though; Cuban intellectual Alejo Carpentier nicknamed Habana the 'city of columns,' Federico Lorca de-clared that he had spent the best days of his life there and Graham Greene concluded that Habana was a city where 'anything was possible.'

But thorn or flower, Habana's mesmerizing powers will quickly lure you in. The opportunities to lose yourself in the melee are limitless – take a guided tour around Habana Vieja's enchanting colonial monuments, experience the pizzazz of a late-night cabaret show, stroll along the Ma-lecón (Av de Maceo) as the waves crash over the sidewalk, or admire the skillful reconstruction job on a sleek, streamlined 1956 Cadillac.

Traditional sights aside, Habana's greatest attraction is its earthy authen-ticity. This is no trussed-up tourist resort or cynically concocted amusement park. There are museums here, of course, along with beautifully preserved palaces, top-notch hotels and rather tasty restaurants. But walk a couple of blocks north of leafy Parque Central and you'll suddenly find yourself on the set of a real-life Elia Kazan movie, a dusty 1950s time warp where working-class mothers still go shopping with their hair in rollers and young kids play baseball in the street with sticks and rolled-up balls of plastic.

While 50 years of Socialism have taken their toll on Habana's fragile so-cial and economic fabric, the indomitable spirit of its citizens is a constant source of inspiration. In a society that invented camel buses, stretch Ladas and steaks made from grapefruit skin, survival is second nature and per-sonal sacrifice almost a rite of passage. But how ever much you fall in love with this flawed yet utterly seductive city, capturing it in a sentence will always be a conundrum. 'Habana is very much like a rose,' said Fico Fellove in the movie *The Lost City*, 'it has petals and it has thorns…so it depends on how you grab it. But in the end it always grabs you.'

'Habaneros love their city and it's not difficult to see why. Amid the warm crystalline waters of the sparkling Caribbean, over 500 years of roller-coaster history have conspired to create one of Latin America's most electric and culturally unique societies'

INTERVIEW 1:
A Sense of Community

NAME	Julio Roque
OCCUPATION	Pediatrician
RESIDENCE	Centro Habana

'Habana has a charm that captures the heart of everyone'

Sum up Habana in one sentence. Aside from its architecture and its people, Habana has a charm that captures the heart of everyone. **What defines a habanero?** Their happiness and their cordiality. **How has Habana changed in the last 10 years?** There has been a lot of restoration, mostly in Habana Vieja. Today the city is much more attractive physically, although it has always had an extraordinary atmosphere. **How do you get about the city?** In many ways: by car (I drive a 1990 Russian Moskvich), by bus, by *camello* [metro bus], taxi and bici-taxi [bicycle taxi]. Public transportation is not just a way of getting around, it is also a way of meeting and conversing with other *habaneros*. **What is the best thing about your neighborhood?** Security – everyone shares, helps out and takes care of each other. **Why is the Cuban health system so good?** Above all, because the government totally prioritizes health: Cuban doctors are trained to take care of patients and are able to get good results out of limited resources. The general public is also very supportive of the health system. **Where can the inquisitive traveler find the 'real' Cuba?** On the intersection of the Prado [Paseo de Martí] and Calle Neptuno; from this corner you can see many of the typical Habana tourist sights and also the daily life of average *habaneros*. **How do you rate Habana's baseball chances this season?** First place. In Habana we always say *Industriales Campeón!* [Habana Champions!]

As related to Brendan Sainsbury

Habaneros gather at a dominoes table (p20) to play out a national obsession

4

Make your own list of icons at the Capitolio Nacional (p79) and Centro Gallego (p80)

TOP FIVE ARCHITECTURAL ICONS

Castillo de los Tres Santos Reyes Magnos del Morro (p93) A classic example of Renaissance military architecture.

Edificio Bacardí (p70) A triumph of art deco architecture.

Catedral de San Cristóbal de la Habana (p70) Described by Alejo Carpentier as 'music set in stone.'

Hotel Nacional (p85) A national icon that mixes art deco, neoclassical and neocolonial styles.

Capitolio Nacional (p79) Based on the United States' Capitol Building, the Capitolio is both taller and richer in detail.

A sleek, sexy and oh-so-cool vintage car adds color to a Vedado (p83) street

Classic Cuba: a 1958 Buick Century and Che Guevara

Puttin' on the glitz: a singer dazzles at the Tropicana (p136)

HABANA'S PLAYLIST

Guajiro Natural
Polo Montañez
Llego
Los Van Van
Unicorno
Silvio Rodríguez
Presagíos
Buena Fe
Yo no me Parezco a Nadie
Bambaleo
A Lo Cubano
Las Orishas
Cancionero
Pablo Milanés
Buena Vista Social Club
Ry Cooder & the Buena Vista Social Club
En La Calle
NG La Banda
Me Sube La Fiebre
La Charanga Habanera
Lo Mejor de Lo Mejor
Benny Moré
King of Mambo
Pérez Prado
La Colección Cubana
Irakere and Chucho Valdés
Rumba Caliente
Los Muñequitos de Matanzas
Caliente Caliente
Adalberto y Su Son

The Music's in the Blood

NAME	Regla Yurisán Pentón Hernández
OCCUPATION	Pianist
RESIDENCE	Habana Vieja

Sum up Habana in one sentence. It Is a place where everyone in the world wants to be. **How has Habana changed in the last 10 years?** Thanks to the restoration work of city historian Eusebio Leal, *habaneros* have been able to rediscover their culture. **What, in your opinion, is the finest Cuban cigar and why?** Populares, for their aroma and taste. **What's the best thing about your neighborhood?** The Café de las Infusiones, the place where I play piano. It reopened in August 2006 after being restored by the city historian. **What is your favorite Habana night out?** The Casa de la Música in Galiano [Av de la Italia], Bar Monserate, and Café Paris in Calle Obispo. **Why are Cubans such skillful dancers?** It's a tradition born out of the union between Indians, Spanish and Africans. It's in our blood. If a Cuban can't sing, they dance; if they can't dance, they sing. **How can the inquisitive traveler find the 'real' Cuba?** Get on a *camello*, go to an agropecuario [free-enterprise vegetable market]; visit a school, hospital, theater or cinema; experience a festival; see an exposition of art; or come to Habana on May 1 and witness a parade. **What do people talk about on the Malecón?** They discuss work or school; they talk about their dreams; they drink rum and talk about love.

As related to Brendan Sainsbury

'If a Cuban can't sing, they dance; if they can't dance, they sing'

A heavenly glow fills the Iglesia y Monasterio de San Francisco de Asís (p73)

A Heart-Stopping Caribbean Beauty

NAME	Enrique Nuñez del Valle
OCCUPATION	Paladar owner
RESIDENCE	Centro Habana

'Habana hasn't changed in the last *50* years'

Sum up Habana in one sentence. One of the most beautiful cities in the world. You see it with your heart. **How has Habana changed in the last 10 years?** Habana hasn't changed in the last *50* years. **What, in your opinion, is the finest Cuban cigar and why?** Cohiba Siglo VI. It's strong and it's the perfect size, taking about 60 to 90 minutes to smoke. **How do you get about the city?** In my 1958 American Pontiac automatic that still retains all its original parts. **What is your favorite Habana night out?** The Casa de la Música in Miramar and the Cabaret Turquino, where I used to go when I was a student at Habana University. **How do you rate Habana's baseball chances this season?** Well the Industriales will win, of course. But my dream is that one day they will get to enter the Baseball World Series – and win that too. **What do most foreign visitors want to see?** Habana is a unique city. They want to see the things that make it different. **What is the best thing about your neighborhood?** Centro Habana is the center of Habana's universe. There are many different people and lots of activity. It's like New York. **What do people talk about on the Malecón?** They talk of different things. In Habana the Malecón is often referred to as the 'cabaret of the poor.'

As related to Brendan Sainsbury

White sand and turquoise water – the Playas del Este (p174) are postcard perfect

Contents

Published by Lonely Planet Publications Pty Ltd
ABN 36 005 607 983

Australia Head Office, Locked Bag 1, Footscray,
Victoria 3011, ☎ 03 8379 8000, fax 03 8379 8111,
talk2us@lonelyplanet.com.au

USA 150 Linden St, Oakland, CA 94607,
☎ 510 893 8555, toll free 800 275 0555,
fax 510 893 8572, info@lonelyplanet.com

UK 72–82 Rosebery Ave, Clerkenwell, London,
EC1R 4RW, ☎ 020 7841 9000, fax 020 7841 9001,
go@lonelyplanet.co.uk

The Author

Brendan Sainsbury

Brendan is a British freelance writer based in British Columbia, Canada. In between penning travel stories for the likes of *Africa Geographic* and the *Sydney Morning Herald,* he has hitchhiked across Mozambique, taught English in Thailand, dug latrines in Angola, and worked as an adventure-travel guide in Spain and Morocco.

Brendan first 'discovered' Cuba in 1997 after throwing in a career running health-and-fitness clubs in central London. Fascinated by the country's exotic mix of melodious *trova* (traditional poetic singing) and bombastic Che Guevara iconology, he returned again in 2002 to lead a succession of cultural and cycling trips. He's been coming back ever since, most recently to pen the 4th edition of *Cuba.*

Brendan's Top Habana Day

With the sun rising above the Malecón (Av de Maceo), I start my day pounding the sidewalks, dodging waves and jumping across holes in the paving. One by one I'll pass the early-morning fishermen, the cigar hustlers, the cavorting couples and the remains of last night's spontaneous salsa party. If I'm feeling flush I'll be staying at the Hostal Conde de Villanueva (p159) in Habana Vieja, and I'll return here for a refreshing shower and breakfast in the magnificent courtyard. The morning's the best time to sightsee, so maybe I'll drop into the Museo de la Revolución (p81) or take a peek at the new exhibits in the Museo Nacional de Bellas Artes (p82). Being a lifelong caffeine junkie, I'll certainly grab a midmorning coffee at Café de las Infusiones (p111) and listen to the great resident pianist tinkle the ivories. Lunch is a movable feast, but the overpriced Hemingway places are best avoided at midday so I'll settle instead for an enormous sandwich at Café O'Reilly (p112). Vedado's a good bet in the afternoon, and getting there via the open-air street theater of Centro Habana and the Malecón is half the fun. I've always had a penchant for the art deco Hotel Nacional (p85) and an indescribable fascination for the ice-cream parlor Coppelia (p119); chances are I'll take in both, then spend a couple of hours strolling along Calle 17 and seeing what's on offer in the local agropecuarios (free-enterprise vegetable markets). Dinner's at a Playa paladar (privately owned restaurant) – La Esperanza (p125), preferably, or La Cocina de Lilliam (p125) – and then, of the 1001 options for nighttime entertainment, I'll plump for the Copa Room cabaret (p136) so I can loll around in the lobby of the Hotel Riviera and imagine I'm back in the 1950s.

City Life

City Life

HABANA TODAY

With Fidel Castro edging ever closer to death, Habana and its controversial socio-political system has once again been thrown into the full glare of the international spotlight. But what direction the city will take if (or when) the much hated 46-year US trade embargo is finally lifted is still anyone's guess.

What few people realize is that Habana has been quietly dusting off its communist cobwebs for more than a decade. Aided by a growing medical and pharmaceutical sector and bolstered by closer political and economic ties with Venezuela and Bolivia, Cuba is no longer the economic basket case that it was in the early 1990s. Subtle signs of the new economic buoyancy are everywhere. Check out the greater choice of consumer goods in the city's shops, or the rapidly expanding waistlines of the better-off *habaneros* (inhabitants of Habana) or, most noticeably, the traffic – 10 years ago you could have quite conceivably sat down and had your lunch in the middle of the Malecón (Av de Maceo), Habana's scenic oceanside drive; these days it'll take you a good five minutes to even cross it.

While the huge growth of tourism has brought plenty of economic benefits to Habana's long-suffering and ever patient inhabitants, the presence of more foreigners on the streets of the capital has presented some prickly problems for the city's once unbreakable social fabric. Che Guevara's socialist 'new man' is looking decidedly old hat these days and, among the younger population, the cultural zeitgeist is gradually changing. Added to this is the emergence of an unofficial class system, a direct consequence of the widening income gap that has exploded between those who have access to tourist money and those who don't.

But despite all of these ticklish issues, Habana has lost none of its refreshing uniqueness and little of its exotic charm. The restoration of Unesco–listed Habana Vieja continues apace, Che Guevara still inspires the reverence of a Catholic saint, and commercialization, globalization and anything resembling a McDonald's restaurant is just a glint in the eye of some wheeling-and-dealing Miami-based marketing magnate. Visit while the legacy is still intact.

LOWDOWN

Population 2.3 million

Time zone Pacific Time (GMT minus eight hours)

Bus ticket CUC$0.25–CUC$0.50

Three-star hotel room CUC$60

Cup of coffee CUC$1

No-no Don't buy cigars off the street, they're nearly always substandard or fake

CITY CALENDAR

Like most Latinos, the inhabitants of Habana aren't shy of holding a fiesta, and through revolution and recession the city calendar has always included its fair share of social shindigs. But it's not all rum and rumba. Indeed, many of Habana's annual get-togethers are internationally renowned cultural extravaganzas that draw movers and shakers from around the globe.

JANUARY

LIBERATION DAY

As well as seeing in the New Year with roast pork and a bottle of rum, Cubans celebrate the *triunfo de la revolución* (triumph of the revolution) on January 1, the day in 1959 when Fidel Castro's rebel army finally dislodged the regime of Fulgencio Batista.

FEBRUARY

FERIA INTERNACIONAL DEL LIBRO DE LA HABANA

The International Book Fair was first held in Cuba in the 1930s and has been growing ever since. In Habana, the event is hosted at the Fortaleza de San Carlos de la Cabaña (p93), ExpoCuba (p96) and various bookstores around the capital. Highlights include book presentations, special readings and the prestigious Premio Casa de las Américas, an awards ceremony for outstanding writers of Latin American origin.

APRIL

FESTIVAL INTERNACIONAL DE COROS

Held in even numbered years, the International Choir Festival brings together different choirs from around the world in a series of workshops and performances. Venues include the Teatro Amadeo Roldán (p131) and the Basilica Menor de San Francisco de Asís (p131).

LA HUELLA DE ESPAÑA

An annual festival that showcases various vestiges of Spanish culture in Cuba, the Huella de España includes dance, music, visual arts, poetry and theater. It kicks off at the Gran Teatro de la Habana (p131) in the last week of April.

MAY

CUBADISCO

Far from being Cuba's interpretation of *Saturday Night Fever*, Cubadisco is an annual get-together for record producers and recording companies (both foreign and Cuban) with musical interests on the island. The itinerary includes a trade fair at the Pabexpo conference center, numerous performances and concerts, and a Grammy-style awards ceremony that encompasses every musical genre from chamber music to pop.

LABOR DAY

Hundreds of thousands of flag-waving Cubans converge on the Plaza de la Revolución every May 1 to witness military parades and listen to Fidel Castro make an impassioned speech. It's a fantastic spectacle, even if you're lukewarm about the political polemics.

FESTIVAL INTERNACIONAL DE POESÍA DE LA HABANA

An opportunity for poets from around the world to convene in Cuba as part of an international cultural exchange, this festival is organized by the Unión Nacional des Escritores y Artistas de Cuba (Uneac; National Union of Cuban Writers & Artists) and is held in the glorious Iglesia y Monasterio de San Francisco de Asís (p73) in Habana Vieja.

JUNE

FESTIVAL INTERNACIONAL BOLEROS DE ORO

Organized by Uneac and held in various Habana theaters, the Boleros de Oro was created by Cuban composer and musicologist José Loyola Fernández in 1986. Groups and individuals from as far away as Japan head to Habana to take part in the largest global celebration of the *bolero* (romantic love song).

JULY

COMMEMORATION OF THE ASSAULT OF THE MONCADA GARRISON

On July 26 every year, the Cubans 'celebrate' Fidel Castro's failed 1953 attack on the Moncada Garrison in Santiago de Cuba. The event is a national holiday and – in the days when Castro enjoyed better health – the loquacious leader was famous for making speeches that went for up to four or five hours. Aside from the political rhetoric, Cubans use the holiday as an excuse to eat, drink, dance and generally be merry.

AUGUST

HABANA CARNIVAL

Parades, dancing, music, colorful costumes and striking effigies – the Cubans certainly know how to throw a party. Habana's annual summer shindig might not be as famous as its more rootsy Santiago de Cuba counterpart, but the celebrations and the joyful processions along the Malecón leave plenty of other city carnivals in the shade.

FESTIVAL INTERNACIONAL HABANA HIP-HOP

Organized by the Hermanos Saíz Association, the youth arm of Uneac, the annual Habana Hip-Hop Festival is now well into its second decade. A chance for the island's young musical creators to improvize and swap ideas, the event has its headquarters in the rough Habana suburb of Alamar, where Cuba's nascent rap scene first emerged, and where it still maintains its spiritual home.

SEPTEMBER

FEAST DAY OF THE VIRGIN OF REGLA

Every September 7, religious devotees from around Habana take part in a pilgrimage to the church of Nuestra Señora de Regla on the eastern side of the harbor to honor the saintly Virgin of Regla, a black Madonna associated with the Santería deity of the ocean, and venerated by both Catholics and followers of Santería. An effigy of the saint is removed from its position on the church's main altar and paraded through the neighborhood.

OCTOBER

FESTIVAL INTERNACIONAL DE BALLET DE LA HABANA

Hosted by the Cuban National Ballet and presided over by dance diva Alicia Alonso (p28), the International Habana Ballet Festival brings together dance companies, ballet dancers, and a mixed audience of foreigners and Cubans for a week of expositions, galas, and classical and contemporary ballet. It has been held in even numbered years since its inception in 1960.

NOVEMBER

MARABANA HAVANA MARATHON

The popular Marabana Havana Marathon gets under starter's orders in late November, and draws between two and three thousand competitors from around the globe. The race begins outside the Capitolio Nacional and proceeds along the oceanside Malecón before switching back toward the airport. It is a two-lap course, though there are also races for 5km, 10km and half-marathon distances. The organization of the marathon is consistently excellent and the sense of camaraderie is second to none.

FESTIVAL INTERNACIONAL DE JAZZ

Intrinsically linked to Cuban jazz maestro Chucho Valdés, the International Jazz Festival has been around for nearly a quarter of a century. Staged in the Casa de las Américas (p84), along with the Teatro Karl Marx (p132), Teatro Mella (p132) and Teatro Amadeo Roldán (p131), the event draws top jazz musicians from around the world, resulting in some truly memorable concerts.

DECEMBER

FESTIVAL INTERNACIONAL DEL NUEVO CINE LATINOAMERICANO
www.habanafilmfestival.com

Cubans love the movies, and this internationally renowned film festival, held in cinemas across Habana, helps illustrate Cuba's growing influence in Latin American cinema. In recent years, the event has showcased such classics as *Viva Cuba*.

PROCESSION DE SAN LÁZARO

There can be few pilgrimages more powerful or disturbing than this devotional crawl to the Santuario de San Lázaro, located in Santiago de las Vegas (p97) on the outskirts of Habana. Every year on December 17, up to 50,000 Cubans descend en masse on the venerated shrine of Saint Lazarus to exorcise evil spirits and pay off debts for miracles granted; some devotees crawl on bloodied knees, others drag themselves prostrate across the asphalt, while still others walk barefoot for kilometers through the night.

HOT CONVERSATION TOPICS

Hit the withered streets of Habana on a sun-streaked Saturday evening and – even if you don't speak Spanish – it's easy enough to discern that the ebullient *habaneros* (inhabitants of Habana) are anything but tongue-tied. But aside from the haranguing hustlers who stalk unsuspecting tourists with offers of cheap taxis and knock-off cigars, what are the locals really talking about?

- Baseball – rarely a day goes by without hotly disputed talk of Habana's two baseball teams, Las Industriales and Los Metropolitanos, and their chances of trouncing each other (or the boys from Santiago) in the upcoming game and/or season.
- New appliances – *habaneros* are still busy comparing their new energy efficient electrical appliances (including refrigerators, light fittings and pressure cookers), which were doled out by the Cuban government in 2006 to usher in the Year of the Energy Revolution.
- Fidel's health – love him or hate him, Fidel is hot news in Habana, especially since a 2006 illness brought him a step closer to death.
- Tonight's party – hang around on the Malecón (Av de Maceo) on a Saturday night and the idle chatter will quickly gravitate to talk about what's happening later, how you're going to get there and who's providing the car.
- Luís Posada Carriles – Cuba's Osama bin Laden is still wanted on terrorist charges in Venezuela for blowing up a Cubana de Aviación passenger plane containing 73 people off Barbados in 1976. The story has dominated Cuban news stories since 2005, when Carriles turned up illegally in the US, and throughout 2006 the Cuban government organized a number of demonstrations in Habana demanding the Cuban-born fugitive be extradited (the US courts have yet to oblige).
- La Cara Oculta de la Luna – Cuba's popular government-sponsored soap opera *La Cara Oculta de la Luna* (The Dark Side of the Moon) features gay characters and has been riveting the nation with its controversial discussion of transvestism and AIDS.

CULTURE

Habana's culture is as dynamic as it is distinct, and its influences have spread far beyond the boundaries of the city – there are few people who haven't heard of Fidel Castro, Che Guevara, salsa music, Cohiba cigars, Havana Club rum or mojitos. Other equally unique aspects of Habana culture, such as Santería and the city's eclectic colonial architecture, are less famous internationally but are just as compelling.

IDENTITY

To the vast majority of its two million inhabitants, Habana *is* Cuba, a cosmopolitan and enormously energetic metropolis that makes the rest of this palm-fringed Caribbean archipelago look like a sleepy bucolic backwater. Renowned for their musicality, hospitality, joviality and glowing civic pride, the *habaneros* are survivors, and their gallant dignity and infectious joie de vivre has seen them battle resourcefully through hell, high water and innumerable economic crises.

Cocooned from the outside world by a 45-year trade embargo and spared much of the ugly urban blight that has engulfed many other 21st-century capitals, Habana remains a quirky and old-fashioned city where neighbor still helps neighbor, young kids play baseball in the street, and old men slap down dominos on potholed sidewalks.

Music is the city's lifeblood and it is rare that you'll come across a *habanero* who can't sing or dance. Rootsy rumba began life on the docks of Habana Vieja, the lilting *habanera* first fused smooth French melodies with raw African rhythms in the city's dusty dance halls, and salsa – perhaps Cuba's greatest cultural export – can trace at least a part of its musical metamorphosis to the colorful streets of Cuba's lively capital.

Descended from a colorful mixture of Spanish colonists, African slaves, French émigrés, Chinese immigrants and the odd surviving Taíno (a settled, Arawak-speaking tribe that inhabited much of Cuba prior to the Spanish conquest), the people of Habana are a vibrant and eclectic lot, and their unique blend of blood, brains and brawn has infused Cuban culture with an unusual degree of creativity and adaptability.

HEALTH WITHOUT WEALTH

In the late 1970s, Fidel Castro boldly declared that his fledgling Caribbean nation would become a pioneer in Third World medicine, rub shoulders with the world's economic giants and provide a realistic challenge to the medical power of the US. He was right on all three counts.

Subsequently, under the dark shadow of the US trade embargo, the Cubans – who languish at 156 on the CIA's list of the world's richest nations, in between St Vincent and Georgia – stuck the lion's share of their resources into health care in an attempt to match their northern neighbor on every health-related index from life expectancy to infant mortality rates. Quite remarkably, they succeeded.

With a doctor:patient ratio of 1:170 and a national pool of 30,000 general practitioners who, skillwise, could knock strips off many of their US counterparts, Fidel's health experts have developed a health-care system that is the envy of many of the world's cash-rich democracies.

Achievements are impressive and wide ranging: homegrown treatment for over 15,000 Chernobyl victims, the successful vaccination of 1.5 million Haitian children against measles, the production of the world's first meningitis B vaccine (subsequently licensed by drug multinational GlaxoSmithKline), heart transplants, cancer research and one of the world's lowest AIDS rates.

'Health care is better now because we can do more with less,' piped the understandably smug health minister, Leoncio Padrón, in 1998. It was a timely and pertinent comment. Thanks primarily to the ongoing US embargo (which since 1992 has included emergency food aid and medications), preventative medicine has become a way of life in Cuba. With 21 medical schools training doctors en masse and a family-doctor program placing thousands of qualified health professionals inside every single community in the country, the government has been able to create both legitimacy in the international arena and greater popularity at home.

Habaneros have long displayed an almost inexhaustible ability to bend the rules and 'work things out' when times get tough. In a country where everything is illegal, anything becomes possible. Two of the most popular verbs in the national phrasebook are *conseguir* (to get, to manage) and *resolver* (to resolve, to work out), and the *habaneros* are experts at doing both. In a small nation where monthly salaries top out at around US$20, survival can often mean getting innovative. Cruise the crumbling streets of Habana Centro during the daytime and you'll see people *conseguir*-ing and *resolver*-ing wherever you go. Here's the mechanic wiring a Lada engine underneath the hood of his 1951 Plymouth, and there's the cigar-factory worker selling cast-off Cohibas to foreigners on a side street. One of the most popular ways to make extra cash is to work with – or work over – the tourists.

But it's not all tribulation and trickery. In Habana, sharing is second nature, and helping out your *compañero* (companion) with a lift, a square meal or a few convertibles when they're in trouble is considered a national duty. Check out the way that strangers interact in queues or at transportation intersections and log how the owner of your casa particular (private houses that let out rooms to foreigners) always refers you onto someone else.

In such an egalitarian system, the notion of fairness is often sacred and the social cohesion that characterized the lean years of the *período especial* (special period; p23) still remains loosely intact. One of the most common arguments you'll see in a Cuban street is over queue jumping – a fracas that won't just involve one or two people, but half the neighborhood.

LIFESTYLE

Cuban socialism dances to its own drummer. While on the surface the citizens of Habana might appear open minded, gregarious and devil may care, dip your toe a little deeper and the reality is often a little more contradictory – and Kafka-esque.

Cuban women have been liberated in the sense that they have access to education and training of whatever sort they desire. In fact, women make up 66.4% of the professional and technical workforce, and specific governmental policies such as one year's guaranteed maternity leave and free day care mean it's easier being a mother *and* a career woman in Cuba. But, like everywhere, a glass ceiling still exists in some fields (eg politics), and home-based tasks, such as cooking, child minding and cleaning, are still largely the woman's responsibility. However, the ongoing economic difficulties have meant that Cuban couples since the early 1990s have only had one or – at most – two children, something that is unprecedented elsewhere in the developing world.

The rapid influx of tourists to the island has affected daily life for *habaneros*, with the lucrative carrot of capitalism being dangled in front of their noses, many people, including women, have turned to hustling to get by. While some *jineteras* (women who attach themselves to male foreigners for monetary or material gain) are straight-up prostitutes, others are just getting friendly with foreigners for the perks they provide: a ride in a car, a night out in a fancy disco or a new pair of jeans. Some are after more, others nothing at all. It's a complicated state of affairs and can be especially confusing for male travelers who get swept up in it. It's unusual – though not unheard of – for a Cuban-foreigner relationship not to have at least some kind of economic motivation.

While housing is free, shortages often mean three or even four generations live under the same roof, and with strict property laws there's little scope to move elsewhere. This domestic claustrophobia also cramps budding love lives, and Cubans will tell you that this is the reason the country has one of the world's highest divorce rates. On the flip side, a full house means there's almost always someone to baby-sit, take care of you when you're sick or do the shopping while you're at work. It also accounts for the unusually close-knit nature of Cuban family life, and partly explains why there are few visible signs in Habana of street gangs or teenage delinquency.

Thanks to the tropical climate, much of Cuban life is lived out in the open, and animated conversation and general good neighborliness are all part of the rhythm of the street. Most homes don't have a phone or computer, and internet access is effectively out of bounds to the general populace. Due to a lack of disposable income, keeping up with the Joneses (in Miami) is a pipe dream and most people must be content with filling their houses with furniture that looks as if it's been dragged kicking and screaming from a 1970s bargain basement.

What makes Cuba different from somewhere like Bolivia or Sweden, though, is that the government heavily subsidizes every facet of life, especially culture. Consider the fact that in Habana there are some 200 movie theaters and a ticket costs 2 Cuban pesos (US$0.08) – or that a front-row seat at the Gran Teatro de la Habana costs 10 pesos (US$0.40), rap concerts cost 2 pesos and a patch of cement bench at the ballpark is 1 peso (US$0.04). Now if only there was the transportation to get there. Still, with a set of dominoes or a guitar, a bottle of rum and a group of friends, who needs baseball or the ballet?

FOOD

Overcooked, frazzled and tasteless, Cuban food is invariably portrayed as the revolution's Achilles heel. There's a certain truth in the rumor that the local chicken are born fried and that salad is a euphemism for 'whatever raw thing is available,' but it's not all burnt-to-a-cinder pork chops and congealed microwave pizzas. Indeed, Habana's much maligned restaurants often get an unfairly bad rap. Look no further than Habana Vieja, where many of the city's eager-to-please chefs can be extraordinarily creative, or Vedado and Playa, where the old-fashioned home cooking in privately run paladares is both plentiful and delicious.

The key is to manage your expectations. Don't arrive in Habana assuming that you'll find New York–standard delis or Singapore-style variety. Food culture in Cuba – or the apparent lack of it – is a direct consequence of the country's *período especial* (p23), when meat was a rare luxury and an average Cuban breakfast consisted of sugar mixed with water. As a result, mealtimes in Habana aren't the drawn-out family occasions so common in France or Italy, and people rarely discuss recipes as they might do in Europe or North America. Eating rather is seen as a basic necessity – and a hastily undertaken one – that acts as a prelude to drinking, music, dancing or some other more exciting form of night-time entertainment.

Food in the classier hotels is a different story. If you're headed to the Hotel Nacional (p167) or the Meliá Habana (p170), there will be cranberry-filled crepes for breakfast and at least a dozen types of exotic fruit for lunch. But eating options shrink astronomically as you scoot down the star ratings. Wake up in an old-town hotel and you can expect a standard 'Cuban' breakfast of eggs and fruit; crash at the two-star Hotel Lincoln and you'll be contemplating a bowl of rice pudding, a cup of lukewarm coffee and ham that looks mysteriously like tinned spam.

Popularly known as *comida criolla*, Cuban meals use a base of *congrí* (rice flecked with black beans, sometimes called *moros y cristianos*) and meat, and invariably come garnished with fried plantains and salad. 'Salad' is limited to seasonal ingredients (outside the posh hotels), and consists mostly of tinned green beans, cucumber slices and/or shredded cabbage.

Protein means pork, and you'll become well acquainted with *lomo ahumado* (aromatic smoked loin), *chuletas* (thin juicy fillets), and pork fricassee with peppers and onions. *Filete Uruguayo* is a deep-fried breaded pork cutlet stuffed with ham and cheese.

Chicken is readily available in Habana, though it's often fried to a crisp, while *pescado* (fish) is surprisingly limited for an island nation. Though you'll come across *pargo* (red snapper) and occasionally octopus and crab in some of the specialist seafood places in Playa, you're more likely to see lobster or shrimp *ajillo* (sautéed in oil and garlic) or *enchilado* (in tomato sauce). *Ostiones*, small oysters served with tomato sauce and lime juice, are also popular. The farming of cows is government controlled, so beef products such as steak are sold only in state-run restaurants. Cuban fast-food chains El Rápido and Pollo make McDonalds look like a health-food store and are best avoided.

Yuca (cassava) and *calabaza* (pumpkinlike squash) are served with an insanely addictive sauce called *mojo*, which is made from oil, garlic and bitter orange. Green beans, beets and avocados (June to August) are likely to cross your lips too.

NUEVA COCINA CUBANA

For legions of taste-deprived gastronomes, Cuban cuisine has always been something of an international joke. From the empty-shelf ration shops of Habana Vieja to the depressing ubiquity of soggy cheese-and-ham sandwiches that seem to serve as the country's only viable lunch option, it's a question of less feast, more famine. But while celebrity chefs might still be in short supply in many of Habana's uninspiring government-run restaurants, a whole new pot of tricks is brewing in the suburbs.

Nueva cocina cubana is a loose term used to describe a new awakening in Cuban cooking. Combining fresh, innovative ingredients and exciting new flavors with a traditional Caribbean base, the ideas have their roots in the US and owe a notable debt to celebrated Cuban-American chefs such as Douglas Rodríguez. But the real engine room of this gourmet-led food revolution lies not in the US, but in Habana's small clutch of congenial but vastly underrated paladares (privately run restaurants; p124).

Legalized in 1994, Habana's paladares faced tough times during the dark days of the *período especial* (special period). But by the late 1990s, as tourism increased and food shortages gradually began to ease, some of the restaurants started to use their new private status to experiment and expand. One such innovator was La Guarida (p118), a private paladar housed in a wonderfully eclectic mansion in Centro Habana. Fostering close ties with gastronomic gurus in France, Spain and the US, La Guarida's chefs keenly absorbed international influences and slowly began to fuse traditional Cuban food with more exotic European and North American flavors. The results were as tasty as they were unexpected: tuna infused with sugarcane, chicken in a lemon and honey sauce, and caimanera (a fish indigenous to the Guantánamo region) panfried in onions and white wine. Word of these delicacies spread rapidly and, before long, a roll call of big names was descending on La Guarida: Jack Nicholson, Uma Thurman, Matt Dillon, Queen Sofía of Spain, plus a plethora of US congressmen. Soon it wasn't a question of whether you had been to Habana, but whether you had been to Habana *and* eaten at La Guarida.

Not to be outdone, other paladares quickly starting jumping on the culinary bandwagon. Housed in old grandiose houses in the neighborhoods of Vedado and Playa, places like La Esperanza (p125) and La Cocina de Lilliam (p125) were soon churning out equally delectable dishes, and recipes were being developed and expanded.

Thanks largely to *nueva cocina cubana*, Cuban food has slowly edged itself back into international reckoning, and visitors to the island are increasingly surprised by the quality of the food on offer. Although Habana might still be a long way from becoming the gourmet capital of Latin America (let alone the Caribbean), by most measures that Cuban stereotype of cheap rum and iron rations could soon be confined to gastronomic history.

Few restaurants do breakfast (although pastries are sold at chains such as Pain de Paris, and the 24-hour Pan.com in Miramar does great eggs), so if this is an important meal for you, stock up at a hotel buffet or arrange for your casa particular to provide it. Most casas do huge, hearty breakfasts of eggs, toast, fresh juice, coffee and piles of fruit for CUC$2 to CUC$3.

Habana has some great coffee houses and more are being opened all the time. The Cubans prefer their coffee strong, black and sweet, but most touristy places will have an espresso machine and will be able to rustle you up a *café con leche* (coffee with milk), especially first thing in the morning. However, the Cubans haven't yet cottoned onto coffee 'to go.'

See p110 for restaurant reviews.

RELIGION

Religion in Cuba is a complex and highly misunderstood topic. Though the Cuban state is nominally secular, the people of Cuba are anything but, and while practicing Catholicism may have taken a nosedive since the 'triumph' of the revolution, spirituality is very much alive.

Before the revolution Cuba, like most other Latin American countries, was staunchly Catholic, with 85% of the population pledging allegiance to Rome, though only 10% attended church regularly. Protestants made up most of the rest of the church-going public though, up until 1959, Habana supported a significant Jewish population of over 12,000. Though never officially banned or persecuted under Castro, the Catholic Church came up against two problems once the new Socialist regime was firmly installed in Habana. Firstly many conservative priests, objecting to Fidel's dogmatic leadership style, quickly identified themselves with the counterrevolution and soon fell foul of the ambitious new leader and his supporters. In the early 1960s, 140 Catholic priests were expelled from the island for reactionary political activities and another 400 left voluntarily. Secondly, by proclaiming the revolution as Marxist-Leninist in 1961, Castro – who had himself been educated at a Jesuit school in his youth – embraced atheism, thus making life increasingly difficult for *creyentes* (believers).

Treated as ideological deviants during the hard-line Soviet days of the 1970s and '80s, practicing Catholics were prohibited from joining the Communist Party and unofficially prevented from holding key posts in national or local government. Certain university careers, notably in the humanities, were also off-limits. In short, while religion itself was never technically banned, admitting that you were a believer could seriously damage your career prospects.

Things took a turn for the better after 1992 when the constitution was revised, removing all references to the Cuban state as Marxist-Leninist. Another hatchet was buried in January 1998 when Pope John Paul II visited Cuba and over one million people turned out to see him say Mass in Habana's Plaza de la Revolución (suggesting that many Cubans had been a lot more religious than they'd let on during the '70s and '80s). Recent statistics suggest that there are currently 400,000 Catholics regularly attending mass in Cuba and 300,000 Protestants from 54 denominations. It's not quite on a par with the rest of Latin America, but it's a giant leap of faith since the 1960s.

The religious beliefs of Africans brought to Cuba as slaves in the colonial period have proved to be far more durable than traditional Catholicism. Santería – or Regla de Ocha as it's sometimes known – first took root on the island in the 17th and 18th centuries, when thousands of Yoruba slaves transported from West Africa brought with them a system of animistic beliefs that they hid beneath a Catholic veneer. Over time the slaves began to practice their own form of religious worship, replacing each Catholic saint with an equivalent Yoruba *orisha* (deity).

It's likely there are more followers of the Afro-Cuban religions than practicing Roman Catholics in contemporary Cuba and, although Regla de Ocha is by far the largest group, it is by no means the only strand. Some even contend that Fidel himself is a practicing *santero* (Santería high priest) and the son of the god of destiny, Elegguá, which might account for his ability to cheat death so often.

SPORTS

In Habana, *pelota* (baseball) is the unofficial religion and, with two rival city sides battling it out for honors in the 18-team national baseball league, there's plenty to get worked up about. Habana's most successful team is Las Industriales, closely followed by Los Metropolitanos, although the most intense rivalry is with the outsiders from Santiago de Cuba. An integral part of baseball folklore is the *esquina caliente* (hot corner), a shady spot in Parque Central (p82) where animated, finger-wagging baseball fanatics come to argue and joke with their rivals. The corner is especially entertaining in the postseason, when funereal wreaths and offerings to *orishas* appear for eliminated teams and those still contending.

Boxing is Cuba's second sport and Habana has produced its fair share of pugilistic greats in the past, including Eligio 'Kid Chocolate' Sardiñas and Florentino 'the Ox' Fernández. Ingrained in the national sporting curriculum, boxing is the primary reason why Cuba's Olympic medal haul has rocketed into the stratosphere since the early 1970s. The crowning moment came in 1992, when the Olympic team brought home 14 gold medals and finished fifth in the overall medals table. It's testament to Cuba's high sporting standards that their 11th-place finish in Athens in 2004 was considered something of a national failure.

Basketball, volleyball and soccer (football) are all popular in Cuba, but *dominó* (dominoes) and chess – which are both considered sports – are national passions. José Raúl Capablanca, touted as the greatest natural chess player that ever lived, became world chess champion in 1921, and you'll see chess matches on the street and read about the masters in the sports pages. *Dominó* is everywhere, and you'll see quartets of old men and young bucks slugging back shots of rum and slamming down their tiles in every Cuban neighborhood. In March 2003, Habana hosted the first annual Campeonato Mundial de Dominó (World Domino Championship), with 10 countries and thousands of players participating. The finals were held in Ciudad Deportiva, where Cuba won it all.

CUBA'S OLYMPIANS

Cuba's Olympians are living proof that success at sport is not just about sponsorship, equipment and million-dollar contracts – hunger, passion and a heartfelt desire to succeed are equally important factors when it comes to bagging the top honors.

The country's awesome athletic accomplishments speak for themselves. Floundering as the world's 105th-largest nation and with a GDP on a par with the African state of Angola, Cuba has achieved a level of sporting prowess way out of proportion to its size. Between 1976 and 2000, the island never fell outside the top 10 in the final medals table at the summer Olympics, finishing in fourth position in 1980 with 20 medals, and turning in an even more impressive performance 12 years later in Barcelona when, in the depths of the *período especial* (special period), the Cubans grabbed 31 medals (including an unprecedented 14 golds) to finish fifth.

Here are some of the island's most celebrated Olympic heroes:

- Teófilo Stevenson – arguably Cuba's greatest Olympian, heavyweight boxer Stevenson won three successive gold medals in Munich (1972), Montreal (1976) and Moscow (1980). He could well have gone one further in 1984 if Cuba, following the lead of the USSR, hadn't boycotted the Los Angeles games.
- Félix Savón – another skillful heavyweight boxer, Savón equaled Stevenson's Olympic tally with three successive boxing golds in Barcelona (1992), Atlanta (1996) and Sydney (2000).
- Men's baseball team – with baseball introduced as an Olympic sport in 1992, the Cubans won the first two baseball tournaments (1992 and 1996) and remained unbeaten in the competition until suffering a narrow defeat against the USA in Sydney in 2000. Not to be outdone, they came back four years later to regain the Olympic gold in Athens.
- Women's volleyball team – as indomitable as the men's baseball team, Cuba's female volleyball players won a hat trick of Olympic golds in 1992, 1996 and 2000.
- Alberto Juantorena – at Montreal in 1976, Juantorena became the first athlete to win Olympic golds at both 400m and 800m track events, and he remains the only male runner to have achieved this feat. He set a new world record for the 800m in the process (1:43:50 minutes). In Cuba he is known affectionately as White Lightening or *El Caballo* (the Horse).
- Javier Sotomayor – the current holder of the world high-jump record (2.45m), Sotomayor brought home gold from Barcelona in 1992. He's dominated the sport ever since, recording 17 of the 24 highest jumps in history.

THE FOREIGN PRESS IN CUBA

There are 120 foreign correspondents in Cuba, although the number of regular working journalists is closer to 35. News agencies with offices in the capital include Reuters, Associated Press, CNN and the BBC; two US newspapers, the *Chicago Tribune* and the *Miami Sun Sentinel,* also have offices. Despite rather restrictive working practices, only one agency is currently banned from the island: the German TV and radio network ARD.

Although there is no official censorship in Cuba, all work inside the country is monitored by the state-controlled Centro Prensa Internacional (who must OK all in-country interviews), and the visas and work permits of journalists who fall out of favor with the Cuban authorities are often not renewed. In February 2007, such a fate befell a writer from the *Chicago Tribune* for filing home news stories that were deemed too negative. The previous year a journalist from the *Financial Times* was similarly banished for writing an article that allegedly 'mocked' Fidel.

Cuba is one of the few countries in the world where it is almost impossible to pick up a copy of any Western newspaper or magazine. Even business hotels such as the NH Parque Central and the Meliá Cohiba don't stock copies of popular periodicals such as the *Economist* or *Newsweek.* Apart from the insipid *Granma* or *Juventud Rebelde,* your only real domestic news source is the internet, which is readily available to foreigners, and the TV, which broadcasts international news networks such as CNN, TV5 and TVE in tourist hotels (Cubans technically have access to neither of these sources).

MEDIA

In a country replete with talented writers and lyrical poets, Cuba's gagged media is something of an oxymoron. With only two wafer-thin national newspapers and a central press agency, which keep an asphyxiating hold on every word, thought and feature that is sent to print, Habana's heavily censored news reporters are little more than state-sponsored minions working for the all-pervading, all-encompassing propaganda ministries of the Cuban Communist Party.

The silencing of the press was one of Castro's first political acts on taking power in 1959. Challenged with the crime of speaking out against the revolution, nearly all of Cuba's – and Habana's – once independent newspapers were either closed down or taken over by the state by the summer of 1960. Many freelance operators faced a similar fate. In 1965 Guillermo Cabrera Infante, one of Cuba's most respected writers, left for an ignominious exile in London while, three years later, Castro's former journalistic guru Carlos Franqui – the man who had been responsible for the setting up of rebel newspaper *Revolución* in the Sierra Maestra – earned his own place on the blacklist for speaking out in opposition to the Soviet invasion of Czechoslovakia.

Though art, music and culture are actively encouraged in Cuban society, writers of all genres are set strict limits. Conformists such as national poet Nicolas Guillén enjoy prestige, patronage and a certain amount of artistic freedom, while dissidents – Franqui and Infante to name but two – face oppression, incarceration and the knowledge that their hard-won literary reputation will be quickly airbrushed out of Cuban history.

Although there has been some opening up of press restrictions since the heavy-handed days of the 1970s and '80s, Cuban journalists must still operate inside strict press laws that prohibit antigovernment propaganda, and ban the seemingly innocuous act of 'insulting officials in public' – a crime that carries a three-year jail term.

Habana's two main dailies are *Granma* and the slightly edgier *Juventud Rebelde.* For more information on these and other publications, see p194.

LANGUAGE

Spanish is the language spoken by most Cubans, and some knowledge of it will enhance your stay in Habana exponentially. Despite high levels of literacy and education, the people of Habana, rather like their counterparts in North America and Britain, are linguistically lazy. While you can expect employees in the tourist sector to understand basic English, it's unlikely that the average *habanero* will know his right from his 'write.' The Cubans will appreciate any attempts to converse with them in their own language, and learning some common Spanish words and phrases will definitely open a few doors; see p202.

¿QUE BOLÁ ASERE?

Informal, heavily accented and rich in slang, Cuban Spanish doesn't always match up to the Spanish in your phrase book. Here are a few useful words and phrases to help you get your tongue round the local lingo:

¡Déjame coño! – Get lost!

¿Dígame? – a more formal form of *Dime?*, normally used by someone answering the phone

¿Dime? – literally means 'Tell me,' but often used as a friendly form of greeting

guagua – bus

guajiro – country person; specifically someone from Pinar del Río province

jamaliche – literally 'food junkie;' someone who's always eating

mamay – literally a delicious, fleshy tropical fruit, but used as a superlative for anything good

mango – a pretty woman

melón – money

No es fácil – It ain't easy

palestino – someone from eastern Cuba

pepe – someone from Spain

por la izquierda – attained via the black market

¿Que bolá asere? – How's it going, man?

¿Qué es la mecánica? – What's the process here? (when buying a ticket, renting a car etc)

¿Quién es último? – Who's last? (used when joining a queue to ascertain who's in front of you)

Tranquilo, man – Cool down, man

yuma – someone from the US

Now for the hard part – Cuban Spanish is notoriously difficult to understand and is riddled with colorful slang. Furthermore, Cubans in general – and *habaneros* in particular – often talk incredibly quickly and are in the habit of dropping vital letters from the ends of their words (most commonly the letter 's,' which can be confusing when you're talking in plurals). A plea to *habla más despacio* (speak slower) usually puts them straight.

The Cubans have enriched their language with many of their own words and phrases. Some of these injections come from Afro-Cuban sources (*cabildo* for 'brotherhood' or *batá* for 'drum'), others are a legacy of the original Taíno natives (the word *cohiba* for 'cigar' and *guajiro* for 'country person').

Cuban Spanish is a lot more informal than the Spanish you will encounter in other Latin American countries. In Habana, for instance, it's not unusual for a female shop assistant to address a (younger) male customer as *mi amor* (literally 'my love') and male clients in restaurants to attract the attention of waitresses by calling them *niña* (girl) or *muñeca* (doll). In a similar fashion, the polite *usted* form of address is less widely used here than in, say, Colombia or Bolivia (Cubans generally favor the pronoun '*tu*').

In common with the rest of Latin America, the Cubans use the pronoun *ustedes* for the second-person plural (as opposed to *vosotros*).

ECONOMY & COSTS

Habana is the proverbial engine room of the Cuban economy, and is by far its richest province. As a result, Cubans from all over the island regularly pour into the city in search of work, security and better living conditions. But to assume that Habana's streets are paved with gold would be a gross miscalculation. On the contrary, the city's relative riches are woefully paltry by Western standards, and foreigners flying in from Europe and North America are often struck by Habana's cheap, scruffy houses and general air of decrepitude.

Nearly destroyed during the economic meltdown that followed the collapse of the Soviet Union in the early 1990s, the Cuban economy has defied all logic by its continued survival. Coaxed out of its coma with a three-pronged recovery plan in 1993 that included the legalization of the US dollar (retracted in 2004), the limited opening up of the private sector and the frenzied promotion of the tourist industry, net advances have been slow but steady, with many of the benefits yet to filter down to the average man on the street.

Throwing off its heavy reliance on old staples such as sugar and tobacco, Cuba's economy has spun inexorably toward Latin America, with new trade agreements such as the 2004 Bolivian Alternative of the Americas (ALBA) accords exchanging Cuban medical know-how for Venezuelan oil. Other modern economic mainstays include nickel mining (Cuba is the world's third-largest producer) and pharmaceuticals.

To the surprise of many, Habana isn't a particularly cheap destination, especially since the US dollar was abolished in 2004 (meaning that all tourists must buy convertible pesos, for which they are charged a 10% commission). While there is nothing to stop you wandering off to anywhere you please, the tourist industry has been specifically designed to herd visitors into posh hotels, where they are encouraged to fork out for overpriced souvenirs and bland organized tours. To stay outside of this vacuum, try traveling on public buses, renting a room in a casa particular with kitchen privileges and changing a small amount of money into Cuban pesos *(moneda nacional)*.

If you stay in a casa, eat from street stalls and hang out with the locals, it is possible to get by in Habana on as little as CUC$40 to CUC$50 a day. Hobnob with the tourists in the Hotel Parque Central, however, and you won't see much change from CUC$250 daily.

Cuba has a sometimes confusing double economy where convertibles and Cuban pesos circulate simultaneously. In theory, tourists are only supposed to use convertibles but, in practice, there is nothing to stop you walking into a *cadeca* (change booth) and changing your convertibles into *moneda nacional*. With approximately 29 pesos per convertible, there are a lot of saving possibilities if you are prepared to sacrifice a little (or a lot!) of quality. Alternatively you can just put aside a small amount of Cuban pesos for small daily items such as ice cream, pizzas and bus fares.

HOW MUCH?

Liter of gas CUC$0.95
Liter of bottled water CUC$1
Bottle of Cristal beer CUC$1.50
Souvenir T-shirt CUC$8
Peso pizza CUC$0.25
Cinema ticket CUC$2
Night at the opera CUC$20
Mojito CUC$3
Tropicana cabaret show CUC$70
Music CD CUC$10

SURVIVING THE SPECIAL PERIOD

Following the demise of the Soviet Union in 1991, the Cuban economy went into free fall. Almost overnight, half of the country's industrial factories closed, the transportation sector ground to a halt and the national economy shrunk by as much as 60%.

Determined to defend the revolution at all costs, Castro battened down the hatches and announced that Cuba was entering a 'special period in a time of peace,' creating a package of extreme austerity measures that reinforced widespread rationing and made acute shortages an integral part of everyday life.

It was a decision that quickly resonated throughout all levels of society. Suddenly Cubans, who had been relatively well-off a year or so earlier, faced a massive battle just to survive.

The stories of how ordinary Cubans got through the darkest days of the *período especial* (special period) are as remarkable as they are shocking. Ask any *habanero* (inhabitant of Habana) over the age of 25 about the years 1991 to 1994 and they will invariably furnish you with torrid tales of hunger, hardship and almost unimaginable personal sacrifice. The changes people made to their living conditions during this period were drastic and dramatic: pigs stored in bathrooms, soap made from cow fat, breakfasts consisting of sugar and water, and power outages that lasted for up to 18 hours a day. In three fearsome years, the average Cuban lost over a third of their body weight and saw meat pretty much eradicated from their diet. Insipid food substitutes included 'steaks' cut from grapefruit skins, beans made from royal palm fruit (normally used as animal feed), and tea concocted from various indigenous leaves and herbs.

It is testament to Cuban spirit and ingenuity that the country didn't just survive the *período especial* – it emerged from the crisis with its head held high and its national dignity still intact. Indeed in many respects Cuba's social cohesiveness was actually strengthened by the crisis, creating the kind of stoic wartime resolve that saw the Russians through the siege of Leningrad and the British through the Blitz.

Socially, the *período especial* saw the emergence of a whole new culture of conservation and innovation, and many elements of this communal belt-tightening still mark Habana today. Unique Cuban adaptations from the 1990s include *camellos* (metro buses), paladares (privately owned restaurants), *casas particulares* (private guesthouses that let out rooms to foreigners), organopónicos (urban vegetable gardens), agropecuarios (vegetable markets), peso pizzas, stretch Ladas and *amarillos* (roadside traffic organizers).

GOVERNMENT & POLITICS

Independent Socialist republic or totalitarian one-man dictatorship? That is the question. The true nature of Cuba's unorthodox political system, with its contradictory list of hard-fought successes (health and education) and dismal failures (the media and elections), has long been a matter of some debate. According to the Cuban constitution, the country is 'a Socialist state of workers and peasants and all other manual and intellectual workers,' but in reality, not much happens on this idyllic Caribbean island that hasn't first been heavily scrutinized by the *Líder Máximo* (Maximum Leader) Fidel Castro and his assorted cronies.

Theoretically the Cuban system largely apes the ex–Soviet Union. The constitution of February 1976 provides for a 601-member Asamblea Nacional del Poder Popular (National Assembly of People's Power) that is elected every five years. In 1992 the constitution was amended to allow direct elections by universal suffrage and secret ballot (previously, the National Assembly was elected indirectly by the municipalities). Half of the candidates are nominated by mass organizations, while the other half are chosen by elected municipal delegates from among their ranks.

TOP FIVE POLITICAL BOOKS

- *Fidel: a Portrait*, by Tad Szulc
- *Che Guevara: a Revolutionary Life*, by John Lee Anderson
- *After Fidel*, by Brian Latell
- *Cuba: The Pursuit of Freedom*, by Hugh Thomas
- *Pleasure Island: Tourism and Temptation in Cuba*, by Rosalie Schwartz

The National Assembly elects the 31-member Consejo de Estado (Council of State), which has a president (currently Ricardo Alarcón), a first vice president, five additional vice presidents and a secretary. This body represents the National Assembly between its twice annual meetings, and the Council's president is the head of government and state. The president, in turn, nominates a 44-member Consejo de Ministros (Council of Ministers), which must be confirmed by the National Assembly. The Council of Ministers is the highest-ranking executive body in the country and is headed by Fidel Castro.

Cuban elections have refined the overcomplicated democratic voting system down to a simple universal choice: Communist or Communist. Existing as Cuba's only political party, the Partido Comunista de Cuba (PCC) was formed in October 1965 by merging cadres from the Partido Socialista Popular (the pre-1959 Communist Party founded by Julio Antonio Mella in 1925) and veterans of the guerrilla campaign, including members of M-26-7 (26th of July Movement; Fidel Castro's revolutionary organization) and the Directorio Revolucionario 13 de Marzo. The present party has close to one million members and is led – you've guessed it – by Fidel Castro.

At the local level, each of Cuba's 14 provinces – including Habana – is represented by a provincial assembly known as the Poder Popular (People's Power), an elected administrative body that deals with local issues such as garbage collection, housing and community services. Far more important at ground level are the Comités de Defensa de la Revolución (CDRs), Cuba's most integral mass organization. The CDRs are a type of neighborhood-watch scheme that mixes excellent community work with plenty of neighbor-on-neighbor snooping (to root out dissidents). They have more than seven million members islandwide and there are more than 15,000 committees in Habana alone. You'll see their graffiti plastered everywhere, usually highlighted with the slogan *En Cada Barrio, Revolución* (Revolution in Every Neighborhood).

Fidel Castro's recent illness has once again served to reignite Cuba's succession debate and to fuel further speculation as to whether Cuba's political system can outlive the man who created it. First in line for the country's top job is Fidel's younger brother Raúl (opposite) but, devoid of any personal charisma and lacking his older sibling's extraordinary popularity, it is unlikely that the younger Castro could rule alone. What is more likely is some form of collective government will emerge, propped up by other key figures such as National Assembly president Ricardo Alarcón, economic guru Carlos Lage, and Fidel's ex-personal secretary and current foreign minister Felipe Pérez Roque. Only time will tell.

WHO IS RAÚL CASTRO?

Small, impish and outwardly unassuming, Raúl Castro has always been the living antithesis of the self-confident and more combative Fidel. Biographer Tad Szulc once described him as resembling a 'self-satisfied Spanish grocer,' while other equally critical observers have dismissed him as Fidel's obsequious minion.

But hiding beneath the neatly trimmed moustache and khaki military fatigues of Cuba's little-known leader-in-waiting, the picture is a bit more complex.

Born in Birán, Holguín province, in June 1931, Raúl was a quiet and unremarkable youth who exhibited few academic leanings and even fewer political ambitions. A good head shorter than his robust and ruggedly athletic older brother, the impassive younger Castro instead nurtured a childhood penchant for cockfighting and a lifelong love of Cuban rum (political opponents claim he's a closet alcoholic).

Yielding to Fidel's domineering influence, in his early 20s Raúl attended the 1953 International Youth Conference in Vienna, where he received his first political awakening under the auspices of KGB spy Nikolai Leonov.

It was an important and retrospectively timely conversion. A self-proclaimed communist by the time of the abortive Moncada attack in 1953, Raúl first introduced Fidel to Che Guevara in Mexico City, and – along with Che – became the most vociferous voice in the push for Soviet-style economic reforms in the years that followed.

Promoted to the rank of *comandante* (commander) during the war in the Sierra Maestra, Raúl's transformation from mild-mannered *guajiro* (country person) to cold-blooded revolutionary was as dramatic as it was rapid. Ruthlessly suppressing an easy-going sentimentality, the increasingly radicalized Castro metamorphosed into Raúl the Terrible, a widely feared military commander who meted out summary trials and executions with chilling detachment.

In June 1958 the 27-year-old Raúl made a daring incursion into Guantánamo naval base, where he audaciously kidnapped 50 US and Canadian servicemen in a carefully planned publicity stunt (Fidel promptly ordered the men returned). Six months later, on the eve of the guerrilla victory in Santiago, Raúl purportedly rounded up 70 officers from Batista's army and ordered them shot by a firing squad – an act that cast him as the revolution's bloody Robespierre.

But such reckless acts of political vengeance were quickly brushed underneath the carpet. With the rebel army victorious and the new revolutionary government safely installed in Habana, Fidel proceeded to confer a plethora of titles upon his industrious younger brother, including the offices of vice president, defense minister, general of the armed forces and the second secretary of the Central Committee of the Communist Party.

For critical observers, the appointments were as shrewd as they were nepotistic. Hard working, meticulous and fanatically loyal, Raúl has long been content to play Mark Anthony to Fidel's Julius Caesar, a ploy that has ensured that both brothers have survived for over 45 years with their political authority virtually unchallenged.

A feared radical in the 1960s and '70s, Raúl has become more pragmatic and flexible with age. In the early '90s he advocated limited free market reforms after the breakup of the Soviet Union, and in 2002 he willingly cooperated with US authorities by promising to extradite any Al-Qaeda prisoners who strayed into Cuban territory from Guantánamo naval base.

Away from the political spotlight, Raúl is said to be humorous, charming and dedicated to his family. Married for nearly 50 years to fellow revolutionary Vilma Espin, Raul has four grown-up children, including wayward daughter Mariela, who is the head of the Cuban National Center for Sex Education and a major advocate of gay rights.

Having lived for so long in the shadow of his pugnacious and internationally recognizable older brother, it is difficult to predict how Raúl will react when – or indeed if – he gets his hands permanently on the powers of state. Patient and a little more forgiving than his volatile older sibling, the younger Castro, insiders claim, is a cagey and diplomatic negotiator who does not share his brother's pathological hatred of the US – a factor that could play an important part in reopening dialogue with Cuba's neighbors to the north. But negotiation skills aside, Raúl is still a formidable political survivor and part of one of the most enduring double acts (and sibling rivalries) in modern history. On the basis of this fact alone, the potential King Castro II shouldn't be underestimated.

ENVIRONMENT

THE LAND

Habana is perched strategically on Cuba's northwestern coast, abutting the choppy Atlantic Ocean. One hundred and fifty kilometers to the north lies the US, the country's longtime political nemesis and ideological antagonist, while 200km to the west is the friendlier Spanish-speaking state of Mexico.

Habana's exact location was originally chosen by the Spanish for its excellent natural harbor and, later on, the city was chosen over Santiago de Cuba as the colonial capital due to its favorable position on the North Atlantic trade routes. Heaving Spanish galleons on

PREVENTING CHILD-SEX TOURISM IN HABANA *By ECPAT*

The exploitation of local children by tourists is becoming more prevalent throughout Latin America, including Cuba. Various socioeconomic factors make children susceptible to sexual exploitation, and some tourists choose to take advantage of their vulnerable position. Sexual exploitation has serious, life-long effects on children. It is a crime and a violation of human rights.

Cuba has laws against sexual exploitation of children. Many countries have enacted extraterritorial legislation that allows travelers to be charged as though the exploitation happened in their home country. Responsible travelers can help stop child sex tourism by reporting it. It is important not to ignore suspicious behaviour. You can report the incident to local authorities and if you know the nationality of the perpetrator, report it to their embassy.

ECPAT (End Child Prostitution, Child Pornography and Trafficking of Children for Sexual Purposes) is a global network working on these issues with over 70 affiliate organizations around the world. You can find its website at www.ecpat .org. Beyond Borders is the Canadian affiliate of ECPAT. It aims to advance the rights of children to be free from abuse and exploitation without regard to race, religion, gender or sexual orientation. Its website can be found at www .beyondborders.org.

their way back home to Spain from Mexico and Peru regularly used the city's port facilities to restock their ships and replenish their hardworking crews.

Located on the narrowest point of Cuba's alligator-shaped Isla Grande, Habana's terrain is relatively flat. Within the city, the neighborhood of Vedado, settled in the late 19th century, is the only definably 'hilly' area, with a collection of gentle inclines that culminate in the breezy Loma de las Catalones (where the Plaza de la Revolución is now situated).

Habana is bisected in the west by the Río Almendares, a 45km-long river that rises in Tapaste to the southeast and provides the bulk of the city's water supply. The Habana coastline is rugged and rocky, though further to the east the shore gives way to a 9km stretch of sandy beaches known collectively as Playas del Este.

Habana today exhibits little of the tropical forest that once covered the entire island, though plenty of indigenous royal palms (the country's national symbol) still dot the surrounding countryside.

Boasting a warm tropical climate, the city's weather is tempered by trade winds and, during the winter, cold fronts blow in from the north, causing the temperature to drop at night into the high teens (centigrade). Thanks to its position in the volatile Caribbean hurricane belt, the city is particularly susceptible to strong storms such as Hurricane Wilma, which caused widespread flooding and damage to Centro Habana in October 2005.

GREEN HABANA

Environmentally, Habana presents a perplexing dichotomy. On the one hand, the city is a model for sustainable development, boasting urban gardens, local organic markets, modest consumption levels and one of the lowest people-to-car ratios in Latin America. In October 2006, the WWF even touted Cuba as the 'world's most sustainable country' (on the merit of its high levels of literacy and life expectancy, and low levels of consumption).

On the other side of the coin, Habana suffers from the traditional growing pains of the economically dispossessed. The city's harbor is filthy, the local industry positively asphyxiating, and most of those streamlined 1950s American cars that ply their way so romantically along the Malecón and down Paseo de Martí (Prado) chuck out a ton of unregulated diesel fumes.

But the portents of change are encouraging. Although Cuba essentially first jumped on the world environmental bandwagon because the strictures of the *período especial* meant it had to, recent efforts to bolster national sustainability have been a lot more credible. In early 2006, Fidel Castro announced that the country was entering the Año de la Revolución de Energia (Year of the Energy Revolution). Starting in Pinar del Río province, every household across the country was refitted with energy-efficient lightbulbs, refrigerators and pressure cookers. Similarly, plans are now afoot to phase out many of the country's fume-belching trucks and buses and replace them with cleaner, more modern Chinese models.

Arts

Arts

Far from dampening Habana's artistic heritage, the Cuban revolution actually strengthened it, ridding the city of insipid foreign commercial influences and putting in their place a vital network of art schools, museums, theater groups and writers unions. Indeed, Cuba is one of the few countries in the world where mass global culture has yet to penetrate and where being 'famous' is usually more to do with genuine talent than good looks, luck or the right agent.

Despite the all-pervading influence of the Cuban government in the country's vibrant cultural life, Habana's art world remains surprisingly experimental and varied. Thanks to generous state subsidies over the past 50 years, traditional cultural genres such as Afro-Cuban dance and contemporary ballet have been enthusiastically revisited and revalued, resulting in the international success of leading Cuban dance troupes such as the Habana-based Conjunto Folklórico Nacional (p139) and the Ballet Nacional de Cuba.

Much of Cuba's best art is exhibited in apolitical genres such as pop art and opera, while more cutting-edge issues can be found in movies such as *Fresa y Chocolate*, a film that boldly questioned social mores and pushed homosexuality onto the public agenda.

DANCE & THEATER

Described by aficionados as 'a vertical representation of a horizontal act,' Cuban dancing is famous for its libidinous rhythms and sensuous moves. It comes as no surprise to discover that the country has produced some of the world's most exciting dancers. With an innate musical rhythm at birth and the ability to replicate perfect salsa steps by the age of two or three, Cubans are natural performers who approach dance with a complete lack of self-consciousness – something that leaves most visitors from Europe or North America feeling as if they've got two left feet. Most Cuban dances are connected with a specific genre of music, including rumba and mambo; see p36 for more details.

ALICIA ALONSO

In a country famous for its machismo, it might seem strange that the traditionally graceful art of ballet has risen to a position of such eminence. Yet not only does Cuba possess one of the world's most prestigious ballet companies, it also boasts one of its oldest, greatest and most enduring ballet divas, Alicia Alonso.

Born Alicia Ernestina de la Caridad del Cobre Martnez Hoya in Habana in 1921, Alonso was a child dancing prodigy who relocated to New York in the 1930s to study at the School of American Ballet. Despite suffering from an eye condition that left her partially blind at the age of 19, she quickly became a regular in such illustrious Broadway shows as *Stars in Your Eyes* and *Great Lady*. Married at the age of 15 to fellow dancer Fernando, Alonso's talent ultimately led her to the American Ballet Theater, with whom she traveled to the Soviet Union in the '40s and '50s, where she became the first American representative to dance with the Bolshoi. She returned to Habana in 1948 where, patronized by Cuban president Fulgencio Batista, she founded the Alicia Alonso Ballet Company. But the institution's early days were far from easy and in 1956, after objecting to the gross excesses of Cuba's Mafia-run capital, she moved into exile.

In stark contrast to other disaffected artists, Alonso was lured back to Cuba in 1959, where she set up the Ballet Nacional de Cuba with a gift of US$200,000 from Fidel Castro. A longtime supporter of both Castro and his revolution, her loyalty has been richly rewarded over the years with state funding, professional recognition, and a countrywide network of teachers and schools.

As synonymous with Cuban ballet as Fidel Castro is with facial hair and military fatigues, Alonso regularly scours the country for bright young protégés to star in her prize-winning and widely lauded dance productions, which cover everything from definitive versions of *Giselle* (which she has taken to the Paris Opera) and *Sleeping Beauty* (showcased in Vienna and Milan) to her own compositions.

A veteran of over 50 foreign tours as both a dancer and choreographer, Alonso is now well into her eighties and is nearly blind. Thanks largely to her skill, foresight and lifelong dedication to the art, she has made ballet one of Cuba's most famous and widely respected international exports. It is hard to imagine Cuban dance without her.

ART & THE REVOLUTION

The marriage of art and communism has rarely been harmonious. In the former Soviet Union, outspoken writers such as Alexander Solzhenitsyn were unceremoniously packed off to Siberia for their literary 'indiscretions,' while in communist China the Cultural Revolution put an end to any realistic freedom of thought.

But Cuba, as ever, presents a confusing dichotomy. On the one hand, art on this colorful and highly literate island has been actively encouraged, while on the other, many liberal freethinkers have been repeatedly suppressed.

After coming to power in 1959, Fidel Castro made a decision to level the social playing field within Cuba's already vibrant cultural life, making good art and entertainment available to all. As a result, entry fees to everything from the baseball to the opera were all but eradicated, and huge state subsides were handed out to bodies such as the Ballet Nacional de Cuba and the Instituto Cubano del Arte e Industria Cinematográphicos (Icaic; Cuban Film Institute).

Founded in 1960, the influential Casa de las Américas was delegated with the task of redefining Cuban intellectualism within a post-1959 sociopolitical reality, while the Unión Nacional des Escritores y Artistas de Cuba (Uneac; National Union of Cuban Writers & Artists) initiated a series of heated debates about the future of art within the new 'framework.'

For a brief period, the experiment appeared to work. Far from being ostracized by Western intellectuals, Castro and his poetry-scribbling cohort Che Guevara were viewed as romantic figures in Europe and America, and few left-leaning writers or artists remained impervious to their charm. Indeed, considered an unreliable hothead by his stern-faced allies in the Kremlin, Fidel often preferred to go his own way in the cultural sphere, hobnobbing with literary luminaries such as Jean-Paul Sartre and forming a lifelong friendship with Nobel Prize–winning author Gabriel García Márquez.

But it wasn't all wine and roses. Determined to promote an ethos of 'in the revolution everything, against the revolution nothing,' Castro's artistic judgment became increasingly bellicose in the late '60s and early '70s, when skeptical writers and critics were treated with growing intolerance. With the press effectively silenced by the mid-'60s and criticism of the revolution viewed as treasonable, many leading intellectuals fled into exile (see p21).

Yet, despite the draconian clampdown, Cuba somehow managed to avoid the artistic famine of the Soviet Union and Eastern Europe. Part of the reason for this is the country's high literacy rate (Cubans are avid readers), as well as its already strong tradition of music and dance. The loyalty of key cultural icons such as ballerina Alicia Alonso, poet Nicolás Guillén and writer Alejo Carpentier has also gone a long way in promoting Cuba's artistic image abroad. Finally, there's Fidel, a vociferous reader who, despite an unhealthy dose of political paranoia, has rubbed shoulders with members of the international arts community, including such famous figures as movie director Oliver Stone and media magnate Ted Turner.

Cuba might not yet be a font of intellectual freedom but, within its limits, it has tackled prickly issues such as homosexuality and individual repression, and continues to lead the world in a whole host of colorful cultural genres.

Cuban ballet is synonymous with prima ballerina Alicia Alonso (opposite). Now well past her pointe days, Alicia cofounded the Ballet Nacional de Cuba in 1948 and her choreography is still in heavy use – classic stuff like *Don Quixote* and *Giselle*, with few surprises save for the powerful dancers themselves.

The Festival Internacional de Ballet de la Habana (p14) takes Habana by storm every other year, when you can see a *Swan Lake* matinee and an evening performance of *Carmen* – a ballet junkie's dream.

Original Cuban theater is limited but the Cubans create excellent interpretations of classic foreign works, including the plays of Federico Lorca and the comedies of Shakespeare. Habana's theaters also put on surprisingly edgy (and funny) comedy shows, professional rumba dancing and music performed by the Conjunto Folklórico Nacional de Cuba, and some fantastic children's theater.

For dance and theater performances, see p131 and p131, respectively.

LITERATURE

In a country strewn with icons like rice at a wedding, José Martí (1853–95) is the master. Visionary, patriot and rebel, he was also a literary giant whose collected plays, essays and poetry fill 30 volumes. Exiled before he was 20, Martí lived most of his life outside Cuba. *Versos Sencillos* (Simple Verses) is, as the title proclaims, full of simple verses and is arguably one of his best works. Though written over a century ago, the essays collected in *Nuestra America* (Our America) and *Los Estados Unidos* are remarkably forward thinking, providing a basis for Latin American self-determination in the face of US hegemony.

LITERARY HABANA

Wild, romantic, vivid and sensuous – Habana has long acted as an inspiration to a whole host of expat writers and poets. Here's a quick expose of two of the city's most erudite literary spokesmen.

Ernest Hemingway

Ernest Hemingway's towering literary ghost is plastered all over Habana. The irrepressible Papa – as he was affectionately known – spent most of the 1930s holed up in the pastel pink Hotel Ambos Mundos (p160), where he put the finishing touches to his Spanish civil war classic *For Whom the Bell Tolls* (Fidel's book of choice in the Sierra Maestra) before buying the hillside Finca Vigía, a splendid colonial villa where he lived from 1940 to 1959. The property now hosts the fascinating Museo Hemingway (p97).

Always a sucker for a lunchtime tipple, Hemingway took his daily daiquirí in El Floridita (p134), while copious mint-laced mojitos were downed later on in the bohemian Bodeguita del Medio (p134), adjacent to the Plaza de la Catedral. Unfortunately both establishments have cashed in shamelessly on their Hemingway-once-got-drunk-in-here reputation and the drink prices have been hiked up accordingly (to a hefty CUC$6 a cocktail in the Floridita).

Other must-see Hemingway haunts in Habana include the cheaper and less touristy Dos Hermanos (p133) in Habana Vieja, the Restaurante La Terraza (p127) in the seaside village of Cojímar and the neoclassical Hemingway bust (p95), situated a short walk along the harbor wall in the same neighborhood.

Graham Greene

Conceived as early as 1938, *Our Man in Havana,* Graham Greene's comic take on British espionage in prerevolutionary Cuba, was originally planned to be set in the Soviet-occupied city of Tallinn in Estonia. But with the long shadows of an impending European conflict gathering pace, Greene temporarily shelved the idea and elected to look elsewhere.

It wasn't until after WWII that the author became acquainted with Habana, a loose-living diplomatic outpost that had already seduced such notable literary luminaries as Federico Lorca and Ernest Hemingway.

For Greene, a former MI6 spy and one of the 20th century's best traveled and most insightful writers, it was an opportunity too good to miss. By the early 1950s, Habana had become the Las Vegas of the Caribbean, a disreputable 'city of sin' caught in the dying throes of a malevolent and laughably corrupt dictatorship run by Fulgencio Batista and a clutch of unscrupulous Mafia henchmen.

'Suddenly it struck me that here in this extraordinary city, where every vice was permissible and every trade possible, lay the true background to my comedy,' Greene wrote enthusiastically in his autobiography *Ways of Escape.*

Greene fans can follow the author's literary ghost in the Hotel Sevilla (p80), where Wormold, the book's protagonist, goes for a secret meeting with British agent Hawthorne in Room 501 (a noisy suite next to the lift shaft). Other favorite Greene hangouts include the Hotel Nacional (p85), where Wormold delivers a speech to the European Traders Association, and the Tropicana cabaret (p136), where he takes his daughter Milly for her 17th birthday.

Like Martí, Nicolás Guillén (1902–89) is considered one of Cuba's world-class poets. Ahead of his time, he was one of the first mainstream champions of Afro-Cuban culture, writing rhythmic poems like *Sóngoro Cosongo* (1931). A communist who believed in social and racial equality, Guillén lived in exile during Batista's regime, writing *Elegía a Jesús Menéndez* and *La Paloma de Vuelo Popular: Elegías.* Some of his most famous poems are available in the English collection entitled *New Love Poetry: Elegy.* He returned after the revolution and cofounded the Unión Nacional de Escritores y Artistas Cubanas (Uneac; National Union of Cuban Writers & Artists). Guillén was Cuba's national poet until his death.

Cubans are crazy for poetry, so don't be surprised when someone starts reeling off verses by Dulce María Loynaz (1902–97), recipient of Spain's coveted Miguel de Cervantes award; Eliseo Diego (1920–94), the poet's poet, whose words give wings to the human spirit; or singer-songwriter Silvio Rodríguez (1946–), who is a good guitar player, but a great poet.

In literature, as in poetry, the Cuban bibliography is awe inspiring. Novelist Alejo Carpentier (1904–80) was another exiled writer, returning after the revolution to write *El Recurso del Método* (Resource of the Method) and *Concierto Barroco* (Baroque Concert), both published in 1974. The latter is considered his masterpiece. Habana fans will want to check out his *Ciudad de las Columnas* (City of Columns), which juxtaposes black-and-white photographs of the city's architectural details with insightful prose.

Paradiso by José Lezama Lima (1910–76) was a 'scandalous novel' when it appeared in 1966 because of its erotic homosexual scenes. Now it's considered a classic. Lezama was a poet and essayist who cofounded the influential magazine *Orígenes* in 1944.

Notable writers who left Cuba after the revolution include queer playwright Reinaldo Arenas, whose autobiography *Before Night Falls* (1943–90) was made into a critically acclaimed drama for the silver screen, and Guillermo Cabrera Infante (1929–), whose *Tres Tristes Tigres* (Three Trapped Tigers) describes cultural decadence during the Batista era. Of course, Cuba's most famous foreign writer-in-residence was Ernest Hemingway, who wrote *For Whom the Bell Tolls* in the Hotel Ambos Mundos (p71) in Habana.

PAINTING

Painting and art is alive and well in Habana, despite more than four decades of asphyxiating on-off censorship. From the classical realism of Guillermo Collazo (1850–96) to the futuristic murals of Amelia Peláez (1896–1968), a colorful and broad-ranging artistic pastiche has been painstakingly conserved through arts schools, government sponsorship and an eclectic mix of cross-cultural influences.

Cuba's art legacy goes back nearly 200 years to 1818, when the San Alejandro National Academy of Arts was founded in Habana. Established as the second-oldest academy of its type in Latin America, the institute had as its first director French painter Jean Baptiste Vermay (1786–1833), the artist responsible for creating the huge historic canvases that decorate the walls of El Templete (p75), a diminutive temple in Habana's Plaza de Armas. Other important 19th-century artists include Miguel Melero (1836–1907) and Esteban Chartrand (1840–83), a Cuban of French descent, both of whom created nostalgic classical landscapes that combined bold European influences with a noticeable Cuban tinge.

The 20th century was a particularly fertile period for Cuban art, with many of San Alejandro's restless academy members rejecting traditional painting ideas and going off on their own to search for new inspiration in Barcelona and Paris. As a result, the decade of the 1920s onwards saw the popularization of many distinct new artistic genres in Cuba, such as cubism, surrealism, pop art, poster art and mural painting.

Cuba's most influential artist of this period was Wifredo Lam (1902–82), a painter, sculptor and ceramicist of mixed Chinese, African and Spanish ancestry. Born in Sagua Grande, Villa Clara province, in 1902, Lam studied art and law in Habana before departing for Madrid in 1923 to pursue his artistic ambitions in the fertile fields of post-WWI Europe. Displaced by the Spanish Civil War in 1937, he gravitated toward France, where he became friends with Pablo Picasso and swapped ideas with the pioneering surrealist André Breton. Having absorbed various cubist and surrealist influences, in 1941 Lam returned to Cuba, where he produced his own seminal masterpiece *La Jungla* (The Jungle), considered by critics to be one of the Third World's most emblematic paintings.

By the 1930s modern art in Habana had been consolidated into a national movement known as the Vanguardia, a group of artists who combined traditional *guajiro* (country) and Afro-Cuban influences with Lam's modern primitivism, René Portocarrero's colorful stained glass and the striking murals of Amelia Peláez.

The revolution ushered in an important sea change in the Cuban art world, but local painters have remained shocking, engaging and visceral. Forced into a corner by the constrictions of the Castro shake-up, budding artists have invariably found that by cooperating with the Socialist regime opportunities for training and encouragement are almost unlimited.

In such a volatile creative climate, graphic art – well established in its own right before the revolution – has evolved almost independently of global artistic trends. Poster art exploded in Cuba after the revolution, using a distinctive style of silk-screening known as serigraphy. Recruited by new cultural bodies such as the Instituto Cubano del Arte e Industria Cinematográficos (Icaic; Cuban Film Institute) and the Editoria Politica, artists were sponsored to create informative posters designed to rally the Cuban population behind the huge tasks needed to create a glowing 'new society.' Cuba's most celebrated exponent of poster art in the 1960s was Raúl Martínez (1927–95), who elevated the genre to a high art form with a series of Warhol-like studies of Castro, Che Guevara, José Martí and others.

Street art is one of Habana's most striking and exciting modern styles. Mixing pop art and mural painting with a sprinkling of Afro-Cuban influences, the genre is wonderfully showcased in Habana's Callejón de Hamel (p139), a lurid alleyway full of Santería symbolism and colorful political graffiti that was the brainchild of local artist Salvador González Escalona.

Habana's unique artistic heritage is lovingly preserved in Habana Vieja's Centro Wifredo Lam (p70) and the Instituto Superior de Arte (p91) in outlying Cubanacán. The capital is also blessed with a splendid national art museum, the sprawling Museo Nacional de Bellas Artes (p82).

CINEMA & TELEVISION

The Cubans are crazy about cinema and this passion is reflected in the plethora of movie houses that dot Habana and its suburbs. Since 1959 the film industry has been run by Icaic, headed up by Alfredo Guevara who, along with other influential filmmakers such as Tomás Gutiérrez Alea (1928–96), is widely recognized as putting cutting-edge Cuban cinema on the international map. Indeed, for years cinema has led the way in cultural experimentation and innovation on the island, exploring themes such as homosexuality, misogyny and bureaucratic paranoia, which are generally considered taboo in other parts of Cuban society.

Cuba's first notable postrevolutionary movie, the Cuban-Soviet-made *Soy Cuba* (I am Cuba) dramatized the events leading up to the 1959 revolution in four interconnecting stories. Once described by an American film critic as 'a unique, insane, exhilarating spectacle,' the movie has been consistently lauded by contemporary Hollywood directors such as Martin Scorcese and Francis Ford Coppela for its innovative tracking shots and poetic plot.

Serving his apprenticeship in the 1960s, Cuba's most celebrated director, Tomás Gutiérrez Alea, cut his teeth directing intellectual art-house movies such as *La Muerte de un Burocrata* (Death of a Bureaucrat), a satire on excessive socialist bureaucratization, and *Memorias de Subdesarrollo* (Memories of Underdevelopment), the story of a Cuban intellectual who is too idealistic for Miami yet too decadent for the austere life of Habana. Teaming up with fellow director Juan Carlos Tabío in 1994, Gutiérrez went on to make the Oscar-nominated *Fresa y Chocolate* (Strawberry and Chocolate), the tale of Diego, a skeptical homosexual who falls in love with a heterosexual communist militant. It remains Cuba's cinematic pinnacle.

HABANA ON SCREEN

Cuba's photogenic capital has long lured American film directors with an eye for the exotic, but of the countless Hollywood movies that have been made about Habana since 1959, less than a handful have actually been filmed in the city itself. More often than not, frustrated film-location managers – bored by the bureaucracy and anxious not to upset draconian US travel restrictions – have searched for potential Habana substitutes elsewhere.

Alternative locations have ranged from the Caribbean to Europe. In 1974, Francis Ford Coppola filmed Michael Corleone's infamous Habana hotel scene in *The Godfather: Part II* in the El Embajador Hotel in Santo Domingo, while Pierce Brosnan's shaken-not-stirred Habana espionage in the Bond movie *Die Another Day* was recreated in Cádiz, Spain. Other Habana wannabes have included Andy García, who filmed his 2005 epic *The Lost City* in the Dominican Republic; Sydney Pollack, who shot 1990's *Havana* with Robert Redford in Florida and Santo Domingo; and Richard Fleischer, who tackled the truly awful Che Guevara biopic *Che* in Puerto Rico.

Indeed, the only notable Habana-themed films that have sneaked past the censors in the years since the revolution are Carol Reed's 1959 adaptation of Graham Greene's *Our Man in Havana*, deemed by a freshly victorious Castro as an appropriate critique of the Batista regime, and Wim Wenders' astounding 1999 account of Ry Cooder's resurrection of the *Buena Vista Social Club* (though Cooder was ultimately stung with a US$25,000 US Treasury Department fine for 'spending US dollars in Cuba').

For incurable Habana junkies, the best way to see the city re-created in glorious Technicolor is to check out a recent Cuban-made movie with English subtitles. Good contemporary flicks include 2006's Benny Moré biopic *El Benny*, 2005's highly underrated *Viva Cuba* and 1994's Oscar-nominated (and truly brilliant) *Fresa y Chocolate*.

Habana's growing influence in the film culture of the American hemisphere is highlighted at the Festival Internacional del Nuevo Cine Latinoamericano (p14), held every December in Habana. Described alternatively as the ultimate word in Latin American cinema or Cannes without the ass kissing, this annual get-together of critics and filmmakers has been fundamental in showcasing recent Cuban classics such as *Viva Cuba*, a study of class and ideology as seen through the eyes of two children, and *El Benny*, a biopic of mambo king, Benny Moré.

To say that Cubans are cinema buffs would be a massive understatement: the crush of a crowd shattered the glass doors of a movie theater during the 2001 film festival and an adoring mob nearly rioted trying to get into Steven Spielberg's *Minority Report* premier in 2002. If you're headed for a flick, queue early.

Cuban TV has three national channels, no commercials and an obligatory nightly dose of unedited speeches by Fidel Castro (or his stand-in). Elsewhere, educational programming dominates, with Universidad Para Todos offering full university-level courses in everything from astronomy to film editing. The news is a predictable litany of good things Cuba has done (eg big tobacco harvest, sending doctors to Africa) and bad things the US is up to (eg mucking around in the Middle East, big corporations buying influence). *Mesa Redonda* (Round Table) is a nightly 'debate' program where several people sharing the same opinion sit around discussing a topic of national or global importance. *Telenovelas* (soap operas) are a national obsession, and the latest favorite, *La Cara Oculta de la Luna* (The Dark Side of the Moon), has been known to bring the country to a virtual standstill.

Music

Music

In Habana, it is often said that if you can't dance you sing, and if you can't sing you play an instrument – and judging by the rich diversity of talented bands that ply their trade in the bars of Habana Vieja, this rings resoundingly true. Music is a given in this most effervescent of cities. Everywhere you go, rhythms and melodies drift tantalizingly out of buildings, squares, hotels and shops: the sharp beat of a *batá* (conical, two-headed drum) in the Callejón de Hamel, the sudden stab of a trumpet in a rehearsal room off the Gran Teatro, the lazy lilt of a guitar as a busker serenades you on the Malecón (Av de Maceo). 'In Cuba music flows like a river,' wrote Ry Cooder in his sleeve notes for the *Buena Vista Social Club* CD. 'It takes care of you and rebuilds you from the inside out.'

Rich, vibrant, hip gyrating and soulful, Cuban music has long acted as a standard-bearer for the sounds and rhythms emanating from Latin America, and Habana has often been its busiest crossroads. From the crowded and *caliente* (hot) rap clubs of Centro Habana to the glittering cabaret shows of Vedado and Playa, everything from *son,* salsa, rumba, mambo and *chachachá* to *charanga* and *danzón* owe at least a part of their existence to the magical musical dynamism that was first ignited here.

Aside from its obvious Spanish and African roots, Cuban music has called upon a number of other important influences in the process of its development; mixed into an already exotic melting pot are genres from France, the US, Haiti and Jamaica. Conversely Cuban music has also played a key role in developing various melodic styles in other parts of the world. In Spain they called this process *ida y vuelta* (literally 'round trip'), and it is most clearly evident in a style of flamenco called *guajira*. Elsewhere the 'Cuban effect' can be seen in forms as diverse as New Orleans jazz, New York salsa and West African Afrobeat.

FOLKLORE ROOTS

Son, Cuba's instantly recognizable signature music, first emerged from the mountains of the Oriente region in the second half of the 19th century, though the earliest known descriptions of the style go back as far as 1570. Famously described by Cuban ethnologist Fernando Ortiz as 'a love affair between the African drum and the Spanish guitar,' the roots of this eclectic and intricately fused rural music lie in two distinct subgenres: rumba and *danzón*.

While drumming in the North American colonies was ostensibly prohibited, the Spanish were slightly less mean-spirited in the treatment of their African brethren. As a result,

---

THE HABANERA: CUBA'S EARLIEST MUSICAL EXPORT

While the city of Santiago de Cuba lays claim to the lion's share of Cuba's musical heritage, Habana's role in the island's grand cultural dissemination has been just as important. Indeed, the locally concocted *habanera* was one of Cuba's earliest and most influential musical exports. Evolving from the French contredanse, which arrived in Cuba from Haiti in the early 1800s, the *habanera* was a hybrid music style that interwove traditional European dance themes with the more earthy rhythms practiced by imported African slaves. Characterized by their suave romantic melodies and repeated anticipated bass line, *habaneras* created catchy and enduring new dance rhythms that sprouted many different offshoots in the late 19th and early 20th centuries, including the *bolero* (romantic love song), *danzón* (traditional Cuban ballroom dance), Argentinean tango and New Orleans jazz.

Brought back to France via Spain in the 1860s, the *habanera* was popularized by Spanish composer Sebastián Yradier, who wrote the classic song 'La Paloma' after a visit to the island in 1860. Embraced enthusiastically by admirers from England to Italy, the music's influence mushroomed, and before long the style had been incorporated into elegant ballroom dances all over Europe. One of the genre's most celebrated advocates was romantic French composer Georges Bizet who famously 'borrowed' the music's distinctive anticipated bass rhythm for his rousing 'Habanera Aria' in the opera *Carmen* in 1875.

RUMBA

Rumba, Cuba's hypnotic dance music, was first concocted in the dock areas of Habana and Matanzas during the 1890s when ex-slaves began to knock out soulful rhythms on old packing cases in imitation of various African religious rites. As the drumming patterns grew more complex, vocals were added, dances emerged and, before long, the music had grown into a collective form of social expression for all Afro-Cubans.

Spreading in popularity throughout the 1920s and '30s, rumba gradually diverged into three different but related dance formats: *guaguancó*, an overtly sexual dance; *yambú*, a slow couples' dance; and *columbia*, a fast, aggressive male dance often involving fire torches and machetes.

Pitched into Cuba's cultural melting pot, these rootsy yet highly addictive musical variants quickly gained acceptance among a new audience of middle-class whites and, by the 1940s, the music had fused with *son* in a new subgenre called *son montuno* which, in turn, provided the building blocks for salsa.

Indeed, so influential was Cuban rumba by the end of WWII that it transposed itself back into African music, with experimental Congolese artists such as Sam Mangwana and Franco Luambo (of OK Jazz fame) using ebullient Cuban influences to pioneer their own variation on the rumba theme – a genre popularly known as *soukous*.

Raw, expressive and exciting to watch, Cuban rumba is a spontaneous and often informal affair performed by groups of up to a dozen musicians. Conga drums, claves, *palitos* (sticks), *marugas* (iron shakers) and *cajones* (packing cases) lay out the interlocking rhythms while the vocals alternate between a wildly improvising lead singer and an answering *coro* (chorus).

The best place to see and hear authentic rumba in Habana is at the Sábados de Rumba performed by the Conjunto Folklórico Nacional (p139) or at the Callejón de Hamel (p139) in Habana Centro. Slightly further out but equally transfixing are the weekend shows at Las Orishas (p139), a bar-restaurant and performance space in the eastern neighborhood of Guanabacoa.

Cuban slaves were able to preserve and pass on many of their musical traditions via influential Santería *cabildos* (association of tribes), which re-enacted ancient African percussive music on simple *batás* or *chekeres* (gourds covered with beads to form rattles). Performed at annual festivals or on special Catholic saint's days, this rhythmic yet highly textured dance music was offered up as a form of religious worship to the *orishas* (deities).

Over time the ritualistic drumming of Santería evolved into a more complex genre known as rumba (above). Rumba was originally viewed as a lewd and unsophisticated form of entertainment for Afro-Cubans only, but while the music itself sat well outside the cultural mainstream, the dances and rhythms of rumba gradually permeated more accepted forms of popular Cuban music such as *son montuno*.

On the other side of the musical equation sat *danzón*, a refined Cuban dance that had taken Europe by storm at the end of the 19th century. Pioneered by innovative Matanzas bandleader Miguel Failde in the 1880s, the Cuban *danzón* quickly developed its own peculiar syncopated rhythm borrowing heavily from Haitian slave influences and, later on, adding such improbable extras as conga drums and vocalists. By the early 20th century, Cuban *danzón* had evolved from a stately ballroom dance into a jazzed-up free-for-all known alternatively as *charanga, danzonete* or *danzón-chá*.

Welded together, rumba and *danzón* provided the musical backbone for *son,* a distinctive blend of anticipated African rhythms and melodic rustic guitars, over which a singer improvised from a traditional 10-line Spanish poem known as a *décima*.

In its pure form, *son* was played by a sextet consisting of guitar, *tres* (guitar with three sets of double strings), double bass, bongo, and two singers who played maracas and *claves* (sticks that tap out the beat). Arising in the mountains of Cuba's east, the genre's earliest exponents were the legendary Trio Oriental, who stabilized the sextet format in 1912 when they were reborn as the Sexteto Habanero. Another early *sonero* was singer Miguel Matamoros, whose self-penned *son* classics such as 'Son de la Loma' and 'Lagrimas Negras' are still de rigueur among Cuba's musical entertainers.

By the 1930s, the sextet had become a septet with the addition of a trumpet, and exciting new musicians such as blind *tres* player Arsenio Rodríguez – who Harry Belafonte once called the 'father of salsa' – were paving the way for mambo and *chachachá*. See p137 for places to hear *son* in Habana.

MAMBO & CHACHACHÁ

In the '40s and '50s, the *son* bands grew from seven pieces to eight and beyond until they became big bands, boasting full horn and percussion sections that played rumba, *chachachá* and mambo. The reigning mambo king was Benny Moré (below) who, with his sumptuous voice and rocking 40-piece all-Black band, was known as *El Bárbaro del Ritmo* (the Barbarian of Rhythm).

Mambo grew out of *charanga* music, which itself was a derivative of *danzón*. Bolder, brassier and altogether more exciting than its two earlier incarnations, the music was characterized by exuberant trumpet riffs, belting saxophones and regular enthusiastic interjections by the singer (usually in the form of the word *dilo!* or 'say it!'). The style's origins are mired in controversy. Some argue that it was invented by native *habanero* (inhabitant of Habana) Orestes López after he penned a new, rhythmically dexterous number called 'Mambo' in 1938. Others give the credit to Matanzas band leader Pérez Prado, who was the first musician to market his songs under the 'mambo' umbrella in the early 1940s. Whatever the case, mambo had soon spawned the world's first universal dance craze and, from New York to Buenos Aires, people couldn't get enough of its infectious rhythms.

A variation on the mambo theme, the *chachachá* was first performed by Habana-based composer and violinist Enrique Jorrín in 1951 while playing with the Orquesta América. Originally known as 'mambo-rumba,' the music was intended to promote a more basic kind of Cuban dance that less-coordinated North Americans would be able to master, but it was quickly mambo-ized by overenthusiastic dance competitors who kept adding complicated new steps.

BENNY MORÉ

No one singer encapsulates Cuban music more eloquently than Bartolomé 'Benny' Moré, a legendary vocalist and showman who blended African rhythms and Spanish melodies with effortless ease, and successfully mastered every musical genre of his age. Born in the small village of Santa Isabel de las Lajas in Cienfuegos province in 1919, Moré first arrived in Habana in 1936, where he earned a precarious living selling damaged fruit on the streets of Cuba's swinging capital. Saving up enough cash to buy a cheap guitar he graduated to playing and singing in the smoky bars and restaurants of Habana Vieja's tough dockside neighborhood, where he passed the hat and made just enough money to get by.

His first big break came in 1943, when his velvety voice and pitch-perfect delivery won him first prize in a local radio singing competition and landed him a regular job as lead vocalist for a Habana-based mariachi band called the Cauto Quartet.

His meteoric rise was confirmed two years later when, while singing at a regular gig in Habana's El Temple bar, he was spotted by Siro Rodríguez of the famed Trio Matamoros, then Cuba's biggest *son-bolero* band. Rodríguez was so impressed by what he heard and saw that he asked Moré to join the band as lead vocalist for an imminent tour of Mexico.

In the late 1940s, Mexico City was like Hollywood for young Cuban performers and Moré wasted no time in making a name for himself. Staying behind when the rest of the band returned home, he was promptly signed up by RCA records and his fame rapidly spread.

Moré returned to Cuba in 1950 a star, and was quickly baptized the Prince of Mambo and the Barbarian of Rhythm by an adoring public, who claimed him as their own. Never one to rest on his laurels, he kept obsessively busy in the ensuing years, inventing a brand-new hybrid sound called *batanga* and putting together his own 40-piece backing orchestra, the explosive Banda Gigante. Along with the Banda, Moré toured Venezuela, Jamaica, Mexico and the US in 1956–57, culminating in a performance at the 1957 Oscars ceremony. But the singer's real passion was always Cuba, and from Santiago to Cienfuegos his beloved countrymen couldn't get enough of him. Indeed, legend has it that whenever Benny performed in Habana's Centro Gallego, hundreds of people would fill the parks and streets around the Capitolio in the hope of hearing him sing.

With his multitextured voice and signature scale-sliding glissando, Moré's real talent lay in his ability to adapt and seemingly switch genres at will. As comfortable with a tear-jerking *bolero* (romantic love song) as he was with a hipgyrating rumba, Moré could convey tenderness, exuberance, emotion and soul all in the space of five tantalizing minutes. Although he couldn't read music, Moré composed many of his most famous numbers, including 'Bonito y Saboroso' and the big hit 'Que Bueno Baila Usted.' When he died in 1963 of cirrhosis of the liver brought on by a lifelong penchant for rum, over 100,000 people turned up at his funeral. Unsurprisingly, no one in Cuba has yet been able to fill his shoes.

NUEVA TROVA

Cuba's original *trovadores* were old-fashioned traveling minstrels who plied their musical trade across the island in the early part of the 20th century, moving from village to village and city to city with the carefree spirit of perennial gypsies. Armed with simple acoustic guitars and furnished with a seemingly limitless repertoire of soft, lilting rural ballads, early Cuban *trovadores* included Sindo Garay, Nico Saquito and Joseíto Fernández, the man responsible for composing the Cuban blockbuster 'Guantanamera.' As the style developed into the 1960s, new advocates such as Carlos Puebla gave the genre a grittier and more political edge, penning classic songs such as 'Hasta Siempre Comandante,' his romantic if slightly sycophantic ode to Che Guevara.

Nueva trova was very much a product of the revolution and paralleled – though rarely copied – folk music in the US and the emerging *nueva canción* (protest song) scene that was taking shape in Chile and Argentina. Stylistically the music also paid indirect homage to the rich tradition of French chansons (cabaret songs) that had been imported into Cuba via Haiti in the 19th century. Political in nature yet melodic in tone, *nueva trova* first burst forth from the Oriental towns of Manzanillo and Bayamo in the early '70s before being driven outwards and upwards by such illustrious names as Silvio Rodríguez and Pablo Milanés. Highly influential throughout the Spanish-speaking world during the 1960s and '70s, *nueva trova* was often an inspirational source of protest music for the impoverished and downtrodden populations of Latin America, many of whom looked to Cuba for spiritual leadership in an era of corrupt dictatorships and US cultural hegemony. This solidarity is echoed in many of Rodríguez' internationally lauded classics, including 'Canción Urgente para Nicaragua,' which supported the Sandinistas in Nicaragua; 'La Maza,' which supported Salvador Allende in Chile; and 'Canción para mi Soldado,' which supported Cuban soldiers in Angola.

SALSA, TIMBA & JAZZ

Salsa is an umbrella term used to describe a variety of musical genres that emerged out of the fertile Latin New York scene in the '60s and '70s, when jazz, *son* and rumba blended to create a new, brassier sound. While not strictly a product of Cubans living in Cuba, salsa's roots and key influences come from *son montuno* and owe an enormous debt to innovators such as Pérez Prado, Benny Moré and Miguel Matamoros. See p137 for places to hear salsa in Habana.

The self-styled 'queen of salsa' was Grammy-award winning singer and performer Célia Cruz. Born in Habana in 1925, Cruz served the bulk of her musical apprenticeship in Cuba before leaving for self-imposed exile in the US in 1960. But due to her longstanding opposition to the Castro regime, Cruz's records and music have remained largely unknown on the island, despite her enduring legacy elsewhere. Far more influential on their home turf are the legendary salsa outfit Los Van Van, formed by Juan Formell in 1969 and still performing regularly at venues across Habana. With Formell at the helm as the group's great improviser, poet, lyricist and social commentator, Los Van Van are one of the few contemporary Cuban groups to have created their own unique musical genre – that of *songo-salsa*. The band also won top honors in 2000 when they memorably took home a Grammy for their classic album, *Llego Van Van*.

Modern salsa evolved further in the '80s and '90s, allying itself with cutting-edge musical genres such as hip-hop, *reggaeton* (Cuban hip-hop) and rap before coming up with some hot new alternatives, most notably *timba* and *songo-salsa*.

Timba is Cuba's own experimental and fiery take on traditional salsa. Mixing New York sounds with Latin jazz, *nueva trova*, American funk, disco, hip-hop and even some classical influences, the music is more flexible and aggressive than standard salsa, and incorporates greater elements of the island's potent Afro-Cuban culture. Many *timba* bands such as Bambaleo and La Charanga Habanera use funk riffs and rely on less conventional Cuban instruments, including synthesizers and kick drums. Others such as NG La Banda, formed in 1988 (and often credited as being the inventors of *timba*), have infused their music with a more jazzy dynamic.

Traditional jazz, considered the music of the enemy in the revolution's most dogmatic days, has always seeped into Cuban sounds. Jesus 'Chucho' Valdes' band Irakere, formed in 1973, broke the Cuban music scene wide open with its heavy Afro-Cuban drumming laced with jazz and *son,* and Habana now boasts a number of decent jazz clubs (p138). Other musicians associated with the Cuban jazz set include pianist Gonzalo Rubalcaba, Isaac Delgado and Adalberto Álvarez y Su Son.

RAP, REGGAETON & BEYOND

The contemporary Cuban music scene is an interesting mix of enduring traditions, modern sounds, old hands and new blood. With low production costs, solid urban themes and lots of US-inspired crossover styles, hip-hop and rap are taking the younger generation by storm.

Born in the ugly concrete housing projects of Alamar in Habana, Cuban hip-hop, rather like its US counterpart, has gritty and impoverished roots.

First beamed across the nation in the early 1980s when American rap from Miami-based radio stations was picked up on homemade rooftop antennae, the new music quickly gained ground among a population of young urban Blacks, who were culturally redefining themselves during the inquietude of the *período especial* (special period). By the 1990s, music from groups such as Public Enemy and NWA were de rigueur on the streets of Alamar, and in 1995 there was enough local hip-hop talent to throw a festival.

Tempered by Latin influences and censored by the parameters of strict revolutionary thought Cuban hip-hop – or *reggaeton* as locals prefer to call it – has shied away from the US mainstream and taken on a progressive flavor all of its own. Instrumentally the music uses *batás,* congas and electric bass, while lyrically the songs tackle important national issues such as sex tourism and the difficulties of the stagnant Cuban economy.

Despite being viewed early on as subversive and antirevolutionary, Cuban hip-hop has gained unlikely support from inside the Cuban government, whose art-conscious legislators consider the music to have played a constructive social role in shaping the future of Cuban youth. Fidel Castro has gone one further, describing hip-hop as 'the vanguard of the revolution' and – allegedly – once tried his hand at rapping at a Habana baseball game.

Today there are upwards of 800 hip-hop groups in Cuba and the Festival Internacional Habana Hip-Hop (p14) is in its second decade. The event even has a sponsor, the fledgling Cuban Rap Agency, a government body formed in 2002 to give official sanction to the country's burgeoning alternative music scene. Groups to look out for include Obsession, 100% Original, Freehole Negro and Anónimo Consejo, while the best venues are Anfiteatro Parque Almendares (p139) and La Madriguera (p140), both in Vedado.

It's hard to categorize Interactivo, a collaboration of young, talented musicians led by pianist Robertico Carcassés. Part funk, jazz and rock, and very 'in the groove,' this band jams them to the rafters – it's a guaranteed good time. Interactivo's bassist is Yusa, a young Black woman whose eponymous debut album made it clear she's one of the most innovative musicians on the Cuban scene today. Other difficult-to-categorize modern innovators include X Alfonso, an ex-student of the Conservatorio Amadeo Roldán, and dynamic *trova*-rock duo Buena Fé, whose guitar-based riffs and eloquent lyrics push the boundaries of art and expression within the confines of the Cuban revolution.

Meanwhile, back at base camp, US guitar virtuoso Ry Cooder inadvertently breathed new life into *son* music 10 years ago with his remarkable *Buena Vista Social Club* album. Linking together half a dozen or so long-retired musical sages from the '40s and '50s, including 90-year-old Compay Segundo (writer of Cuba's second-most-played song, 'Chan Chan') and pianist Rúben González (ranked by Cooder as the greatest piano player he has ever heard), the American producer sat back in the studio and let his ragged clutch of old-age pensioners work their magic. Over two million albums later, European and North American audiences are still enraptured by their sounds.

Architecture ■

Architecture

Habana is, without doubt, one of the most attractive and architecturally diverse cities in the world. Shaped by a colorful colonial history and embellished by myriad foreign influences from as far afield as Italy and Morocco, the Cuban capital gracefully combines Mudéjar, baroque, neoclassical, art nouveau, art deco and modernist architectural styles into a visually striking whole.

But it's not all sweeping vistas and broad tree-lined boulevards. Habana doesn't have the architectural uniformity of Paris or the instant knock-out appeal of Rome. Indeed, two decades of economic austerity has meant many of the city's finest buildings have been left to fester in an advanced state of dilapidation. Furthermore, attempting to classify Habana's houses, palaces, churches and forts as a single architectural entity is extremely difficult. Cuban building – rather like its music – is unusually diverse. Blending Spanish colonial with French belle epoque, and Italian Renaissance with Gaudí-esque art nouveau, the overriding picture is often one of eclecticism run wild. While basic themes mix and merge, for architectural experts it's almost impossible to recognize any purity of style.

Thankfully, none of this takes away from the wonder of Habana's glorious urban pastiche. In their architecture, the *habaneros* (inhabitants of Habana) have acquired an uncanny habit of taking a theme, reinventing it for their own purposes and coming up with some utterly enchanting alternatives. Thus, rather than following traditional baroque styles, Habana produced 'Cuban baroque', a sturdier and notably less decorative form of the European original. As well as pursuing streamlined art deco, the *habaneros* came up with Cuban art deco, a skillful blend of neocolonialism, neoclassicism and modernism, best exemplified in the magnificently eclectic Hotel Nacional (p85).

Emerging relatively unscathed from the turmoil of three separate revolutionary wars, Habana's well-preserved historical core has survived into the 21st century with the bulk of its original colonial features remarkably intact. The preservation was helped initially by the nomination of Habana Vieja as a Unesco World Heritage site in 1982 and has been

HABANA VIEJA'S SOCIAL PROJECTS

In the streets and squares of majestic Habana Vieja, remodeled buildings are only half the story. Unique among restoration projects of its type, the city's ambitious preservation program has come out firmly in favor of a 'living' historic center. Of the US$160 million that government-run agency Habaguanex generates annually in tourist profits, only 45% goes back into further restoration efforts; the other 55% is earmarked for deserving social programs elsewhere in the neighborhood.

For the long-suffering inhabitants of Habana's oldest neighborhood, the rehabilitation has been long overdue. With a population of over 70,000 crammed into an area of just 4.5 sq km, Habana Vieja is one of the most crowded quarters in Latin America; over 45% of the people in the neighborhood live in houses deemed unfit for human habitation. Since 1994, when eminent city historian Eusebio Leal set up Habaguanex, the situation has been improving dramatically, with renovation projects providing employment for over 10,000 workers. On top of this, the restoration and repairs have also enhanced education and health facilities, fostered better community services and improved vast tracts of the city's infrastructure.

Examples of Habaguanex successes exist everywhere. Amid the tourist sights on Calle Mercaderes is the Hogar Materno Infantil, a maternity home where high-risk pregnant women are sent for expert medical provision and care. A block further north in the Casa de Obrapía, local women practice the traditional art of embroidery in a government-built cooperative that doubles as a tourist souvenir outlet. The neighborhood's youth are another important focus. A slum little more than a decade ago, Plaza Vieja is now home to the Angela Landa elementary school, where local children rub shoulders with busloads of foreigner visitors. Meanwhile a few blocks further west on Calle Lamparilla, the Centro de Rehabilitación Infantil treats children with disabilities relating to the central nervous system.

To get the lowdown on Habana Vieja's groundbreaking social projects, you can organize a specialist tour of the various facilities with Habaguanex travel agency San Cristóbal (p67).

enhanced further by the work and vision of longstanding city historian Eusebio Leal Spengler. Acting in tandem with government-sponsored agency Habaguanex, Leal has been meticulously putting Habana Vicja's classical palaces and baroque town houses back together, square by square and street by street (see p62). Rather fortuitously, he has been aided in his work by the economic peculiarities of the Cuban revolution. Due to the asphyxiating 45-year US trade embargo, Habana has largely missed out on the rampant modernization so common in other Latin American cities. Left to languish in a historical time warp, the city has nurtured an architectural legacy that is wonderfully unique. Undisturbed by the braying bulldozers of modern property development, the city's streets are nothing short of mesmerizing.

THE DEVELOPMENT OF THE COLONIAL CORE

Habana grew up in the late 16th and early 17th centuries on the western shores of the harbor channel, fanning out from the area surrounding present-day Plaza de Armas. As most of the settlement's earliest houses were made of wood, the only surviving buildings from this initial construction boom are a small clutch of churches and a network of Spanish fortresses erected around the city to deter attacks from pirates and corsairs. Notable examples of forts include the Castillo de la Real Fuerza (p69), the second-oldest fort in the Americas; the Castillo de los Tres Santos Reyes Magnos del Morro (p93), designed by Italian military architect Giovanni Bautista Antonelli; and the massive Fortaleza de San Carlos de la Cabaña (p93), the largest fort on the American continent. Fully restored by the City Historian's Office during the 1980s and '90s, these forts now act as major tourist sites and present visitors with some of the best surviving examples of Renaissance military architecture in the world.

Habana Vieja's cityscape in the 17th and 18th centuries was dominated by ecclesial architecture, reflected in the noble cloisters of gargantuan colonial buildings such as the Convento de Santa Clara (p73), built in 1632, and the Convento Nuestra Señora de Belén (p72), built in 1718. Early churches, including the Iglesia Parroquial del Espíritu Santo (p72), were equally decorative, with beautifully gilded altars and delicately chiseled facades, though the baroque influence reached its apex in the 1770s with the magnificent Catedral de San Cristóbal de la Habana (p70), considered by many as the country's most outstanding religious monument. Some of the best architecture from this period can be viewed in Habana Vieja, whose peculiar layout around *four* main squares – only two of which boasted a church – set it apart from other Spanish colonial capitals.

Neo-Gothic architecture never really gained a foothold in Cuba, although a couple of impressive churches were built in Habana in this style during the late 19th and early 20th centuries. The most distinguished example is the soaring Iglesia del Sagrado Corazón de Jesús (p81) in Centro Habana, a building so un-Cuban in its design that it could quite conceivably have been lifted out of a medium-sized English city. Another white elephant worth checking out is the neo-Romanesque Iglesia Jesús de Miramar (p90) in Playa.

MUDÉJAR

Most of Habana's earliest permanent structures exhibited recognizable Mudéjar features. Built during the 16th and 17th centuries, before the islandwide sugar boom inflated the lackluster Cuban economy, Mudéjar buildings were relatively modest in size, consisting of one or two levels that opened out onto a shady central courtyard or patio. Stylistically the genre, which was imported from Andalucía in Spain, incorporated strong Moorish influences such as *azulejos* (glazed tiles), wooden window grilles, large doors and often a small storage well. Mudéjar houses differed from later baroque constructions in that they were smaller and less decorative.

The best surviving examples of Mudéjar architecture in Habana can be found in Habana Vieja, in buildings such as the Casa de los Arabes (now the Al Medina restaurant; p111) on Calle Oficios, the Casa del Mayorazgo de Recio (now the Museo de Pintura Mural; p74) in Calle Obispo, and the Museo de Naipes (p74) on Plaza Vieja.

CUBAN BAROQUE

Baroque architecture arrived in Cuba via Spain in the early 1700s, a good 50 years after its high-water mark in Europe. Fuelled by the rapid growth of the island's nascent sugar industry, Habana's nouveau riche slave owners and sugar merchants used their juicy profits to construct larger and more grandiose urban buildings. The finest examples of baroque in Cuba adorn the homes and public buildings of Habana Vieja, including the Catedral de San Cristóbal de la Habana (p70) and the surrounding Plaza de la Catedral (p77).

Due to various climatic and stylistic considerations, traditional baroque (the word is taken from the Portuguese noun *barroco*, which means 'elaborately shaped pearl') was quickly 'tropicalized' in Cuba, with local architects adding their own personal flourishes to the new municipal structures that were springing up all over Habana Vieja. Indigenous features included *rejas* (wooden window grilles), *vitrales* (colorful stained glass), *entresuelos* (mezzanine floors) and elegantly arched *portales* (galleried exterior walkways that provided pedestrians with shelter from the sun and the rain). Signature baroque buildings, such as the Palacio de los Capitanes Generales (p76) in Plaza de Armas, were made from hard local limestone dug from the nearby San Lázaro quarries and constructed using slave labor. As a result, the intricate exterior decoration that characterized baroque architecture in Italy and Spain was noticeably toned down in Cuba, where local workers lacked the advanced stonemasonry skills of their more accomplished European counterparts.

NEOCLASSICISM

Neoclassicism first evolved in the mid-18th century in Europe as a reaction to the lavish ornamentation and ostentation of baroque. Conceived in the progressive academies of London and Paris, the movement's early adherents advocated sharp primary colors and bold symmetrical lines, coupled with a return to the architectural 'purity' of ancient Greece and Rome. The style eventually reached Habana at the beginning of the 19th century via groups of French émigrés who had fled from Haiti following a violent slave rebellion in 1791 and, within a couple of decades, it had established itself as the city's primary architectural style.

Habana's first true neoclassical building was El Templete (p75), a diminutive Doric temple constructed in Habana Vieja in 1828 next to the spot where Fray Bartolomé de las Casas is said to have conducted the city's first Mass. As the city gradually spread westward in the mid-1800s, outgrowing its 17th-century walls, use of the style quickly mushroomed, including in buildings such as the Palacio de Aldama in Centro Habana, the famous Hotel Inglaterra (p80) overlooking Parque Central, and the Partagás tobacco factory (p83). With neoclassicism bringing into vogue new residential design features such as spacious classical courtyards and rows of imposing street-facing colonnades, Habana grew in both size and beauty during this period, leading seminal Cuban novelist Alejo Carpentier to christen it the 'city of columns.'

A second neoclassical revival swept Habana at the beginning of the 20th century, spearheaded by the growing influence of the US on the island. Prompted by the ideas and design ethics of the American Renaissance (1876–1914), the city underwent a full-on building explosion, sponsoring such gigantic municipal buildings as the Capitolio Nacional (p79), the Universidad de la Habana (p89), and the dense cluster of banks and trust companies in Habana Vieja known colloquially as 'Little Wall Street.'

ART NOUVEAU

The dynamic curves of art nouveau first materialized in Europe during the 1890s before crossing the Atlantic approximately half a decade later. While the style is most closely associated with the Catalan architect Antoni Gaudí, Cuban art nouveau made its own local adaptations, often sculpting ornate Gaudí-esque facades onto existing neoclassical bases.

An important transitional architectural style in Habana, art nouveau flourished on pivotal east–west axis streets such as Av Simón Bolívar (Reina) and the Malecón (Av de Maceo) as the new city expanded rapidly westward in the 1910s and '20s. For sharp-eyed observers, some fantastic examples of the genre, now dilapidated after 50 years of virtual neglect, can still be seen amid the tightly packed apartment blocks and townhouses of Centro Habana.

The city's most recognizable art nouveau structure is the wonderfully ornate Palacio Cueto (p76) in Plaza Vieja, a former hotel and hat shop that has been recently earmarked by Habaguanex for a full makeover.

ART DECO

Art deco was an elegant, functional and modern architectural movement that originated in France at the beginning of the 20th century and reached its apex in America in the 1920s and '30s. Drawing from a vibrant mix of cubism, futurism and primitive African art, the genre promoted lavish yet streamlined buildings with sweeping curves and exuberant sunburst motifs.

Brought to Cuba via the US, Habana quickly acquired its own clutch of signature art deco buildings, including one of Latin America's finest: the magnificent Edificio Bacardí (p70) in Habana Vieja, built in 1930 to provide a Habana headquarters for Santiago de Cuba's world-famous rum-making family. Another striking art deco creation was the Rockefeller Center–inspired, 14-story López Serrano building (p85) in Vedado, constructed as the city's first real *rascacielo* (skyscraper) in 1932. Other more functional art deco skyscrapers followed, including the Teatro América (p132) on Av de la Italia (Galiano), the Teatro Fausto (p132) on Paseo de Martí and the Casa de las Américas (p84) on Calle G (Av de los Presidentes). A more diluted and eclectic interpretation of the genre can be seen in the famous Hotel Nacional (p85), whose sharp symmetrical lines and decorative twin Moorish turrets dominate the view over the Malecón.

ECLECTICISM

Eclecticism is the term often applied to the nonconformist and highly experimental architectural zeitgeist that grew up in the US during the 1880s. Rejecting 19th-century ideas of 'style' and categorization, the architects behind this revolutionary new genre promoted flexibility and an open-minded 'anything goes' ethos, drawing their inspiration from a wide range of historical precedents.

Thanks to the strong US presence in Cuba in the decades before 1959, Habana quickly became a riot of modern eclecticism with rich American and Cuban landowners constructing huge Xanadu-like mansions in the burgeoning upper-class residential district of Miramar. Expansive, ostentatious and, at times, outlandishly kitschy, these fancy new homes were garnished with crenellated walls, oddly shaped lookout towers, rooftop cupolas and leering gargoyles. Classic examples of eclecticism in Habana include La Maison (p138) in Miramar, the Palacio Presidencial (now the Museo de la Revolución; p81) in Centro Habana, and the Centro Asturianos (now the Museo Nacional de Bellas Artes; p82) on the east side of Parque Central.

In Cuba, the term 'eclectic' is also applied to buildings that exhibit a mixture of different architectural styles or, alternatively, constructions that revisit an older genre outside of its original historical timeframe. Hence hybrid buildings such as the neocolonial-neoclassical–art deco Hotel Nacional (p85) are often confusingly described as 'eclectic,' as is the neobaroque Centro Gallego (p80), a Spanish social-club-theater that was built over 200 years after the baroque period fizzled out.

MODERNISM

Habana's brief flirtation with modernism began in earnest in the early 1950s, before being cut short by the revolution. Historically speaking, the abrupt change was a blessing in disguise. If the process had been allowed to continue unchecked – experts argue – Habana today would look more like Las Vegas than one of Latin America's best-preserved Unesco World Heritage sites.

Modernist Habana revolves around the rather ugly nexus of the Plaza de la Revolution (p87). Laid out in the 1950s during the presidency of Fulgencio Batista, this gargantuan urban square was based loosely on the plans of Belgian urbanist Jean Forestier, who had drawn up designs for a progressive new city 30 years earlier. But, while Forestier had envisaged a refined modern cityscape on a par with Paris or Madrid, what Habana actually got was something more akin to an uninspiring Soviet housing development. Those in doubt should check out the gray concrete Biblioteca Nacional José Martí (p84), the hideous Ministerio del Interior building (p86) and the insipid Teatro Nacional de Cuba (p88), a building eerily reminiscent of London's Festival Hall.

Elsewhere, Habana's myriad modernist skyscrapers are a little easier on the eye. Lauded for its groundbreaking use of function over form, the Hotel Habana Libre (p85) is an angular concrete and glass high-rise that first opened its doors as the Havana Hilton Hotel in 1958. Close by, the similarly lofty Edificio Focsa (p84) was built with revolutionary new construction techniques between 1954 and 1956 and, for a time, was the tallest building of its type in the world. Between them, these two indomitable concrete giants completely altered the Habana skyline during the 1950s.

POSTREVOLUTIONARY

Habana's small collection of postrevolutionary buildings is modest and relatively unimpressive. Thirty years of Soviet domination followed by a decade and a half of severe economic austerity has shunted inspirational architecture well down the list of government priorities. Most of the minor successes have focused on the tourist sector and include large hotels such as the spacious Hotel Meliá Cohiba (p168), built in 1994, and the highly contemporary Meliá Habana (p170), which opened in 1998.

Cuba's brief flirtation with Soviet architectonics threw up some interesting and highly incongruous buildings. Concrete oddities from this period include the 28-floor Hospital Nacional Hermanos Ameijeiras (p85) overlooking the Malecón, the obelisk-like Russian embassy (p91) in Miramar, and the flying-saucer-shaped Coppelia ice-cream parlor (p84) in Vedado. In a land of picturesque palm trees and diamond-dust beaches, none of them are particularly attractive.

A slightly more adventurous architectural experiment can be seen in Las Ruinas (p127), a restaurant in Parque Lenin where the ruins of an 18th-century sugar mill have been incorporated into a funky postmodern building that pays more than a passing nod to the influence of American architect Frank Lloyd-Wright. The structure, which was the work of Cuban modernist Joaquin Galvcin in 1972, also showcases colorful stained-glass windows designed by noted Habana artist René Portocarrero.

History ∎

History

Habana's 488-year history is a classic tale of invasion, colonization, revolution and rebirth. Perched on the storm-lashed shores of the strategically important Straits of Florida, the city has been successively ransacked by pirates, fortified by the Spanish, conquered by the British, turned into a disreputable gambling den by the Americans and used as a mass exodus point by thousands of fleeing Cuban refugees. Action, adventure, drama and intrigue – Habana has it all. Read on...

THE RECENT PAST

Not much happens in Habana these days that isn't prefaced by the health and fitness of Cuba's ailing octogenarian leader, Fidel Castro. Emerging from a recent bout of acute diverticular disease, Castro is either making a miraculous recovery or suffering from a debilitating terminal illness; it all depends on which TV network you happen to be watching.

But with or without the faltering Fidel at the helm, the Cuban economy is in far better shape these days than it was 15 years ago. Fuelled by growing trade ties with India and China, and reignited by a 'new left tide' in Latin American politics spearheaded by groundbreaking alliances with Venezuela and Bolivia, the effects of the hated US *bloqueo* (embargo) – while still felt widely across Habana society – have lessened dramatically since the dark days of the *período especial* (special period; p23).

In the political sphere, Cuba has enjoyed an equally unlikely renaissance. After decades of lolling around in the diplomatic wilderness, the formerly friendless Castro – a dangerous liability less than a decade ago – is suddenly back on everyone's Christmas-card list. From São Paulo to Caracas, Cuba's gnarly bearded global warrior has become every wannabe Latin American strongman's inspiration and mentor – a feisty survivor of the Cold War, crippling economic crises and several hundred failed assassination attempts.

First in the line of fans is Venezuelan president Hugo Chávez, a fervent anti-American and, more importantly, the man with his finger in some of the world's largest oil wells. Famous for spouting the nationalist rhetoric of Latin American liberator Simon Bolívar, Chávez has pledged to supply cash-strapped Cuba with a valuable supply of cheap oil (to the tune of 90,000 barrels a day) in return for the medical services of thousands of Cuban doctors.

The Cuban-Venezuelan alliance culminated in the 2004 Bolivian Alternative of the Americas (ALBA) accords which, as well as strengthening the countries' nascent oil trade, gifted Cuba with US$500 million in credit to buy Venezuelan consumer goods. Further initiatives included a joint venture to build cheap housing, the promise of Cuban assistance in developing the Venezuelan sugar industry, and the pioneering Misión Milagros (p189), a program to provide free eye treatment for poor Venezuelans in Cuban hospitals.

The new alliance got further boosts throughout 2005–06 with the victory of Michelle Bachelet in Chile, the reincarnation of Daniel Ortega in Nicaragua and the emergence of Evo Morales in Bolivia, all potential Castro-philes.

Meanwhile, daily life in Habana continues in the shimmering light of a faded 1950s time capsule. While ostensibly little has changed here since Fidel first rolled into the city atop an American jeep in 1959, international tourism has left its bloody mark on a tired and worn-down populace. With the carrot of capitalism dangled in front of the Cubans in the form of all-inclusive tourism, limited private enterprise and the legalization of the US dollar (1993–2004), the psychology of Cuban socialism has been irrevocably damaged and people have gradually started to look elsewhere for inspiration.

TIMELINE	2000 BC	1492
	Guanahatabey people live in the caves of western Cuba	Christopher Columbus 'discovers' Cuba, where he finds the local Taínos smoking rolled up tobacco leaves

Over two million visitors arrived on the island in 2006, the majority of whom spent at least part of their time in Habana. The upside of the tourist growth is that the restoration of Habana Vieja has been allowed to continue largely unhindered. The downside is that, exposed to 21st-century capitalism, Habana's inhabitants been given a tantalizing glimpse of the things they ultimately can't have (new cars, consumer goods, the freedom to travel). What happens next in this embattled yet enduringly beautiful city is anybody's guess.

FROM THE BEGINNING

PRE-COLUMBIAN HISTORY

According to exhaustive carbon dating, Cuba has been inhabited by humans for over 4000 years. The first known civilization to settle on the island were the Guanahatabeys, a primitive Stone Age people who lived in caves not far west of present-day Habana and eked out a meager existence as hunter-gatherers. At some point over the ensuing 2000 years, the Guanahatabeys were gradually displaced by the arrival of the Siboneys, a significantly more developed group of fishermen and small-scale farmers who settled comparatively peacefully on the archipelago's sheltered southern coast.

The island's third and most important pre-Columbian civilization, the Taínos, first started arriving in Cuba around 1100AD in a series of waves, concluding a migration process that had begun in the Orinoco River delta in South America several centuries earlier. Taíno culture was far more developed and sophisticated than its two archaic predecessors. Related to the Greater Antilles Arawaks, the new natives were skillful farmers, weavers and boat builders, and their complex society boasted an organized system of participatory government that was overseen by a series of local *caciques* (chiefs). Taínos are thought to be responsible for pioneering approximately 60% of the crops still grown in Cuba today, and they were the first pre-Columbian culture to nurture the delicate tobacco plant into a form that could be processed for smoking.

Despite never reaching the heights of the Aztec or Inca civilizations in South America, the Taíno culture left its indelible mark on the island. Cuba's traditional *guajiros* (country people, from a Taíno word meaning 'one of us') still industriously work the land for a living, and evidence of Taíno ancestry in modern Cuban bloodlines remains surprisingly intact in the villages of eastern Guantánamo. Furthermore, in keeping with their tobacco-addicted predecessors, a whole generation of Cuban cigar aficionados continues to obsessively smoke *cohibas* (cigars) for their aroma and taste.

THE ARRIVAL OF THE SPANISH

When Columbus neared the Cuban coast at Gibara in present-day Holguín province on October 27, 1492, he described it as 'the most beautiful land human eyes had ever seen.' But deluded in his search for the kingdom of the Great Khan, and finding little gold in Cuba's lush and heavily forested interior, the great explorer quickly abandoned the territory in favor of Hispaniola.

The colonization of Cuba didn't begin until nearly 20 years later. In 1511, Diego Velázquez de Cuéllar led a flotilla of four ships and 400 men from Hispaniola destined to conquer the island for the Spanish Crown. Docking near present-day Baracoa, the conquistadors promptly set about establishing seven pioneering settlements throughout their new colony in Baracoa, Bayamo, Trinidad, Sancti Spíritus, Puerto Príncipe (Camagüey), Habana and Santiago de Cuba. From the safety of their *bohíos* (thatched-roof huts), a scattered population of Taínos looked on with a mixture of fascination and fear.

Despite Velázquez's attempts to protect the local Indians from the gross excesses of the Spanish swordsmen, things quickly got out of hand and the invaders soon found that they

1508	1519
Sebastián de Ocampo charts the current location of Habana during his pioneering circumnavigation of Cuba	The settlement of San Cristóbal de la Habana is founded on its present site on the western shores of Bahía de la Habana

had a full-scale rebellion on their hands. Leader of the embittered and short-lived insurgency was the feisty Hatuey, an influential Taíno *cacique* and the archetype of the Cuban resistance, who was eventually captured and burned at the stake, Inquisition style, for daring to challenge the iron fist of Spanish rule.

With the resistance decapitated, the Spaniards set about emptying Cuba of its relatively meager gold and mineral reserves, using the beleaguered natives as forced labor. As slavery was nominally banned under a papal edict, the Spanish got around the various legal loopholes by introducing a ruthless *encomienda* system, whereby thousands of hapless natives were rounded up and forced to work for Spanish landowners on the pretext that they were receiving free 'lessons' in Christianity. The brutal system lasted 20 years before 'Apostle of the Indians' Fray Bartolomé de Las Casas appealed to the Spanish Crown for more humane treatment, and in 1542 the *encomiendas* were abolished. Catastrophically the call came too late for the unfortunate Taínos. Those who had not already been worked to death in the gold mines quickly succumbed to fatal European diseases such as smallpox, and by 1550 only about 5000 scattered survivors remained.

THE EMERGING CAPITAL

The area now occupied by the city of Habana was first charted by Europeans in 1508 during an exploratory circumnavigation of the island of Cuba by Spanish navigator Sebastián de Ocampo. Established as the westernmost of Diego Velázquez' seven settlements in August 1515, the original village of Habana was founded on Cuba's south coast near the present-day town of Surgidero de Batabanó. A disaster from the start, the site – which was mired in a mosquito-infested swamp – was moved a few years later to the north coast between present-day Vedado and Miramar. Only in 1519 did the town finally re-establish itself at its third and present site, 8km further east at the Puerto de Carena – the name originally given by de Ocampo to Bahía de la Habana (Habana Bay). On November 25, 1519, San Cristóbal de la Habana was officially christened by Fray Bartolomé de las Casas, who convened a solemn Mass under a ceiba tree on the ground now occupied by Plaza de Armas (p77) in Habana Vieja.

Testimonies suggest that Habana was originally named by Spanish conquistador Pánfilo de Nárvaez by combining the city's patron saint, San Cristóbal (St Christopher), with the name of the daughter of a local Taíno *cacique;* the chief was called Habaguanex and his daughter was known colloquially as Habana.

Despite its early foundation, Habana's growth was slow and ponderous in the early years. Cuba was colonized from the east and its three most important towns up until the 1550s were Baracoa, Bayamo and Santiago de Cuba, all of which lay closer to the Spanish colony of Hispaniola. Stuck out on the northwest corner of the island, Habana appeared isolated and remote and when Baracoa relinquished its role as Cuban capital in the 1520s, the mantle passed without argument to Santiago de Cuba.

It took the Spanish conquest of Mexico and Peru to swing the pendulum in Habana's favor. As Spanish trade with the Americas grew in the 1530s and '40s, increasing numbers of heaving galleons laden down with gold, silver, dyes and spices plied their way east through the Straits of Florida, where they became prime fodder for pirates and buccaneers. One of their more audacious brethren, Frenchman Jacques de Soros, attacked Habana itself in 1555, where he kidnapped a group of its richest citizens and demanded a ransom of 80,000 gold pieces. When the demand wasn't met, he razed the city.

The Spanish responded with two history-defining decisions. Firstly they built a network of formidable forts around Habana, spearheaded by the Castillo de San Salvador de la Punta (p79) and the Castillo de los Tres Santos Reyes Magnos del Morro (p93) on either side of the harbor channel. Secondly a royal decree in 1561 stipulated that all ships heading for Spain should, in future, congregate in Habana harbor before making the voyage east to Spain as part of a huge communal treasure fleet. The new measures enhanced Habana's

1555	1592
Habana is sacked by French pirate Jacques de Soros, who holds many of the city's inhabitants to ransom	King Philip II of Spain confers the title of 'city' on Habana

commerce and trade exponentially, and in 1556 the settlement replaced Santiago as the seat of the Spanish captain general. More progress followed. Benefiting from its new strategically important position in the Spanish Indies, Habana was declared a city in 1592, and in 1607 the capital of the colony was officially moved there. The stage was finally set: for the next 200 years, Habana was the most important port in the Americas and the key to the vast Spanish colonial empire.

THE BRITISH WREST CONTROL

Habana expanded rapidly in the late 17th and early 18th centuries, spreading out around the four main squares of Plaza Vieja, Plaza San Francisco de Asís, Plaza de Armas and Plaza de la Catedral. Riches from the New World financed the construction of lavish new buildings and intricately decorated churches, and gave birth to the resplendent city that still forms the basis of today's Unesco World Heritage site. Between 1674 and 1740 Habana, ever wary of the threat of attack, sprouted a 5m-long defensive wall and by 1750 it was the third-biggest city in the Americas – behind Mexico City and Lima, and ahead of New York.

In 1762, Spain joined in the Seven Years' War on the side of France against the British. For Habana the intervention quickly turned out to be disastrous. Unperturbed by their new Spanish foes and sensing an opportunity to disrupt trade in Spain's economically lucrative Caribbean empire, 20,000 British troops homed in on the city on June 6, landing in the small village of Cojímar, and attacking and capturing the seemingly impregnable castle of El Morro from the rear. Worn down and under siege, the Spanish reluctantly surrendered Habana two months later, leaving the British to become the city's (and Cuba's) rather unlikely new overlords.

The British occupation turned out to be brief but important. Bivouacking themselves inside Habana's formidable city walls for 11 months, the enterprising occupiers flung open the doors to free trade and sparked a new rush of foreign imports into the colony in the form of manufacturing parts and consumer goods. Not surprisingly, it was the sugar industry that benefited most from this economic deregulation and in the years that followed the British handover (they swapped Habana for Florida at the Treaty of Paris in 1763), the production of sugarcane boomed like never before.

SUGAR HIGH

When the Spanish regained Habana in 1763, they began a crash program to upgrade the city's defenses in order to avoid a repeat performance of the previous year's military debacle. A gargantuan new fortress, Fortaleza de San Carlos de la Cabaña (p93), was built along the harbor ridge from where the British had shelled El Morro, and by the time the work was finished in 1766, Habana had become the most heavily fortified city in the New World. It was also during this period that many of the city's finest buildings were constructed on the huge profits that were being generated by the burgeoning sugar industry. In 1787, Habana's magnificent baroque cathedral (p70) was completed and the city became a bishop's seat. In the 1790s, the neighborhoods of El Prado and Parque Central took Habana outside of its traditional colonial walls for the first time. Then, in 1837, Cuba became only the sixth country in the world to construct a fully functioning railroad, a 51km track that stretched from Habana Vieja to the outlying town of Bejucal.

By the 1820s, Cuba was the world's largest sugar producer and the freshly inaugurated United States – hooked on sugar and spice and all things nice – was its most prestigious market. Situated just 90 miles from the American mainland, Habana became the focus of a growing movement inside the US to annex Cuba. In 1808, Thomas Jefferson became the first of four US presidents to offer to buy the island from its increasingly beleaguered Spanish owners, and in 1845 President Polk upped the ante further when he slapped down a massive US$100 million bid for the jewel of the Caribbean.

1607	1674
Habana succeeds Santiago de Cuba as the colony's new capital	Work on Habana's city walls begins

For better or for worse, Spain refused to sell, preferring instead to import more slaves and bank more pesetas. By 1840 there were 400,000 slaves incarcerated on the island, the bulk of them of West African origin.

In 1862 the British finally began enforcing the ban on slave trading across the Atlantic that they had first enacted in 1820. Most slaves in Cuba still arrived on US ships, but with the distraction of the US Civil War in 1861–65 the British were able to act without fear of major repercussions. To plug the new labor gap, indentured Chinese workers and Mexican Indians were brought to the island to serve as *macheteros* (sugarcane cutters). The first Chinese laborers arrived in Cuba in 1847, and by the 1880s there were tens of thousands of them, living primarily in Habana in a neighborhood centered on the Zanja canal that quickly became known as Barrio Chino (Chinatown).

THE FIRST WAR OF INDEPENDENCE

Fed up with Spain's reactionary policies and enviously eyeing Lincoln's new American dream, *criollo* (Spaniards born in the Americas) landowners around the eastern city of Bayamo began plotting rebellion in the late 1860s. The spark was lit on October 10, 1868, when Carlos Manuel de Céspedes, a lawyer, sugar-plantation owner and budding poet, launched an uprising from his Demajagua sugar mill near Manzanillo in the Oriente. Calling for the abolition of slavery, and freeing his own slaves in an act of solidarity, Céspedes proclaimed the famous *Grito de Yara*, a cry of liberty for an independent Cuba, encouraging other disillusioned separatists to join him. For the colonial administrators in Habana, such a bold and audacious bid to wrest control from their grasp was an act tantamount to treason. The furious Spanish reacted accordingly.

Fortuitously for the loosely organized rebels, the cagey Céspedes had done his military homework. Within weeks of the historic *Grito de Yara,* the diminutive lawyer-turned-general had raised an army of over 1500 men and marched defiantly on Bayamo, taking the city in a matter of days. But initial successes soon turned to lengthy deadlock. A tactical decision not to invade western Cuba, along with an alliance between *peninsulares* (Spaniards born in Spain but living in the Americas) and the Spanish, soon put Céspedes on the back foot. Temporary help arrived in the shape of mulatto general Antonio Maceo, a tough and uncompromising *santiagüeno* (inhabitant of Santiago de Cuba) nicknamed the 'Bronze Titan' for his ability to defy death on countless occasions, and the equally formidable Dominican Máximo Gómez, but although they were able to disrupt the economy and periodically destroy the sugar crop, the rebels lacked a dynamic political leader capable of uniting them behind a singular ideological cause.

With the loss of Céspedes in battle in 1874, the war dragged on for another four years, reducing the Cuban economy to tatters and leaving an astronomical 200,000 Cubans and 80,000 Spanish dead. Finally in February 1878, a lackluster pact was signed at El Zanjón between the uncompromising Spanish and the militarily exhausted separatists, a rambling and largely worthless agreement that solved nothing and gave little to the rebel cause. Maceo, disgusted and disillusioned, made his feelings known in the 'Protest of Baraguá,' but after an abortive attempt to restart the war briefly in 1879, both he and Gómez disappeared into a prolonged exile.

Spared any direct fighting in the war, Habana rose in grandeur during the 1880s as conditions on the rest of the island continued to plummet. The long-superfluous city wall had been knocked down in 1863 and, fuelled by strong sugar prices and the lofty ambitions of its prosperous inhabitants, Habana burst its boundaries into the once forbidden forests of Vedado. Punctuated by theaters, palaces, broad boulevards and verdant parks, the new city cut a pretty picture by the end of the 19th century with its colonnaded streets and distinctive neoclassical architecture. But it wasn't all one-way traffic. A fall in the price of sugar on the world market in the late 1880s precipitated an economic crisis and forced many of the island's old landowning oligarchy to sell out to a newer and slicker competitor – the

1728	1762
The University of Habana is founded	Habana is attacked and taken by the British, who occupy the city for 11 months before exchanging the island of Cuba for Florida

US. By the end of the 19th century, US trade with Cuba was larger than US trade with the rest of Latin America combined and Cuba was America's third-largest trading partner after Britain and Germany. The island's sweet-tasting mono-crop economy – a thorn in its side since time immemorial – was translating into a US monopoly and some wealthy Cuban landowners were readvocating annexation.

THE SECOND WAR OF INDEPENDENCE

Cometh the hour, cometh the man; José Martí – poet, patriot, visionary and *habanero* (inhabitant of Habana) – was a patriotic figure of Bolívarian proportions, not just in Cuba, but in the whole of Latin America.

After his arrest at the age of 16 during the First War of Independence for a minor indiscretion, Martí had spent 20 years formulating his revolutionary ideas abroad in places as diverse as Guatemala, Mexico and the US. Although impressed by American business savvy and industriousness, he was equally repelled by the country's all-consuming materialism, and was determined to present a workable Cuban alternative.

Dedicating himself passionately to the cause of the resistance, Martí wrote, spoke, petitioned and organized tirelessly for the island's independence for well over a decade, and by 1892 he had created enough momentum to coax Maceo and Gómez out of exile under the umbrella of the Partido Revolucionario Cubano (PRC). At last, Cuba had found its Bolívar.

Predicting that the time was right for another revolution, Martí and his compatriots set sail for Cuba in April 1895, landing near Baracoa two months after PRC-sponsored insurrections had tied down Spanish forces in Habana. Raising an army of 40,000 men, the rebels headed west engaging the Spanish on May 19 in a place called Dos Ríos. It was on this bullet-strafed and strangely anonymous battlefield that Martí, conspicuous on his white horse and dressed in his trademark black dinner suit, was shot and killed as he charged suicidally toward the Spanish lines. Had he lived he would certainly have become Cuba's first president; instead, he became a hero and a martyr whose life and legacy would inspire generations of Cubans in the years to come.

Conscious of mistakes made during the First War of Independence, Gómez and Maceo stormed west toward Habana, utilizing a scorched-earth policy that left everything from the Oriente to Matanzas in flames. Early victories quickly led to a sustained offensive, and by January 1896 Maceo had broken through to Pinar del Río province, while Gómez was tying down Spanish forces near Habana. But once again the city escaped any major damage.

Unleashing a devastating counterpunch, the Spanish dispatched to Cuba a ruthless general named Valeriano Weyler, who quickly set about building countrywide north–south fortifications and attempted to break the underground resistance by herding *guajiros* into camps in a process called *reconcentración*. The brutal tactics started to show results and on December 7, 1896, the *Mambíses* (rebels) suffered a major military blow when Antonio Maceo was killed in a field near Santiago de las Vegas, south of Habana, trying to break out to the east.

By this time Cuba was a mess: thousands were dead, the countryside was in flames and William Randolph Hearst and the tub-thumping US tabloid press were leading a hysterical war campaign to draw America into the fray.

Preparing perhaps for the worst, the US battleship *Maine* was sent to Habana in January 1898 on the pretext of 'protecting US citizens.' But its peacekeeping mission never came to fruition. On February 15, 1898, the *Maine* exploded in Habana harbor, killing 258 US sailors and bringing the country to the brink of war (p54).

After the *Maine* debacle, the US scrambled to take control. They offered Spain US$300 million for Cuba and, when this deal was rejected, demanded a full withdrawal. The long-awaited US-Spanish showdown that had been simmering imperceptibly beneath the surface for decades had finally ended in war.

1796	1837
The remains of Christopher Columbus are transported to Habana, where they rest in the cathedral until 1898	Cuba becomes only the sixth country in the world to get a railroad, with a 51km line running from Habana to Bejucal

REMEMBER THE MAINE – AND TO HELL WITH SPAIN

Few attacks on American interests abroad have provoked as much anger and controversy as the explosion of the battleship *Maine* in Habana harbor in 1898, which sparked an international conflict, fuelled a bitter newspaper circulation war and left 258 of the ship's 350-strong crew dead.

Dispatched to Habana in January 1898 by US President McKinley on the pretext of protecting US interests in Cuba, the *Maine* – which measured 319ft in length and displaced 6682 tons – was the largest battleship ever constructed in a US shipyard.

But on February 15, 1898, while undertaking routine duties in Habana harbor, a massive explosion ripped the giant vessel apart, causing it to start sinking within minutes.

Suspicion for the explosion fell immediately on the Spanish, whose relationship with the US had become increasingly fraught since the reignition of the Cuban independence war in 1895. But the real backlash was caused by a vitriolic newspaper war between William Randolph Hearst's *New York Journal* and Joseph Pulitzer's *New York World,* both of which shamelessly whipped up American public opinion into a hysterical prowar frenzy in a desperate bid to become the first periodical to achieve one million subscribers.

Journalistically speaking, the tactics were far from ethical. Ever keen to fan the political flames, Hearst had for months been planting his reporters in Cuba, where they had cabled home stories of macabre Spanish atrocities that dangerously distorted the truth. But such was the *Journal* owner's enduring national influence that not only was he able to masterfully manipulate public opinion, he was also able to wield considerable political pressure within the higher echelons of the US government.

With the *Maine* explosion, Hearst finally had his damning scoop. 'Remember the Maine and to hell with Spain' screamed the headlines of the *Journal* over the ensuing few weeks, inventing a new catchphrase and stifling any serious political dialogue about what really happened. Indeed, before any form of independent inquiry could be undertaken, US public opinion had unceremoniously declared the Spanish guilty of sabotage and President McKinley found himself sliding into a war that he was powerless to stop.

Modern analyses suggest that the explosion of the *Maine* was an accident caused by badly packed gunpowder – though this hasn't stopped various conspiracy theorists from speculating that the Americans blew the ship up themselves to invent a pretext for invading Cuba via the back door. Some cynics even hold Hearst himself responsible.

A monument to the 258 American sailors killed in the *Maine* explosion (Map pp224–5) adorns a traffic island on the Malecón (Av de Maceo) in front of the Hotel Nacional.

The only important land battle of the conflict was on July 1 in Santiago, when the US Army attacked Spanish positions on San Juan Hill, just east of the city. Despite vastly inferior numbers and limited, antiquated weaponry, the Spanish held out bravely for over 24 hours before future US president Theodore Roosevelt broke the deadlock by leading a celebrated cavalry charge of the Rough Riders up San Juan Hill. It was the beginning of the end, and an unconditional surrender was offered to the Americans on July 17, 1898.

On December 12, 1898, a peace treaty ending the war was signed in Paris by the Spanish and the Americans. Despite three years of blood, sweat and sacrifice, no Cuban representatives were invited. After a century of trying to buy Cuba from the Spanish, the US, wary of raised voices among short-changed Cuban nationalists, decided to appease the situation temporarily by offering the island a form of quasi-independence that would dampen internal discontent while keeping any future Cuban governments on a tight leash. In November 1900, the US governor of Cuba, General Leonard Wood, convened a meeting of elected Cuban delegates, who drew up a constitution similar to that of the US. Connecticut senator Orville Platt attached a rider to the US Army Appropriations Bill of 1901, giving the US the right to intervene militarily in Cuba whenever they saw fit. This was approved by President McKinley, and the Cubans were given the choice of accepting what became known as the Platt Amendment or remaining under a US military occupation indefinitely. The US also used their significant leverage to secure a naval base in Guantánamo Bay in order to protect their strategic interests in the Panama Canal region.

1838	1853
Teatro Tacón (now the Gran Teatro de la Habana) opens; it's generally believed to be the oldest surviving theater in the Americas	Cuban national hero José Martí is born in a small house in Habana Vieja on January 28

MARRIED TO THE MOB

Habana entered the 20th century on the cusp of a new beginning. Despite gaining nominal independence in 1902, Cuba became inexorably linked both politically and economically to the US. Intervening militarily three times between 1906 and 1923, the US walked a tightrope between benevolent ally and exasperated foreign meddler. There were, however, some coordinated successes, most notably the eradication of yellow fever using the hypotheses of Cuban doctor Carlos Finlay and the transformation of the ravaged Cuban economy from postwar wreck into nascent sugar giant.

Cuba's early-20th-century economic growth was nothing short of astounding and Habana was once again its main beneficiary. Thanks to substantial financial aid from the dollar-wielding *Yanquis,* the Malecón (Av de Maceo; p86) was laid out in 1901, the Presidential Palace (now the Museo de la Revolución; p81) was opened in 1920 and, nine years later, the champagne corks popped over the Capitolio Nacional (p79), a carbon copy of the US's Capitol Building that was actually a few inches taller. By the late 1920s, US companies owned two-thirds of Cuba's farmland and most of its mineral resources, and close to 20,000 rich Cuban-American businessmen were living in Habana's new garden suburbs of Miramar and Marianao.

With the economy booming and the US gripped by Prohibition, the Mafia homed in on Habana in the 1920s, and gangsters such as Al Capone began to milk the lucrative tourist sector by setting up hotels and clubs based on drinking, gambling and prostitution. One such venture was the Hotel Nacional (p85), which opened in 1930 and was designed with an art deco influence that was very much in vogue in the US at the time.

But there were setbacks ahead. When commodity prices collapsed in 1929, Habana was plunged into chaos and president-turned-dictator Gerardo Machado y Morales (1925–33) went on a terror campaign to root out the detractors. But Machado was no Mussolini (upon whom he allegedly modeled himself). When he was toppled during a spontaneous general strike in August 1933, it was left to a seemingly innocuous army sergeant named Fulgencio Batista to step into the power vacuum after a swiftly enacted military coup.

Batista was a wily and shrewd negotiator who presided over Cuba's best and worst attempts to establish an embryonic democracy in the 1940s and '50s. Elected president in a relatively free and fair election in 1940, Batista began to enact a wide variety of social reforms and set about drafting Cuba's most liberal and democratic constitution to date. But neither the liberal honeymoon nor Batista's good humor were to last. Stepping down in 1944, the former army sergeant handed over power to the politically inept President Ramón Grau San Martín, and corruption and inefficiency soon reigned like never before.

Aware of his underlying popularity and sensing an easy opportunity to line his pockets with one last big paycheck, Batista cut a deal with the American Mafia in Daytona Beach, Florida, and positioned himself for a comeback. Grau would be paid off (with a 'gift' of US$250,000), Batista would regain the presidency, and organized-crime boss Meyer Lansky would be left to run Habana's hotels and gambling syndicates pretty much as he pleased. But it began to look like Batista would lose the scheduled elections, and on March 10, 1952, three months before the election, he staged a second military coup. Wildly condemned by opposition politicians inside Cuba but recognized by the US government two weeks later, Batista quickly let it be known that his second incarnation wasn't going to be quite as enlightened as his first.

REVOLUTION

After Batista's second coup, a revolutionary circle formed in Habana around the charismatic figure of Fidel Castro, a qualified lawyer and gifted orator who had been due to stand in the cancelled 1952 elections. Though Castro himself was an 'easterner' from the bucolic province of Holguín, most of his early followers hailed from Habana, where they used the

1863	1898
Habana's city walls are demolished	The US battleship *Maine* explodes in Habana harbor

house of his trusty lieutenant Abel Santamaría (later tortured to death by Batista's thugs) on the corner of Calle 25 and O in Vedado as a clandestine meeting place. Appalled by Batista's corruption, Castro saw no alternative to the use of force in ridding Cuba of its detestable dictator. Low on numbers but adamant to make a political statement, he led 119 rebels in an attack on the strategically important Moncada army barracks in Santiago de Cuba on July 26, 1953. The audacious and poorly planned assault failed dramatically when the rebel's driver (who was from Habana) took the wrong turning in Santiago's badly signposted streets and the alarm was raised.

Fooled, flailing and hopelessly outnumbered, 64 of the Moncada conspirators were rounded up by Batista's army, and brutally tortured and executed. Castro and a handful of others managed to escape into the nearby mountains, where they were found a few days later by a sympathetic army lieutenant named Sarría, who had been given instructions to kill them. 'Don't shoot, you can't kill ideas,' Sarría is alleged to have shouted on finding Castro and his exhausted colleagues. By taking him to jail instead of doing away with him, Sarría – a foresighted and highly principled man – ruined his military career, but saved Fidel's life. (One of Fidel's first acts after the revolution triumphed was to release Sarría from the prison where Batista had incarcerated him and to give him a commission in the revolutionary army.) Castro's capture soon became national news, and he was put on trial in

THE 1946 HABANA CONFERENCE

Deported from the US in February 1946 on a charge of pandering, notorious New York Mafia don Salvatore 'Lucky' Luciano made a beeline for Sicily, where he sought out the local crime bosses and surreptitiously plotted his return. In the early fall of 1946 the opportunistic mobster received a note from his childhood friend and associate Meyer Lansky containing just three words: 'December – Hotel Nacional.' For the ambitious Luciano, the message needed no further explanation. Taking a necessarily circuitous route in order to avoid US police detection, he was on the next plane bound for Habana, Cuba.

Met by the corpulent Lansky at Habana airport, Luciano quickly retook control of the North American crime syndicate by buying a $150,000 stake in a lucrative casino situated in the Hotel Nacional, co-owned at the time by Lansky and his silent partner, Cuban president Fulgencio Batista. The cash for the venture was raised via a series of 'gifts' brought out to Habana by visiting mobsters from the US, who were congregating in the Cuban capital on Luciano's orders for the biggest get-together of North American hoods in Mafia history.

Convened on the mezzanine floor of the Hotel Nacional on December 22, 1946, the infamous Habana Conference was attended by every major figure in the US postwar Mafia hierarchy and was to play a pivotal role in organized crime activity in the decades that followed. In order to provide a pretext for such a heavy Italian-American presence in the Cuban capital (and to cover the tracks of Luciano, who US authorities had prohibited from leaving Italy), the Mob brought in rising singing star Frank Sinatra for a Christmas Eve concert. Sinatra allegedly flew in with the Fischetti brothers (Al Capone's cousins) from Chicago, stoking rumors about the singer's supposed Mob connections and setting alight a controversy that haunted him until his death.

The main focus of the conference was to relaunch Luciano as a major North American crime figure, or the 'Boss of Bosses' as he was known in popular Mafia folklore. Additional business included discussions on Mob involvement in the global narcotics trade (using Cuba as a base) and the planned assassination of mobster Bugsy Siegel, whose new hotel venture in a small Nevada desert town called Las Vegas had turned out to be an embarrassing flop (and had cost the Mob millions).

With the big business settled, Luciano elected to remain in Habana while awaiting a convenient opportunity to return to the US. But when federal drug agent Harry Anslinger got wind of the mobster's presence in the city, he asked President Truman to put pressure on the Cuban government to expel the already deported Italian. Acting under Lansky's and ex-president Batista's influence, the Cuban government initially refused the order, causing the Truman administration to halt deliveries of medical supplies to Cuba. In retaliation, Luciano hired an attorney and concocted a plan to stop Cuban sugar shipments to the US, but with the Americans undiplomatically turning the screws, he found himself in a lose-lose situation and desisted. In April 1947, in order to avoid any further international incidents, Salvatore 'not-so-lucky' Luciano was placed on a slow transatlantic cargo ship to Italy where he served out an ignominious exile.

1902	1930
Cuba gains independence from Spain under the auspices of the US	The Hotel Nacional, one of Habana's greatest landmarks, opens

the full glare of the media spotlight. A lawyer by profession, the loquacious Fidel defended himself in court with an eloquent and masterfully executed speech that he later transcribed into a comprehensive political manifesto entitled *History Will Absolve Me*. Basking in his new-found legitimacy and backed by a growing sense of restlessness with the old regime in the country at large, Castro was sentenced to 15 years imprisonment on Isla de Pinos. Cuba was well on the way to gaining a new national hero.

In February 1955, Batista won the presidency in what were widely considered to be fraudulent elections and, in an attempt to curry favor with growing internal opposition, agreed to an amnesty for all political prisoners, including Castro. Realizing that Batista's real intention was to assassinate him once out of jail, Castro fled Habana for Mexico. Behind him he left a small band of loyal supporters trapped in a city that – thanks to Batista's ever spiraling corruption – had degenerated into a decadent all-night gambling den that was scooping crooked fortunes into the pockets of American mobsters such as Meyer Lansky.

But despite its moral decline, Habana's expansion continued apace. The 1950s saw the final institution of the plans of Belgian urbanist Jean Forestier, who 30 years earlier had drawn up a Parisian-style street layout for Vedado based along the three modern-day axes of Paseo, Calle G (Av de los Presidentes) and the Plaza de la Revolución. Elsewhere, the city grew outwards and upwards with a frenzied New York–skyscraper-building craze that culminated in the completion of the Focsa building (p84) in 1956 and the Havana Hilton hotel (now the Habana Libre; p85) in 1958. Not to be outdone, the Mob used their own money to emulate the lurid hotel strips of Las Vegas with the lavishly decorated Hotel Capri and the ritzy Hotel Riviera (p167). Habana's skyline was changed forever.

Meanwhile, cocooned in Mexico, Fidel and his compatriots plotted and planned afresh, drawing in key new figures such as Camilo Cienfuegos and the Argentine doctor-turned-revolutionary Ernesto 'Che' Guevara, both of whom added strength and panache to the nascent army of disaffected rebel soldiers. On the run from the Mexican police and determined to arrive in Cuba in time for an uprising that underground leader Frank País had planned for late November 1956 in Santiago, Castro and 81 companions set sail for the island on 25 November in an old and overcrowded leisure yacht named *Granma*. After seven dire days at sea, they arrived at Playa Las Coloradas near Niquero on December 2, two days late. Three days later, after a catastrophic landing – 'it wasn't a disembarkation it was a shipwreck,' a wry Guevara later commented – they were spotted and routed by Batista's soldiers in a sugarcane field at Alegría de Pío.

Of the 82 rebels who had left Mexico, only 12 managed to escape. Splitting into three tiny groups, the survivors wandered around hopelessly for days half-starved, wounded and assuming that the rest of their compatriots had been killed in the initial skirmish. 'At one point I was commander in chief of myself and two other people,' commented Fidel years later. However, with the help of the local peasantry, the dozen or so hapless soldiers finally managed to reassemble two weeks later in Cinco Palmas, a clearing in the shadows of the Sierra Maestra, where a half-delirious Fidel gave a rousing and premature victory speech. 'We will win this war,' he proclaimed confidently. 'We are just beginning the fight!'

The comeback began on January 17, 1957, when the guerrillas scored an important victory by sacking a small army outpost on the south coast. This was followed in February by a propaganda coup when Fidel persuaded *New York Times* journalist Herbert Matthews to come up into the Sierra Maestra to interview him. The resulting article made Castro internationally famous and gained him much sympathy among liberal Americans. On March 13, 1957, university students led by José Antonio Echeverría attacked the Presidential Palace (now the Museo de la Revolución) in Habana in an unsuccessful attempt to assassinate Batista. Thirty-two of the 35 attackers were shot dead as they fled, and reprisals were meted out on the streets of Habana with a new vengeance. Cuba was rapidly disintegrating into a police state run by military-trained thugs.

Back in the Sierra Maestra, Fidel's rebels overwhelmed 53 Batista soldiers at an army post in El Uvero in May and captured more badly needed supplies. The movement seemed to be

1940	1952
Ernest Hemingway purchases La Finca Vigía, a private villa in the Habana suburb of San Francisco de Paula	Batista stages his second coup and opens the doors to widespread repression and corruption

gaining momentum and despite losing Frank País to a government assassination squad in Santiago in July, support and sympathy around the country was starting to mushroom. By the beginning of 1958, Castro had established a fixed headquarters in a cloud forest high up in the Sierra Maestra and was broadcasting propaganda messages from Radio Rebelde (710AM and 96.7FM) all across Cuba. The tide was starting to turn.

Sensing his popularity waning, Batista sent an army of 10,000 men into the Sierra Maestra in May 1958 on a mission known as Plan FF (*Fin de Fidel* or 'End of Fidel'). The intention was to liquidate Castro and his merry band of loyal guerrillas, who had now burgeoned into a solid fighting force of 300 men. Outnumbered 30 to one, and fighting desperately for their lives, the rebels – with the help of the local *campesinos* (country people) – gradually halted the onslaught of Batista's young and ill-disciplined conscript army. With the Americans increasingly embarrassed by the no-holds-barred terror tactics of their one-time Cuban ally, Castro sensed an opportunity to turn defensive into offensive and signed the groundbreaking Caracas Pact with eight leading opposition groups, calling on the US to stop all aid to Batista. Che Guevara and Camilo Cienfuegos were promptly dispatched to the Sierra del Escambray to open up new fronts in the west, and by December, with Cienfuegos holding down troops in Yaguajay and Guevara closing in on Santa Clara, the end was in sight. It was left to Che to seal the final victory, employing classic guerrilla tactics to derail an armored train in Santa Clara and split the country's battered communications system in two. By New Year's Eve 1958, the game was up, a sense of jubilation filled the country, and Che and Cienfuegos were on their way to Habana unopposed.

In the small hours of that night, Batista fled by private plane to the Dominican Republic, taking US$40 million in embezzled government funds with him. Materializing in Santiago on January 1, meanwhile, Fidel made a rousing victory speech from the town hall in Parque Céspedes before jumping into a jeep and traveling across the breadth of the country to Habana in a Caesar-like cavalcade. The triumph of the revolution was complete. Or was it?

CONSOLIDATING POWER

On January 5, 1959, the Cuban presidency was assumed by Manuel Urrutia, a judge who had defended the M-26-7 (the 26th of July Movement; Fidel Castro's revolutionary organization) prisoners during the 1953 Moncada trials, though the leadership and real power remained unquestionably with Fidel. Riding on the crest of a popular wave, the self-styled *Líder Máximo* (Maximum Leader) began to mete out revolutionary justice with an iron fist, and within a matter of weeks hundreds of Batista's supporters and military henchmen had been rounded up and executed inside the walls of Fortaleza de San Carlos de la Cabaña in Habana. Already suspicious of Castro's supposed communist leanings, the US viewed these openly antagonistic developments with a growing sense of alarm and when Fidel visited Richard Nixon in the White House on a state visit in April 1959, the vice president gave him a decidedly cool and terse reception.

As Castro's star ascended, the cautious President Urrutia was forced to resign in July 1959 after denouncing the new regime's increasingly communist credentials. Riding on the crest of a populist wave, Fidel handed the presidency to Osvaldo Dorticós Torrado, a Cienfuegos lawyer, who held the post until 1976 (when Fidel became president). But despite a rather industrious work ethic, Dorticós was realistically little more than a token figurehead who bowed to Castro's every whim.

After closing down Habana's casinos and brothels, the new government largely turned its back on the once decadent Cuban capital, preferring instead to focus its energies on instituting the much lauded First Agrarian Reform Act, a piece of landmark legislation that nationalized all rural estates over 400 hectares (without compensation) and infuriated Cuba's largest landholders, the bulk of whom were American. Habana, meanwhile, slipped into a long period of decline, with former city mansions stripped down and redistributed among the urban poor as their once powerful proprietors headed north for Miami.

1959	1977
Che Guevara and Camilo Cienfuegos enter Habana on behalf of Fidel Castro's victorious guerrilla army	The US opens up an Interests Section in Habana

Back on the political scene, entities with vested interests in Cuba were growing increasingly bellicose. Perturbed by Castro's intransigent individual style and increasingly alarmed by his gradual and none-too-subtle shift to the Left, dissidents started voting with their feet. Between 1959 and 1962, approximately 250,000 judges, lawyers, managers and technicians left Cuba, primarily for the US, and throughout the top professions Cuba began to experience an economically debilitating brain drain. Fidel, meanwhile, hit back at the counterrevolutionaries with draconian press restrictions and the threat of arrest and incarceration for anyone caught being outwardly critical of the new regime.

Crisis begot crisis, and in June 1960 Texaco, Standard Oil and Shell refineries in Cuba buckled under US pressure and refused to refine Soviet petroleum. Sensing an opportunity to score diplomatic points over his embittered American rivals, Castro dutifully nationalized the oil companies. President Eisenhower was left with little choice: he cut 700,000 tons from the Cuban sugar quota in an attempt to get even. Rather worryingly for Cold War relations, the measure played right into the hands of the Soviet Union. Already buttered up by a 1959 visit from Che Guevara, the USSR stepped out of the shadows the following day and promised to buy the Cuban sugar at the same preferential rates. The tit-for-tat war that would come to characterize Cuban-Soviet-US relations for the next 30 years had well and truly begun.

The diplomatic crisis heated up again in August when Cuba nationalized US-owned telephone and electricity companies, and 36 sugar mills, including US$800 million in US assets. Outraged, the American government forced through an Organization of American States (OAS) resolution condemning 'extracontinental' (Soviet) intervention in the Western hemisphere, while Cuba responded by establishing diplomatic relations with communist China and edging ever closer to its new Soviet ally, via a hastily signed arms deal.

By October 1960, 382 major Cuban-owned firms, the majority of its banks and the whole rental housing market had been nationalized, and both the US and Castro were starting to prepare for the military showdown that by this point seemed inevitable. Turning the screw ever tighter, the US imposed a partial trade embargo on the island as Che Guevara nationalized all remaining US businesses. In the space of just three short years, Fidel had gone from darling of the American liberals to US public-enemy number one. The stage was set.

CONFLICT WITH THE USA

The brick finally hit the window in early 1961 when Castro ordered US embassy staff reductions in Habana. Barely able to conceal their fury, the Americans broke off diplomatic relations with Cuba, banned US citizens from traveling to the island and abolished the remaining Cuban sugar quota. At the same time, the government and the CIA began to initiate a covert program of action against the Castro regime that included invasion plans, assassination plots and blatant acts of sabotage. At the center of subterfuge lay the infamous Bay of Pigs invasion, a poorly conceived military plot that honed 1400 disaffected Cuban exiles into a workable fighting force in the jungles of Guatemala. On April 14, 1961, deemed sufficiently armed and ready to fight, the émigrés sailed with a US navy escort from Puerto Cabeza in Nicaragua to the southern coast of Cuba. But military glory wasn't forthcoming. Landing at Playa Girón and Playa Larga three days later, the US-backed expeditionary forces took a conclusive drubbing, in part because President Kennedy canceled US air cover during the landings, a decision that has since been the subject of much revisionist analysis.

Rocked and embarrassed by what had been a grave and politically costly military defeat, the Americans declared a full trade embargo on Cuba in June 1961, and in January 1962 the US used diplomatic pressure to expel the island from the OAS. Much to the Americans' chagrin, their closest neighbors, Mexico and Canada, refused to bow to US pressure to sever diplomatic relations with Cuba completely, thus throwing the country a valuable lifeline that – in the case of Canada – still exists to this day. Spinning inexorably into the Soviet sphere of influence,

1980	1982
Between April and October, 125,000 Cubans depart for the US from the port of Mariel, 30km west of Habana	Habana Vieja is listed as a Unesco World Heritage site

Castro began to cement closer relations with Khrushchev and upped the ante even further in April 1962 when, exploiting American weakness after the Bay of Pigs fiasco, he agreed to effect the installation of Soviet-made medium-range missiles on the island.

The Americans were understandably furious and, anxious not to loose any more face on the international scene, the Kennedy administration acted quickly and decisively. On October 22, 1962, President Kennedy ordered the US Navy to detain Cuba-bound Soviet ships and search for missiles, provoking the Cuban Missile Crisis, which brought the world closer to the nuclear brink than it had ever been before or has been since. Six days later, after receiving a secret assurance from Kennedy that Cuba would not be invaded, Khrushchev ordered the missiles dismantled. Castro, who was not consulted nor informed until it was a done deal, was livid and reputedly smashed a mirror in his anger.

BUILDING SOCIALISM

The learning curve was steep in the revolution's first decade. The economy continued to languish in the doldrums despite massive injections of Soviet aid, and production was marked by all of the normal inconsistencies, shortages and quality issues that characterize uncompetitive socialist markets. As National Bank president and later the minister of industry, Che Guevara advocated centralization and moral (rather than material) incentives for workers. But despite his own tireless efforts to lead by example and sponsor voluntary work weekends, all attempts to create the 'new man' ultimately proved to be unsustainable.

The effort to produce a 10-million-ton sugar harvest in 1970 was equally misguided and almost led to economic catastrophe as the country ditched everything in pursuit of one all-encompassing obsession.

Determined to learn from its mistakes, the Cuban government elected to diversify and mechanize after 1970, ushering in a decade of steadier growth and relative economic prosperity. As power was decentralized and a small market economy was permitted to flourish, people's livelihoods gradually began to improve and, for the first time in decades, *habaneros* (inhabitants of Habana) started to live more comfortably, due in no small part to burgeoning trade with the Soviet bloc, which increased from 65% of the total trade in the early 1970s to 87% in 1988.

COMMUNISM IN CRISIS

After almost 25 years of a top-down Soviet-style economy, it was obvious that quality was suffering and ambitious production quotas were becoming increasingly unrealistic. In 1986, Castro initiated the 'rectification of errors' campaign, a process that aimed to reduce malfunctioning bureaucracy and allow more local-level decision. Just as the process was reaping some rewards, the Eastern bloc collapsed in the dramatic events that followed the fall of the Berlin Wall in Europe. As trade and credits amounting to US$5 billion vanished almost overnight from the Cuban balance sheet, Castro – determined to avoid the fate of Honecker in East Germany and Ceauşescu in Romania – declared a five-year *período especial* austerity program (p23) that sent living standards plummeting and instituted a system of rationing that would make the sacrifices of wartime Europe almost pale in comparison.

Sniffing the blood of a dying communist animal, the US tightened the noose in 1992 with the draconian Torricelli Act, which forbade foreign subsidiaries of US companies from trading with Cuba and prohibited ships that had called at Cuban ports from docking at US ports for six months. Ninety percent of the trade banned by this law consisted of food, medicine and medical equipment, which led the American Association for World Health to conclude that the US embargo has caused a significant rise in suffering – even deaths – in Cuba.

In August 1993, with the country slipping rapidly into an economic coma and Habana on the verge of riot, the US dollar was legalized, allowing Cubans to hold and spend foreign currency and open US-dollar bank accounts. Spearheaded by the unlikely figure

1991	1994
Habana hosts the Pan American games	The Habana-made film *Fresa y Chocolate* (Strawberry and Chocolate) becomes the first Cuban movie to be nominated for an Oscar

of Raúl Castro, other liberal reforms followed, including limited private enterprise, self-employment, the opening of farmers markets and the expansion of the almost nonexistent tourist sector into a mainstay of the burgeoning new economy.

But the recovery was not without its problems. Class differences reemerged as people with US dollars began to gain access to goods and services not available in pesos, while touts and prostitutes took up residence in tourist areas where they preyed upon rich foreigners.

Although some of the worst shortages have been alleviated thanks to the reinvestment of tourist revenue into public services, the *período especial* has left a nasty scar. Much to the popular chagrin, the government also started to go back on some of its earlier liberalization measures in an attempt to re-establish an updated brand of old socialist orthodoxy.

Following the 1994 *balsero* crisis (when thousands of Cubans attempted to escape to the US on barely seaworthy rafts) and a handful of further shots in the ongoing diplomatic war that had been plaguing US-Cuban relations for decades, the US pulled the embargo a notch tighter in 1996 by signing the Helms-Burton Bill. Widely condemned by the international community, and energetically leapt upon by Castro as a devastating propaganda tool, the bill allows US investors to take legal action in the American courts against foreign companies utilizing their confiscated property in Cuba. It also prevents any US president from lifting the embargo until a transitional government is in place in Habana.

THE MARIEL BOATLIFT

On April 1, 1980, Hector Sanyustic – a disgruntled Cuban dissident – drove a public bus through the fence of the Peruvian embassy in downtown Habana in an audacious escape bid. Despite being fired upon by guards in the street outside (one of whom was killed in the cross fire), Sanyustic and his four accomplices made it safely inside the embassy perimeter where they successfully claimed political asylum.

Hearing the news, a furious Castro immediately demanded that Sanyustic and his colleagues be handed back to the Cuban authorities to be tried on charges of manslaughter. When Peru refused, Fidel decided to remove the guards from the embassy gates.

Few observers – Fidel included – could have predicted the chaos that followed. As word of the new security arrangements quickly spread among other disaffected Cubans, the grounds of the Peruvian embassy filled up with over 11,000 Cuban refugees determined to leave the island in the wake of a worsening economic crisis and a thaw in US-Cuban relations that had been orchestrated by the Carter administration.

With a major confrontation brewing, Castro did what he always does best: he passed the problem onto the US. On April 9, incensed at a comment by US president Jimmy Carter that had stated that America would 'welcome the refugees with open arms,' Fidel announced that the port of Mariel, 45 km west of Habana, would be open to any Cubans wanting to leave, as long as they had someone to pick them up. Moving quickly to bail out their beleaguered compatriots, Cuban exiles in Miami and Key West resourcefully rustled up a Dunkirk-like flotilla of ships that was dispatched off to Mariel on a spontaneous rescue mission.

It was a lengthy and highly disorganized evacuation. Within weeks, the US had been inundated with Cuban refugees, many of whom – it later turned out – had been released from Cuban jails and mental institutions in a cynical bid by Castro to rid the island of its so-called undesirables. Indeed, by the time the two governments finally ended the debacle in October 1980, the US had accepted approximately 125,000 Cuban immigrants from an estimated flotilla of 1700 dangerously overloaded boats. Twenty-seven people died during the sea crossing, while over 2700 were denied asylum on the grounds that they were violent felons.

In America the episode became known as the Mariel Boatlift and the refugee crisis that it created – along with the ongoing Iranian hostage affair – played a major part in Jimmy Carter's diminishing popularity. Meanwhile Castro, in a shrewd act of damage limitation, embarked upon a series of fiery nationalistic speeches that lambasted the emigrants as *lumpen* (traitors) and vowed to continue defending the revolution at all costs.

The Mariel Boatlift is fictionally portrayed in the 1983 Brian de Palma movie *Scarface*, which starred Al Pacino in the role of Tony Montana, an unscrupulous cocaine-addicted *marielito* (Cuban who came to the US as part of the Mariel Boatlift) who is let out of a Cuban jail to run amok in Miami.

1998	2003
Pope Jean Paul II visits Habana and address over one million people in the Plaza de la Revolución	Three Cubans attempting to hijack a cross-harbor Habana ferry in an audacious escape bid are foiled by authorities

REVIVAL & RESTORATION

Up until the 1970s, Habana Vieja was a poor and physically uninspiring urban neighborhood that had been in decline for the best part of a century. The slide was precipitated in the mid-19th century when the city burst its old colonial walls and sent coachloads of rich sugar barons spilling west into Vedado and Miramar. Abandoned on the shores of the harbor, Habana Vieja was left to fester in a dust-coated time capsule, its soul sequestered and its historical significance temporarily forgotten

The 'saving' of Habana Vieja is often put down to the work of one individual: Eusebio Leal Spengler, city historian, dedicated taskmaster and – perhaps more importantly – a man with a voice close to the ear of one Fidel Castro. The program that he initiated in the '70s and '80s shouldn't be underestimated. Architectural preservation wasn't a priority when the revolutionary government rolled triumphantly into the capital in a fug of cigar fumes, but Leal had other ideas. Succeeding Dr Emilio Roig de Leuchsenring as city historian in 1967, his first big project was to restore the Palacio de los Capitanes Generales (p76), a task that he completed in 1979, uncovering a museum's worth of treasures in the process. By this point he had already co-opted the Cuban government into declaring Habana Vieja 'national monument,' and in 1982, thanks primarily to his tireless lobbying, Habana Vieja, along with Habana's eastern forts, was declared a Unesco World Heritage site.

With more money and greater publicity, the master plan could now be confidently put into place. But Leal's primary motivation has never just been tourist money. 'The most important aspect of a city for tourists should be a knowledge of its own culture,' he stated portentously in the 1990s, and much of his work has reflected this theme (see p42).

Since 1982, Leal has been piecing Old Habana back together brick by brick with the aid of Unesco and a variety of foreign investors. The development isn't as straightforward as it might first appear. Leal must fight against the odds in a country where shortages are part of everyday life and money for raw materials is often scarce. Furthermore, many buildings of historical significance have long been homes for Cuban families and, in a state where it is not permissible to either buy or sell property for profit, these people must first be moved and rehoused elsewhere. The cultural and architectural results, however, are clear. Habana Vieja is a triumph of urban regeneration and a mini Rome in the making.

THE 21ST CENTURY

Cuba entered the new millennium in the throes of the Elián González drama, a tragic family crisis that became an allegory for the all-pervading senselessness of the ongoing Cuban-US immigration showdown. Not that much changed.

Failing to learn the lessons of its nine predecessors (all of whom had tried and failed to 'get rid of' Castro), the Bush administration came out all guns blazing in November 2000, following the victory-clinching Florida vote recount – a state in which conservative Cuban exiles have always punched way above their weight.

Promising to crack down on Cuba's purported human-rights abuses, George W Bush's rhetoric turned venomous after September 11, when the president began mentioning the Castro regime in the same breath as North Korea and Iraq. Subsequently, US policy was rolled back to resemble that of the worst of the Cold War years, with draconian travel restrictions, damaging financial constraints and no-compromise political rhetoric.

Rather than score much-needed capital out of Bush's belligerence, Castro elected to shoot himself in the foot by proceeding to arrest scores of so-called dissidents who had – allegedly – been sponsored by US Special Interests Office chief James Cason to spread social unrest across the island. Whether or not this was true, the trials and hefty prison sentences meted out to over 100 or more of these 'dissidents' horrified human-rights groups worldwide, and Castro's heavy-handed crackdown was condemned by everyone from Amnesty International to the Vatican.

2004	2006
The US dollar is taken out of circulation	The WWF declares Cuba to be the world's most sustainable country

Sights

Sights

Central Habana consists of three main neighborhoods. The most interesting for visitors is Habana Vieja, a magnificent Unesco World Heritage site that juxtaposes fascinating museums and gorgeous architecture with the lives over 70,000 proud *habaneros* (inhabitants of Habana). Habana Vieja is where most of the city's signature sights are located and hence is where most travelers spend the bulk of their time.

Flanking Habana Vieja to the west is Centro Habana, a crowded grid of weathered tenements and transitional 20th-century architecture that is home to the massive Capitolio building, the famous Partagás cigar factory and one of the most romantic stretches of the Malecón (Av de Maceo), Habana's dreamy sea drive. Here you can witness Habana without the tourist-brochure wrapping, a city of beguiling insights and confounding contradictions that is forever fascinating, but not always pretty.

Along Centro Habana's western border lies the central district's third main neighborhood, Vedado, a leafy suburb that was taken over by the American Mafia in the 1940s and '50s, when US mobsters such as Meyer Lanksy attempted to turn Cuba's colonial capital into a Caribbean version of Las Vegas. Posing today as a fashionable, if slightly faded, commercial district, Vedado boasts a university, some choice nightspots and a handful of interesting museums. Though quieter and more spread out than bustling Habana Vieja, Vedado is no less alluring, with picturesque parks and imposing American-era apartment blocks.

West of the Río Almendares, central Habana folds gently into the garden suburbs of Playa and Marianao. Here, elegant eclectic mansions rub shoulders with thick-trunked fig trees amid the wide boulevards and rocky shorelines of Habana's ubertrendy diplomatic

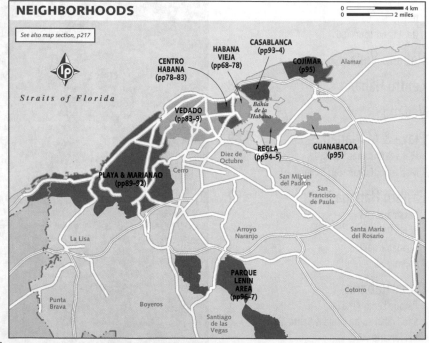

NEIGHBORHOODS

See also map section, p217

CENTRO HABANA (pp78–83)

HABANA VIEJA (pp68–78)

CASABLANCA (pp93–4)

COJÍMAR (p95)

Alamar

Straits of Florida

VEDADO (pp83–9)

Bahía de la Habana

Diez de Octubre

REGLA (pp94–5)

GUANABACOA (p95)

PLAYA & MARIANAO (pp89–92)

Cerro

San Miguel del Padrón

San Francisco de Paula

La Lisa

Arroyo Naranjo

Santa María del Rosario

Punta Brava

Boyeros

PARQUE LENIN AREA (pp96–7)

Cotorro

Santiago de las Vegas

district. Once a bastion of rich American businessmen, Playa has been recolonized in recent years by foreign embassies and fancy hotels and, although tourist sights might be a little thin on the ground, the neighborhood is not bereft of its own salubrious charms.

Other areas of Habana of interest to travelers include the eastern neighborhoods of Regla, Guanabacoa, Cojímar and Casablanca, plus the outlying suburbs of Parque Lenin, Santiago de las Vegas, San Francisco de Paula and Santa María del Rosario.

For information about transportation within Habana, see p184.

ITINERARIES
One Day

Fortify yourself with an early morning coffee in the elegant **Café de las Infusiones** (p111), with its hissing espresso machines and talented resident pianist.

The **Museo de la Revolución** (p81) will take up most of the morning, but you can clear your head afterwards with a revitalizing stroll through Habana Vieja, taking in the four 16th-century plazas. Grab a snack lunch alfresco in the gorgeous **Restaurante El Patio** (p114) before hailing a yellow coco-taxi (distinctive egg-shaped taxi) to whiz you over to the quirky **Callejón de Hamel** (p139) in Centro Habana.

After digesting a raw and hypnotic dose of Afro-Cuban rumba, stroll over to Vedado, where you can break up a leisurely afternoon with an ice cream at the **Coppelia** (p119) or a mojito in the **Hotel Nacional** (p85). After a pleasant sunset stroll back along the **Malecón** (p86), taxi it to **Fortaleza de San Carlos de la Cabaña** (p93) for the 9pm *cañonazo* (shooting of the cannons) and get back to Habana Vieja in time for a late dinner at the **Restaurante La Dominica** (p115).

Three Days

Follow the one-day itinerary, then split day two between the **Plaza de la Revolución** (p87) and the **Real Fábrica de Tabacos Partagás** (p83). In the evening, buy a copy of *Cartelera* to check out the nighttime activities at **El Hurón Azul** (p137) or the **Casa de la Música Centro Habana** (p137) before hitting the Miramar **paladar** (privately run restaurant; p124) scene for a wonderfully delicious dinner.

On day three, spend the morning examining the monuments, graves and religious iconology in the **Necrópolis Cristóbal Colón** (p106) before whetting your appetite with a light lunch at the nearby **Café Fresa y Chocolate** (p133). The afternoon can be spent soaking up the free musical entertainment in Calle Obispo or wandering around the secondhand book market (p152) in Plaza de Armas. Make a reservation at the **Paladar Guarida** (p118) for dinner and round the evening off with a glamorous nighttime cabaret show at the glitzy **Copa Room** (p136) in the Hotel Riviera.

HABANA STREET NAMES

Confusingly, many main avenues around Habana have two names in everyday use – a new name that appears on street signs and in this book, and an old name overwhelmingly preferred by locals. See below to sort it all out.

Old name	New name
Zulueta	Agramonte
Someruelos	Aponte
Av del Puerto	Av Carlos Manuel de Céspedes
Egido & Monserrate	Av de Bélgica
Vives	Av de España
Galiano	Av de Italia
Av de Rancho Boyeros	Av de la Independencia
Monserrate	Av de las Misiones
Cristina	Av de México
Carlos III (Tercera)	Av Salvador Allende
Reina	Av Simón Bolívar
Teniente Rey	Brasil
La Rampa	Calle 23
Av de los Presidentes	Calle G
Cárcel	Capdevila
Estrella	Enrique Barnet
Paula	Leonor Pérez
Av de Maceo	Malecón
Monte	Máximo Gómez
Belascoaín	Padre Varela
Paseo del Prado	Paseo de Martí
San José	San Martín

HABANA FOR CHILDREN

Bring your kids to Habana and you'll quickly discover that they'll be more of a help than a hindrance. Cubans love children and bringing a small family along with you will open up many doors that otherwise would have remained closed. Kid-friendly sights include the following:

- Acuario Nacional (p90)
- Aquarium (p68)
- Cinecito (p142)
- Circo Trompoloco (p142)
- Coppelia (p119)
- Parque Lenin (p96)
- Parque Almendares (p87)
- Teatro Nacional de Guiñol (p133)

Other kid-specific parks include **Holá Ola** (Map pp224-5; Malecón btwn Principe & Vapor; ⏲ 11am-sunset), which has minigolf for CUC$2, and **Parque La Maestranza** (Map p220; Av Carlos Manuel de Céspedes; admission CUC$2; ⏲ 9am-5pm), which is open to under-fours only.

At the time of writing, there was also a huge new amusement park being built in Playa next to Circo Trompoloco.

One Week

Follow the three-day itinerary and on day four hit the road for an out-of-town excursion to **Las Terrazas** (p179), Cuba's model ecovillage. Partake in a short hike to the **Cafetal Buenavista** (p181) or visit the **Peña de Polo Montañez** (p181) down by the lake, but don't forget to sample one of island's best cups of coffee in the friendly **Cafe de María** (p181). Return to Habana in the evening and, if you're still feeling sociable, head for a quick (expensive) daiquirí in the world-famous **El Floridita** (p134) bar.

Stay close to the city center on day five where you might want to consider a specialized tour with Habaguanex travel agency San Cristóbal. Its **architectural** (opposite) and **social programs** (opposite) excursions are highly recommended. Spend the afternoon browsing through the souvenirs at the **Feria de la Artesanía** (p151) before heading over to the **Barrio Chino** (Chinatown; p81) for a cheap and tasty dinner.

Kick off day six with a **dance lesson** (p145) at the **Museo del Ron** (p75), and stick around afterwards to take a peep at the fascinating museum. After a couple of glasses of Havana Club drunk straight up at the museum bar, stroll a block or two south to the ferry terminal and board a boat bound for Regla. Disembarking at the dock you'll see the **Iglesia de Nuestra Señora de Regla** (p94) directly in front of you. After paying your respects to the venerated Virgin of Regla, hike a few blocks up Calle Martí to the **Museo Municipal de Regla** (p94), where you can unlock the secrets of Santería. If you've still got any energy left, press on a kilometer or so to the rarely visited **Colina Lenin** (p94) for stellar views over Habana. Take the ferry back across the harbor to Habana Vieja and finish your day with a home-brew beer in the **Taberna de la Muralla** (p135) or a cup of something sweeter in the **Museo del Chocolate** (p113).

On day seven try to keep your options open. If you've had your fill of culture, organize a trip to the **Marina Hemingway** (p185) for a boat 'seafari' (p144) or a **diving excursion** (p144). For those who just can't get enough of colonial forts and historic museums, make your way over to the **Castillo de los Tres Santos Reyes Magnos del Morro** (p93) or home in on the **Museo Nacional de Bellas Artes** (p82). In the evening check out the concert program at the **Gran Teatro de la Habana** (p131) for ballet and opera or, for something a little less formal, hail a taxi to the **Café Cantante Mi Habana** (p140).

ORGANIZED TOURS

Since all of Habana's half-dozen or so tourist agencies are government run, competition between them is minimal and the itineraries they offer are much the same. The main exception to this rule is the San Cristóbal Agencia de Viajes, which is run by the City Historian's Office and offers some of the best packages in the city.

Most of the main hotels have representatives from the Cubatur, Cubanacán,

Gaviota and Havanatur agencies. Additionally, a San Cristóbal rep can be found in any of the city's Habaguanex hotels.

City Sights

CUBANACÁN Map pp224-5

☎ 873-2686; www.cubanacan.cu; Hotel Nacional, cnr Calles O & 21

The famous *cañonazo* (shooting of the cannons) is held nightly in the Fortaleza de San Carlos de la Cabaña, and is one of Habana's oldest traditions. If you go it alone, you'll pay a CUC$6 entry fee, plus taxi hire there and back. With Cubanacán's CUC$15 organized trip, however, you can throw in all of the above plus a side visit to the Castillo de Tres Santos Reyes Magnos del Morro. Cubanacán also has an office at **Hotel NH Parque Central** (Map p222; Calle Neptuno btwn Paseo de Martí & Agramonte).

CUBATUR Map pp224-5
☎ 833-3170/1; www.cubatur.cu; Calle 23 btwn Calles L & M
If you're short on time, but keen to see as much of Habana as possible, a guided city tour (CUC$15) is worth the gamble. Itineraries include a manageable mix of walking and driving, and take in such notable Habana landmarks as the Plaza de la Revolución, the Capitolio, the Malecón and Habana Vieja's four main colonial squares.

GAVIOTA Map pp228-9
☎ 204-4411; Hotel Kohly, cnr Av 49 & Calle 36
Habana's Jardín Botánico Nacional (National Botanical Garden), situated 20km south of the city, is notoriously inaccessible by public transportation, and Gaviota's organized trip is the easiest way to get there. The standard package (CUC$19) includes transportation to the gardens, entry fee, a guided tour, and a free cocktail when you arrive. The gardens themselves are surprisingly interesting and varied.

Cultural Tours
HAVANATUR Map pp228-9
☎ 203-9770, 830-8227; www.havantur.cu; Edificio Sierra Maestra, Av 1 btwn Calles 0 & 2
All of Habana's main travel agencies offer a Hemingway tour, and the packages are much the same. The itinerary (CUC$20) includes a visit to the author's house La Finca Vigía, a side trip to the fishing village of Cojímar (where Papa moored his boat), plus

---

> ### TOP FIVE MUSEUMS
> - Museo de la Revolución (p81)
> - Museo Nacional de Bellas Artes (p82)
> - Museo de la Ciudad (p74)
> - Fundación Naturaleza y El Hombre (p90)
> - Museo del Ron (p75)

---

an opportunity to down copious mojitos and daiquirís in Hemingway's two favorite watering holes, the overhyped Bodeguita del Medio and El Floridita.

SAN CRISTÓBAL AGENCIA DE VIAJES Map p220
☎ 861-9171/2; www.viajessancristobal.cu; Oficios No 110 btwn Lamparilla & Armagura
The city historian's travel agency runs a number of cultural tours, including an illuminating architectural tour (CUC$19) that is quite possibly the best specialized trip Habana has to offer. The three- to four-hour jaunt around the city's famous and not-so-famous architectural sites takes in a riot of art deco, art nouveau and eclectic architecture, and concludes with a walking tour through the beautiful baroque squares of Habana Vieja. The guides on this excursion are superb and their knowledge of the city's history and architecture is encyclopedic.

The agency also runs a tour that provides a rundown of religion in Cuba (CUC$45/23 per person for one/two people), and includes some unlikely ports of call, such as the Museo Municipal de Regla, Callejón de Hamel, the Museo de Arte Religioso, and the Adhat Israel Synagogue. And you thought all Cubans were atheists...?

And then there's the 'Art of Rum' tour (CUC$15), which involves a visit to the Museo del Ron, followed by drinks, cocktails and yet more complimentary drinks. It's for serious drinkers only.

Social Programs
SAN CRISTÓBAL AGENCIA DE VIAJES Map p220
☎ 861-9171/2; www.viajessancristobal.cu; Oficios No 110 btwn Lamparilla & Armagura
This fascinating ramble through some of Habana Vieja's groundbreaking social projects (p42) is as educational as it is unique. Negotiated on foot, the three-hour tour (CUC$10) uncovers a range of projects that have benefited from money raised via the city's tourist sector. There are visits to a maternity home, a rehabilitation center for children with diseases of the central nervous system, an embroiderers' workshop and the beautiful Convento de Nuestra Señora de Belén, now used as a residence and community center for the elderly.

HABANA VIEJA

Eating p111; Shopping p151; Sleeping p158; Walking Tours p100

Studded with architectural jewels from every era, Habana Vieja offers visitors one of the finest collections of urban edifices in the Americas. At a conservative estimate, the old town contains over 900 buildings of historical importance, with myriad examples of illustrious architecture ranging from intricate baroque to glitzy art deco.

But Habana Vieja is far more than just a living museum. Home to over 70,000 *habaneros,* who live squeezed into an area of just 4.5 sq km, the neighborhood is also one of the most condensed living spaces in Latin America. Rubbing shoulders with the rising star of tourist Habana are crumbling buildings, run-down ration shops and potholed streets.

Founded as one of Cuba's original seven settlements in 1519, Habana Vieja contained the full extent of the city until the growth of Centro Habana in the early 19th century. Between 1674 and 1863, the quarter was ringed by a 5km-long defensive wall and huge ships weighed down with precious metals from Mexico and Peru were regular visitors to the city's busy harbor.

As the city expanded westward in the 19th and 20th centuries, Habana Vieja became something of a forgotten district. Its renaissance began in the early 1980s when Unesco, in association with the talented city historian Eusebio Leal, instituted a plan to restore the old town to its former glory.

These days Habana Vieja is in the midst of one of the most extensive and ambitious renovation projects in the Americas.

TRANSPORTATION

Bus Bus 400 from Playas del Este and eastern Habana drops you on the corner of Calles Agramonte (Zulueta) and Gloria, near the train station. The M-1 from Alamar and eastern Habana also stops in Calle Agramonte near the tunnel.

Ferry The ferry from Casablanca and Regla arrives and departs from the Muelle Luz on Calle San Pedro.

Horse Carriage Horse carriages congregate in Plaza de San Francisco de Asís, and on the corner of Calle Obispo and Mercaderes.

Taxi The best place to hail a cab is in Parque Central or on the northeast corner of Plaza de Armas.

Characterized by its narrow cobbled streets and punctuated by striking churches and pretty colonial plazas, the district – particularly at night – is truly transfixing, and you'll need little imagination to summon up the images of centuries past.

Orientation

Habana Vieja sits on the western side of the harbor channel in an area once bounded by 17th-century city walls, which ran along present-day Av de Bélgica (Egido and Monserrate) and Av de las Misiones (Monserrate). The district is laid out in a rough diamond-shaped grid; its main artery is pedestrianized Calle Obispo, while most of the more interesting tourist sights are clustered around the four main squares of Plaza de la Catedral, Plaza Vieja, Plaza de San Francisco de Asís and Plaza de Armas, which lie at the eastern end of the neighborhood.

AQUARIUM Map p220

☎ 863-9493; Brasil No 9 btwn Mercaderes & Oficios; admission CUC$1; ⊙ 9am-5pm Tue-Sun
This small freshwater aquarium in a tasteful old building in Habana Vieja contains eight tanks and a varied collection of fish from around the world; it's great for the kids.

CÁMARA OSCURA Map p220

cnr Mercaderes & Brasil; admission CUC$2; ⊙ 9am-5pm Tue-Sat, 9am-1pm Sun
Situated on the corner of Plaza Vieja in the eye-catching Gómez Vila building, this fun old-town diversion provides 360-degree views of the city from a telescopic lens atop a 35m-tall tower. Sheets flap in the breeze, old cars amble by, and the docent does an admirable job explaining Habana's architectural highlights in Spanish and English during a 10-minute 'virtual' tour.

CASA DE ÁFRICA Map p220

☎ 861-5798; Obrapía No 157; admission CUC$2; ⊙ 9:30am-7:30pm
This is a small museum that houses artifacts presented to Fidel Castro during his 1977 Africa tour. Objects from no fewer than 26 countries are presented here. Also on display are objects relating to the Afro-Cuban religion Santería, which were formerly in the collection of celebrated Cuban ethnographer Fernando Ortíz.

CASA DE ASIA Map p220

☎ 863-9740; Mercaderes No 111; admission free;
🕑 10am-6pm Tue-Sat, 9am-1pm Sun

Sometimes known as the Museo de Asia, or the Museo de Arte del Lejano Oriente, this quirky cultural house exhibits painting and sculpture from Asia, with a special focus on China and Japan. The building dates from 1688, and the museum opened in 1997.

CASA DE LA OBRA PÍA Map p220

Obrapía No 158; admission CUC$1, camera CUC$2;
🕑 9am-4:30pm Tue-Sat, 9:30am-12:30pm Sun

This typical Habana aristocratic residence was originally built in 1665, and was rebuilt in 1780, soon after the British occupation. It is named for the piety of its original owner, Martín Calvo de la Puerta, who was well known for lending economic support to orphans over a period of many years (obra pía means 'charitable work'). Baroque decoration – including an intricate portico, which was made in Cádiz, Spain – covers the exterior facade, and at 1480 sq m this grandiose home was the largest in the neighborhood at the time it was erected.

As well as its historical connections, the house today also contains one of the city historian's most commendable social projects, a sewing-and-needlecraft cooperative that has a workshop inside and a small shop selling clothes and textiles on Calle Mercaderes.

CASA DE LOMBILLO Map p220

cnr Empedrado & Mercaderes

This resplendent casa (house) is one of Habana's oldest, dating from 1741, although there has been a building on this site since 1618. Named after one of its 18th-century owners, the count of Lombillo, who made his fortune in the slave trade, the building is most notable for its exquisite interior balconies and stately Tuscan-style columns. During the mid-19th century the palace served as Habana's main post office (it was the city's first), and a stone-mask mailbox in one of the outside walls is still in use. In late 2000, the Casa de Lombillo was gutted and restored. It now functions as the main office for the city historian, Eusebio Leal Spengler.

CASA DE LOS CONDES DE JARUCO
Map p220

☎ 861-8544; Muralla No 107; admission free;
🕑 10am-5pm Mon-Fri, 10am-2pm Sat

With its wide gallery, this house is said to be typical of aristocratic residences built around 1737. Although the house is named after the counts of Jaruco, its most famous resident was María Mercedes de Santa Cruz y Cárdenas, who was born in the mansion and went on to become one of the city's early literary greats. Today the building houses La Casona Centro de Arte (p152).

CASA DE MÉXICO BENITO JUÁREZ
Map p220

☎ 861-8166; cnr Obrapía & Mercaderes; admission CUC$1; 🕑 10:15am-5:45pm Tue-Sat, 9am-1pm Sun

Named after Mexico's long-serving indigenous president and hero, the Casa de Benito Juárez exhibits Mexican folk art in an 18th-century palace. However, there's not a whole lot about Señor Juárez himself at the museum bearing his name.

CASA OSWALDO GUAYASAMÍN
Map p220

☎ 861-3843; Obrapía No 111; donations accepted;
🕑 9am-2:30pm Tue-Sun

This is the former workshop and home of the notable Ecuadorian painter Oswaldo Guayasamín, who lived in Habana for many years before his death in March 1999. Guayasamín is most famous for paintings of Fidel produced during the '80s and '90s; one of them is normally displayed in the Fundación Naturaleza y El Hombre (p90). The Ecuadorian also painted many other famous figures, including Raúl Castro, Eusebio Leal and Colombian novelist Gabriel García Márquez, but unfortunately you won't find any of these portraits here. Instead the house showcases exhibits of Cuban and international art, although the place is actually more impressive for its finely worked iron railings, marble staircases, graceful arches and other architectural features.

CASTILLO DE LA REAL FUERZA
Map p220

☎ 861-6130; Plaza de Armas; admission CUC$2;
🕑 9am-6pm

The oldest existing fort in the Americas, the Castillo de Real Fuerza was built between

HABANA VIEJA TOP FIVE

- Museo de la Ciudad (p74)
- Museo del Ron (p75)
- Plaza de la Catedral (p77)
- Edificio Bacardí (right)
- Iglesia de San Francisco de Asís El Nuevo (p72)

1558 and 1577 on the site of an earlier fort destroyed by French privateers in 1555. The west tower is crowned by a copy of a famous bronze weather vane called La Giraldilla; the original was cast in Habana in 1632 by Jerónimo Martínez Pinzón and is popularly believed to be of Doña Inés de Bobadilla, the wife of gold-explorer Hernando de Soto. It is now kept in the **Museo de la Ciudad** (p74), and the figure also appears on the Havana Club rum label. For the first 200 years of its existence, the Castillo was the residence of the Spanish captains general, until they finally got around to constructing a palace of their own across the square. Imposing and indomitable, the castle is ringed by an impressive moat and its walls, like those of other forts facing the Caribbean, are made from blocks of coral. Today, La Fuerza shelters the **Museo de la Cerámica Artística Cubana**, along with a bar, snack stand and souvenir shop.

CATEDRAL DE SAN CRISTÓBAL DE LA HABANA Map p220
cnr San Ignacio & Empedrado
Dominated by two unequal towers and framed by a theatrical baroque facade designed in the style of Italian architect Francesco Borromini, Habana's graceful Catedral de San Cristóbal was once described by Cuban novelist Alejo Carpentier as 'music set in stone.'

When the Jesuits began construction of the church in 1748, Habana was still under the ecclesiastical control of Santiago de Cuba. Work continued despite the expulsion of the Jesuits from Cuba in 1767, and the diocese of Habana was finally created when the building was finished in 1787. A year later the city became a bishop's seat, elevating the church to a cathedral – one of the oldest in the Americas. Legend has it that the cathedral contained a dramatic funeral monument dedicated to Christopher Columbus, which held the great explorer's remains. It's said that the monument was

shipped to Spain in 1898, where it is interred in Seville's cathedral.

One of the cathedral's many curiosities is its surprisingly austere classical interior, the work of a pious bishop at the beginning of the 19th century. To take a peep at the pews and altar your best bet is to slip inside at 10:30am during Sunday Mass. Otherwise opening times can be sporadic.

Pope John Paul II said one of his four Cuban Masses at the cathedral in January 1998 during a groundbreaking papal tour of the island.

CENTRO CULTURAL PABLO DE LA TORRIENTE BRAU Map p220
☎ 861-6251; Muralla No 63; admission free; ☯ Tue-Sat 9am-5:30pm
A leading cultural institution that was formed under the auspices of the Unión Nacional des Escritores y Artistas de Cuba (Uneac; National Union of Cuban Writers & Artists) in 1996, this center hosts a variety of expositions of substance, including poetry readings and a live acoustic music series called Guitarra Limpia. Its **Salón de Arte Digital** is renowned for its groundbreaking digital art.

CENTRO WIFREDO LAM Map p220
☎ 862-2611; San Ignacio No 22 cnr Empedrado; admission CUC$3; ☯ 10am-5pm Mon-Sat
This exhibition center is named after Cuba's most famous painter (p31), though these days it is more likely to display works by lesser-known Latin artists. A Cuban of Chinese and African ancestry, Lam (1902–82) was strongly influenced by Pablo Picasso, whom he met in Paris in 1936 and under whom he studied for a brief period. Much of the artist's best work can be viewed today at the **Museo Nacional de Bellas Artes** (p82). This venue, just off Plaza de la Catedral, also contains a small shop and a patio café that was being renovated at the time of writing.

EDIFICIO BACARDÍ Map p220
Av de las Misiones btwn Neptuno & Empedrado
Finished in 1929, the magnificent Edificio Bacardí is a triumph of art deco architecture, with a whole host of lavish furnishings that somehow manage to blend the kitsch with the cool. Hemmed in by other buildings, it's hard to get a full kaleidoscopic view of

the structure from street level, though the opulent bell tower can be glimpsed from all over Habana. There's a bar in the lobby and for a few convertibles you can travel up to the tower for a bird's-eye view.

EDIFICIO SANTO DOMINGO Map p220
Mercaderes btwn Obispo & O'Reilly
Across Obispo from the Hotel Ambos Mundos lies the site of Habana's original university, which stood at this intersection from 1728 until 1902, after which it was moved to its present location in Vedado. It was housed in the now defunct Santo Domingo convent, a huge building that had been commissioned in 1574 by Father Santo Domingo de Guzmán and altered radically to fit in with the new baroque style in 1777. The convent was partly demolished in 1919 and razed completely 30 years later when the Americans sponsored the building of a grotesque and totally incongruous 1950s-style office block whose roof was used as a helicopter landing pad. Accepting one of its biggest challenges yet, the City Historian's Office completed an ambitious restoration project in 2006 that rebuilt the convent's original bell tower and inserted an elaborate baroque doorway into the ugly modern building. The result provides an interesting juxtaposition of old against new. As well as housing a number of relocated departments from Habana University, the restored Edificio Santo Domingo also contains a scale model of the old convent and – in the adjoining tower – the original antique bell.

ESTACIÓN CENTRAL DE FERROCARRILES Map p220
Av de Bélgica cnr Arsenal
Train lovers will adore Cuba, the only country in the Caribbean with a fully functioning rail system. In 1837 it was the first place in Latin America (and the sixth in the world) to install a railway network; ironically, colonial masters Spain didn't open their own railway network until nearly a decade later. Built upon the ruins of an old Spanish shipyard with two renaissance-style towers, Habana's central station first opened its doors for business in 1912 (an older station had stood on the site of the present-day Capitolio). The spacious waiting rooms and wide platforms have seen few alterations in the 100 years since.

FARMACIA MUSEO TAQUECHEL
Map p220
☎ 862-9286; Obispo No 155 btwn San Ignacio & Mercaderes; admission free; ☺ 9am-7pm
This old-fashioned store dating from 1898 is one of several restored 19th-century pharmacies in Habana Vieja. Inside you'll find shelves lined with rows of fine French porcelain jars. The pharmacy also sells natural therapeutic products and homeopathic medicines.

FOTOTECA DE CUBA Map p220
☎ 862-2530; Mercaderes No 307; admission free; ☺ 10am-5pm Tue-Fri, 9am-noon Sat
In the Casa de Juan Rico de Mata on Plaza Vieja, this photo gallery run by the Fototeca de Cuba displays intriguing exhibits by local and international artists.

FUNDACIÓN ALEJO CARPENTIER
Map p220
Casa de la Condesa de la Reunion; Empedrado No 215 btwn Aguiar & Cuba; admission free; ☺ 8:30am-4:30pm Mon-Fri
The small Carpentier foundation is named for one of Cuba's most lauded writers, Alejo Carpentier (1904–80), the son of a French man and a Russian woman, who was born in Lausanne, Switzerland, but moved to Cuba as a child. Built in 1809, this house – where Carpentier once kept an office – has a small museum displaying some of the writer's personal effects. Carpentier was a magic-realist writer who also dabbled in nonfiction. His works include *La Consagración de la Primervera* and his seminal work *Music in Cuba*.

HOTEL AMBOS MUNDOS Map p220
Obispo No 153
As well as being a restored Habaguanex hotel (p160), the Ambos Mundos is also a shrine to the late, great Ernest Hemingway who 'lived' here on and off throughout the 1930s. Real suckers for the legend can visit Room No 511 (admission CUC$2; ☺ 9am-5pm Mon-Fri), where the expat American began writing *For Whom the Bell Tolls,* though you're probably better off investigating the bar downstairs, where there is an interesting photo wall (including a snapshot of Hemingway and Fidel at a 1960 fishing tournament) and a fine resident pianist who'll serenade you with Sinatra tunes on a shiny grand.

IGLESIA DE SAN FRANCISCO DE ASÍS EL NUEVO Map p220

cnr Cuba & Amargura

Still in the throes of a lengthy restoration, this unique church near Plaza Vieja was once known as the Iglesia de San Agustín. Built in 1633, it was reconsecrated in 1842 and taken over by the Franciscan order, which had recently lost its tenancy in the Iglesia de San Francisco de Asís a few blocks to the east. Thanks to its earlier incarnation under Augustine monks, the church still retains a notable Mexican flavor, including ochre pillars, intricate stained glass, haunting frescoes and a gorgeously painted inner dome.

IGLESIA DE SAN FRANCISCO DE PAULA Map p220

cnr Leonor Pérez & Desamparados

Standing on a traffic island on Calle Desamparados, this church, dating from 1664, is all that remains of the San Francisco de Paula women's hospital. Rebuilt after a hurricane in 1730, the hospital was demolished in the 1940s, but the church remained as an architectural oddity until a 2000 restoration transformed it into a classical-music venue. Lit up at night for concerts (most notably by the medieval ensemble Ars Longa), the church's stained glass, heavy cupola and baroque facade are utterly romantic and inviting.

IGLESIA DEL SANTO ANGEL CUSTODIO Map p220

☎ 861-0469; Compostela No 2

Originally constructed in 1695, the Santo Angel was pounded by a ferocious hurricane in 1846, after which it was entirely rebuilt in neo-Gothic style. Among the notable historical and literary figures that have passed through its handsome doors are 19th-century Cuban novelist Cirilo Villaverde, who set the main scene of his novel *Cecilia Valdés* here, and Felix Varela and José Martí, who were baptized in the church in 1788 and 1853, respectively.

IGLESIA PARROQUIAL DEL ESPÍRITU SANTO Map p220

☎ 862-3140; Acosta No 161; ⏱ 8am-noon & 3-6pm

Habana's oldest surviving church was built as a chapel with slave labor in 1638, but was extensively altered in 1674 when it was declared a parish church. While the exquisite baroque wooden lattice gate outside is eye-catching, the true masterpieces lie within, including a modern sculpture by Alfredo Lozano and a large painting by Cuban artist Arístides Fernández. The finely carved ceiling also deserves a look. Catacombs run on both sides of the nave, supported by the stumps of buried trees, and there are many burials in the crypt. A royal decree issued by King Charles III of Spain in the late 18th century gave the automatic right of asylum to anyone who set foot in the church.

IGLESIA Y CONVENTO DE NUESTRA SEÑORA DE BELÉN Map p220

☎ 861-7283; Compostela btwn Luz & Acosta; admission CUC$2; ⏱ 9am-5pm Mon-Sat, 9am-1pm Sun

Completed in 1718, the Convento Belén was used initially by nuns from the Order of Bethlehem as a convalescent home. When the order was suppressed in 1842, the convent was passed onto to the Spanish government who, in turn, passed it over to the Jesuits. In the ensuing years, the structure was substantially enlarged to occupy a full city block and a school was added. The church inside has a nave with vaulted transepts and the gate is adorned with stone statues that display various images of the saints. The structure is also known for a unique baroque arch – the Arco de Belén – that stands at the corner of Acosta and Compostela.

The City Historian's Office's biggest social project, the convent today is (once again) a convalescent home where elderly people from the surrounding neighborhood come to relax, paint, enjoy live theater and receive occupational therapy; there are even some live-in residents.

IGLESIA Y CONVENTO DE NUESTRA SEÑORA DE LA MERCED Map p220

Cuba No 806; ⏱ 8am-noon & 3-5:30pm

Built over a period of a century, this small but compact church was completed by monks in 1867. Traditionally a bastion of the Habana aristocracy, the Merced is a long-favored site for weddings due to its stunningly beautiful interior, which includes colorful trompe l'oeil frescoes, elaborate dome paintings and a magnificent altar. The best time to visit the church is on September 24, the feast day of the Virgin of the

Merced. On this day, Catholic and African beliefs come together in the veneration of two saints in one image: the Virgin Mary and Ohatalá, the Yoruba goddess of the earth. The statue of the Virgin sporting a flowing white robe stands on the altar.

IGLESIA Y CONVENTO DE SANTA CLARA Map p220

☎ 866-9327; Cuba No 610 btwn Luz & Sol; admission CUC$2; ☺ 9am-4pm Mon-Fri

This huge construction – which covers four city blocks – was the first nunnery in Habana. Built from 1638 to 1643, it was founded by nuns from Cartagena de Indias. Look out for the marvelous beamed ceiling in the nave, and the handsome columns and pleasing arches in the main cloister. Among the many residences here is the Casa del Marino (Sailor's House), in the second cloister. According to records, this house (the current residence of academics) was built by a pirate-turned-respectable-shipowner who gave the building to his devout daughter.

Ceasing to be a convent in 1920, the Santa Clara became the Ministry of Public Works. Today the team in charge of the restoration of colonial Habana is based here, and the complex also offers a small guesthouse, the **Residencia Académica de Santa Clara** (p158), one of Habana Vieja's cheapest budget hotels.

IGLESIA Y MONASTERIO DE SAN FRANCISCO DE ASÍS Map p220

Plaza de San Francisco de Asís

Originally constructed as a church in 1608 and rebuilt in the baroque style from 1719 to 1738, the Iglesia San Francisco de Asís was taken over by the Spanish state in 1841 as part of a political move against the powerful religious orders of the day. It ceased to be a consecrated church, and later served as a warehouse and post office. Protected from the public gaze are three former cloisters, spacious courtyards and more than 100 tiny apartments for members of the monastery. Today the church serves as a **concert hall** (p131), featuring classical, chamber and choral music. The **Museo de Arte Religioso** (unguided/guided CUC$2/3; ☺ 9am-6pm) is replete with religious paintings, silverware, wood carvings and ceramics. The admission price for the museum includes access to the tallest bell tower in Habana.

LONJA DEL COMERCIO Map p220

Plaza de San Francisco de Asís

This large box-shaped building on Plaza de San Francisco is a former commodities market erected in 1909. In 1996 the building was completely renovated by Habaguanex and today it provides office space for foreign companies with joint ventures in Cuba. You can enter the Lonja to admire its central atrium and futuristic interior. It also houses the excellent café-restaurant **El Mecurio** (p113), named after the bronze figure of the god Mercury that sits atop a dome on the roof.

MAQUETA DE LA HABANA VIEJA Map p220

Mercaderes No 114; unguided/guided CUC$1/2; ☺ 9am-6pm

This is a scale model of Habana Vieja, complete with an authentic soundtrack that is meant to replicate a day in the life of the city. It's incredibly detailed and provides an excellent way to geographically acquaint yourself with what the central historical district has to offer. Come here first!

MUSEO CARLOS FINLAY Map p220

Cuba btwn Amargura & Brasil; admission CUC$2; ☺ 8:30am-5pm Mon-Fri, 9am-3pm Sat

Named after Cuba's most famous scientist, this engaging museum on Calle Cuba is also home to the Academia de Ciencias Médicas, Físicas y Naturales (Academy of Medical, Physical & Natural Sciences). A physician of French and Scottish descent, Finlay (1833–1915) was the first scientist to identify the mosquito as the organism that caused yellow fever. Later on he became Cuba's chief medical officer and a respected figure within the Latin American scientific community. The museum displays numerous busts and paintings related to the scientist's remarkable life, along with a stash of over 95,000 medical books.

MUSEO DE ARTE COLONIAL Map p220

☎ 862-6440; San Ignacio No 61; guided/unguided CUC$2/3; ☺ 9am-6:30pm

On the south side of the Plaza de la Catedral, this is a small museum displaying colonial furniture and decorative arts in the former Palacio de los Condes de Casa Bayona (Palace of the Counts of Casa Bayona); it's the oldest house on the square, dating from 1720. Among the finer exhibits are pieces of china with scenes of colonial Cuba, a collection of ornamental flowers, and many colonial-era dining room sets. To wander the rooms of the Palacio de los Condes de Casa Bayona today is to get an accurate picture of the interiors of 18th- and 19th-century Habana mansions.

MUSEO DE LA CIUDAD Map p220

☎ 861-6130; Tacón No 1; unguided/guided CUC$3/4; ☯ 9am-6pm
Located in the Palacio de los Capitanes Generales (p76) and set around a splendid central courtyard adorned with a white marble statue of Christopher Columbus, this is one of Habana's most comprehensive and interesting museums, and is worthy of a good couple of hours of your time. The rooms are richly decorated with period furniture, military uniforms, 19th-century horse carriages and personal artifacts of citizens past, while old photos vividly re-create events from Habana's rich history, such as the 1898 sinking of US battleship *Maine* in the harbor. War buffs will appreciate the rooms dedicated to Cuba's independence struggles from 1868 until 1959. The guided tour takes you into several otherwise inaccessible areas.

MUSEO DE LA FARMACIA HABANERA
Map p220

☎ 866-7556; cnr Brasil & Compostela; admission free; ☯ 9am-7pm
Founded in 1886 by Catalan José Sarrá and once considered the second-most important pharmacy in the world, this old-fashioned store on Calle Brasil (Teniente Rey) got the Habaguanex makeover in 2004 when a small museum was incorporated into the existing structure. Aside from the elegant mock-up of an old drugstore with long wooden counters and well-polished glass display jars, the store still acts as an important working pharmacy for the people of the neighborhood.

MUSEO DE LA ORFEBRERÍA Map p220

☎ 863-9861; Obispo No 113 btwn Mercaderes & Oficios; donations accepted; ☯ 9am-4:30pm Tue-Sat, 9am-12:30pm Mon
The museum of silverware is located in the former house of silversmith Gregorio Tabares, who had a workshop here from 1707.

Various items made by Habana silversmiths between the 18th and 20th centuries are displayed inside, and they're not half bad considering the island's notable lack of the precious metal. Curios include jewels, clocks, ashtrays and desktops.

MUSEO DE NAIPES Map p220

☎ 860-1534; Muralla No 101; admission CUC$1; ☯ 9am-6pm Tue-Sun
Exhibited in one of Plaza Vieja's oldest structures, dating from the 17th century, is one of Habana's more obscure museums. Dedicated to a collection of playing cards, it has everything from rock stars to rum drinks to round cards – there are 2000 of them here.

MUSEO DE NUMISMÁTICO Map p220

☎ 861-5811; Obispo btwn Aguilar & Habana; admission CUC$1; ☯ 9am-4:45pm
Numismatists will love this well-presented museum on Habana Vieja's main thoroughfare. It brings together various collections of medals, coins and banknotes from around the world, including a stash of 1000 mainly American gold coins (ranging in date from 1869 to 1928) given to Fidel Castro by eminent Swiss biologist Dr Albert Thut. Other highlights include Greek, Roman and early Spanish coins, plus a full chronology of Cuban banknotes from the 19th century to the present, including the infamous peso bills signed by the former president of the National Bank, Che Guevara.

MUSEO DE PINTURA MURAL Map p220

Obispo btwn Mercaderes & Oficios; donations accepted; ☯ 10am-6pm
Hidden in the Casa del Mayorazgo de Recio – popularly considered to be Habana's oldest surviving house – this museum tracks the history in Cuba of wall paintings and frescoes, a style that was vogue throughout the 18th and 19th centuries, particularly in the cities of Habana, Trinidad and Camagüey. The building itself dates from the 1570s, when it belonged to Antón de Recio, a Spaniard from Huelva province in Andalucía, who owned one of the island's oldest sugar mills and married the daughter of a local *cacique* (chief). Originally a one-story construction, a second floor was added in the 17th century, though the house retains many of its earlier Mudéjar elements, including a patio, storage

well, wooden window grilles and some beautifully restored frescoes.

MUSEO DE SIMÓN BOLÍVAR Map p220

Mercaderes No 160; admission CUC$1; 9am-5pm Tue-Sat

A diminutive museum dedicated to Latin America's great liberator, who remains a perennial hero to most Cubans. Downstairs there are panels containing text in English, French and Spanish that describe Bolívar's life and his many accomplishments. Upstairs there's a reproduction of his sword, a coin minted in his honor and paintings of him by contemporary artists. There is a bronze statue of Simón Bolívar in a small park across the road.

MUSEO DE TABACO Map p220

861-5795; Mercaderes No 120; admission free; 10am-5pm Mon-Sat

Inside here you'll find a standard cigar salesroom plus displays of assorted cigar paraphernalia. Among the many Casa del Habano cigar stores in the city, this is one of the best.

MUSEO DEL AUTOMÓVIL Map p220

Oficios No 13; admission CUC$1; 9am-7pm

One of Habana's most amusing sights is this small and vaguely surreal museum, stuffed full of ancient Thunderbirds, Pontiacs and Ford Model Ts, at least half of which appear to be in better shape than the asthmatic automobiles that ply the streets outside. It's even got the green Chevrolet Bel Air that Che Guevara once drove (very badly apparently) after he was installed as a member of the revolutionary government in 1959. Other notable vehicles include a 1930 La Salle Model 340, a 1926 Willy's Overland Whippet 96, a horse-drawn fire engine dating from 1894 and the 1918 Ford Model T truck that belonged to Castro's father.

MUSEO DEL RON Map p220

861-8051; San Pedro No 262; admission incl guide CUC$5; 9am-5pm Mon-Fri, 10am-4pm Sat & Sun

Even for teetotalers, this intriguing museum in the Fundación Havana Club is worth a turn. The interesting bilingual guided tour shows rum-making antiquities (check out the funky terracotta flask), and explains the entire brewing process, from cane cutting to quaffing amber Añejo Reserva in the museum's tasting room. The scale model of the Central La Esperanza sugar mill factory, with working train, is especially cool. The dancing lessons (p145) here are some of the best in Habana.

MUSEO EL TEMPLETE Map p220

Plaza de Armas; admission CUC$2; 8:30am-6pm

This tiny neoclassical Doric chapel on the east side of the Plaza de Armas was erected in 1828 at the point where Habana's first Mass was held beneath a ceiba tree in November 1519. A similar ceiba tree has now replaced the original. Inside the chapel are three large paintings of the event by the French painter Jean Baptiste Vermay.

MUSEO NACIONAL DE HISTORIA NATURAL Map p220

863-9361; Obispo No 61; admission CUC$3; 9:30-7pm Tue-Sun

This average museum in Plaza de Armas contains examples of Cuba's flora and fauna. Next door is the Biblioteca Pública Provincial Rubén M Villena (p193), a public library.

MUSEO NACIONAL DE LA MÚSICA Map p220

863-0052; Capdevila No 1; 10am-5:45pm

The collection of Cuban musical instruments exhibited in this glittering 1905 residence built in Italian Renaissance style includes vintage pianos, bongo drums, guitars, maracas, claves and even a xylophone from Laos. There's a small shop near the entrance that sells recordings of Cuban music, and concerts – including some great rumba – take place in the music room a couple of nights a week. The museum was temporarily closed for renovation at the time of writing.

MUSEO-CASA NATAL DE JOSÉ MARTÍ Map p220

861-3778; Leonor Pérez No 314; admission CUC$1, camera CUC$2; 9am-5pm Tue-Sat

The apostle of Cuban independence was born in this humble, two-story dwelling on the edge of Habana Vieja on January 28, 1853. Today it's a small museum that displays letters, manuscripts, photos, books and other mementos of his life. While it's not as comprehensive as the Memorial a José Martí (p86) in Plaza de la Revolución, it's a charming little house and is well worth the walk.

OLD CITY WALL Map p220
Av de Bélgica

At the southern end of Av de Bélgica, close to the train station, lies the longest remaining stretch of the old city wall. The wall, which was designed to deter attacks from pirates and buccaneers, was begun in 1674 and took over 60 years to build. On its completion, it measured 1.5m thick, 10m high and 5km long. A bronze map at the remnants of the wall shows the outline of the original layout. Among the defenses erected along its course were nine bastions and some 180 big guns aimed toward the sea. The only way in and out of the city from 1740 until the demolition of the wall began on August 8, 1863, was through 11 highly guarded gates that closed every night and opened every morning at the sound of a solitary gunshot. Many of the stones used to pave Habana's streets and construct the city's buildings were pulled from the monstrous wall, much of which still stood five decades after its demolition began.

PALACIO CUETO Map p220
cnr Muralla & Mercaderes

Habana's finest art nouveau building was constructed in 1906, based on the designs of architect Arturo Márquez. Located on the southeast corner of Plaza Vieja, it exhibits distinct Gaudí-esque features. Its outrageously ornate facade housed a warehouse and a hat factory before it was rented by a Señor José Cueto as the Palacio Vienna hotel a decade or so later. The property has been empty and unused since the early '90s, but Habaguanex has pledged to restore the property as a period hotel. Scaffolding suggests work is already underway.

PALACIO DE GOBIERNO Y VAGÓN MAMBÍ Map p220
☎ 863-4352; Oficios No 211; admission free; ⏰ 8:30am-4:45pm

This eclectic palace on Calle Oficios was the former seat of the Cuban government from 1902 until 1929 (when the Capitolio was completed). Furnished with decorative baroque details and an Italian marble floor, the museum contains a parliament room, the former president's office and the original Cuban flag used by Carlos Manuel de Céspedes. To the side of the building on Churruca is the Vagón Mambí, a train

car built in the US in 1900 and brought to Cuba in 1912. Put into service as the presidential car, it's a palace on wheels, with a formal dining room, louvered wooden windows and, back in its heyday, fans that cooled the car with dry ice.

PALACIO DE LOS CAPITANES GENERALES Map p220
Tacón No 1

Filling the whole west side of the Plaza de Armas, this former palace is one of Cuba's most majestic baroque buildings. It stands on the site of Habana's original church, the Parroquial Mayor, which was established in 1574 but was damaged by the explosion of the *Invencible* in Habana harbor in 1741. Due to ongoing damage, the church was subsequently demolished in 1776. The current building dates from the late 1770s and it has served many purposes over the years. From 1791 until 1898, it was the residence of the Spanish captains general. From 1899 until 1902, the US military governors were based here, and during the first two decades of the 20th century the building briefly became the presidential palace. In 1920 the president moved to the palace now housing the Museo de la Revolución and the Palacio de los Capitanes Generales became the city hall. The municipal authorities moved out in 1967, and since 1968 it has been home to the Museo de la Ciudad (p74).

PALACIO DE LOS CONDES DE SANTOVENIA Map p220
Calle Baratillo No 9

Habaguanex' five-star Hotel Santa Isabel (p162) is a historic building in its own right and a former stately palace of the counts of Santovenia. It dates from the 1780s and was converted into a luxurious hotel in 1867, making it one of Habana's oldest hotels. Habaguanex gave the place a much needed makeover in the 1990s, which was good enough for ex–US president Jimmy Carter, who stayed here during his groundbreaking 2002 visit.

PALACIO DE LOS MARQUESES DE AGUAS CLARAS Map p220
San Ignacio No 54

Situated on the western side of the Plaza de la Catedral, this majestic building completed in 1760 was a one-time baroque palace widely lauded for the beauty of its shady Andalucian patio. Today it houses the Restaurante El Patio (p114), a choice spot for an alfresco drink or meal in front of the ethereal cathedral. You'll be serenaded 24 hours a day by live music – three bands alternate eight-hour shifts.

PALACIO DEL MARQUÉS DE ARCOS
Map p220
Plaza de la Catedral
Completed in 1746, this luxurious former residential mansion is a perfect example of a typical Spanish-American colonial house, with a spacious main room with a wide staircase that hugs two walls as it winds up to the 2nd floor. Five arcades of Doric columns adorn the ground floor and lovely porticoes above the arcades overlook the square. The main entrance to the building is on Calle Mercaderes.

PALACIO DEL SEGUNDO CABO
Map p220
Calle O'Reilly No 4; admission CUC$1;
🕑 10am-5:30pm Mon-Sat
Situated on the northwest corner of the Plaza de Armas, this is the former head-quarters of the Spanish vice-governor, constructed in 1772. For a time the building acted as a post office, then during the 20th century it variously served as the palace of the Senate, the nation's Supreme Court, the National Academy of Arts & Letters, and, for a brief period, the seat of the Cuban Geographical Society. Today most of the building is used by the Instituto Cubano del Libro and houses a well-stocked bookstore just inside the entrance. Architectural buffs should check out the lovely inner courtyard.

PLAZA DE ARMAS Map p220
Habana's oldest square was conceived in the early 1520s, soon after the city's foundation. It was originally known as Plaza de Iglesia after the church – the Parroquial Mayor – that once stood on the site of the present-day Palacio del los Capitanes Generales. The name Plaza de Armas (Parade Ground) wasn't adopted until the late 16th century, when the governor of the Castillo Real de la Fuerza used the site to conduct military exercises. The modern plaza, along with most of the buildings around it, dates only from the late 1700s when, minus its

church, it became a park that filled nightly with lilting music and carriages used by ladies and their suitors.

In the center of the square, which is lined with royal palms and characterized by a daily (except Sunday) secondhand book market (p152), is a marble statue of Carlos Manuel de Céspedes, the man who set Cuba on the road to independence in 1868. Long a favored rest spot for travelers and inquisitive Cubans, this is a pleasant place to sit on a bench and listen to the typical Cuban music drifting across the square from the restaurant La Mina (p113).

PLAZA DE LA CATEDRAL Map p220
Habana Vieja's most uniform square is a museum to Cuban baroque, with all the surrounding buildings – including the city's magnificent cathedral (p70) – dating from the 1700s. Despite this homogeneity, it is actually the newest of the four squares in the old town, with its present layout dating from the 18th century. Attractive, diminutive and spine-tinglingly atmospheric, the plaza is best enjoyed at nighttime, when the winking lanterns lend the shadowy walls an almost timeless quality and, with a little imagination, you can transport your-self back to the days of beer-swilling pirates and horse-drawn carriages.

PLAZA DE SAN FRANCISCO DE ASÍS
Map p220
Facing Habana harbor, the breezy Plaza de San Francisco de Asís first grew up in the 16th century, when New World prospectors disembarked at the quayside and Spanish galleons stopped by on their passage through the Indies to Spain. A market took root on this spot in the 1500s, followed by a church in 1608, though when the pious monks complained of too much noise the market was moved a few blocks south to Plaza Vieja. The Plaza de San Francisco underwent a full restoration in the late 1990s and is most notable for its uneven cobbles and the white-marble Fuente de los Leones (Fountain of Lions), carved by the Italian sculptor Giuseppe Gaginni in 1836. A more modern statue outside the square's famous church depicts El Caballero de Paris, a well-known street person who roamed Habana during the 1950s, with his unkempt beard and rough bag of belongings, engaging passers-by with his philosophies on life,

religion, politics and current events. On the eastern side of the plaza stands the Terminal Sierra Maestra, which dispatches shiploads of tourists once or twice a week.

PLAZA DEL CRISTO Map p220

Habana Vieja's fifth (and most overlooked) square lies at the west end of the neighborhood, a little apart from the bustling historic core. The city historian's renovation project hasn't reached this far yet, as the plaza's clutch of dilapidated (and, in some cases, collapsing) buildings graphically testify. That's not to say it isn't worth a look. The plaza's main highlight is the **Parroquial del Santo Cristo del Buen Viaje**, a church dating from 1732, although there has been a Franciscan hermitage on this site since 1640. Currently undergoing some long-awaited repairs, the church is most notable for its intricate stained-glass windows and brightly painted wooden ceiling. The Plaza del Cristo also boasts a children's school (hence the noise) and the blue-and-yellow restaurant **Hanoi** (p113), a longtime travelers' hangout.

PLAZA VIEJA Map p220

Laid out in 1559, Plaza Vieja (Old Sq) is Habana's most architecturally eclectic square, juxtaposing the baroque **Casa de los Condes de Jaruco** (p69) with the Gaudí-inspired **Palacio Cueto** (p76). Planned as a 'living' public space in the 16th century, Plaza Vieja – in contrast to other Latin American plazas – contains no church and was designed with the houses and private dwellings overlooking the central action. Initially known as Plaza Nueva (New Sq), it was a public square and a popular gathering place used for military exercises. It then served as an open-air marketplace until 1835, when the market moved and the square again became a popular place to gather and converse. More recently the Batista regime constructed an ugly underground parking lot here that engineers demolished in 1996. A massive renovation project began in the late 1990s and, as of 2006, only the Palacio Cueto and a rather scruffy dwelling on the west side were still awaiting the restorer's paintbrush. Sprinkled liberally with bars, restaurants and cafés, Plaza Vieja boasts its own microbrewery – **La Taberna de la Muralla** (p135) – and the Angela Landa children's school (the square itself doubles as a school play-

ground), which is housed in a decorative neoclassical–art nouveau building. The beautiful fountain in the centre is a copy of an earlier fountain on this site.

CENTRO HABANA

Eating p116; Shopping p153; Sleeping p162; Walking Tours p101

Centro Habana, which borders Habana Vieja to the west, was built up in the mid-19th century when the burgeoning colonial city gradually outgrew its defensive walls. Its signature street is Paseo de Martí, laid out in the 1770s, while its nexus point is the diminutive Parque Central, ringed by a clutch of top-end hotels and crowned by a white-marble statue of Cuban national hero José Martí.

The area immediately to the west of the old town features some of Centro Habana's oldest architecture and is replete with interesting tourist attractions, including a cigar factory, a fine-arts museum and the famous Capitolio Nacional. West of Paseo de Martí lies a highly populated residential area that languishes in varying states of disrepair, but whose evocative backstreets pulsates with sultry Cuban atmosphere and the gritty essence of everyday city life. A stroll around this quarter during the daytime will quickly put you in touch with the sounds and secrets of the 'real' Habana: ration shops with antiquated cash registers, flailing lines of household washing, keys being lowered on string from upstairs windows, or groups of men of all ages slapping down dominoes on foldaway tables on the sidewalk. Centro Habana's best walking street is the famous oceanside Malecón, closely followed by Av de Italia (Galiano), which boasts a theater and a top-notch live-music venue. Its most polluted thoroughfare is Av Simón Bolívar (Reina), and its most quintessentially Cuban street is the pedestrianized shopping quarter of Calle San Rafael.

Architecturally Centro Habana is a transitional area linking the old with the new. In the east, grandiose neoclassical edifices mingle picturesquely with glorious neo-baroque while, further west, exuberant art nouveau town houses lie half-hidden under decades of dirt and dust. Tucked away behind the Capitolio, the colorful Barrio Chino (Chinatown) provides one of the neighborhood's quirkiest and most unexpected surprises.

TRANSPORTATION

Bus Bus 400 from Playas del Este and eastern Habana stops on the corner of Calles Agramonte (Zulueta) and Gloria, a few blocks south of Parque Central. Bus M-1 from Alamar and eastern Habana stops on Agramonte on the Vieja–Centro border. Bus M-2 from Santiago de las Vegas, bus M-4 from western Playa via Marianao and Nuevo Vedado, and bus M-7 from San Francisco de Paula converge on Parque de la Fraternidad.

Taxi Taxis, bici-taxis (bicycle taxis) and coco-taxis (distinctive yellow egg-shaped taxis) congregate in Parque Central, Parque Fraternidad and In front of the Capitolio Nacional.

Orientation

While its boundaries are often a little blurred, Centro Habana officially begins at the Av de las Misiones and runs west as far as Calzada de Infanta. To the north the neighborhood is bounded by the Straits of Florida and to the south it stretches as far as Arroyo (Av Manglar), though few travelers venture beyond Av Simón Bolívar. The main north–south thoroughfares are Calzada de Infanta, Padre Varela (Belascoaín), Av de Italia and Paseo de Martí. Running east–west are the Malecón, Av Simón Bolívar and Neptuno. San Rafael is a pedestrian shopping street that runs between Paseo de Martí and Av de Italia. The bustling Barrio Chino is centered on Calle Cuchillo.

ASOCIACIÓN CULTURAL YORUBA DE CUBA Map p222

☎ 863-5953; Paseo de Martí No 615; admission CUC$6; ⏰ 9am-4pm Mon-Sat

The museum in this center provides a worthwhile overview of the Santería religion and the saints' powers, with 30-plus terracotta statues of the most important *orishas* (deities), including Changó, god of war, and Yemayá, goddess of the sea. There are free *tambores* (drum-jams-cum-ceremonies) on alternate Fridays at 4:30pm (when you can check out the museum for free), and you can also arrange consultations with a *santero* (Santería high priest). Note that there's a church dress code for the *tambores* – no shorts or sleeveless T-shirts.

CALLE SAN RAFAEL Map p222

The pedestrian street between the Hotel Inglaterra and the Gran Teatro – popularly known as El Bulevar – is Centro Habana's main shopping precinct for Cubans, and offers a great insight into life away from the tourist haunts. Here you'll find local cinemas, peso-pizza stalls, and old 1950s department stores offering modest selections of imported clothing.

CAPITOLIO NACIONAL Map p222

☎ 863-7861; unguided/guided CUC$3/4; ⏰ 9am-8pm

The incomparable Capitolio is Habana's most ambitious and grandiose building. Similar to the US Capitol Building in Washington, DC, but (marginally) taller and much richer in detail, the work was initiated by Cuba's US-backed dictator Gerardo Machado in 1926 and took 5000 workers three years, two months and 20 days to build at a cost of US$17 million. Formerly it was the seat of the Cuban Congress but, since 1959, it has housed the Cuban Academy of Sciences and the National Library of Science & Technology.

Constructed with white Capellanía limestone and block granite, the entrance is guarded by six rounded Doric columns atop a staircase that leads up from Paseo de Martí. A stone cupola rising 62m and topped with a replica of 16th-century Florentine sculptor Giambologna's bronze statue of Mercury looks out over the Habana skyline. Directly below the dome is a copy of a 24-carat diamond set in the floor. Highway distances between Habana and all sites in Cuba are calculated from this point.

The entryway opens up into the Salon de los Pasos Perdidos (Room of the Lost Steps), so named because of the room's unusual acoustics. At the center of the *salon* is the 'Statue of the Republic,' an enormous bronze woman standing 11m tall and representing the mythic guardian of virtue and work. In size, it's smaller only than the gold Buddha in Nava, Japan, and the Lincoln Monument in Washington, DC.

Tours of the Capitolio take in the entrance halls, the mahogany-covered library, and the former chamber of the Senate and deputies, and are well worth the small fee.

CASTILLO DE SAN SALVADOR DE LA PUNTA Map p222

☎ 860-3196; cnr Av del Puerto & Paseo de Martí; admission CUC$5; ⏰ 10am-6pm Wed-Sun

Designed by the Italian engineer Giovanni Bautista Antonelli and built between 1589

CENTRO HABANA TOP FIVE

- Museo de la Revolución (opposite)
- Museo Nacional de Bellas Artes – Collección de Arte Cubano (p82)
- Capitolio Nacional (p79)
- Iglesia del Sagrado Corazón de Jesus (opposite)
- El Prado (Paseo de Martí; below)

and 1600, this fort is a fine example of 16th-century Renaissance military architecture. In days of yore, a chain was stretched 250m to the castle of El Morro on the other side of the channel every night to close the harbor mouth to shipping. The castle's **museum** displays artifacts from sunken Spanish treasure fleets, a collection of model ships and information on the slave trade.

CENTRO GALLEGO Map p222
cnr Paseo de Martí & San Rafael
It might look unmistakably baroque, but the Centro Gallego, which was erected as a Galician social club in 1914, is a relatively modern 20th-century creation. The center, which contains myriad arcades, columns, balconies and sculptures, was built around the existing Teatro Tacón, which opened in 1838 with five masked Carnival dances. This history is the basis of claims by the present 2000-seat **Gran Teatro de la Habana** (☎ 861-3077; guided tours CUC$2; ☻ 9am-6pm) that it's the oldest operating theater in the western hemisphere. History notwithstanding, the architecture is brilliant, as are many of the weekend **performances** (p131). The National Ballet of Cuba and the State Opera are based here. Upcoming shows are listed on the boards outside.

EL PRADO Map p222
Paseo de Martí
Construction of this stately European-style boulevard (officially known as Paseo de Martí) began outside the city walls in 1770, and the work was completed in the mid-1830s during the term of Captain General Miguel Tacón. He also constructed the original Parque Central. The idea behind El Prado was to create in Habana a boulevard as splendid as any found in Paris, Florence or Madrid. The famous bronze lions that guard the central promenade at either end were added in 1928.

FUENTE DE LA INDIA Map p222
Paseo de Martí
Don't miss this white Carrara marble fountain, carved by Giuseppe Gaginni in 1837 for the count of Villanueva, situated on a traffic island in front of the Hotel Saratoga. It portrays a regal indigenous woman adorned with a crown of eagle's feathers and seated on a throne surrounded by four gargoylesque dolphins. In one hand she holds a horn-shaped basket filled with fruit, in the other she holds a shield bearing the city's coat of arms – a golden key between two mountains, a sun above the sea, three stripes emblazoned on a white background, and a royal palm.

HOTEL INGLATERRA Map p222
Paseo de Martí No 416
Habana's oldest **hotel** (p164) first opened its doors in 1856 on the site of a popular bar called El Louvre. Facing leafy Parque Central, the building exhibits the neoclassical design features that were in vogue at the time, though the decor inside is distinctly Moorish. At a banquet here in 1879, José Martí made a speech advocating Cuban independence and, much later, US journalists covering the so-called Spanish-American War stayed at this hotel. War hero Antonio Maceo was another famous guest, and a letter he wrote on hotel notepaper is proudly displayed in the lobby. **El Louvre** (☻ 11am-midnight), named after the hotel's predecessor, is the Hotel Inglaterra's popular downstairs alfresco bar; it's situated under a colonnaded porch outside the hotel.

HOTEL SEVILLA Map p222
Trocadero No 55
The **Sevilla** (p164), one of Habana's most famous hotels, first opened as the Sevilla-Biltmore in 1908 and was embellished with tiles and stucco to resemble a Spanish-Moorish palace. Steeped in history, the hotel has boasted many famous guests over the years, including gangster Al Capone, Italian opera singer Enrico Caruso and British novelist Graham Greene (a full roll call can be found on a photo wall close to the main reception area). Greene even used the Sevilla and Room 501 (a noisy room next to the lift shaft) as a setting in his 1958 novel *Our Man in Havana*. The Sevilla's **Patio Sevillana** is a great place to come to have a snack, catch some live music and sample one of Cuba's most

famous cocktails, the Mary Pickford (rum, pineapple juice and grenadine), which was invented at the hotel's bar.

IGLESIA DEL SAGRADO CORAZÓN DE JESUS Map p222

Av Simón Bolívar btwn Gervasio & Padre Varela
Constructed between 1914 and 1923, the city's finest neo-Gothic building is an inspiring marble creation with a distinctive white steeple. The church is rightly famous for its stained-glass windows, and the light that penetrates through the eaves first thing in the morning (when the church is deserted) gives the place an almost ethereal quality. You can enjoy a few precious minutes of quiet contemplation away from the craziness of the street here.

MUSEO DE LA REVOLUCIÓN Map p222

Refugio btwn Agramonte & Av de las Misiones; unguided/guided CUC$5/7; ⏰ **10am-6pm Tue, 10am-5pm Wed-Sun**
Habana's largest and most definitive museum is housed in the former Presidential Palace, which was constructed between 1913 and 1920 and used by a string of

cash embezzling Cuban presidents, culminating in Fulgencio Batista. The world-famous Tiffany's of New York decorated the interior, and the shimmering Salón de los Espejos (Room of Mirrors) was designed to resemble the room of the same name at the Palace of Versailles. In March 1957 the palace was the site of an unsuccessful assassination attempt on Batista led by revolutionary student leader José Echeverría.

The museum itself descends chronologically from the top floor, starting with Cuba's pre-Columbian culture and extending to the present-day Socialist regime. Much emphasis is placed on the plethora of US plots against the island, along with the various achievements of the revolution. The downstairs rooms have some interesting exhibits on the 1953 Moncada attack and the life of Che Guevara, and highlight a Cuban penchant for displaying blood-stained military uniforms. Most of the labels are in English and Spanish. In front of the building is a fragment of the former city wall, as well as an SAU-100 tank used by Castro during the 1961 Battle of the Bay of Pigs. In the space behind the museum you'll find the **Pavillón Granma**, a memorial to

CHINATOWN

While the noodles might be a little soggy and the crispy vegetables conspicuous by their absence, Habana's Chinatown – or Barrio Chino (Map p222), as it's more popularly known – provides a fascinating glimpse into the cultural makeup of a city where the term 'Far East' is more likely to mean Santiago than Shanghai.

Hired initially as contract laborers on the island's sprawling sugar plantations, the first Chinese immigrants arrived in Cuba in 1847 to fill in the gaps left by the decline of the transatlantic slave trade. By the 1880s there were over 100,000 Chinese in Spain's longstanding Caribbean colony, working in conditions little better than those of their African counterparts. But as employment contracts were opened up and business opportunities expanded, many workers laid down roots and a small Chinese community grew up on Habana's periphery.

At the advent of the 1920s, Habana's Chinatown had burgeoned into the biggest Asian neighborhood in Latin America, a booming and bustling hub of human industry that boasted its own laundries, pharmacies, theaters and grocery stores.

But the prosperity wasn't to last. By the early 1960s, Castro's ambitious nationalization plans quickly took the wind out of Chinatown's entrepreneurial sails and caused thousands of business-minded Chinese to relocate to the US. The Barrio Chino – which at its peak had stretched across 44 city blocks and published four independent newspapers – fell into a long decline, with many second- and third-generation immigrants marrying into Hispanic families – a demographic shift that left Chinese speakers numbering only in the hundreds.

Reversing the slide during the *período especial* (special period), the Cuban government – recognizing the lucrative tourist potential of Habana's ailing Chinese quarter – invested money and resources into rejuvenating the district's distinct historical character. From the mid-1990s onwards, new bilingual street signs were erected, a huge pagoda-shaped arch appeared at the entrance to Calle Dragones, and incentives were given to local Chinese businessmen in order to promote restaurants, community groups and tai chi classes.

Barrio Chino today centers on the narrow pedestrian thoroughfare of Calle Cuchillo and its surrounding streets, and the atmosphere and services have been improving by the year. Head here for cheap restaurants, plentiful food and an interesting slice of authentic Cuban life with a quirky Asian twist.

the 18m yacht that carried Fidel Castro and 81 other revolutionaries from Tuxpán, Mexico, to Cuba in December 1956. It's encased in glass and guarded 24 hours a day, presumably to stop anyone from breaking in and making off for Florida in it. The pavilion is surrounded by other vehicles associated with the revolution and is accessible from the Museo de la Revolución.

MUSEO NACIONAL DE BELLAS ARTES Map p222

A cultural tour de force, Cuba's magnificent arts museum showcases everything from ancient Greek pots to modern Cuban pop art. Indeed, so extensive are the myriad exhibits in this fascinating collection that it takes two formidable buildings to house them.

Arranged inside the fabulously eclectic Centro Asturianas (a former Spanish social club that dates from 1927), the Colección de Arte Universal (☎ 863-9484; cnr Agramonte & San Rafael; adult/under 14yr CUC$5/free; ☼ 10am-6pm Tue-Sat, 10am-2pm Sun) exhibits international art from 500 BC to the present day on three separate floors. Highlights include an extensive Spanish collection (with a canvas by El Greco), some 2000-year-old Roman mosaics, Greek pots from the 5th century BC and a suitably refined Gainsborough canvas in the British Room.

The Colección de Arte Cubano (☎ 861-3858; Trocadero btwn Agramonte & Av de las Misiones; adult/under 14yr CUC$5/free; ☼ 10am-5pm Tue-Sat, 10am-2pm Sun) displays purely Cuban art and, if you're pressed for time, is the best one to visit. Works are displayed in chronological order starting on the 3rd floor and are surprisingly varied. Artists to look out for are Guillermo Collazo, considered to be the first truly great Cuban artist; Rafael Blanco, with his cartoonlike paintings and sketches; and Raúl Martínez, a master of 1960s Cuban pop art. Housed in a modern, spacious building dating from 1956, the highlight of this museum is the section put aside for Wifredo Lam (p31), Cuba's modern artistic genius, whose paintings evoke those of Picasso.

PARQUE CENTRAL Map p222
Paseo de Martí btwn Neptuno & San Martín
A small but scenic haven from the belching buses and roaring taxis that ply their way along Paseo de Martí, Parque Central has long been a microcosm of daily Habana

life. The park was expanded to its present size in the late 19th century after the city walls were knocked down, and the marble statue of José Martí at its center was the first of thousands to be erected in Cuba. Raised in 1905 on the 10th anniversary of the poet's death, the monument is ringed by 28 palm trees planted to signify Martí's birth date, January 28. Hard to miss is the group of baseball fans who linger, seemingly 24 hours a day, within ball-pitching distance of the statue's marble base at the famous esquina caliente (literally 'hot corner'), animatedly debating statistics, play-off predictions and the chances of US-defector Liván Hernández coming home for Christmas.

PARQUE DE ENAMORADOS Map p222
cnr Paseo de Martí & Capdevila
Preserved in 'Lover's Park,' surrounded by streams of speeding traffic, lies a surviving section of the colonial Cárcel (Tacón Prison), built in 1838, where many Cuban patriots, including José Martí, were imprisoned. A brutal place that sent unfortunate prisoners off to perform hard labor in the nearby San Lázaro quarry, the prison was finally demolished in 1939, and the park that took its place is dedicated to the memory of those who had suffered so horribly within its walls. Two tiny cells and an equally minute chapel are all that remain of the hated prison today. The beautiful wedding cake–like building (art nouveau with a dash of eclecticism) behind the park, flying the Spanish flag, is the old Palacio Velasco (1912), now the Spanish embassy.

PARQUE DE LA FRATERNIDAD Map p222
Dragones btwn Paseo de Martí & Industria
'Fraternity Park' was established in 1892 to commemorate the fourth centenary of the Spanish landing in the Americas. A few decades later, it was remodeled and renamed to mark the 1927 Pan-American Conference. The name was meant to signify American brotherhood, hence the many busts of Latin and North American leaders that have been set up around the park – including one of US president Abraham Lincoln. The ceiba tree protected by a high iron fence in the center was planted in a mixture of soil from all the countries of the Americas. Ceiba trees, the giants of jungles and savannas, have been revered as life givers throughout Latin America for centuries, from the ancient

Incas to contemporary Mayas. Followers of the Santería religion also consider the trees to be sacred, due mainly to the legacy of slaves who noted their resemblance to the African baobab. Today the park is the terminus of numerous *camello* (buses named for their two humps) routes, and is sometimes referred to as 'Jurassic Park' for the plethora of photogenic old American cars that congregate here.

REAL FÁBRICA DE TABACOS PARTAGÁS Map p222

☎ 862-0086; Industria No 520 btwn Barcelona & Dragones; tours CUC$10; ⏰ every 15min btwn 9:30-11am & 12:30-3pm Mon-Fri

One of Habana's oldest cigar factories and certainly its most famous, this neoclassical Habana landmark was founded in 1845 by a Spaniard named Jaime Partagás. Today some 400 workers toil here for up to 12 hours a day, rolling such famous cigars as Montecristos and Cohibas. As far as tours go, Partagás is the most popular and reliable factory to visit. Tour groups first check out the ground floor, where the leaves are unbundled and sorted, before proceeding to the upper floors to watch the tobacco get rolled, pressed, adorned with a band, and boxed. Though interesting in an educational sense, the tours here are often rushed and a little robotic, and some visitors find they smack of a human zoo. Still, if you have even a passing interest in tobacco, Cuban work environments or economies of scale, it's probably worth a peep.

VEDADO

Eating p118; Shopping p153; Sleeping p165; Walking Tours p102, p106

Vedado is Habana's commercial hub and much sought-after residential district. Compared to Habana Vieja, it isn't particularly old; in fact, the first houses penetrated this formerly protected forest in the 1860s, with the real growth spurt beginning in the 1920s and continuing into the 1950s.

The name Vedado derives from the Spanish verb *vedar* (to forbid); during the colonial era, the area was a forest reserve where the cutting down of trees was forbidden. This situation changed at the conclusion of the 'Spanish-American' War in 1898, when a peace treaty between Spain and the US

placed Cuba under US military occupation. With US troops in control of the island, rich and prosperous Americans flocked to Habana in their droves to invest money in sugar mills, rum factories and real estate. Many of them built their grandiose Miami-style mansions on the low hills and rocky shores of Vedado.

Laid out in a near-perfect grid, Vedado has more of a North American feel than other parts of the Cuban capital and is largely a product of the half century or so of US domination. The suburban streets are classified in a simple number and letters system à la the US while the distinctive skyline – which contains Cuba's premier clutch of *rascacielos* (skyscrapers) – draws its inspiration from the art deco giants of Miami and New York.

During the 1940s and '50s, Vedado was where Habana's prerevolutionary gambling party reached its heady climax, and its Mafia-run hotels were where most of the biggest deals were cut. The Hotel Nacional once boasted a Las Vegas–style casino, the ritzy Hotel Riviera was the former stomping ground of influential mobster Meyer Lansky, while the now defunct Hotel Capri was masterfully managed by Hollywood actor (and sometime Mob associate) George Raft. Then, in January 1959, everything went a bit awry as Fidel Castro rolled into town with his scruffy army of bearded rebels and set up shop on the 24th floor of the spanking new Havana Hilton hotel (which was promptly renamed the Hotel Habana Libre).

Today Vedado is a mostly residential neighborhood with a population of approximately 175,000, although the area still retains the Universidad de la Habana, myriad theaters and nightspots, and a plethora of decent paladares and restaurants. Unlike Centro Habana, the streets here are wide, leafy and relatively quiet while the

TRANSPORTATION

Bus Bus M-6 from Centro Habana stops at the corner of Calles 21 & L. Bus M-1 from Alamar and eastern Habana stops on the corner of Calles G and 23, and bus M-5 from western Playa stops on Calle 23 (La Rampa).

Taxi Taxis congregate outside Hotel Nacional, around the Coppelia and along the Malecón (Av de Maceo).

houses – which boast spacious lots and plenty of well-manicured gardens – have a tendency to be grander and more eclectic. The neighborhood is bisected by two wide Parisian-style boulevards, Calle G (Av de los Presidentes) and Paseo, and there is a liberal sprinkling of pleasant parks, each one filling an entire block. Locals will tell you that their beloved district is cleaner and more intimate than other parts of the city, and they're not far wrong.

Orientation

Like Centro Habana, Vedado faces the sea and is bordered to the north by the sweeping curves of the Malecón. To the east the neighborhood is marked by Calzada de Infanta and to the west by the Río Almendares. For the purposes of this book, we have extended the district south of the Calzada de Zapata to include the Necrópolis Cristóbal Colón and the Plaza de la Revolución. Southwest of here, the mainly residential neighborhood of Nuevo Vedado continues as far as the Víazul bus terminal.

BIBLIOTECA NACIONAL JOSÉ MARTÍ
Map pp224-5
Plaza de la Revolución; admission free;
🕑 8am-5:45pm
Cuba's national library is housed in a modernist tower block overlooking the Plaza de la Revolución. There is sometimes a photo exhibit in the lobby.

CASA DE LAS AMÉRICAS
Map pp224-5
☎ 55-27-06; Calle G btwn Calles 3 & 5; admission CUC$2; 🕑 10am-4pm Tue-Sun, 9am-1pm Sun
This cathedral-like art deco structure just off the Malecón on Calle G is a major cultural institution set up by Haydee Santermaría in 1959 to sponsor literary and artistic seminars, conferences and musical events (p137). It's also home to one of Cuba's largest publishing houses. Inside there's a small bookstore, as well as an art gallery and library.

VEDADO TOP FIVE

- Hotel Nacional (opposite)
- Universidad de la Habana (p89)
- Necrópolis Cristóbal Colón (p87)
- Memorial a José Martí (p86)
- Museo de Artes Decorativas (p86)

CASTILLO DEL PRÍNCIPE Map pp224-5
cnr Calzada de Zapata & Calle G
The Castillo del Principe (1767–79) is an irregularly shaped fortress constructed to protect nearby valleys. It is said to contain moats, underground passageways, vaulted galleries, cisterns and all sorts of other intriguing stuff, but today it serves as a police headquarters and is off-limits to tourists.

COMITÉ CENTRAL DEL PARTIDO COMUNISTA DE CUBA Map pp224-5
Plaza de la Revolución
A long, uninspiring concrete structure that glowers from behind the Martí memorial, the modern HQ of the Cuban government doesn't match the architectural splendor of the Capitolio or the Presidential Palace. This is where the affairs of the Cuban government are sorted out and where the elusive Fidel maintains an office. Not surprisingly, it's strictly out of bounds for foreigners (and most Cubans, for that matter).

COPPELIA Map pp224-5
Calle 23 cnr Calle L; 🕑 11am-11pm
Habana's much-loved ice-cream parlor (p119) sits in the middle of a park in a building that looks more like a flying saucer than a café-restaurant. Erected in the 1960s, the Coppelia faced hard times during the período especial (special period), but it managed to stay open throughout the 1990s despite the rather gruesome queues.

EDIFICIO FOCSA Map pp224-5
cnr Calles N & 19
Hard to miss on the Habana skyline, the modernist Focsa building was built between 1954 and 1956 in a record 28 months using pioneer computer technology. In 1999 it was listed as one of the seven modern engineering wonders of Cuba. With 39 floors housing 373 apartments, on its completion it was the second-largest concrete structure of its type in the world, entirely constructed without cranes. The Focsa fell on hard times in the early '90s – its upper floors became nests for vultures and in 2000 an elevator cable snapped, killing one person. Sparkling once more after a recent renovation project, this giant contains refurbished apartments and – in top-floor restaurant La Torre (p122) – one of the city's most celebrated eating establishments.

GRAN SYNAGOGA BET SHALOM

Map pp224-5

☎ 832-8953; Calle I btwn Calles 13 & 15;
☯ services 6pm Fri, 10.30am Sat

There are approximately 1500 Jews living in Cuba today, and about 85% of them reside in Habana. It's a far cry from the 1950s, when Habana's Jewish population peaked at around 12,000. Though never directly persecuted under the Castro regime, the island's Jews suffered the same business fall out as other Cubans and many of them left. Those who remained were similarly peeved when Israel and Cuba cut off diplomatic relations in 1973. The Gran Synagoga is one of three remaining synagogues in Habana and, although not a tourist sight in itself, its comprehensive library and friendly staff should be able to enlighten interested parties further on Cuba's fascinating Jewish history.

HOSPITAL NACIONAL HERMANOS AMEIJEIRAS Map pp224-5

San Lázaro No 701

A bastion of the Cuban medical system, this 24-story hospital was completed in 1982 during Cuba's Soviet honeymoon and is the tallest occupied building in Centro Habana. One of the few post-1959 structures in this part of the city, the hospital is said to house a different specialty on every floor, and contains good facilities for treating foreigners (see p193).

HOTEL HABANA LIBRE Map pp224-5

cnr Calles L & 23

This classic modernist hotel (p167) – the former Havana Hilton – was commandeered by Castro and his triumphant revolutionaries in 1959, just nine months after it had opened, and promptly renamed the Habana Libre. During the first few months of the revolution, Fidel effectively ruled the country from a luxurious suite on one of the upper floors.

The art here, starting with the 670-sq-m Venetian tile mural by Amelia Peláez splashed across the front of the building, is visually arresting and worth a look. Upstairs is Alfredo Sosa Bravo's *Carro de la Revolución*, made from 525 ceramic pieces, plus a rotating painting exhibit. The shopping arcade has a good liquor store and there are some great 1959 black-and-white photos of the all-conquering *barbudos* (members

of Castro's rebel army) lolling around with their guns in the hotel's lobby.

HOTEL NACIONAL Map pp224-5

cnr Calle O & 21

Built in 1930 in an eclectic style that fused art deco with neoclassical and neocolonial elements, the Hotel Nacional (p167) is a national monument that – along with the Castillo de Morro – is one of the city's most recognizable 'postcard' sights. In fact, its design is an almost direct copy of the Breakers Hotel in Palm Beach, Florida. Illustrious former guests include Winston Churchill, Frank Sinatra, Errol Flynn, Ernest Hemingway, Naomi Campbell...the list goes on.

The hotel's checkered history began in August 1933, when US-backed dictator Gerardo Machado was overthrown during a popular uprising, and a young army sergeant named Fulgencio Batista stepped into the presidential role. On October 2, 1933, some 300 army officers displaced by Batista's coup sought refuge in the newly opened Hotel Nacional, where the US ambassador Sumner Wells was staying. Aware that the reins of power had changed hands, Wells found urgent business elsewhere, and Batista's troops attacked the officers, many of whom were shot after surrendering.

In December 1946, the hotel gained notoriety of a different kind when it hosted the largest ever get-together of North American Mafia hoods under the guise of a Frank Sinatra concert (see The 1946 Havana Conference, p56). These days the hotel maintains a more reputable face and the once famous casino is long gone, though the Cabaret Parisién (p136) is still a draw. Non-guests are welcome to admire the Moorish lobby, stroll the breezy grounds overlooking the Malecón and examine the famous photos of past guests on the walls inside.

LOPEZ SERRANO BUILDING

Map pp224-5

Calle L btwn Calles 11 & 13

Resembling a miniature Empire State Building with the bottom 80 floors chopped off, the Lopez Serrano apartment building is Vedado's most distinctive art deco construction. Raised in 1932, it was the first skyscraper in a two-decade-long Habana love affair with the buildings.

THE MALECÓN

The Malecón (Av de Maceo; Map pp224-5), the evocative 8km-long sea drive that wraps its way like a weathered fortress around the choppy Straits of Florida, is one of the city's most soulful and quintessentially Cuban thoroughfares.

Long a favored meeting place for assorted lovers, philosophers, poets, traveling minstrels, fishermen and wistful Florida-gazers, the street party that is the Malecón reaches its apex at sunset when the weak yellow light from Vedado filters like a dim torch onto the buildings of Habana Centro, lending their dilapidated facades a distinctly ethereal quality.

Laid out in the early 1900s as a salubrious oceanside boulevard for Habana's pleasure-seeking middle classes, the Malecón expanded rapidly eastward in the century's first decade with a mishmash of eclectic architecture that mixed sturdy neoclassical with whimsical art nouveau. By the 1920s the road had reached the outer limits of Vedado and, by the early 1950s it had metamorphosed into a busy six-lane traffic highway that carried streams of wave-dodging Buicks and Chevrolets from the grey hulk of the Castillo de San Salvador de la Punta to the borders of the opulent diplomatic quarter.

Today, aside from being one of the world's most scenic running routes, and *the* best place on the planet to pledge undying love to your starry-eyed partner, the Malecón remains Habana's most authentic open-air theater, a place where the whole city comes to meet, greet, date and debate.

Fighting an ongoing battle with the corrosive effects of the salty ocean, which regularly sends brine-filled waves splashing like mini tsunamis over the slime-covered sea wall, many of the thoroughfare's magnificent buildings now face decrepitude, demolition or irrevocable damage. To combat the problem, 14 blocks of the Malecón have recently been given special status (despite lying outside the Unesco World Heritage site) by the City Historian's Office in an attempt to stop the rot. For the fading facades of Habana's romantic hurricane-lashed sea drive, it's a race against time.

MEMORIAL A JOSÉ MARTÍ Map pp224-5
☎ 59-23-47; Plaza de la Revolución; museum/ museum & tower CUC$3/5; ☼ 9am-5pm Mon-Sat
At 138.5m high, this noble monument is Habana's tallest structure and is fronted by an impressive 17m marble statue of a seated Martí in pensive *Thinker* pose, the work of artist Juan José Sicre. Constructed between 1953 and 1958 (during the Batista era) using gray marble from the Isla de la Juventud, the memorial houses a beautifully laid-out museum with access to a 129m lookout, reached via a small lift, which affords fantastic views over Habana. The museum – the definitive word on Martí in Cuba – contains handwritten letters, a host of rare photos and a brief overview of Jean Claude Forestier's grand plans for Habana's urban development.

MINISTERIO DEL INTERIOR Map pp224-5
Plaza de la Revolución
The ugly concrete block on the northern side of the Plaza de la Revolución is famous for its huge mural of Che Guevara, a copy of Alberto Korda's famous 1960 photograph, with the words *Hasta la Victoria Siempre* (Always toward Victory) emblazoned underneath. The mural was fitted in 1995 on the side wall of the Ministry of the Interior, where Che once kept an office.

MONUMENTO A JULIO ANTONIO MELLA Map pp224-5
Calle Neptuno cnr San Lázaro
At the bottom of the university's famous *escalinata* (stairway) lies a monument to the student leader who founded the first Cuban Communist Party in 1925. In 1929, dictator Machado had Mella assassinated in Mexico City. More interesting are the black-and-white Mella portraits mounted in the wall in the park across San Lázaro.

MUSEO DE ARTES DECORATIVAS
Map pp224-5
☎ 830-9848; Calle 17 No 502, btwn Calles D & E; admission US$2; ☼ 11am-7pm Tue-Sat
This museum is slightly isolated but worth a visit. The stately mansion, completed in 1927, was formerly owned by the countess of Revilla de Camargo, and exhibits rococo, Regency, neoclassical, English, Asian and art deco styles. The rooms are filled with antique furniture, most of it European from the 18th and 19th centuries, including plenty of elegant porcelain.

MUSEO DE LA DANZA Map pp224-5
☎ 831-2198; Linea No 365 cnr Calle G; admission CUC$2; ☼ 11am-6:30pm Tue-Sat
Four blocks from the Museo de Artes Decorativas, this place claims to be the only

museum in the Western Hemisphere devoted entirely to dance. You'll find exhibits portraying Cuban ballerinas, as well as dancers from Russia, Spain and Mexico. There are also some personal effects of Cuban ballet diva Alicia Alonso (p28). The museum is housed in a beautiful colonial-style two-story building.

MUSEO NAPOLEÓNICO Map pp224-5

☎ 879-1460; San Miguel No 1159; unguided/guided CUC$3/5; ☾ 9am-4:30pm Tue-Sat, 9am-noon Sun

There's no record of Napoleon ever visiting Cuba, although some of his more dogmatic traits may have rubbed off on the island's current leader. Perhaps that's what makes this four-story Italian-style mansion (1928) containing 7000 objects associated with the life and death of Napoleon Bonaparte so compelling. Amassed by Cuban sugar baron Julio Lobo and politician Orestes Ferrera, the collection of objects – which come mostly from Napoleon's period of exile on St Helena – includes one of several bronze Napoleonic death masks made two days after the emperor's death by his personal physician, Dr Francisco Antommarchi, who later lived in Cuba. Other highlights include sketches of Voltaire, paintings of the battle of Waterloo, china, furniture, and an interesting re-creation of Napoleon's study and bedroom.

NECRÓPOLIS CRISTÓBAL COLÓN

Map pp224-5

cnr Calzada de Zapata & Calle 12; admission CUC$1; ☾ 9am-5pm

Cuba's largest cemetery is famous the world over for its stunning sculptures and decorative mausoleums. Covering 56 hectares the graveyard is the final resting place for over a million souls, though people are being disinterred daily due to lack of space. Laid out like a mini city in the 1860s and '70s, the cemetery's graves read like a who's who of Cuban history, and a visit here justifies a walking tour in its own right (p106).

PARQUE ALMENDARES Map pp224-5

cnr Calles 47 & 49C

Running along the banks of the Río Almendares below the bridge on Calle 23 (La Rampa), this wonderful oasis of greenery and negative-air ions in the heart of chaotic Habana is sometimes referred to as the lungs of the city. The park was restored in 2003 and a beautiful job has been done: benches line the river promenade, plants grow profusely in the shade and there are many facilities here, including an antiquated miniature golf course, the Anfiteatro Parque Almendares (p139) and a children's playground. There are also several good places to eat. Take a 20-minute stroll through old-growth trees in the Bosque de la Habana and you'll feel transported (take a friend, though: this is a very isolated spot and is considered unsafe by locals).

PARQUE LENNON Map pp224-5

Calle 17 btwn Calles 6 & 8

It may come as a surprise to some, but there are only three statues of Lenin in Habana: Colina Lenin (p94), one in suburban Parque Lenin (p96), and one (by deftly swiveling a couple of letters in the surname) in this peaceful urban space set in a pleasant corner of Vedado. The hyper-realistic bronze statue of ex-Beatle John (as opposed to Vladimir) Lennon was unveiled by Fidel Castro in December 2000 on the 20th anniversary of the singer's death. Culturally speaking, it was one of the Cuban leader's more remarkable policy U-turns, as the Beatles' music had been banned in Cuba in the 1960s for being too 'decadent.' But following Lennon's strong social activism and opposition to US involvement in the Vietnam War, he quickly became a hero among Cuban music fans, causing Castro to quickly rebrand him as a 'revolutionary.' The 21st-century reincarnation of Lennon in bronze has suffered the ignominy of having his glasses stolen on a number of occasions and a guard has now been employed to keep a regular watch.

PLAZA DE LA REVOLUCIÓN Map pp224-5

Conceived by French urbanist Jean Claude Forestier in the 1920s, this gigantic modern urban space was part of Habana's 'new city,' which grew up in the 1920s, '30s, '40s and '50s. As the nexus point of Forestier's ambitious plan, the square was built on a small hill (the Loma de los Catalanes) in the manner of Paris' Place de Charles de Gaulle, with various avenues fanning out toward the Río Almendares, Vedado and the Parque de la Fraternidad.

Sights

VEDADO

Surrounded by modern office buildings constructed in the late 1950s (the original plan took 30 years to reach fruition), the square today is the base of the Cuban government and its ministries, and a place where large-scale political rallies are held (including lengthy speeches by Fidel Castro). In January 1998, close to one million people (nearly 10 percent of the Cuban population) crammed into the square to hear Pope John Paul II say Mass.

Grey, utilitarian and rather ugly, the plaza on a cloudy day has a barren and rather officious feel. When the sun's out, on the other hand, it's famously hot. Small on beauty but big on grandiosity, it's a regular stop for the ubiquitous tour buses that dispatch crowds of camera-clutching tourists who make a beeline for the famous Che Guevara mural (p86).

QUINTA DE LOS MOLINOS Map pp224-5
cnr Av Salvador Allende & Luaces

The former residence of General Máximo Gómez, hero of the independence wars, this building and its extensive grounds is a now museum that was undergoing a lengthy restoration at the time of writing. The house is surrounded by what were once Habana University's botanical gardens. It also houses La Madriguera (p140), the headquarters of the Asociación Hermanos Saíz, the youth arm of Uneac.

REAL FÁBRICA DE TABACOS H UPMANN Map pp224-5
☎ 862-0081; Calle 23 btwn Calles 14 & 16; tours CUC$10; ☽ 9:30am-2:30pm Mon-Fri

Upmann's cigars are legendary in Cuba and have been produced in the country since 1844, when two German bankers and avid cigar smokers, Hermann and August Upmann, bought a factory in Habana. Indeed, the popular Petit Upmann brand was a longtime favorite of US president John F Kennedy. Currently one of only two cigar factories offering tours in Habana, the grand neoclassical Upmann building is a little out of the way and generally only accepts organized groups. Inquire first at Real Fabrica de Tabacos Partagás (p83) or at your hotel travel desk rather than turn up here in person.

TEATRO NACIONAL DE CUBA
Map pp224-5

☎ 879-6011; cnr Paseo & Calle 39

Cuba's national theater (p132) doesn't quite live up to the grandiosity of the Gran Teatro, and its removed position in the Plaza de la Revolución is a little inconvenient for nighttime shows. The theater opened on March 16, 1960, with the show The Respectful Hooker, with its famous author Jean-Paul Sartre in attendance. Among a host of cultural activities staged here are jazz, theater

VOICES OF HABANA: ANY GARCÍA VIERA

Sales and promotions, Vedado

Sum up Habana in one sentence. Crowded, colorful and full of life. What defines a habanero? A habanero [inhabitant of Habana] is a person who is proud to be from Habana; they will go out of their way to boast about it. How has Habana changed in the last 10 years? There's more renovation in the historical center. What are the hottest sounds in Habana right now? Where can you hear them? Trova [traditional poetic singing] is ever popular, with artists such as Silvio Rodríguez and pop-fusion duo Buena Fe. Also reggae fusion with Alfonso X, who has played at open-air venues such as Parque Lennon. Other good places to catch live music are the Casa de la Música and the Jazz Café. How do you get about the city? I use my car – a 1974 Russian Lada. How can the inquisitive traveler find the 'real' Cuba? Centro Habana is a good slice of typical Habana life. Look around El Prado [Paseo de Martí] and also Parque Central and you'll see different people talking about different things – especially baseball. The Malecón [Av de Maceo] is busiest after midnight and is most popular with the young. What is the best thing about your neighborhood? The view of the ocean over the Malecón from my window. Is the food here so terrible? It's not caviar, but it's not terrible. Try going to an agropecuario [free-enterprise vegetable market] or a local inexpensive paladar [privately run restaurant] such as Los Amigos in Vedado.

As related to Brendan Sainsbury

and ballet festivals. There's also a popular dance club, the **Café Cantante Mi Habana** (p140), and a piano bar, the **Piano Bar Delirio Habanero** (p139), on the premises.

TORREÓN DE SAN LÁZARO Map pp224-5
cnr Malecón & Vapor
This tiny watchtower was built by the Spanish in the 18th century. Like La Chorrera, the San Lázaro tower quickly fell to British troops during the invasion of 1762. You can admire it from the outside only.

TORREÓN DE SANTA DOROTEA
DE LA CHORRERA Map pp224-5
Malecón btwn Calles 18 & 20; 🕙 **noon-2am**
One of a number of small battlements that once guarded Habana from pirates and warships, this small two-story tower at the mouth of Río Almendares contained sentry posts, artillery emplacements, storage rooms and a military barracks. Records indicate that it rarely housed more than 100 troops. The tower was designed by Italian engineer Juan Bautista Antonelli – who also designed a similar tower in Cojímar, east of town – and was completed during the administration of Álvaro de Luna y Sarmiento. In 1762 the tower was taken by the British prior to their attack on the Castillo de los Tres Santos Reyes Magnos del Morro. Today it houses a small restaurant, **Mesón la Chorrera** (p120).

UNIVERSIDAD DE LA HABANA
Map pp224-5
cnr Neptuno & San Lázaro
Founded by Dominican monks in 1728 and secularized in 1842, Habana University began life in Habana Vieja before moving to its present site in 1902. The existing neoclassical complex dates from the second quarter of the 20th century, and today some 30,000 students (2000 of them foreigners), taught by 1700 professors, follow courses in the social sciences, humanities, natural sciences, mathematics and economics here.

Perched on a hill at the top of the famous stairway, the university's central quadrangle, the Plaza Ignacio Agramonte, displays a tank captured by Castro's rebels in 1958. Directly in front is the *biblioteca* (library) and to the left the Edificio Felipe Poey, with two unusual museums. The **Museo de Historia Natural** (admission CUC$1; 🕙 9am-noon & 1-4pm

Mon-Fri Sep-Jul), downstairs, is Cuba's oldest museum, founded in 1874 by the Academia de Ciencias Médicas, Físicas y Naturales. Many of the stuffed specimens of Cuban flora and fauna date from the 19th century. Upstairs is the **Museo Antropológico Montané** (admission CUC$1; 🕙 9am-noon & 1-4pm Mon-Fri Sep-Jul), established in 1903, with a rich collection of pre-Columbian artifacts. The most important objects are the wooden 10th-century Ídolo del Tabaco, discovered in Guantánamo province, and the stone Ídolo de Bayamo. The exhibits are color coded to indicate the three periods of Indo-American civilization in Cuba: Pre-Ceramic (red), Proto-Ceramic (green) and Ceramic (yellow).

US INTERESTS OFFICE Map pp224-5
Calzada btwn Calles L & M
Set up in 1977 during a brief thaw in Cuban-American relations under President Jimmy Carter, the US Interests Office remains a huge source of controversy between the two countries, with the Cubans accusing its US neighbor of sponsoring all kinds of political dissent across the island from behind its heavily guarded doors. Surrounded by billboards displaying hysterical graffiti that liken George W Bush to Adolf Hitler, the building is the site of some of the worst tit-for-tat finger wagging on the island. Facing the office on the Malecón is the **Plaza Tribuna Anti-Imperialista**, built during the Elián González affair to host major in-your-face protests (earning it the local nickname 'Protestódromo'). Seventy-three somber flags currently fly here in honor of the 73 Cubans killed in a 1976 plane bomb in the Bahamas. The main perpetrator, Luís Posada Carriles, is currently residing in the US.

PLAYA & MARIANAO
Eating p122; Shopping p154; Sleeping p168
The municipality of Playa, west of Vedado across the Río Almendares, is a paradoxical mix of prestigious residential streets and tough proletarian housing schemes. There are a handful of worthwhile sights here, including a top-notch aquarium and one of the city's most idiosyncratic yet fascinating museums, the Fundación Naturaleza y El Hombre. The district also boasts a spanking new trade center and a burgeoning strip of high-class hotels.

TRANSPORTATION

Bus Bus M-5 from Vedado stops along Calle 41 and carries on through Marianao to Cubanacán; bus 132 goes from the corner of Dragones and Industria, beside the Capitolio in Centro Habana, to the same destination.

Taxi You can get a Taxi OK taxi on Calle 8 between Av 1 and 3, or you can hail a taxi along Av 5 or outside Miramar Trade Center (Av 3 between Calles 78 and 84).

Gracious Miramar is the municipality's leafiest quarter, a neighborhood of broad avenues and weeping fig trees where the traffic moves sedately and diplomats' wives – clad in sun visors and Lycra leggings – go for gentle afternoon jogs along Av Quinta. Many of Habana's foreign embassies are housed here in old prerevolution mansions, and business travelers and conference attendees flock here from around the globe to make use of some of Cuba's grandest and most luxurious facilities. If you're interested primarily in sightseeing and entertainment, commuting to Vedado or Habana Vieja is a nuisance and an expense. However, some of the best salsa clubs, discos and restaurants are out this way, and the casas particulares (private houses that let out rooms to foreigners) are positively luxurious.

Cubanacán plays host to many of Habana's business and scientific fairs and conventions, and it is also where several specialized medical institutes are situated. Despite the austerity of the *período especial*, vast resources have been plowed into biotechnological and pharmaceutical research institutes in this area. Yachties, anglers and scuba divers will find themselves using the Marina Hemingway (p185) at Playa's west end. Marianao is world famous for the Tropicana Nightclub, but locally it's known as a tough, in parts rough, neighborhood with a powerful Santería community and a long history of social commitment.

Orientation

Playa is a large, sprawling urban area that is bordered in the east by the Río Almendares and to the north by the Straits of Florida. Subdistricts from east to west include the embassy district of Miramar, Buena Vista, Cubanacán, Siboney, Flores, Barlovento (where Marina Hemingway is

situated) and Santa Fe. Marianao is a tougher working-class neighborhood to the south that stretches as far as the Autopista Nacional.

PLAYA & MIRAMAR

ACUARIO NACIONAL Map pp228-9
☎ 202-5872; cnr Av 3 & Calle 62; adult/child CUC$5/4; 🕙 10am-10pm Tue-Sun
A Habana institution founded in 1960, the aquarium gets legions of annual visitors, particularly since its 2002 revamp. Environmentally speaking, the place leaves all other Cuban aquariums in the shade (although that isn't saying much). For a start, it's designed to be both educational and conservationist. Saltwater fish are the specialty, but there are also sea lions, dolphins and lots of running-around room for kids. Dolphin performances are almost hourly from 11am, with the final show at 9pm; admission includes the show. There's also a decent restaurant here.

FUNDACIÓN NATURALEZA Y EL HOMBRE Map pp228-9
☎ 204-0438; Av 5B No 6611 btwn Calles 66 & 70; admission CUC$3; 🕙 10am-4pm Mon-Fri
This museum collects artifacts from a 17,422km canoe trip from the Amazon source to the sea led by Cuban intellectual and nature-lover Antonio Nuñez Jiménez. The canoe in which they made the trip is displayed, along with headdresses, weapons and adornments used by the indigenous communities the team encountered along the way, plus scores of ceramic figurines in all stages and positions of sexual arousal – the Latin American Kamasutra. The *fundación* (foundation) itself is mind-blowing, with one of Cuba's largest photography collections, plus all the titles written by Nuñez Jiménez, (he was damn prolific!), the famous Fidel portrait by Guayasamín, stalactites in the foyer and glass cases collecting all kinds of intriguing ephemera from the founder's life. Though small, the museum is one of Habana's most rewarding.

IGLESIA JESÚS DE MIRAMAR
Map pp228-9
cnr Av 5 & Calle 82
It's difficult to miss the domed roof of this gigantic neo-Romanesque church, an architectural rarity in Habana. Despite its

eye-catching facade the church, which dates from the 20th century, has little historic significance.

PABELLÓN PARA LA MAQUETA DE LA CAPITAL Map pp228-9

☎ 202-7303; Calle 28 No 113 btwn Avs 1 & 3; admission CUC$3; ⊙ 9:30am-5:15pm Tue-Sat

If you thought the **Maqueta de la Habana Vieja** (p73) was impressive, check out this ultramodern pavilion containing a huge 1:1000 scale model of the whole city, originally created for urban-planning purposes but now a tourist attraction in its own right. Measuring 22m long and 8m wide, it's one of the largest scale models in the world. You can rent binoculars to check out all the color-coded buildings, parks and monuments.

RUSSIAN EMBASSY Map pp228-9

Av 5 No 6402, btwn Calles 62 & 66

The strikingly ugly Russian embassy sticks out like a sore thumb in the graceful avenues of Playa and Miramar, casting its dark Stalinist shadow over an otherwise quiet and attractive neighborhood. With its imposing double tower visible for miles around, this monstrous structure is testament to the once weighty influence of Cuba's superpower patron on the island.

MARIANAO, CUBANACÁN & FLORES

CENTRO DE INGENERÍA GENÉTICA Y BIOTECNOLOGÍA Map pp228-9

☎ 271-8008; www.cigb.edu.cu; cnr Av 31 & Calle 190

The ultramodern Centro de Ingenería Genética y Biotecnología, 1km south of the Palacio de las Convenciones, is the focus of Cuba's genetic engineering and biotechnology research. Cuba first became involved in biotechnology in 1981, and this center opened in 1986 after an initial investment of US$140 million. Since then, the 400 Cuban scientists employed in this enormous complex have developed a number of unique methods of medical treatment and several new vaccines. It's the largest of its kind in Latin America. Visits can be made by prior arrangement.

CENTRO NACIONAL DE INVESTIGACIONES CIENTÍFICAS

Map pp228-9

Cenic; ☎ 208 2553; www.cnic.edu.cu; cnr Av 25 & Calle 158

Two blocks away is the Centro Nacional de Investigaciones Científicas, where the anticholesterol wonder drug Ateromixol, or PPG, was created. This remarkable work has been conducted without foreign assistance, and it possibly holds the key to a world-class pharmaceutical industry of the future. Visits can be made by prior arrangement.

CLUB HABANA Map pp228-9

☎ 204-5700; Av 5 btwn 188 & 192; daily pass CUC$20

This fabulously eclectic mansion in Flores dating from 1928 once housed the Havana Biltmore Yacht & Country Club. In the 1950s the establishment gained brief notoriety when it famously denied entry to Cuban president Fulgencio Batista on the grounds that he was 'Black' (Batista was in fact of mixed blood with a Black mother and a part-Chinese father). Castro had better luck when he dropped by for dinner some 30 years later and the club remains one of the few places where he has dined in public. These days the history of the establishment seems to have swung full circle and it is again a popular hangout for foreign correspondents and diplomats. The club has its own beach, swimming pool, tennis courts, bar, boutiques and health club. Annual membership is CUC$1500, but should you wish to hobnob spontaneously with the high and mighty, you can get a daily pass for CUC$20.

INSTITUTO SUPERIOR DE ARTE

Map pp228-9

ISA; Calle 120 No 1110

Cuba's leading art academy was established here in the former Habana Country Club in 1961, and elevated to the status of institute in 1976. The Faculty of Music occupies the original country-club building, and after the revolution a number of other facilities were erected on the site of a former 18-hole championship golf course. This cluster of buildings, some unfinished, some half-restored, but all gloriously graceful due to the arches, domes and profuse use of red brick, was the brainchild of Che

Guevara and a team of architects. Among them was Richard Porro, who designed the striking Faculty of Plastic Arts, with long curving passageways and domed halls in the shape of a reclining woman. Across a small stream from the main building is the Faculty of Theater & Dance. There are some 800 students; it is also possible for foreigners to study (p191) here. It is accessible only from the northwest.

MUSEO DE LA ALFABETIZACIÓN

Map pp228-9

☎ 260-8054; Ciudad Libertad; admission free; ☽ 8am-noon & 1-4:30pm Mon-Fri, 8am-noon Sat

The former Cuartel Colombia military airfield at Marianao is now a school complex called Ciudad Libertad. You may enter to visit the Museo de la Alfabetización, which describes the 1961 literacy campaign, where 100,000 *brigadistas* (student volunteers) aged 12 to 18 spread out across Cuba to teach reading and writing to farmers, workers and the aged. In the center of the traffic circle, opposite the entrance to the complex, is a tower in the form of a syringe in memory of Carlos Juan Finlay, who discovered the cause of yellow fever in 1881.

MUSEO DEL AIRE   Map pp228-9

Calle 212 btwn Avs 29 & 31, La Coronela; unguided/guided CUC$2/3; camera CUC$2; ☽ 9am-4pm Tue-Sun

The substantial Museo del Aire has 22 planes and helicopters on display, most of them ex-military aircraft. Don't miss Che Guevara's personal Cessna 310, or the space suit used by Cuba's first cosmonaut.

PABEXPO   Map pp228-9

☎ 271-6614; Av 17 btwn Calles 174 & 184

Opened in 1987, Pabexpo is a 20,000-sq-m exhibition space housed in four interconnecting pavilions that are filled with about 15 business or scientific shows a year. Events include tourism fairs, cigar festivals and music awards. The excellent restaurant El Palenque (p123) is situated nearby.

PALACIO DE LAS CONVENCIONES

Map pp228-9

Calle 146 btwn Avs 11 & 13

The Habana Convention Center is one of Cuba's most dramatic modern buildings. Built for the Nonaligned Conference in 1979, the four interconnecting halls contain an auditorium with 2101 seats, and there are also 11 smaller halls. The 589-member National Assembly meets here twice a year.

EASTERN HABANA

Eating p126; Sleeping p170

East of Habana harbor the city mixes historic 17th- and 18th-century forts with the grittier working-class neighborhoods of Regla and Guanabacoa. Further afield lie newer developments strung out around the Estadio Panamericano, and further still is the small fishing village of Cojímar.

Despite their relative isolation on the other side of the harbor channel, Habana's eastern forts, referred to collectively as the Parque Histórico Militar Morro-Cabaña, are linked to Habana Vieja via a traffic tunnel and share Unesco World Heritage site status. They're a must-see for anyone with a passing interest in Habana's history.

Further south, the old neighborhood of Regla, just across the harbor from Habana Vieja, is an industrial port town known as a center of Afro-Cuban religions, including the all-male secret society Abakúa. Long before the triumph of the 1959 revolution, Regla was heralded as the Sierra Chiquita ('Little Sierra,' after the Sierra Maestra) for its revolutionary traditions. Free of the standard tourist trappings, Regla makes a nice afternoon out of the city; the skyline views from this side of the harbor offer an entirely different perspective on the Cuban capital.

Three kilometers to the east is Guanabacoa, a town founded in 1607 that later went on to become a center of the slave trade. In 1762 the British occupied Guanabacoa on their way through to Habana, but not without a fight from its mayor, José Antonio Gómez Bulones (better known as Pepe Antonio), who attained almost legendary status by conducting a guerrilla campaign behind British lines. Guanabacoa today is a sleepy yet colorful place that feels more like a small town than a splaying city suburb. There are no hotels here, and access on public transportation is not easy, but a visit is worthwhile if tied in with an excursion to nearby Regla, which is easily accessible by ferry.

Ten kilometers east of Habana is the little port town of Cojímar, famous for harboring Ernest Hemingway's fishing boat *El Pilar* in the 1940s and '50s; it was also (supposedly)

TRANSPORTATION

Bus For Cojímar, the Habana Vieja–Playas del Este bus 400 and the Vedado–Alamar M-1 stop on the Via Monumental near the Estadio Panamericano. Bus M-3 runs from the Terminal de Omnibus to Alamar, and stops on the Via Blanca near Regla. Bus 3 from Parque de la Fraternidad in Centro Habana, and buses 195 and 295 from Vedado all go to Guanabacoa.

Ferry Ferries leave from the Muelle Luz in Habana Vieja every 15 minutes, and dock in Regla and Casablanca.

Taxi The best place to find a cab is outside the Hotel Panamericano near Cojímar, or along the Via Monumental.

Train The *Hershey Train* leaves Casablanca five times daily and stops in Guanabacoa.

the prototype for the fishing village in Hemingway's novel *The Old Man and the Sea*. Founded in the 17th century at the mouth of a river, Cojímar was where the invading British army landed in 1762 en route to Habana. In 1994, thousands of *balseros* (rafters) split from the village's sheltered but rocky bay, lured to Florida by US radio broadcasts and promises of political asylum.

Orientation

Eastern Habana comprises all the neighborhoods east of the harbor channel and the Bahía de la Habana. These include Casablanca and the eastern forts (technically part of the Unesco World Heritage site) immediately across the water; Regla, another harborside settlement further south; and Guanabacoa, a suburb set further inland and separated from Regla by the arterial Via Blanca. Further east lies the Estadio Panamericano complex and the adjacent seaside village of Cojímar, which faces the Boca de Cojímar. Across the bay and delineated by the Río Cojímar lie the modern working-class high-rises of Alamar.

CASABLANCA

CASTILLO DE LOS TRES SANTOS REYES MAGNOS DEL MORRO Map p227

☎ 863-7941; Parque Histórico Militar Morro-Cabaña; admission CUC$4; ☺ 8am-8pm

This imposing castle was erected between 1589 and 1630 to protect the entrance to Habana harbor from pirates such as

Frenchman Jacques de Sores, who had sacked the city in 1555 (the Castillo de San Salvador de la Punta across the harbor was constructed at approximately the same time). Perched high on a rocky bluff above the ebbing Atlantic, the fort – with its irregular polygon shape, 10ft-thick walls and deep protective moat – is a classic example of Renaissance military architecture. Built by African slaves who hacked the foundations straight out of the surrounding rock, El Morro served as Habana's leading line of defense until the completion of the neighboring Fortaleza de San Carlos de la Cabaña in 1774. For more than a century, the fort withstood numerous attacks by French, Dutch and English privateers. But in 1762, after a bloody siege that lasted 44 days, a British force led by Admiral George Peacock consisting of 173 ships and 14,000 men captured El Morro by attacking from the landward side and digging a tunnel under the walls. The famous **lighthouse** (admission CUC$2; ☺ 8am-8pm) – which has made the castle one of Habana's signature sights – was added in 1844.

Renovated in the 1980s, the fort is now open to the public and is ever popular on the tour bus circuit. Aside from the fantastic views over sea and city, El Morro also hosts a **maritime museum**, covered by the entrance fee.

FORTALEZA DE SAN CARLOS DE LA CABAÑA Map p227

☎ 862-0617; Parque Histórico Militar Morro-Cabaña; admission before/after 6pm CUC$4/6, guide CUC$1; ☺ 8am-11pm

An 18th-century colossus, the Fortaleza de San Carlos de la Cabaña was built between 1763 and 1774 on a long, exposed ridge on the east side of Habana harbor to fill a weakness in the city's defenses. In 1762 the British had taken Habana by gaining control of this strategically important ridge and it was from here that they shelled the city mercilessly into submission. In order to prevent a repeat performance, the Spanish king Charles III ordered the construction of a massive fort that would repel future invaders. Measuring 700m from end to end and covering a whopping 10 hectares, it is the largest Spanish colonial fortress in the Americas.

Not surprisingly, the fort was so awesome that no one ever dared to attack it, though during the 19th century Cuban patriots faced firing squads here. Dictators Machado and Batista used the fortress as a military prison, and immediately after the revolution Che Guevara set up his head-quarters inside to preside over another catalogue of grisly executions (this time of Batista's officers).

These days the fort has been restored for visitors and you can spend at least half a day checking out the wealth of attractions here. As well as bars, restaurants, souvenir stalls and a cigar shop (containing the world's longest cigar), La Cabaña boasts the **Museo Fortificaciones y Armas** and the **Museo de Comendancia de Che**, both covered by the entrance fee. The nightly *cañonazo* at 8:30pm is a popular evening **excursion** (p66).

ESTATUA DE CRISTO Map p230

This white-marble statue of Christ that dominates the Bahía de la Habana (Habana Bay) was created in 1958 by J Madera. It was allegedly promised to President Batista by his wife after the US-backed dictator had survived an attempt on his life in the Presidential Palace in March 1957. As you disembark the Casablanca ferry, follow the road uphill for about 10 minutes until you reach the statue. The views from up here are stupendous, and it is a favorite nighttime hangout for locals. Behind the statue is the **Observatorio Nacional** (closed to tourists).

REGLA

COLINA LENIN Map p230
cnr Calle 24 de Febrero & Lenin

About 1.5km from the ferry you'll see a high metal stairway that gives access to one of only two monuments in Habana to Vladimir Ilich Ulyanov, better known to his friends and enemies as Lenin. Conceived in 1924 (before onetime Soviet stooge Fidel Castro was even born) by the Socialist mayor of Regla, Antonio Borsch, the monument was created to honor Lenin's death, and was one of the first of its kind outside the USSR. Above the monolithic image of Lenin is an olive tree planted by Bosch surrounded by seven lithe figures; unlike many other Soviet-inspired monuments you'll find in Cuba, this one creates hope. A small **exhibition** on the history of Colina Lenin is in a pavilion on the back side of the hill (it's often closed).

IGLESIA DE NUESTRA SEÑORA DE REGLA Map p230

☎ 97-62-88; cnr Santuario & Calle Martí; ⌚ 7:30am-6pm

As important as it is diminutive, this church, which lies just behind the boat dock in the municipality of Regla, has a long and colorful history. Inside on the main altar you'll find La Santísima Virgen de Regla, a Black Madonna venerated in the Catholic faith and associated in the Santería religion with Yemayá, the *orisha* of the ocean and the patron of sailors (always represented in blue). Legend claims that this image was carved by St Augustine 'the African' in the 5th century, and that in the year AD 453 a disciple brought the statue to Spain to safeguard it from barbarians. The small vessel in which the image was traveling survived a storm in the Strait of Gibraltar, so the figure was recognized as the patron of sailors. These days, *balseros* attempting to reach the US also evoke the protection of the Black Virgin.

A hut was first built on this site in 1687 by a pilgrim named Manuel Antonio to shelter a copy of the image, but this structure was destroyed during a hurricane in 1692. A few years later a Spaniard named Juan de Conyedo built a stronger chapel and in 1714 Nuestra Señora de Regla was proclaimed patron of the Bahía de la Habana. In 1957 the image was crowned by the Cuban cardinal in Habana cathedral. Every year on September 8, thousands of pilgrims descend on Regla to celebrate the saint's day and the image is taken out for a procession through the streets.

The current church dates from the early 19th century and it is always busy with both Catholic and Santería devotees from both religions stooping in silent prayer before the images of the saints that fill the alcoves. In Habana, there is probably no better (public) place to see the layering and transference between Catholic beliefs and African traditions.

MUSEO MUNICIPAL DE REGLA Map p230

☎ 97-69-89; Martí No 158; admission CUC$2; ⌚ 9am-5pm Mon-Sat, 9am-1pm Sun

If you've come across to see the church, you'd do well to check out this quirky museum that is spread over two sites, one on the corner of Santuario and Calle Martí (adjacent to the church), and the other (better half) a couple of blocks straight up the main street from the ferry. Recording the history of Regla and its Afro-Cuban religions, the museum has an interesting, small exhibit on Remigio Herrero, first *babalawo* (Santería priest) of Regla, and a bizarre statue of Napoleon with his nose missing. An **Observatorio Astronómico** was established in the museum building in 1921. Price of admission includes both museum outposts and the **Colina Lenin exhibition** (opposite).

GUANABACOA

IGLESIA DE GUANABACOA Map p231
Iglesia de Nuestra Señora de la Asunción; cnr Pepe Antonio & Adolfo del Castillo Cadenas
Guanabacoa's main church, on Parque Martí in the center of town, was designed by Lorenzo Camacho, and built between 1721 and 1748. The gilded main altar and nine lateral altars are worth a look, and there's a painting of the Assumption of the Virgin at the back. Notice the Moorish-influenced wooden ceiling. The main doors are usually closed, but you can try asking at the parochial office on the back side of the church.

MUSEO DE MÁRTIRES Map p231
Martí No 320; admission free; ⏰ 10am-6pm Tue-Sat, 9am-1pm Sun
Effectively an arm of Guanabacoa's municipal museum, this place is on the road to Regla and displays material relevant to the Cuban revolution. Pop in only if you're passing.

MUSEO MUNICIPAL DE GUANABACOA Map p231
☎ 97-91-17; Martí No 108; admission CUC$2; ⏰ 10am-6pm Mon, Tue-Sat, 9am-1pm Sun
Two blocks west of Parque Martí, Guanabacoa's small museum is the neighborhood's most interesting draw card. Founded in 1964, it tracks the development of the neighborhood throughout the 18th and 19th centuries, and is famous for its rooms on Afro-Cuban culture, slavery and Santería, with a particular focus on the *orisha* Elegguá.

COJÍMAR

BUST OF ERNEST HEMINGWAY
Map p231
Calle 1D Final
Next to the Torreón de Cojímar and framed by a neoclassical archway is a gilded bust of Ernest Hemingway erected by the residents of Cojímar in 1962. Hemingway came here regularly in the 1940s and '50s and moored his boat in the nearby harbor. His friend and sea captain, Gregorio Fuentes, lived in the green-and-white house at Calle 98 until 2002, when he died aged 101.

TORREÓN DE COJÍMAR Map p231
Calle 1C Final
Overlooking the harbor, this old Spanish fort dating from 1649 is presently occupied by the Cuban coast guard. It was the first fortification taken by the British when they attacked Habana from the rear in 1762.

OUTER HABANA

Outer Habana is a caustic mix of splaying suburbs and small colonial towns – most of them engaging, but all frustratingly difficult to get to without using your own transportation.

Parque Lenin, located off the Calzada de Bejucal in Arroyo Naranjo, 20km south of central Habana, is the city's largest recreational area. Constructed between 1969 and 1972 on the orders of Castro's muse Célia Sánchez, it is one of the few developments in Habana from this era. The 670 hectares of green parkland and beautiful old trees surround an artificial lake, the Embalse Paso Sequito, situated just west of the much larger Embalse Ejército Rebelde, which was formed by damming the Río Almendares.

Although the park itself is attractive enough, the mishmash of facilities inside has fallen on hard times since the onset of the *período especial*. Taxi drivers will wax nostalgic about when Parque Lenin was an idyllic weekend getaway for scores of pleasure-seeking Habana families; these days the place has more of a neglected and surreal air. Fortunately, help is on the way. New management and millions of pesos of Chinese investment is currently financing

TRANSPORTATION

Bus Bus M-7 goes from the Parque de la Fraternidad in Centro Habana to Santa María del Rosario and San Francisco de Paula; bus M-2 goes from the same place to Santiago de las Vegas. Bus 88 from Vibora and bus 113 from Marianao go right through Parque Lenin.
Taxi Taxis cost CUC$15 to Parque Lenin and CUC$20 to Santiago de la Vegas.

of a major renovation project to bring the park back to its former glory.

Santa María del Rosario, 19km southeast of central Habana, is an old colonial town founded in 1732. Unlike most other towns from that period it has not become engulfed in modern suburbs, but stands alone in the countryside. The charms of this area were recognized by one of Cuba's greatest living painters, Manuel Mendive, who selected it for his personal residence. You can also see the countryside of this area in Tomás Gutiérrez Alea's metaphorical critique of slavery in his movie *La Última Cena* (The Last Supper).

In 1940 Ernest Hemingway bought a villa called Finca Vigía on a hill at San Francisco de Paula, 15km southeast of central Habana. He lived and wrote at the property until 1960, a year before his death. Recently reopened after a lengthy renovation, the Museo Hemingway is must-see for all literary fans.

PARQUE LENIN AREA

EXPOCUBA Map p232

Carretera del Rocío; admission CUC$1; 🕙 9am-5pm Wed-Sun

A visit to Parque Lenin can easily be combined with a trip to ExpoCuba, 3km south of Las Ruinas restaurant. Opened in 1989, this large permanent exhibition showcases Cuba's economic and scientific achievements in 25 pavilions based on themes such as sugar, farming, agriculture, animal science, fishing, construction, food, geology, sports and defense. Despite the hype ExpoCuba is poorly maintained and replete with government propaganda. The bulk of its clientele are schoolchildren (who come under duress) and Cubans who flock to the amusement park at the center of the complex. Don't make a special trip.

JARDÍN BOTÁNICO NACIONAL
Map p232

☎ 54-93-65; Carretera del Rocío; admission CUC$1; 🕙 8:30am-4:30pm Wed-Sun

Directly across the highway from Expo-Cuba is the 600-hectare Jardín Botánico Nacional, a surprisingly extensive collection of trees, plants and flowers from around the world. Highlights include the **Pabellones de Exposición** (opened in 1987), a series of greenhouses with cacti and plants native to Cuba, as well as the harmonious **Japanese Garden**, which was the brainchild of Japanese designer Yoshikuni Arake in 1992. This portion of the National Botanical Garden was a gift from Japan's government in 1989 as a token of friendship to the people of Cuba. As the gardens are rather large, a tractor train around the park departs four times a day and costs CUC$3. You can also join ecotourists for an organic, vegetarian buffet lunch in **Restaurante El Bambú** (p127) for CUC$15. Gaviota runs **tours** (p67) to the gardens.

PARQUE LENIN Map p232

Sights in Parque Lenin are scattered around and in dire need of a face-lift. Aside from horseback riding (p146) and a new **amusement park** for kids currently being rebuilt with Chinese money, there's an **aquarium** (admission CUC$2; 🕙 10am-5pm Tue-Sun) with freshwater fish and crocodiles, a dramatic white **monument to Lenin**, a smaller bronze **monument to Célia Sánchez** (Castro's onetime muse who was largely responsible for having the park built), and the scruffy-looking **Rodeo Nacional**, which has sporadic rodeo events. Nestled near the lake is the **Galería de Arte Amelia Peláez** (admission CUC$1; 🕙 10am-5pm). However, the park's best feature is undoubtedly the expansive open spaces that are enjoyed so enthusiastically by Cuban families at weekends during the summer.

PARQUE ZOOLÓGICO NACIONAL
Map p232

Av Zoo-Lenin; adult/child CUC$3/2, vehicle incl occupants CUC$5; 🕙 9am-3:15pm Wed-Sun

The extensive Parque Zoológico Nacional is 2km west of Parque Lenin. Worlds away from the inner-city zoo in Nuevo Vedado, with its stagnant crocodile ponds and jail cells for cages, this is more of a zoo-cum-safari-park where rhinos, hippos and other imported fauna have free rein. A trolley bus tours the grounds all day (included in admission).

SANTUARIO DE SAN LÁZARO
Map pp218-19

El Rincón; 7am-6pm

The object of one of Cuba's most important pilgrimages, this small, sparkling church in the village of El Rincón just outside Santiago de las Vegas is the venerated shrine of San Lázaro, a Christian saint known for his ministrations to lepers and the poor. Every year on December 17 (Saint Lazarus' feast day), thousands of Cubans descend on the sanctuary en masse, some on bloodied knees, others walking barefoot for kilometers through the night to exorcise evil spirits and pay off debts for miracles granted. San Lázaro is paralleled in Santería by the *orisha* Babalú Ayé, the Yoruba god of sickness. A statue of the saint made of wood with gold and marble finishes stands on the church's main altar, and the shrine is busy year-round with people laying flowers and making donations.

SAN FRANCISCO DE PAULA & SANTA MARÍA DEL ROSARIO

IGLESIA DE NUESTRA SEÑORA DEL ROSARIO Map pp218-19
Catedral de los Campos de Cuba, Santa María del Rosario; 5:30-7:30pm

This church on Santa María del Rosario's old town square was built in 1720 near the Quiebra Hacha sugar mill, of which nothing remains today. Inside are a gilded mahogany altar and a painting by Veronese. It's one of suburban Habana's most attractive secrets.

MUSEO HEMINGWAY Map pp218-19
 91-08-09; San Francisco de Paula, Carretera Central Km 12.5; unguided/guided CUC$3/4, camera/video CUC$5/25; 9am-4:30pm Wed-Mon)

Recently reopened after a lengthy renovation, this unique museum in the Finca Vigía, set in the quiet Habana suburb of San Francisco de Paula, is the most interesting stop on the Cuban Ernest Hemingway trail. Having stayed on and off in the Hotel Ambos Mundos for nearly a decade, Hemingway finally bought the Finca Vigía in 1940 and lived here permanently until 1960. The house sits on a lush hilltop 11km southeast of Habana Vieja with gorgeous views over the city. Although visitors are not allowed in the house (which has been left as it was the day Hemingway departed), there are enough open doors and windows to allow an interesting glimpse into Papa's universe. Inside there are books everywhere (including beside the toilet), a large Victrola and record collection, wall-mounted animal heads, a gun collection and an astounding number of knickknacks. A stroll through the garden is worthwhile to see the surprisingly sentimental dog cemetery, Hemingway's fishing boat *El Pilar* and the pool where actress Ava Gardner once swam naked. If you're tired, you can chill out on a chaise longue below whispering palms and bamboo.

Walking &
Cycling Tours

Walking & Cycling Tours

So much of Habana's daily life is acted out in the streets and squares of the captivating Cuban capital that to miss a stroll through the atmospheric neighborhoods of Habana Vieja, Centro Habana and Vedado is to miss out on the gritty essence of the city itself. Fortunately for walking enthusiasts, Cuba's majestic capital is a compact and relatively safe city that is easily negotiated on foot. Furthermore, should your legs (and spirits) start to flag at any point, there are always plenty of passing taxis to whisk you quickly back to your casa particular (private house that lets out rooms to foreigners) or hotel.

HABANA VIEJA BY NIGHT

Music is what Habana does best and there is no better way of summoning up the sultry spirit of rumba, mambo, salsa and chachachá than to take a walk through the atmospheric streets of Habana Vieja after dark.

Warm up with a cocktail in the **El Louvre 1** (p80), the alfresco bar outside the Hotel Inglaterra, and a longtime meeting place for travelers of all types. With your mojito swiftly dispatched, head east across Parque Central, to the top end of Obispo where, if you're feeling flush, you can sink a quick CUC$6 daiquirí in **El Floridita 2** (p134), one of Ernest Hemingway's favorite watering holes. Back outside, the music revs up, and for the next 10 blocks on Calle Obispo myriad sights and sounds – not to mention overzealous waiters – will lure you enthusiastically from bar to bar.

La Casa del Escabeche 3 (cnr Obispo & Villegas; 🕙 11am-midnight), on your right at the intersection with Villegas, is a good early diversion, a tiny bar with an accompanying restaurant that somehow manages to squeeze a guitarist, singer, drummer and double bass into its packed and smoky interior. Enjoy the music from the street outside as it drifts through the wooden grilles. If you fancy a bite to eat, the **Bosque Bologna 4** (p133), where energetic local bands perform 24/7 in front of a mixed audience of drinkers and diners, is a good pit stop; the fare is Cuban-Italian. **La Dichosa 5** (p135) on the corner of Obispo

WALK FACTS

Start El Louvre
End Taberna de la Muralla
Distance 1.5km
Duration One hour and up

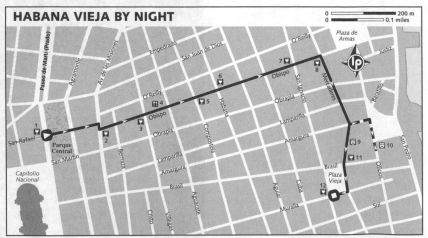

HABANA VIEJA BY NIGHT

and Compostela is another vibrant, if claustrophobic, Habana drinking joint that churns out good thumping music morning, noon and night, and often showcases a skillful flautist.

One block further east and you'll encounter the busy **La Lluvia de Oro 6** (p135), a longtime travelers' haunt and a popular stomping ground for legions of haranguing *jineteras* (women who attach themselves to male foreigners for monetary or material gain) – not that this detracts from the regular live music. Another old favorite is the **Café Paris 7** (p133), on the corner of Obispo and San Ignacio, where you might even get a seat and where you can tune into old Buena Vista Social Club favorites such as 'Chan Chan' and 'Cuarto de Tula.'

If you want to take the beat down a little, the **Hotel Ambos Mundos 8** (p71), a block further east, has some talented resident pianists who can rally flagging spirits (and eardrums) with excellent renditions of old Sinatra classics on a full-size grand. Head right on Mercaderes and you'll happen upon the **Mesón de la Flota 9** (p131), the font of Habana's earthy flamenco scene, where feisty 9pm singing-and-dancing extravaganzas rival anything in Spain.

If its refined classical music you're after, divert along Calle Amargura to the magnificent **Basilica Menor San Francisco de Asís 10** (p131), which holds regular chamber concerts (advance bookings are recommended). For salsa with a jazzy touch, stay on Mercaderes until Plaza Vieja, where the **Café Taberna 11** (p134) pays homage to the late, great Benny Moré, with big, brassy bands raising the roof every weekend in honor of the erstwhile *Bárbaro del Ritmo* (Barbarian of Rhythm).

It would be a shame to get this far and miss Habana's only microbrewery, the **Taberna de la Muralla 12** (p135), which sits pretty on the southwest corner of Plaza Vieja. Cool down amid the lilting musical mélange with a glass of the local amber nectar, or reinforce yourself with a couple of *Cuba libres* (rum and Cokes) before heading off elsewhere.

CENTRO HABANA'S ARCHITECTURE

This leisurely amble through some of Centro Habana's eclectic architectural sights begins at the end of Paseo de Martí, a salubrious tree-lined avenue known to locals by its old name, **El Prado 1** (p80).

Heading south toward Parque Central, the more interesting buildings lie initially to your left. Exhibiting the sharp lines and pure cubist simplicity of Depression-era America, the **Teatro Fausto 2** (p132), on the corner of Paseo de Martí and Colón, is an art deco classic. Still a functioning performance venue for a new generation of budding thespians, the theater is famous for its light plays and hilarious comedy shows.

One block further down on the left, the **Casa del Científico 3** (p162), now a budget hotel, is an eclectic masterpiece that was once the residence of former Cuban president José Miguel Gómez. Furnished with sweeping staircases, elaborate balconies and an eye-catching rooftop lookout, this veritable urban palace is dripping with diverse architectural influences ranging from art nouveau to Italian Renaissance.

Contrasting sharply with other modern architectural styles on Calle Trocadero, the neo-Moorish **Hotel Sevilla 4** (p80) harks back to a bygone age of Spanish stucco and intricate Mudéjar craftsmanship. A glimpse inside its gilded lobby, with its blue-tinted *azulejos* (glazed tiles) and decorative wooden ceilings, calls to mind a scene from Granada's Alhambra, though the hotel itself was built in 1908.

Turn right on Agramonte (Zulueta), and detour down Animas and Av de los Misiones (Monserrate) for Habana's – and perhaps Latin America's – most emblematic art deco building, the kitschy **Edificio Bacardí 5** (p70), a vivid and highly decorative incarnation of this popular interwar architectural genre garnished with granite, Capellanía limestone and multicolored bricks.

On the northwest corner of Parque Central, the royal blue **Hotel Telégrafo 6** (p164), renovated in 2002 by the City Historian's Office, retains many features of an earlier hotel constructed on this site in 1886. Take a peep inside its airy lobby to admire the funky furnishings and intricate bar mosaic.

Eclecticism meets neobaroque at the flamboyant **Centro Gallego 7** (p80), erected as a Galician social club in 1915 around the existing Teatro Tacón. Facing it across leafy Parque Central is the equally eclectic **Centro Asturianas 8** (now part of the Museo Nacional de Bellas Artes; p82), with four separate rooftop lookouts and a richly gilded interior. According to in-the-know locals, these

CENTRO HABANA'S ARCHITECTURE

0 ————— 200 m
0 ————— 0.1 miles

two Spanish social clubs entered into silent competition during the 1910s and '20s to see who could come up with the most grandiose building. The winner? You decide.

Habana's **Capitolio Nacional 9** (p79), built between 1926 and 1929, captures Latin America's neoclassical revival in full swing, with sweeping stairways and Doric columns harking back to a purer and more strident Grecian ideal.

Few travelers venture down Calle Cárdenas behind the Fuente de los Indios, but those who do quickly fall upon some of Habana's most engaging art nouveau and art deco town houses. For pure artistic cheek, check out the pink-and-white wedding-cake structure on the southeast corner of **Cárdenas and Apodaca 10** before heading along Calle Cienfuegos to the Parque de la Fraternidad.

Av Simón Bolívar (Reina) is another architectural mishmash that will leave modern-day urban designers blinking in bewilderment. It also contains one of Habana's finest Gaudí-esque buildings, an outrageously ornate apartment dwelling on the southwest corner of **Bolívar and Campanario 11**.

Go north on Campanario, right on Salud and left on San Nicolas, and you're in the Barrio Chino, Habana's bustling Chinatown. **Cuchillo 12** is the main drag here, a short, narrow pedestrian street with plenty of color, but few buildings of architectural note. Merge into Zanja and proceed one block southeast to the next junction. Here on the corner of **Zanja and Av de Italia 13** is one of Habana's zaniest art deco creations, a narrow turreted town house with cubelike balconies, and sharply defined vertical and horizontal lines.

Turn left on Av de Italia (Galiano to locals) and stroll north to the **Teatro América 14** (p132), one of a trio of classic art deco *rascacielos* (skyscrapers) put up in the 1920s and '30s to house new shops and apartments. Continue north on Av de Italia for six more blocks and turn right at the Hotel Deauville into the **Malecón 15** (Av de Maceo; p86). Habana's storm-lashed sea drive is a museum of brilliant eclecticism, with each building differing defiantly from the last. The style reaches its apex two buildings from the junction with Paseo de Martí in the faux-Egyptian **Centro Hispano Americano de Cultura 16**. Admire the gaudy granite gargoyles before heading off for a well-earned drink.

VEDADO

In Habana, different neighborhoods have different flavors, but few are as intimate as the commercial district of Vedado, which lies between Centro Habana and the Río Almendares.

In order to uncover some of the quarter's most tantalizing sights, start this land-based voyage on the **Malecón 1** (p86) in front of the Hotel Nacional before tracking inland along arterial Calzada de Infanta. The eye-catching church on the corner of Infanta and Neptuno is the **Parroquial de Nuestra Señora del Carmen 2**, notable for its lofty bell tower crowned with an imposing statue of the Virgin Mary holding the baby Jesus. Turn right on Neptuno and head northwest up the hill to the Plaza de Mella, which contains the **Monumento a Julio Antonio Mella 3** (p86), a small obelisk in memory of the founder of the Cuban Communist Party, who was assassinated by government agents in Mexico City in 1929. Towering atop a hill to your left is the **Universidad de la Habana 4** (p89), a formidable neoclassical building fronted by the famous *escalerita,* a sweeping concrete stairway where earnest students come daily to linger, flirt, study and debate.

The proliferation of traffic on San Lázaro and Neptuno signals your proximity to Habana's busiest road intersection, at **Calle L and Calle 23 5**. The latter street, more popularly known as La Rampa (the Ramp), is a wide four-lane thoroughfare that climbs gently 400m uphill from the glistening Malecón. In the 1950s this is where Habana's famously lewd nightlife was lit up in neon in a plethora of casinos, nightclubs, brothels and hotels. A 360-degree turn on Calles L and 23 reveals three of the city's most striking sights. To the east stands the **Hotel Habana Libre 6** (p85), a functional modernist skyscraper that was requisitioned by Castro's rebel army in 1959. To the north lies the **Cine Yara 7** (p142), Cuba's most prestigious movie house and the headquarters of the annual Habana film festival. Finally, to the west, are the leafy confines of the **Coppelia 8** (p119), the city's famous ice-cream parlor, which is housed in a structure that looks more like a flying saucer than a restaurant.

Staying on Calle L, continue one block west before turning right onto Calle 21. Two blocks down is the now empty **Hotel Capri 9**, a former Mafia crash pad run by Hollywood actor George Raft that was fictionally depicted in the movie *The Godfather: Part II* (in the scene when Michael Corleone travels to Habana to meet Hyman Roth).

The Mafia connections continue in the **Hotel Nacional 10** (p85) on Calles 21 and O, one of Habana's most famous architectural icons, which in December 1946 hosted the largest get-together of North American hoods in Mob history (p56). Rest your feet awhile and admire the resplendent Moorish lobby or grab a cool mojito in the breezy Galería Bar.

Turn right when you exit the hotel and then hang a left on Calle 19. The concrete colossus directly in front of you is the **Edificio Focsa 11** (p84), constructed between 1954 and 1956 from the bottom up with no cranes. A right turn on Calle M and a left on **Calle 17 12** will bring you onto an archetypal Vedado street, lined by rows of gnarly laurel trees and embellished by a clutch of impossibly ornate eclectic mansions. Two of the most magnificent piles are **Uneac 13**, the headquarters of Cuban artists and writers union, located on the corner of Calles 17 and H, and the **Museo de Artes Decorativas 14** (p86), on the corner of Calles 17 and E. To earn your cooldown drink, stroll along Calle 17 to Paseo until you reach the **Casa de la Amistad 15** (p137), where beers and music await in a beautiful Italian Renaissance style garden.

WALK FACTS

Start Corner Calle 23 and Malecón
End Casa de la Amistad
Distance 6km
Duration 3½ hours

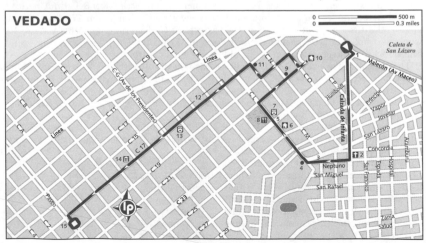

VEDADO

HABANA'S STATUES

Statues can tell an important historical story in any major city and the Cuban capital is no exception. This monumental cycling tour starts at **El Orbe 1** (p145), Habana's friendly bike-hire store in the Manzana de Gómez shopping arcade, and proceeds north along Paseo de Martí. Just before you merge with the busy Malecón in front of the Castillo de San Salvador de la Punta you'll see a large equestrian statue of **General Máximo Gómez 2** on the right-hand side. Gómez (p52) was a war hero from the Dominican Republic who fought tirelessly for Cuban independence in both the 1868 and 1895 conflicts against the Spanish. The impressive statue of him sitting atop a horse faces heroically out to sea and was created by Italian artist Aldo Gamba in 1935. On a small traffic circle close by is the **Memorial a los Estudiantes de Medicina 3**, a fragment of wall encased in marble at the spot where eight Cuban medical students chosen at random were shot by the Spanish in 1871 as a reprisal for allegedly desecrating the tomb of a Spanish journalist (in fact, they were innocent).

Proceed carefully along the Malecón for 14 blocks and you'll reach Parque Maceo, a large traffic island dominated by the **Monumento a Antonio Maceo 4**, the mulatto general (p52) who, along with Gómez, cut a blazing trail across the whole of Cuba during the First War of Independence. Erected in 1916, the monument was sculpted by another talented Italian, Domenico Boni.

Continue west along the Malecón and, soon after passing the Hotel Nacional, you'll come to another traffic island. This one contains the **Monumento a las Víctimas del Maine 5** erected in 1926 to honor the 258 American men who were killed when the US battleship *Maine* mysteriously exploded in Habana harbor in 1898 (p54). The structure once boasted an American eagle atop its two classical pillars, but the figurine was decapitated in 1959 and now resides in the garden of the American ambassador in the suburb of Cubanacán.

Pedal west past the Plaza Tribuna Anti-Imperialista and you'll fall upon the Malecón's third major equestrian statue, the **Monumento a Calixto García 6**, dedicated to the valiant Cuban general who was prevented by US military leaders in Santiago de Cuba from attending the Spanish surrender in 1898. Twenty-four bronze plaques around the base of the structure provide a history of García's 30-year struggle for Cuban independence.

Many busts and statues line Calle G (Av de los Presidentes). The first, outside the Hotel Presidente, isn't actually a monument at all, but rather an empty plinth that formerly displayed a statue of Cuba's first president **Tomás Estrada Palma 7**. Despite being a lifelong friend of José Martí, Palma is now considered a traitor in Cuba for selling out national interests to the Americans in the early 1900s. As a result, his statue has been toppled and all that remains are his shoes.

A few blocks further south you'll spy three statues in quick succession adorning the boulevard's wide central walkway. The first is a memorial to **Simón Bolívar 8**, Latin America's great liberator; the second is a sculpture of **Benito Juárez 9**, Mexico's first non-White president; and the third is a more modern memorial to Socialist Chilean president **Salvador Allende 10**, who was toppled in a US-backed military coup in 1973, after which he – allegedly – shot himself with a rifle given to him by his old friend Fidel Castro.

The crowning glory of Calle G is the **Monumento a José Miguel Gómez 11**, which sits atop a hill below the Castillo del Príncipe. This wonderful classical memorial is the work of another industrious Italian, Giovanni Nicolini, and was sculpted from Boltiano and Carrera marble in 1936. Ironically Gómez is yet another disgraced former president and his bronze figure has also been removed from its plinth.

Merge with Av Salvador Allende (Carlos III) and continue until it becomes Av Simón Bolívar. After about 1km you'll emerge in the Parque de la Fraternidad (p82), a popular green space that is replete with bronze busts of American leaders through the ages. The most interesting and ironic statue here (considering Cuba's recent history) is that of **Abraham Lincoln 12**, which stands authoritatively on a white base opposite the Hotel Saratoga; apparently it's Cuba's only public nod to a US president, living or dead.

CYCLE FACTS

Start La Manzana de Gómez
End Parque Central
Distance 12km
Duration Three hours

HABANA'S STATUES

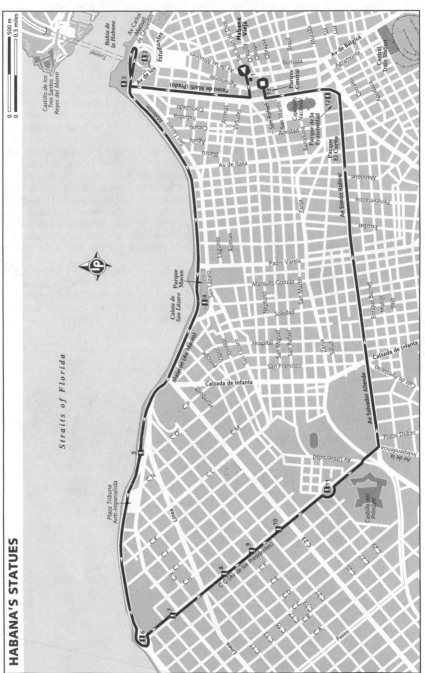

Saving the best till last, pedal the last few hundred meters past the Capitolio and you'll end up where you began in the Parque Central. Here you can grab a well-earned drink in the Hotel Inglaterra (p80) or the Hotel Telégrafo (p164), and admire the white marble statue of Cuban national hero **José Martí 13** (p82) that gleams from behind a ring of 28 royal palms in the middle of the park.

NECRÓPOLIS CRISTÓBAL COLÓN

Declared a national monument in 1987, the Necrópolis Cristóbal Colón (p87) is one of Latin America's most fascinating cemeteries, renowned for its striking religious iconology and elaborate marble-sculpted statues. The cemetary is far from being eerie though, and a walk through these 56 hallowed hectares can be an educational and captivating stroll through the annals of Cuban history.

The Romanic-Byzantine **Puerta de la Paz 1** (Door of Peace) on Calle 12 and Zapata was designed by Spanish architect Calixto de Loira Cardoso in 1871 and is said to have been inspired by the Triumphal Arch in Rome. Pay your CUC$1 entry fee at the door before turning left and proceeding along Calle A parallel to the cemetery's northeast wall. A short walk from the entrance you'll find the grave of Cuban novelist **Alejo Carpentier 2** (1904–80), a white marble tomb topped by a simple cross and surrounded by a white metal fence. The inscription on the grave reads *Hombre de mi tiempo soy y mi tiempo trascendent es el de la revolución Cubana* (I am a man of my time and my historic time is that of the Cuban revolution).

Turn right on Calle 5 and left on Calle B and walk four blocks to the intersection with Calle 15, where you'll find the grave of pioneering Cuban physician and scientist **Carlos Finlay 3** (1833-1915), the first person

WALK FACTS

Start Corner Calle 12 and Zapata
End Corner Calle 12 and Zapata
Distance 2.5km
Duration 1½ hours

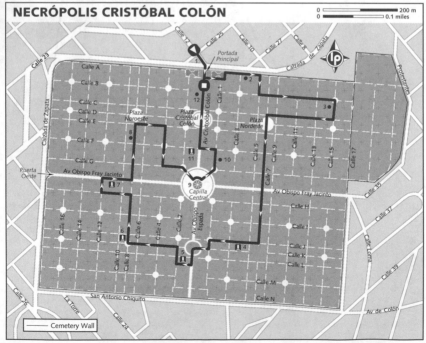

NECRÓPOLIS CRISTÓBAL COLÓN

Cemetery Wall

to identify the mosquito as the carrier of the organism that caused yellow fever. It's an understated grass-covered family plot with a dedication from the Oficina Sanitaria Panamericano added in 1946.

Doubling back along Calle C, turn left at the Plaza Nordeste and head seven blocks south to Calle J, where you turn right. The strange modern sculpture ahead of you integrating elements of the Cuban flag is in honor the **Martyrs of the Assault on the Presidential Palace 4** who, led by student leader José Echeverría, staged an abortive plot to assassinate President Batista in March 1957.

Continue two blocks to the west, turn left and then right and you'll find yourself on Av Obispo Espada, the cemetery's central thoroughfare. Just west of here lies the **Mausoleum of the Revolutionary Armed Forces 5**, a large memorial to Cuban soldiers killed in action in various wars. It consists of a simple arch guarded by two palm trees and a couple of military figures carved in bronze. The many vaults here are often decorated with flowers. Head north on Calle 2 and turn left on Calle K to reach the **Martyrs of Granma 6** memorial. This monument, in honor of the men killed when Fidel's yacht arrived in Cuba in December 1956 to start the revolutionary war, is well tended and includes a carved image of the famous boat, along with the names of 19 deceased.

An earlier conflict is remembered three blocks to the north on Av Obispo Fray Jacinto at a memorial to the **Veterans of the Independence Wars 7**. This large monument commemorates those who fought in the two independence wars of 1868–78 and 1895–98. Backed by five royal palms and fronted by two prickly cacti, the edifice depicts the deaths of Carlos Manuel de Céspedes, José Martí and Antonio Maceo in battle and contains a quote from the latter: *La libertad se conquista con el filo de machete, no se pide* (Freedom is won with the blade of a machete, not by asking for it).

Cutting up Calle 8 you'll see the family grave of former Orthodox party leader **Eduardo R Chibás 8** (1907–51), a relentless anticorruption campaigner in the 1940s and '50s who shot himself dead during a radio broadcast as a form of protest. At his funeral in 1951 – which was attended by thousands – fellow Orthodox Party member Fidel Castro jumped up onto Chibás' grave and made a fiery speech denouncing the old establishment.

Cut east on Calle E, south on Calle 4 and east again on Calle G and you'll arrive at the neo-Romanesque **Capilla Central 9**, Cuba's only octagonal church, where more often than not a funeral service will be taking place. Close to here at Calle 1 and F is the cemetery's most visited tomb, that of Señora Amelia Goyri or **La Milagrosa 10** (Miraculous One), a Habana woman who died while giving birth on May 3, 1901. When the bodies were exhumed one year later, the baby – who had been buried at her feet – was said to be in her arms. Señora Amelia thus became the focus of a miraculous cult, and to this day flowers adorn her tomb and local devotees maintain a regular attendance.

Go left on Calle F and continue straight up the Av Cristóbal Colón. On your left you'll spy one of the cemetery's tallest structures, the **Monument to the Firefighters 11**, which honors a group of firemen who were killed in the line of duty in 1890. Among the many garlands and figures depicted here are a pelican (to signify self-sacrifice) and an angel atop a lofty column clasping an injured fireman.

Heading back toward the entrance gate, don't miss the surprisingly inconspicuous grave of Dominican-born Cuban war hero **General Máximo Gómez 12** (1836–1905). The plot, which is on your left, is distinguished by a brown marble obelisk that sports Gómez' bronze image on a circular medallion. The entrance gate, and the end of this tour, is 100m to the north.

Eating ∎

Eating

Habana is not renowned for its cuisine and, although the food here isn't universally awful, don't bank on it being a highlight of your trip. Fifty years of austerity, rationing and on-off food shortages has left most of the city's state-controlled restaurants stumped for ingredients and starved of creativity. And, with a lack of any real incentive to perform, the service often isn't that much better.

There are, of course, some welcome exceptions to this rule. Habana Vieja has a growing clutch of attractive government-run restaurants set up by the City Historian's Office, Habaguanex, with the palates of foreign visitors in mind, while Playa and Vedado boast a plethora of inviting and gastronomically adventurous paladares (privately run restaurants; p124). If you want to excite your taste buds and try something a bit different, these are the places to head.

See p17 for information about food in Habana.

Opening Hours

As a general rule, most restaurants are open 10:30am to 11pm daily. Paladares tend to open at noon and stay open a little later, often until midnight.

How Much

In Cuba simple street food and light lunchtime snacks are normally relatively cheap, as long as you steer clear of the main tourist hubs (or any bar associated with the late, great Ernest Hemingway). Real aficionados can even swap their convertibles for Cuban pesos and go shopping at the agropecuarios (free-enterprise vegetable markets; p112), thus saving pocketfuls. In and around the tourist areas the picture is a little different. Here you'll find meals and drinks priced at similar rates to Europe and North America. Count on CUC$4 to CUC$6 for a cocktail in a posh hotel and don't expect much change from CUC$20 for a full dinner in one of the city's more upscale paladares or restaurants.

PRICE GUIDE

The price symbols in this chapter indicate the price of a two-course meal for one person, excluding drinks.

$$$	over CUC$15
$$	CUC$8-15
$	under CUC$8

Booking Tables

Booking tables is only necessary in the evenings at the more popular paladares where space is limited. Reservations are recommended at Paladar La Guarida (p118) in Centro Habana, Paladar El Hurón Azul (p121) and Paladar Gringo Viejo (p121) in Vedado, and any of the half-dozen or so paladares in Playa and Miramar.

Tipping

Remembering to tip is important in Cuba where leaving a couple of convertibles in the bread basket at the end of the meal can effectively make or break a person's week. As most Cubans earn their salaries (the equivalent of US$10 to US$25 a month) in Cuban pesos, access to hard currency is vital in order to make up the shortfall. However mediocre your food, a convertible or two isn't just a show of appreciation; it's a vital contribution to the local economy.

In Cuba, a 10% tip is usually sufficient, with CUC$1 being the appropriate minimum in a restaurant that accepts convertibles. Tipping in peso restaurants is not compulsory, but is greatly appreciated. Leaving 10 pesos or CUC$0.50 in convertibles is a generous tip.

Groceries

You're rarely spoilt for choice in Habana's uninspiring grocery stores. Certainly don't expect the jam-packed supermarket shelves that you might be familiar with back home. Imported goods such as pasta and cereal are often hard to come by and fresh produce – while organically grown and relatively abundant – is normally only seasonal.

The best-stocked grocery store in Habana Vieja is **Harris Brothers** (Map p220; O'Reilly No 526; 9am-9pm Mon-Sat), which sells everything from fresh pastries to diapers.

Supermarkets in Centro Habana include **Almacenes Ultra** (Map p222; Av Simón Bolívar No 109; 9am-6pm Mon-Sat, 9am-1pm Sun), **La Época** (Map p222; cnr Av de Italia & Neptuno; 9am-9pm Mon-Sat, 9am-noon Sun) and **Supermercado Isla de Cuba** (Map p222; cnr Máximo Gómez & Factoría; 10am-6pm Mon-Sat, 9am-1pm Sun).

In Vedado **Supermercado Meridiano** (Map pp224-5; Galerías de Paseo, cnr Calle 1 & Paseo; 10am-5pm Mon-Fri, 10am-2pm Sun) has a good wine and liquor selection, and rather overpriced bread.

Supermercado 70 (Map pp228-9; cnr Calle 70 & Av 3; 9am-6pm Mon-Sat, 9am-1pm Sun), in Playa, is still known as the 'Diplomercado' from the days when you had to show a foreign passport to be able to shop here; it's gigantic and has a large selection. There is also a row of simple restaurant kiosks facing the supermarket.

See p112 for Habana's best agropecuarios.

HABANA VIEJA

What it lacks in quality paladares, Habana Vieja makes up for in wonderfully atmospheric and meticulously restored government-run restaurants. Housed in old colonial buildings and offering such (relatively) adventurous culinary alternatives as pasta, pizza and Moroccan tagine, these places have an ambience that is is invariably excellent, even if the food isn't quite cordon bleu standard.

AL MEDINA Map p220   Middle Eastern $
867-1041; Oficios No 12, btwn Obrapía & Obispo; noon-midnight
Habana takes on Middle Eastern cuisine in one of the city's oldest and most architecturally engaging Mudéjar buildings. Tucked into a beautiful patio off Calle Oficios, Al Medina is where you can dine like a Moroccan sheik on lamb couscous (CUC$10) and chicken tagine (CUC$5) with a spicy twist. It's especially recommended for its massive veggie platter that comes with hummus, tabouleh, dolmas, pilaf and falafel.

CAFÉ DE LAS INFUSIONES
Map p220   Café $
Mercaderes btwn Obispo & Obrapía; 8am-11pm
Wedged into Calle Mercaderes, this recently restored Habaguanex coffeehouse is a caffeine addict's heaven and boasts a wonderful resident pianist. Fancier than the Café Habano and more comprehensive

HABANA VIEJA TOP FIVE
- Restaurante La Dominica (p115)
- Museo del Chocolate (p113)
- Mesón de la Flota (p114)
- Café de las Infusiones (left)
- Al Medina (left)

than the Escorial, here you can order more than a dozen different cuppas, including Irish coffee (CUC$3.50), punch coffee (CUC$5), mocha (CUC$1) and cappuccino (CUC$1.75).

CAFÉ EL ESCORIAL Map p220   Café $
868-3545; Mercaderes No 317; 9am-9pm
Habana Vieja's newest coffee bar is housed in a finely restored colonial mansion on the corner of Plaza Vieja and serves some of the best caffeine infusions in the city. Aside from *café cubana* (strong, sweet black coffee), *café con leche* (strong coffee with hot milk) and an eye-wateringly strong Cuban espresso, you can get frappés, coffee liquor and even a *daiquirí de café* (coffee daiquirí) here. There's also a small selection of sweet pastries.

CAFÉ HABANO Map p220   Café $
cnr Mercaderes & Amargura; 10am-9pm
A gritty, no-nonsense coffee bar on Calle Mercaderes, frequented mainly by Cubans, the Habano serves sweet, strong early-morning *café cubana* that gets plunked

HABANA'S BEST AGROPECUARIOS

Agropecuarios are free-enterprise markets where farmers sell their surplus produce to private consumers (after selling a set quota to the state). They are not to be confused with organopónicos, which are urban vegetable gardens run by local community groups that sell organic produce from small on-site kiosks.

Agros are not only good for buying raw, fresh foods; they are also handy for getting Cuban pesos (every large market has a change booth), *cajitas* (full meals of salad, baked vegetables, rice flecked with black beans, and pork cutlets sold in little take-away boxes), fresh meat, bread, cut flowers and other natural products such as herbs, honey, spices and beeswax candles. Every market also has a *protección de consumidor* section with a scale where you can weigh what you've purchased. Go here if you think you've been ripped off (a merchant caught three times cheating is booted from the market). Most markets are closed Monday.

The following are some of Habana's biggest agropecuarios:

Agropecuario Calle 17 & K (Map pp224–5; Calle 17 & K, Vedado) A 'capped' market; prices are set by the government, so they're cheap, but selection is limited.

Agropecuario Calles 19 & A (Map pp224–5; Calle 19 btwn Calles A & B, Vedado) Habana's 'gourmet' market, with cauliflower, fresh herbs and rarer produce during shoulder seasons; prices reflect the selection.

Agropecuario Calles 21 & J (Map pp224–5; cnr Calles 21 & J, Vedado) Good selection, including potted plants; watch for overcharging.

Agropecuario Sol (Map p220; Sol btwn Habana & Compostela, Habana Vieja) A compact, well-stocked market with decent variety.

Mercado Agropecuario Egido (Map p222; Av de Bélgica btwn Corrales & Apodaca, Centro Habana) A gigantic market; the action is over by 2pm.

Organopónico Plaza (Map pp224–5; cnr Av de Colón & Panorama, Plaza) One of Habana's biggest organic farms with a retail market.

Plaza de Marianao (Map pp228–9; Av 51 & Calle 124, Marianao) Friendly local market with produce downstairs, and flowers and plants upstairs. Head east up Av 51 for amazingly varied peso shopping.

---

down straight in front of you on the bar. Don't expect anything fancy here – like, um, milk.

CAFÉ O'REILLY Map p220   Cuban $
O'Reilly No 203; ⏱ 11am-3am
The O'Reilly is a good-old-fashioned 'spit-and-sawdust' café that sells drinks and snacks morning, noon and night. The bar is spread over two floors connected by a spiral staircase, with most of the action taking place upstairs. Grab an O'Reilly special sandwich (CUC$3) and a beer, and listen out for the roaming troubadours.

CAFÉ SANTO DOMINGO
Map p220   Café $
Obispo No 159; ⏱ 9am-9pm
Nestled above a popular bakery, the Santo Domingo is an easy-to-miss café-restaurant that knocks up simple tasty snacks – fast! There are excellent sandwiches and creamy fruit shakes, and you can also grab a few pastries from the patisserie downstairs to enjoy with your coffee.

CAFETERÍA TORRE LA VEGA
Map p220   Cuban $
Obrapía No 114a; ⏱ 9am-9pm
A travelers' staple in the heart of Habana Vieja, Torre La Vega is the perfect place to catch a quick lunch while you're exploring the sights and sounds of intimate Calle Obrapía. Most tables are alfresco and there's a pleasant little park directly opposite where customers can sit and relax. Large bowls of spaghetti, pork, chicken and *ropa vieja* (shredded beef with tomatoes and onions) go for CUC$3 or less, and while the food's not gourmet, it's a palatable snack in between sightseeing stops.

LA BARRITA Map p220   Cuban $
Edificio Bacardí, Av de las Misiones; ⏱ 9am-7pm
If you're keen to stick your nose inside one of Latin America's finest art deco buildings, consider having a snack in this comfortable bar-restaurant on a mezzanine floor just inside the lobby of the illustrious **Edificio Bacardí** (p70). The simple menu churns out standard Cuban staples such as *bocadito*

de queso (cheese sandwich) but, with its leather chairs, friendly waiters and polished mahogany bar, there's oodles of old-world ambience to be had here. Sample one of the bar's many rum cocktails.

MUSEO DEL CHOCOLATE

Map p220   Café $

cnr Amargura & Mercaderes; ☺ 9am-8pm
Chocolate addicts beware. This quirky 'museum' in the heart of Habana Vieja offers a lethal dose of chocolate, chocolate and yet more chocolate. (And it's all made on the premises too.) Situated – with no irony intended – on the corner of narrow Calle Amargura (Bitterness St), this venerable sweet-toothed establishment is actually more a café than a museum, with a small cluster of marble tables set among an interesting assortment of chocolate paraphernalia. Not surprisingly everything on the delicious menu contains one all-pervading ingredient – have it hot, cold, white, dark, rich, or smooth, the stuff is divine whatever way you choose.

RESTAURANTE HANOI

Map p220   Cuban $

☎ 867-1029; cnr Brasil & Bernaza; ☺ noon-11pm
The name might be demonstrating solidarity with formerly communist Vietnam, but the food certainly isn't. Straight-up Cuban cuisine with a couple of fried rice dishes thrown in for good measure characterize this old-town favorite, which mixes Cuban clientele with a liberal smattering of travelers with their noses in their Lonely Planets. Set meals of chicken and pork start at CUC$3, the tasty paella goes for CUC$6.50, while the lobster (which the waiter will probably tell you is the house special) is a hefty CUC$12.

RESTAURANTE PUERTO DE SAGUA

Map p220   Seafood $

☎ 867-1026; Av de Bélgica No 603; ☺ noon-midnight
Restaurante Puerto de Sagua is a nautical-themed eating joint in Habana Vieja's grittier southern quarter. It's characterized by its small porthole-style windows and serves mostly seafood at reasonable prices (CUC$5 to CUC$8). The jacketed waiters are courteous and friendly.

BAR-RESTAURANTE CABAÑA

Map p220   Cuban $$

☎ 860-5670; Tacón; ☺ 11am-midnight
A longtime favorite with Habana bus drivers on the run to and from Varadero, the Cabaña is an unfussy Habaguanex place with alfresco seating and pleasant views across the harbor to the eastern forts. Main dishes highlight beef and come in fairly modest portions; they include *filet de res* (beef fillet; CUC$5.50) and filet mignon (CUC$8.50). There's a bar with a karaoke machine upstairs.

EL CAFÉ MERCURIO

Map p220   International $$

☎ 860-6188; Lonja del Comercio, Plaza de San Francisco de Asís; ☺ 24hr
El Café Mercurio is an elegant indoor-outdoor café-restaurant with cappuccino machines, air-conditioning, intimate booths, smooth marble finishes and waiters in black ties. You can get decent main dishes here such as lobster and steak tartare, but it's also a great place for lunch or a snack. The formidable Cuban sandwich with ham, cheese and pork (CUC$4.50) will easily keep you going until dinnertime. There are also some great desserts.

EL SANTO ANGEL Map p220   Cuban $$

☎ 862-0617; cnr Brasil & San Ignacio; ☺ noon-midnight
Often overlooked by restaurant-seeking travelers, El Santo Angel – which is situated in a gorgeous colonial house on Plaza Vieja's northwest corner – specializes in seafood, offering such dishes as *langosta mariposa* (butterflied lobster; CUC$27), as well as fish in green sauce, and fish with roasted almonds, prawns and vinaigrette (both CUC$10). It's a lovely spot to watch the goings-on in the square.

LA MINA Map p220   Cuban $$

☎ 862-0216; Obispo No 109, btwn Oficios & Mercaderes; ☺ 24hr
Despite a rather mediocre menu, La Mina has always been a popular place for travelers thanks to its privileged position on the corner of Plaza de Armas. The building itself, which is of great historical value, used to be a girl's school and was one of the first structures in the old town to get the City Historian's makeover. The varied menu,

displayed on a stand in the street outside, contains chicken, pork and prawns cooked in a variety of ways, and the prices, which range from CUC$7 to CUC$10, are perfectly respectable. Once you've finished, there's a tempting heladería (ice-cream parlor) around the corner in Calle Oficios.

LA TORRE DE MARFIL

Map p220   Chinese $$

☎ 867-1038; Mercaderes No 111, btwn Obispo & Obrapía; ☽ noon-10pm Mon-Thu, noon-midnight Fri-Sun

Often dubbed Habana's best Chinese restaurant (though the chefs in Calle Cuchillo might disagree), this place, with its beaming waiters and bubbling fish tank, always seems to be at least three-quarters empty. But don't let the vacant tables put you off. The chop suey and chow mein plates – when they arrive – are huge, and the vegetables unusually fresh and crisp. After the hustle and bustle of the Barrio Chino (Chinatown) restaurants, the Torre feels infinitely quieter and more discreet.

LA ZARAGOZANA

Map p220   Cuban, Spanish $$

☎ 867-1040; Av de Bélgica btwn Obispo & Obrapía; ☽ noon-midnight

Established in 1830, La Zaragozana is Habana's oldest restaurant – though it's a long way from being its best. Behind its well-varnished wooden doors in noisy Av de Bélgica (Egido and Monserrate) lies an ample (and often deserted looking) seating area, plus what must be one of the city's longest bars. The Spanish-themed food – which includes the obligatory paella – is OK, but the ambience, amid assorted Iberian flags and memorabilia, can be a little dark and gloomy.

MESÓN DE LA FLOTA

Map p220   Cuban, Spanish $$

☎ 863-3838; Mercaderes btwn Amargura & Brasil; ☽ noon-midnight

Hotel, restaurant, bar, musicfest…is there no end to the Mesón de la Flota's talents? The primary reason to come to this venerable old coaching inn on cobbled Calle Mercaderes is for the masterful flamenco shows (p131), but on top of its well-known musical credentials, the Mesón can also churn out a mean dinner. The house specialty is tapas, with plenty of tasty options, including calamari,

garlic mushrooms, tortilla (potato omelet) and fried chickpeas with chorizo (CUC$2 to CUC$3 per plate), but there are also some excellent main courses too.

PALADAR LA JULIA

Map p220   Cuban $$

☎ 862-7438; O'Reilly No 506A btwn Bernaza & Villegas, ☽ noon-midnight

With an abundance of top government-run restaurants to choose from, Habana Vieja is something of a letdown in terms of paladares. Best of a meager bunch is the longstanding La Julia, an inconspicuous yet homely place wedged into a small downstairs room on Calle O'Reilly. The house specialty is pork with all the trimmings for approximately CUC$10.

PALADAR LA MULATA DEL SABOR

Map p220   Cuban $$

☎ 867-5984; Sol No 153; ☽ noon-midnight

This OK paladar is hidden away behind Plaza Vieja on the corner of Sol and San Ignacio. The decor inside is quirky and the food refreshingly tasty; it includes plenty of egg-based vegetarian options. It's worth a turn if you've been overdosing on historic Habaguanex restaurants and want some authentic home cooking.

RESTAURANTE EL CASTILLO DE FARNÉS
Map p220   Spanish $$

☎ 867-1030; Av de Bélgica No 361; ☽ noon-midnight

Advertising itself as a Spanish-orientated restaurant (it was founded by a Catalan), El Castillo de Farnés has average food, with house specialties such as chickpeas and chorizo lacking the bite of the versions at Restaurante La Paella or the Mesón de la Flota; suffice to say it's usually busy. The varied seafood menu is in the CUC$7 to CUC$20 price range. Next door, the sidewalk bar that sits alongside traffic-choked Av de Bélgica is OK for a beer, although the car fumes can sometimes be asphyxiating.

RESTAURANTE EL PATIO

Map p220   Cuban $$

☎ 867-1034/5; San Ignacio No 54; ☽ restaurant noon-midnight, terrace 24hr

Possibly one of the most romantic settings on planet Earth when the hustlers stay away, the mint stalks in your mojito are pressed to perfection and the band breaks spontaneously into your favorite tune, this place on the Plaza de la Catedral must be experienced at least once in the course of your Habana visit. Housed in the splendid **Palacio de los Marqueses de Aguas Claras (p76)**, a onetime Spanish governor's mansion, El Patio relies more on its setting than its food, which isn't on a par with other less atmospheric places. But, for romantics, that's not the point. Anyone who wants to connect in any way with the dreamy essence of historic Habana Vieja should enjoy at least one drink at an alfresco table here.

RESTAURANTE LA DOMINICA

Map p220 Italian $$

☎ 860-2918; O'Reilly No 108; ✆ noon-midnight
Despite its tendency to be a little overgenerous with the olive oil, La Dominica – with its wood-fired pizza oven and al dente pasta – could quite legitimately stake its claim as Habana's finest Italian restaurant. Located in an elegantly restored establishment on Calle O'Reilly, the restaurant offers everything from spaghetti and pizza (CUC$5 to CUC$7) to shrimp and lobster (CUC$10 to CUC$18). Professional bands serenade diners with music that occasionally departs from the obligatory Buena Vista Social Club staples.

RESTAURANTE LA PAELLA

Map p220 Spanish $$

☎ 867-1037; cnr Oficios & Obrapía; ✆ noon-11pm
Attached to the rustic Hostal Valencia, the theme of this classic Habaguanex restaurant is that great Valencian gift to the culinary world – paella. Though popular elsewhere in Habana, the Spanish rice concoctions here are generally considered to be the city's best, and come in six different varieties ranging in price from CUC$8 to CUC$15. Decorated with plenty of Mediterranean greens and yellows, and continuing the old-world Spanish theme that characterizes the adjoining hotel, the restaurant has a very special ambience.

CAFÉ DEL ORIENTE Map p220 French $$$
☎ 860-6686; Oficios No 112; ✆ noon-11pm
Forget the 'café' title – this place is no wannabe Starbucks. In fact, you'll have to pinch

yourself to remember you're still in Cuba when you enter the doors of the confusingly named Café del Oriente restaurant on breezy Plaza de San Francisco de Asís. Firstly there's the fancy decor, which includes marble floors, an ornate plaster ceiling, mahogany paneling, a resident pianist (or string quartet) and powerful air-conditioning. Then there's the menu, a culinary extravaganza that includes smoked salmon, caviar (yes, caviar!), goose-liver pâté, lobster thermidor, steak au poivre (pepper steak), cheese and port. To top it all, service comes in a tux. There's just the small problem of the price, which starts at around CUC$14 and maxes out in the CUC$40 bracket...but what the hell!

EL TEMPLETE Map p220 Seafood $$$
cnr San Pedro & Narciso López; ✆ 11am-midnight
This upscale restaurant opened in late 2004 and is situated less than 100m from its namesake temple, where the city of Habana was founded in 1519. Overlooking the harbor, the eating space is split into two halves: an outdoor alfresco area accommodated under a large awning, and a pleasant indoor dining room with starched tablecloths and expensive-looking wine glasses. For once the food quality lives up to the pretensions of the fancy decor, with seafood specialties spearheaded by shrimps and lobster. Count on forking out CUC$15 minimum for a main course here.

LA BODEGUITA DEL MEDIO

Map p220 Cuban $$$

☎ 867-1374; Empedrado No 207;
✆ noon-midnight
Habana's most celebrated restaurant is a cramped and markedly overrated eating establishment that was a relatively low-key bar until a certain Ernest Hemingway starting drinking here in the late 1930s. Reinventing itself from a seedy, bohemian drinking dive, La Bodeguita del Medio is now ground zero for the snap-happy tour bus crowd, with sightseers coming here in their droves to down a few icy mojitos and scrawl their signatures on the wall alongside those of illustrious visitors such as Nat King Cole, Salvador Allende and Harry Belafonte. The menu specialty is comida criolla (rice, beans and pork) – the full monty, Cuban style.

CENTRO HABANA

Many of Centro Habana's best restaurants are clustered around Parque Central and Paseo de Martí (Prado), although visitors shouldn't overlook the growing clutch of Chinese places over on narrow Calle Cuchillo. Further west on Calle Concordia is the exquisite Paladar La Guarida, arguably one of the finest eating establishments in the city.

ASOCIACIÓN CANARIA DE CUBA

Map p222   Cuban $

☎ 862-5284; Av de las Misiones No 258 btwn Neptuno & Ánimas; ☼ noon-8:30pm Wed-Sun
One of a number of Spanish social clubs that serve food, the Asociación Canaria de Cuba, behind the Hotel Plaza, is housed in a venerable red-bricked building with a rather fancy lobby. By contrast the restaurant upstairs is a far more basic affair with strip lighting, plastic flowers and crummy tablecloths. But for regulars, the ambience is only secondary – the main reason to come here is for the food. The grilled lobster for CUC$6.50 is one of the city's biggest bargains; add in shrimp enchiladas for CUC$5, and beef stew or pork steak for CUC$2, and you're laughing all the way to the change booth.

EL GRAN DRAGON Map p222   Chinese $

☎ 861-5396; Cuchillo No 1 btwn Rayo & Zanja; ☼ 11am-midnight
First on the left as you enter Calle Cuchillo from Calle Zanja, this is as good an introduction as any to the energetic pulse of Habana's Barrio Chino (p81). Specialties include wonton soup, chop suey, chow mein and fried rice, and the prices come in at less than CUC$5 a dish; it's a good place for vegetarians. The restaurant is spread over three floors and has alfresco dining options.

FERIA LOS FORNOS Map p222   Cuban $

☎ 861-5924; Neptuno btwn Paseo de Martí & Consulado; ☼ 24hr
Shoehorned behind a clothes shop on Calle Neptuno, where tourist Habana meets the gritty reality of bustling Centro, Los Fornos is cheap, simple and usually open. Beyond that pickings are thin, unless you're keen to see what 45 years of rationing has done to Cuban cooking.

LOS GIJONÉS Map p222   Cuban $

Paseo de Martí No 309; ☼ noon-midnight
A good restaurant run by the Asturianas Society, Los Gijonés is situated upstairs in a dark mahogany dining room in the Centro Asturianos on Paseo de Martí and Virtudes. The *ropa vieja* with rice, potatoes and salad (CUC$5) is tasty here, as are the prawns. Service is a little slow, but there's a charming resident violinist who'll keep you entertained with some wonderfully melancholy renditions of Mozart and Vivaldi.

LOS NARDOS Map p222   Cuban $

☎ 863-2985; Paseo de Martí No 563; ☼ noon-midnight
Directly opposite the Capitolio but easy to miss, Los Nardos has been in operation since 2002 and is one of a handful of semi-private Habana restaurants operated by the Spanish Asturianas society; there is another restaurant called Los Asturianitos (☼ noon-midnight) in the same building. Touted in some quarters as one of the best eateries in the city, this unprepossessing but well-designed property is decked out in cedar, mahogany and leather, and serves up such astoundingly delicious dishes as lobster in a Catalan sauce, garlic prawns with sautéed vegetables and authentic Spanish paella. Portions are huge and the prices, which start at CUC$3 to CUC$4 for chicken and pork dishes, are unbelievably cheap.

LOS PORTALES Map p222   International $

☎ 860-8583; Hotel Plaza, Agramonte No 267; ☼ noon-10pm
The primary – nay only – reason to come to this ground-floor restaurant in the four-star Hotel Plaza is for the pizza, which – rather surprisingly – is among the best and cheapest in Habana. Don't be put off by the restaurant's fancy decor (the tables and chairs look as if they've been decked out for a wedding) – the prices here are very reasonable. A decent pizza with one or two

extra toppings shouldn't cost you more than CUC$4. The *flan* (baked custard with caramel glaze) makes for a nice dessert.

PALADAR AMISTAD DE LANZAROTE

Map p222   Cuban $

☎ 863-6172; Amistad No 211 btwn Neptuno & San Miguel; ✆ noon-midnight

Paladar Amistad de Lanzarote charges CUC$6 for most meals. The portions are large, the staff speak English, and you can enjoy your pork and rice amid the cheerful clutter of crowded Centro Habana.

PASTERLERÍA FRANCESA

Map p222   Café $

Paseo de Martí No 411; ✆ 9am-11pm

With a great location among the five-star hotels, this place sells delicious pastries, sturdy sandwiches and OK coffee. The swarming *jineteras* (women who attach themselves to male foreigners for monetary or material gain) spoil the French flavor a little and the service is slow, but for convenience it can't be beaten.

RANCHO COQUITO Map p222   Cuban $

Malecón No 107 btwn Genios & Crespo; ✆ 6pm-midnight

At last, a decent restaurant on the Malecón (Av de Maceo). Run by the Spanish Asturianas society, the Rancho is an unpretentious and inconspicuous food joint (look for the waiter posted outside) that overlooks Habana's dreamy 8km sea drive and is frequented mainly by Cubans. Hidden upstairs with a balcony containing outdoor seating that looks out over the wild and tempestuous Straits of Florida, the restaurant serves food that is both tasty and unbelievably cheap. Paella goes for CUC$7, *garbanzos fritos* (fried chickpeas) for CUC$5, *tortilla* for CUC$3 and a reasonably sized portion of lobster pan-fried in butter for a mere CUC$6.

RESTAURANTE OASIS Map p222   Cuban $

☎ 863-3829; Paseo de Martí No 256; ✆ 2pm-3am

The Oasis is housed in the Centro Cultural de Arabe, but don't be fooled by the Middle Eastern myth. The food here is bog-standard Cuban, and not particularly good at that – unless you have a penchant for dodgy hot dogs or soggy sandwiches – but it's the kind of place where's you'll see Cubans eating, and it makes no provision for 'Western'

palates. The shop downstairs is handy for late-night groceries, but the weekend disco is a *jinetera*-fest.

RESTAURANTE TIEN-TAN

Map p222   Chinese $

☎ 861-5478; Calle Cuchillo No 17, btwn Zanja & San Nicolás; ✆ 11am-11pm

One of the Barrio Chino's best authentic Chinese restaurants, Tien-Tan (Temple of Heaven) is a Cuban institution run by a Chinese-Cuban couple that offers diners an astounding 130 different dishes. With such a complex and varied menu you might have thought that a) you would be in for a long wait, and b) the food would, at best, be average, but thankfully neither is the case. Service is lightening fast and the food – which includes crispy vegetables and real Chinese sauces – is tasty. Try chop suey with vegetables or chicken with cashew nuts, and sit outside in action-packed Cuchillo, one of Habana's most colorful and fastest-growing food streets.

VIEJO AMIGO (LOU PANG YAU)

Map p222   Chinese $

☎ 861-8095; Dragones No 356 btwn Manrique & San Nicolás; ✆ noon-midnight

Situated in a large upstairs room in Calle Dragones, Viejo Amigo wins plenty of kudos for decor, with waitresses in Chinese-style dresses and a large painting of Sun Yat Sen hung reverently on the wall. The downside is the menu, which is a little limited, particularly when compared to some of the Cuchillo joints nearby. As if to make amends, portions sizes are absolutely huge. Fortunately the staff will box up any leftovers for you to take away afterwards.

CENTRO ANDALUZ Map p222   Spanish $$

☎ 863-6745; Paseo de Martí No 104 btwn Genios & Refugio; ✆ 8-11pm Tue-Sun

Another Spanish social club with a restaurant, the Centro Andaluz resembles an old 19th-century Andalucian flamenco bar, with a chipped wooden stage, equally chipped *azulejos* (glazed tiles) and soulful music. The center serves reasonable meals, including a house paella for two, various fish dishes, and pork fillets with rice and beans, and you can see good flamenco dancing (p131) here most evenings. Opening times can be a little sporadic.

Eating   CENTRO HABANA

PALADAR BELLAMAR

Map p222   Cuban $$

☎ 861-0023; Virtudes No 169; ⏰ noon-10pm
A friendly family-run paladar, this tiny
eating joint is squeezed into a front room
that looks out onto the street. Inside the
walls have been scribbled on, Bodeguita
del Medio style, with the comments and
signatures of customers past. However,
unlike its more famous culinary cohort, the
Bellamar is usually deserted. This is a shame
considering the food (which includes clas-
sic chicken, pork and fish dishes) is rather
tasty and starts at a very reasonable CUC$6
a plate.

PALADAR DOÑA BLANQUITA

Map p222   Cuban $$

Paseo de Martí No 158 btwn Colón & Refugio;
⏰ noon-midnight
Paladar Doña Blanquita overlooks Paseo de
Martí and is one of Centro Habana's best-
placed paladares. On entry, you'll be handed
a proper typewritten menu listing main
plates in the CUC$7 to CUC$9 range. You can
dine in the elegant salon or on the pleasant
terrace overlooking the promenade.

PALADAR TORRESSÓN

Map p222   Cuban $$

Malecón No 27; ⏰ noon-midnight
Situated at the eastern end of the Malecón
with a great view of the Castillo de los
Tres Santos Reyes Magnos del Morro, the
Paladar Torressón takes up the 2nd floor of
a suitably dilapidated seafront tenement.
Complete meals of meat or fish cost
between CUC$10 and CUC$15, but the
views are free and – not surprisingly –
stupendous.

PRADO Y NEPTUNO Map p222   Italian $$

☎ 860-9636; cnr Paseo de Martí & Neptuno;
⏰ noon-5pm & 6:30-11:30pm
The pizza at this Italian-themed restaurant
is not nearly Habana's best although, judging by the crowds, you could be forgiven
for thinking that the cooks were native
Neapolitans. None of this detracts from
the restaurant's popularity, however, or its
comfortable decor characterized by dark
tinted windows, colorful tiles and green
ceiling lamps that hang low over the individual tables. Just off Parque Central, the
P & N is a good place to escape the hotel
buffet for a night. There's a good selection
of Italian wines in the bar.

PALADAR LA GUARIDA

Map p222   International $$$

☎ 866-9047; Concordia No 418 btwn Gervasio
& Escobar; ⏰ noon-3pm & 7pm-midnight
Located on the top floor of a spectacularly
dilapidated Habana tenement, La Guarida's
lofty reputation rests on its movie-location
setting (*Fresa y Chocolate* was filmed in this
building) and a clutch of swashbuckling
newspaper reviews (including the *New
York Times* and the *Guardian*). The food, as
might be expected, is up there with Haba-
na's best, shoehorning its captivating blend
of Cuban *nueva cocina* (p18) into dishes
such as sea bass in a coconut reduction,
and chicken with honey and lemon sauce.
Reservations required.

VEDADO

Better than Centro Habana, but not in the
same bracket as Playa and Miramar, Vedado
is hit-and-miss in the paladar stakes. Shop
around until you find something appetizing.
The state-run sector includes two vegetarian
restaurants, an Italian trattoria and even a
place that specializes in rabbit dishes.

BIKI VEGETARIAN RESTAURANT

Map pp224-5   Vegetarian $

☎ 879-6406; cnr Calzada de Infanta & San Lázaro,
⏰ noon-10pm Tue-Sun
This vegetarian buffet that charges in Cuban
pesos is one of Habana's more unusual
restaurant offerings. Biki has dozens of good
selections laid out cafeteria style in easy-
to-reach trays; join the line and pick from
several fresh juices and salads, veggie paella,
fried rice or stuffed peppers, root vegetables
and desserts such as rice pudding.

BIM BOM Map pp224-5   Ice-Cream Parlor $

☎ 879-2892; cnr Calzada de Infanta & Calle 23;
⏰ 10am-midnight
The famous Coppelia isn't Cuba's only ice-
cream institution. Somewhere down the list
in the 'not-half-bad' category is Bim Bom,
an islandwide *helado* (ice cream) chain that
serves a deliciously creamy version of the
stuff in flavors such as coffee, condensed
milk, and rum and raisin. Try it and see.

CAFÉ TV Map pp224-5 International $

☎ 33-44-99; cnr Calles N & 19; ☯ 10am-9pm

In the bowels of the Focsa building lies one of Habana's best-kept secrets. Café TV is an up-and-coming performance space lauded by those in the know for its hilarious comedy nights, but it's also a cheap and tasty eating option if you're willing to brave the frigid air-conditioning and rather forbidding underground entry tunnel. Head here for fresh burgers (CUC$2), healthy salad (CUC$1.50), pasta (CUC$4) and Gordon Bleu (chicken stuffed with ham and cheese; CUC$5). The tables are laid out simply in a café style, and the walls are adorned with black-and-white Cuban TV and movie memorabilia.

CAFETERÍA SOFÍA Map pp224-5 Cuban $

cnr Calles 23 & 0; ☯ 24hr

The 24-hour Cafetería Sofía is on busy Calle 23 (La Rampa), resulting in an above-average amount of noisy passing trade. It's a cheap, if slightly seedy, central option with regular live music. Look out for the special breakfast offers. The people-watching potential here is excellent.

COPPELIA Map pp224-5 Ice-Cream Parlor $

☎ 832-6184; cnr Calles 23 & L; ☯ 11am-11pm

To come to Habana and not visit the Coppelia is like going to New York and missing the Empire State Building. Why? Well, firstly, it's a city institution and a fascinating glimpse into the intricacies of everyday Cuban life and, secondly, the ice cream is mouthwateringly delicious. See also p120.

EL LUGAR Map pp224-5 Cuban $

☎ 204-5162; cnr Calles 49C & 28A; ☯ noon-midnight

If you're in leafy Parque Almendares, check out this restaurant, which offers fantastic value. For under CUC$5 you get a juicy pork filet, a whole heap of *congrí* (rice flecked with black beans), salad, *tostones* (fried plantain patties), ice cream and coffee. There's a talented trio playing nights. The attached **pizza place** is good too.

G-CAFÉ Map pp224-5 Café $

cnr Calles 23 & G; ☯ 10am-11pm

This café is the ultimate student hangout, with arty wall drawings and a modernist mural, a patio with lots of greenery, and more than 400 books and magazines to

VEDADO TOP FIVE

- Restaurante La Torre (p122)
- La Rampa Cafetería (p120)
- Coppelia (left)
- Paladar Le Chansonnier (p122)
- Café TV (left)

read, borrow and buy. As well as deftly concocted mojitos and chunky sandwiches, there is *trova* (traditional poetic singing), jazz and poetry.

PALMARES CENTRO

Map pp224-5 Cuban $

cnr Calles 23 & P; ☯ 24hr

The Palmares group has many incarnations in Cuba – from the internationally lauded **El Aljibe** (p123) in Miramar to greasy little beach barbecues in Santiago and Baracoa. This café on busy Calle 23 falls into the latter category, and is OK if you're desperate for a 2am *perro caliente* (hot dog). Otherwise you're better off satisfying your hunger pangs elsewhere.

PAN.COM Map pp224-5 International $

☎ 53-50-40; cnr Calles 17 & 10; ☯ 10am-2am

A new Habana fast-food joint with two branches, Pan.com is a great place to find comfort food if you're missing chunky burgers, fresh club sandwiches and authentic French fries. Even the cheese-and-ham sandwiches here are good. The original, better branch is in **Miramar** (p122).

RESTAURANTE VEGETARIANO CARMELO Map pp224-5 Vegetarian $

☎ 832-4495; Calzada btwn Calles D & E; ☯ noon-midnight Tue-Sun

This place has the same menu as **Biki** (opposite), but is in a much nicer locale opposite the Teatro Amadeo Roldán, and has patio dining and a full bar. Be careful with overcharging; prices should be in Cuban pesos rather than convertibles.

CAFÉ CONCERTO EL GATO TUERTO

Map pp224-5 Cuban $$

☎ 66-22-24; Calle 0 No 14 btwn Calles 17 & 19; ☯ noon-midnight

Café Concerto El Gato Tuerto (the One-Eyed Cat) is a chic café and bar that hosts

MAKING CENTS OF COPPELIA

Until you've gone slack jawed watching a young woman with a model's body wolf down nine scoops of ice cream followed by a cake à la mode with childish delight, you haven't eaten at Coppelia (p119). It is truly a cultural phenomenon without equal, and waiting a near eternity to enter the weirdly futuristic but retro halls of this Habana ice-cream institution is an essential part of getting to know Cuba and the Cubans. Loitering around the perimeter, strategically positioned security guards try to usher foreigners toward the Coppelia's sterile convertibles café but, with a little persistence and a few persuasive words in Spanish, there's no reason why you can't join one of the long and seemingly disorganized queues on the periphery of the peso part. Ah…the queues. Hard though it may be to believe, there *is* a system, which many foreigners don't observe or get. Here's how it works.

There are several entrances to Coppelia, each with their own menu, line and dining area. Diehards cruise the different entrances to see what's on each menu. What the menu says and what's actually on offer once you're inside is another story, but more often than not you'll encounter *fresa y chocolate* (strawberry and chocolate), coconut, banana and orange-pineapple, so it's not just vanilla (though Coppelia's vanilla is luscious). Shout out *¿Quien es último?* (Who is last?) as you approach the line and remember to log the face of whoever is in front of you. Sections are seated all at once, so some 20 people are let in en masse and are shown to their section. A server comes around, tells you what's available, takes your order and brings back the goods. They come around afterward to collect your money. Rainy days are traditionally slow here, so you might minimize wait times by showing up then.

The language of ice-cream love is complex here. Suffice to say, a movie at Cine Yara across the street, followed by a *jimagua* (two scoops of ice cream) at Coppelia is the classic Habana date.

live music (p137) on Fridays and Saturdays. The restaurant upstairs, meanwhile, serves good soup, reasonably priced *ropa vieja,* and excellent lobster fried in butter with a little sweet-and-sour sauce (CUC$20).

EL CONEJITO Map pp224-5   Cuban $$
☎ 832-4671; Calle M No 206; ☽ noon-midnight
This surreal restaurant-bar housed in a red-bricked Tudor-style mansion in central Vedado serves rabbit (CUC$8), rabbit and yet more rabbit, along with a few more standard Cuban staples such as chicken, beef, fish and lobster. Ambience is German-meets-Cuban-meets-Tudor, with an amiable resident pianist serenading all comers. If all this doesn't sound too freaky, give it a whirl.

LA CASONA DE 17 Map pp224-5   Cuban $$
☎ 33-45-29; Calle 17 No 60; ☽ noon-2am
Housed in a wonderful eclectic mansion opposite the modernist Edificio Focsa, this small restaurant offers reasonable, if overpriced, food in an attractive early-20th-century setting. The menu specializes in chicken and rice dishes.

LA RAMPA CAFETERÍA
Map pp224-5   International $$
cnr Calles 23 & L; ☽ 24hr
One of Vedado's most welcome culinary oases is this authentic American-style diner

tacked onto the side of the Hotel Habana Libre. Superfast service and surgical cleanliness are second nature here and the no-nonsense kitchen serves up excellent milk shakes (CUC$4), filling – and healthy – salads (CUC$6), a mean club sandwich (CUC$6) and to-die-for chocolate brownies in hot fudge sauce (CUC$3). If you just can't handle another mouthful of rice, beans and deep-fried chicken, this is your get-out-of-jail card.

MESÓN LA CHORRERA
Map pp224-5   Cuban, Spanish $$
☎ 33-45-21; Malecón btwn Calles 18 & 20; ☽ noon-2am
The Mesón La Chorrera is in the Torreón de Santa Dorotea de la Chorrera (p89), an old fortified tower that marks the western extremity of the Malecón. The restaurant serves up a Spanish-influenced menu in a unique oceanside setting, and sometimes lays on music.

PALADAR ARIES Map pp224-5   Cuban $$
☎ 831-9668; Ave Universidad No 456 btwn Calles J & K; ☽ noon-midnight
Serving traditional Cuban fare mixed with what are generously referred to as 'international dishes,' this nicely decked-out place in a house dating from 1925 is conveniently located behind the university. There are occasionally wandering troubadours.

PALADAR DECAMERON

Map pp224-5   Italian $$

☎ 832-2444; Línea No 753 btwn Paseo & Calle 2;
🕒 noon-midnight

Ugly from the outside but far prettier within, the Decameron is an intimate Italian restaurant where you can order from the varied menu with abandon. Veggie pizza, lasagna bolognese, a sinful *calabaza* (pumpkinlike squash) soup – it's all good. There's a decent wine selection and vegetarians will find heavenly options. Figure on CUC$10 to CUC$12 per person.

PALADAR EL HELECHO

Map pp224-5   Cuban $$

☎ 831-3552; Calle 6 No 203 btwn Línea & Calle 11;
🕒 noon-10:30pm Wed-Thu

Tucked in a tree-lined side street in western Vedado, this romantic little place is a longtime favorite. The nice atmosphere is complemented by decent prices (around the CUC$5 mark) and good portions. The food is remarkably tasty; try the chicken soup.

PALADAR GRINGO VIEJO

Map pp224-5   Cuban $$

☎ 831-1946; Calle 21 No 454 btwn Calles E & F;
🕒 noon-11pm

Paladar Gringo Viejo offers a good atmosphere and large portions of invariably brilliant food. It has recently reopened after a lengthy refurbishment and appears to have lost none of its culinary creativity.

PALADAR LOS AMIGOS

Map pp224-5   Cuban $$

Calle M No 253; 🕒 noon-midnight

Situated in the back of a prerevolutionary house near the Hotel Victoria, Paladar Los Amigos serves good Cuban meals for CUC$10, including side plates. It is regularly recommended by locals.

PALADAR NEREI Map pp224-5   Cuban $$

cnr Calles 19 & L; 🕒 noon-midnight Mon-Fri, 6pm-midnight Sat & Sun

Ah, the Nerei, the only paladar in central Habana where you can get whole roast pig on a spit (or so the owners will tell you). The pluses here are numerous: huge portions (almost too huge), an extensive menu, and a pleasant alfresco seating area arranged around a sleepy veranda that overlooks

quiet(ish) Calle 19. The downside is the price piracy; insist on seeing a written menu first.

RESTAURANTE 1830

Map pp224-5   Cuban $$

☎ 55-30-90; Calzada No 1252 cnr Calle 20;
🕒 noon-10pm

One of Habana's most elegant restaurants is this glittering old stalwart, refurbished in 2001. Chandeliers, antique furniture and palacelike table settings are two a penny here, and the food includes duck, pork and chicken in lemon-and-honey sauce (which is rapidly becoming Cuba's gourmet specialty). After the kitchen closes at 10pm, there's live music and salsa dancing in the garden behind the restaurant (don't come on a windy night).

RESTAURANTE WAKAMBA

Map pp224-5   Cuban $$

☎ 878-4526; Calle O btwn Calles 23 & Humboldt;
🕒 24hr

One of several restaurants in Calle O, the Wakamba has been serving customers since 1956. It is named after an African tribe and subregion in Kenya and, prior to the revolution, it was a famous nightclub. Today it serves good cheap food such as chicken stuffed with ham, chorizo, olives and cheese for approximately CUC$7. An adjacent cafeteria (🕒 24hr) has hot dogs and other snacks.

TRATTORÍA MARAKAS

Map pp224-5   Italian $$

☎ 33-37-40; Calle O No 260 btwn Calles 23 & 25;
🕒 10am-11pm

Don't be put off by the cheap Formica tables and the dodgy map of Italy on the wall; real olive oil, parmesan and mozzarella cheese, plus a wood oven, mean that the pizza in this Italian trattoria is among the city's best. Also on offer are Greek salads, tortellini with red sauce, and spinach-stuffed cannelloni; the menu is long and few items are over CUC$8.

PALADAR EL HURÓN AZUL

Map pp224-5   Cuban $$$

☎ 879-1691; Humboldt No 153; 🕒 noon-midnight

This place is often touted as one of Habana's best private restaurants and, although the food might be tasty, the windowless interior combined with the preponderance of after-dinner smokers can leave your meal tasting more like nicotine than chicken in orange sauce. Nonetheless the Hurón Azul (Blue Ferret) boasts plenty of original food and is locally famous for its adventurous smoked pork served with a pineapple salsa. That said, it's not cheap, averaging CUC$15 a pop, plus a 10% service charge is added to every bill. You may want to consider booking ahead as there isn't much room for waiting.

PALADAR LE CHANSONNIER

Map pp224–5   French $$$

☎ 832-1576; Calle J No 257 btwn Calles 13 & 15; ☽ 12:30pm-12:30am

A great place to dine if a) you can find it (there's no sign), and b) it's open (the staff seem to be in the habit of taking regular sabbaticals). Hidden in an elegant dining room in a faded mansion-turned-paladar, it's not just the name of this place that's French; French wine, French furniture and French flavors also predominate. House specialties include rabbit in red-wine sauce, chicken smothered in mushrooms, Dijon pork chops, and gigantic salads for herbivores. It's also one of Habana's few truly gay-friendly establishments. Phone ahead to check it's open.

PALADAR MARPOLY

Map pp224–5   Cuban $$$

☎ 832-2471; Calle K No 154 btwn Línea & Calle 11; ☽ noon-1am

An unsignposted – and hence hard-to-find – paladar just off Linea, the Marpoly offers good food, including a seafood platter, and a great selection of wines in luxurious surroundings.

RESTAURANTE LA TORRE

Map pp224–5   French $$$

☎ 832-2451; Edificio Focsa, Calle 17 No 55; ☽ noon-midnight

One of Habana's tallest and most talked about restaurants is perched high above downtown Vedado atop the 36-story Edificio Focsa (p84). A colossus of modernist architecture and French-Cuban haute cuisine, this lofty fine-dining extravaganza combines sweeping city views with a progressive French-inspired menu that serves everything from artichokes to foie

gras to almond tart. The prices at CUC$30 a pop are as distinctly un-Cuban as the ingredients, but with this level of service, it's probably worth it.

PLAYA & MARIANAO

Playa is paladar heaven and boasts the best selection of quality private restaurants in Cuba. Not to be outdone, the Cuban government has also set up some excellent state-run eating establishments here.

CAFETERÍA 3 Y 62

Map pp228–9   Cuban $

☎ 204-0369; cnr Av 3 & Calle 62; ☽ 8am-11pm

If you're staying in one of the pricey hotels and want a cheaper place to eat, then try this place on the eastern side of the Russian embassy. It's a varied mix of five or six cheap permanent booths selling beer, biscuits, fried chicken and sandwiches, and the prices are rarely more than a couple of convertibles.

PAIN DE PARIS

Map pp228–9   Bakery, Café $

Marina Hemingway, cnr Av 5 & Calle 248; ☽ 8am-6pm

Next door to Pizza Nova, just past the entrance to Marina Hemingway, is a branch of Cuba's best bakery chain. It sells chocolate croissants, pastries, soft drinks, cakes and coffee. There's another good branch in Vedado (Calle 25 No 164 btwn Calzada de Infanta & Calle O; ☽ 8am-midnight).

PAN.COM

Map pp228–9   International $

☎ 204-4232; Av 7 cnr Calle 26, Miramar; ☽ 24hr

One of two Pan.com establishments presently operating in Habana, the clean and friendly Miramar branch is easily the best. Set on tree-lined Av 7 opposite El Aljibe, the menu at this Cuban version of the Subway sandwich chain is extensive and includes hearty sandwiches, fantastic burgers and ice-cream milk shakes to die for. Seating is in a shaded outdoor patio and service is surprisingly warm and efficient – it's the ultimate Habana comfort-food haven. The other branch is in Vedado (p119).

PIZZA NOVA

Map pp228–9   Pizza $

☎ 204-1150; Marina Hemingway, cnr Av 5 & Calle 248; ☽ noon-midnight

Best of a scanty choice of restaurants in Marina Hemingway and billing itself as the

PLAYA & MARIANAO TOP FIVE

- Paladar La Cocina de Lilliam (p125)
- Paladar La Fontana (p126)
- El Aljibe (below)
- Paladar La Esperanza (p125)
- Paladar Calle 10 (p124)

best pizza joint in Habana, Pizza Nova is a great place to end up after an all-day fishing or diving outing. Otherwise the pepperoni (which is allegedly imported from Canada) isn't worth the 20km journey to get here

DON CANGREJO Map pp228-9   Seafood $$
☎ 204-4169; Av 1 No 1606 btwn Calles 16 & 18; ☺ noon-midnight

Perched strategically on the rocky shores of Miramar, this unique seafood restaurant is run by the Ministry of Fisheries and scores high points for atmosphere and service. Fresh fish dishes include red snapper, grouper and prawns (CUC$8 to CUC$12), while lobster plucked from the pit on the terrace comes in at CUC$20 to CUC$25. There's a pool table and swimming pool, an inexpensive pizza-and-grill menu, and one of Habana's classic signs out front.

DOS GARDENIAS
Map pp228-9   Chinese, Pizza $$
El Rincón del Bolero; ☎ 204-2353; cnr Av 7 & Calle 28; ☺ noon-midnight

Next door to El Aljibe is Dos Gardenias, an upscale complex with several restaurants, bars and shops; you'll have a choice of pizza and Chinese food. Dos Gardenias also has nightly shows beginning at 9pm.

EL ALJIBE Map pp228-9   Cuban $$
☎ 204-1583/4; Av 7 btwn Calles 24 & 26; ☺ noon-midnight

On paper a humble Palmares restaurant, in reality a rip-roaring culinary extravaganza, El Aljibe has been delighting both Cuban and foreign taste buds for years. The hype surrounds the gastronomic mysteries of just one dish, the *pollo asado* (roast chicken), which is served up with as-much-as-you-can-eat helpings of white rice, black beans, fried plantain, French fries and salad. The accompanying bitter-orange sauce is said to be a state secret.

EL CHELO Map pp228-9   Cuban $$
☎ 204-3301; Av 5 btwn Calles 188 & 192, Flores; ☺ noon-midnight

El Chelo is situated in the swanky **Club Habana** (p91), 18km west of the city center. Perched in front of the sparkling Straits of Florida and a well-raked scimitar of private beach, El Chelo serves everything from a CUC$5 *ropa vieja* to a CUC$25 lobster. The decor is suitably luxurious.

EL PALENQUE Map pp228-9   Cuban, Italian $$
☎ 208-8167; cnr Calles 17 & 190; ☺ 10am-10pm

Located next to the Pabexpo exhibition center, this huge place sprawls beneath a series of open-sided *bohíos* (thatched huts) and offers an extensive menu at prices cheap enough to attract both Cubans and foreigners. The cuisine is Cuban-Italian, with pizzas starting at CUC$3, steak and fries coming in at CUC$9, and *langosta mariposa* maxing out at CUC$22. As well as sit-down tables there are smaller booths, and stores that sell everything from cigars to imported apples.

LA CECILIA Map pp228-9   Cuban $$
☎ 204-1562; Av 5 No 11010 btwn Calles 110 & 112; ☺ noon-midnight

Opposite the Servi-Cupet gas station in Playa, La Cecilia is an upscale garden restaurant run by government company Palmares. The menu features mainly Cuban cuisine, especially lobster and steak; prices vary, but you can pick up quality meat bruschettas and tender *ropa vieja* here for as little as CUC$6, making it much cheaper than most Miramar eating joints. On occasion La Cecilia hosts excellent live music in its attractive back garden; however, rather than hiring the usual staid guitar trios, the management promotes full-on dance bands that knock out classic Benny Moré hits, with hip-gyrating rhythms and stabbing trumpets, well into the night. On quieter evenings the La Cecilia is equally alluring, with acres of tables laid out under the romantic thatched-roof garden and large parrots squawking in their cages.

LA PAILA Map pp228-9   Cuban $$
☎ 267-1771; Ave 51A No 8827 btwn Calles 88B & 88C; ☺ noon-midnight

If this place wasn't so off the beaten track, it would be in Habana's top five. With just a few tables ensconced in a garden replete

PALADARES

Paladares are small family-run restaurants that are permitted to operate as private entities on the payment of a monthly tax to the government. First established in 1995 during the economic chaos of the *período especial* (special period), paladares owe much of their success to the sharp increase in tourist traffic on the island, and the bold experimentation of the local chefs who, despite a paucity of decent ingredients, have heroically managed to keep the traditions of Cuban cooking alive.

Legally paladares are only supposed to offer 12 seats and are prohibited from selling lobster, beef or shrimps (which are government monopolies). The reality, however, is often rather different. Through secrecy, guile, or a surreptitious bending of the rules, most Habana paladares pack well over a dozen people into carefully concealed dining rooms or romantically lit back gardens and, with meal prices hovering in the CUC$15 to CUC$20 bracket, business has never been better.

Although the atmosphere in various paladares can differ significantly, the food in these unique private restaurants is almost always of a superior quality to the uninspiring rations offered elsewhere. Indeed, following big reviews in the *New York Times,* the *Guardian* and *Cigar Aficionado*, leading paladares such as La Guarida (p118), La Cocina de Lilliam (opposite) and La Fontana (p126) have even started to attract international attention.

with soft-lit lanterns, this is the most romantic paladar no one knows about. And the food is infallible. It does a great *bistec Uruguayo* (fried, breaded pork stuffed with ham and cheese), and its pizzas are famous; both dishes are less than CUC$5.

LE SELECT Map pp228-9   Cuban $$
☎ 207-7410; Av 5 cnr Calle 30; ☽ restaurant 10am-9pm, bar 10am-midnight
This minicomplex – complete with swimming pool, boutiques, bars and restaurant – is spread across the grounds of a 1950s Miramar mansion that was used after the revolution by a certain Ernesto 'Che' Guevara. Reopened a few years back to serve the neighborhood's affluent diplomatic community (what would Che have said?), the fancily named Le Select hasn't yet lived up to the hype. While the architecture might be quasi-Italian Renaissance, you'll get far better food elsewhere.

PALADAR CALLE 10
Map pp228-9   Cuban $$
☎ 205-3970; Calle 10 No 314, btwn Avs 3 & 5; ☽ noon-midnight
Paladar Calle 10 is situated in – um – Calle 10 and, while the name might be a little unimaginative, the food certainly isn't. In fact, the meals served up in this rather fetching mansion-cum-gourmet-restaurant could well be some of the best in Cuba. Set up barbecue style in the owner's back garden, the paladar has alfresco seating arranged under an attractive thatched canopy. The printed menu is both varied and

adventurous, and delicious dishes include *ropa vieja* (CUC$7), chicken in balsamic vinegar (CUC$8), and chicken in lemon-and-honey glaze (CUC$7.50). Portions are huge and arrive with assorted roasted vegetables and memorable pureed potato. There are even profiteroles for dessert.

PALADAR EL BUGANVIL
Map pp228-9   Cuban $$
☎ 271-4791; Calle 190 No 1501 btwn Calles 15 & 17; ☽ noon-midnight
For Habana's old hands, El Buganvil is what you'll have come to expect from a choice Playa paladar, but for comparative newbies this will still be a rare treat. Take the house special *loma ahumado* (smoked pork) with piles of rice and yucca outside amid the blooming bougainvillea, and all those memories of bad tinned ham and insipid melted cheese will quickly fade away.

PALADAR MI JARDÍN
Map pp228-9   Mexican $$
☎ 203-4627; Calle 66 No 517; ☽ noon-midnight
It's a rare Cuban menu that offers chicken mole, tacos and quesadillas, which makes this Mexican place a keeper. Dining beneath the vine-covered trellis in the garden is recommended, as is the fish Veracruz.

EL RANCHO PALCO
Map pp228-9   Cuban $$$
☎ 208-9346; cnr Av 19 & Calle 140; ☽ noon-11pm
Situated in a forest near the Palacio de las Convenciones, El Rancho Palco has one of

the finest thatched roofs you'll likely ever see. This place has terrific ambience all the time, but it's particularly good at night, when live salsa music fills the air. Ceiling fans help keep the atmosphere cool. Beef is the specialty here, with fillets ranging in price from CUC$15 to CUC$35. Fish dishes, chicken and shrimp are also good.

EL TOCORORO

Map pp228-9   International, Japanese $$$
☎ 202-4530; Calle 18 No 302; ☽ noon-midnight
Once considered (along with El Aljibe) to be one of Habana's finest government-run restaurants, El Tocororo has lost ground to its competitors in recent years and is often criticized for being overpriced. Nonetheless the candlelit tables and inviting garden are still worth a visit, while the unprinted menu, with such luxuries as lobster's tail and (occasionally) ostrich, still has the ability to surprise. Bank on paying for everything right down to the bread basket, and be aware of a 10% service charge. As an added bonus, El Tocororo now has a small attached sushi bar and restaurant called Sakura (meals over CUC$15; ☽ noon-midnight). It's the only place in Cuba where you can find real Japanese food.

LA CASA DE QUINTA Y 16

Map pp228-9   International $$$
☎ 206-9509; Av 5 cnr Calle 16; ☽ noon-10:30pm
La Casa de Quinta y 16 is an upscale ranch-style restaurant tacked onto a Casa del Habano (p155) cigar shop. Housed in a funky modernist building with a pleasant wood interior, the restaurant presents its food as daily specials, including prawns (CUC$9), grilled fish (CUC$17), paella (CUC$18) and fettuccini alfredo (CUC$12). All mains are served with a glass of wine. Owners of local casas particulares (private houses that let out rooms to foreigners) always rave about this place.

LA FERMINIA
Map pp228-9   Cuban $$$
☎ 33-67-86; Av 5 No 18207; ☽ noon-11pm
Habana gets swanky at this memorable restaurant set in an elegant converted colonial mansion along one of Av 5's leafier stretches. Dine inside, in one of a handful of beautifully furnished rooms, or outside on a glorious garden patio – it doesn't really matter. The point is the food. A wonderful

mixed grill pulled straight from the fire, or a thick filet mignon will set you back more than CUC$20, but it will be money well spent. It also offers lobster tails panfried in breadcrumbs. Not surprisingly La Ferminia is considered to be one of Habana's finest restaurants and the establishment operates a strict dress code: no shorts or (for guys) sleeveless T-shirts. Fidel Castro has – allegedly – dined here.

LA MAISON Map pp228-9   Cuban $$$
☎ 204-1543; cnr Calle 16 & Av 7; ☽ noon-midnight
If you're out in Miramar, it would be a shame to pass over the opportunity to dine in La Maison (p138, p155), Habana's premier fashion house. A full meal in the restaurant followed by a fashion show and music performance will set you back CUC$30. The 'chic' menu includes chicken, pork and turkey dishes.

PALADAR LA COCINA DE LILLIAM

Map pp228-9   International $$$
☎ 209-6514; Calle 48 No 1311 btwn Calles 13 & 15; ☽ noon-midnight
Slick service, secluded ambience and freshly cooked food to die for, La Cocina de Lilliam has all the ingredients of a prize-winning restaurant par excellence. It's no wonder that Jimmy Carter made a pit stop here during his landmark 2002 visit (for the record he had ropa vieja). Set in an illustrious villa and surrounded by a garden of trickling fountains and lush tropical plants, the restaurant has such Cuban rarities as chicken mousse and tuna bruschetta, and an atmosphere more European than Caribbean. Not a cheese-and-ham sandwich in sight!

PALADAR LA ESPERANZA

Map pp228-9   Cuban $$$
☎ 202-4361; Calle 16 No 105 btwn Avs 1 & 3; ☽ 6:30-11pm Fri-Wed
Few would disagree that the food, ambience and gastronomic creativity showcased at this unassuming Miramar paladar puts it among Habana's (and undoubtedly Cuba's) best eating establishments. While unspectacular from the street, the house is a riot of quirky antiques, old portraits and refined 1940s furnishings inside. It's almost as if the decor has been left untouched since the day Castro's guerillas marched past in 1959

and nationalized the whole neighborhood. The food, which is produced in a standard-sized family kitchen, includes such exquisite dishes as *pollo luna de miel* (chicken flambéed in rum), fish marinated in white wine, lemon and garlic, and lamb brochette. It's expensive but memorable.

PALADAR LA FONTANA

Map pp228-9   International $$$

☎ 202-8337; Calle 3A No 305; ⌚ noon-midnight
Habana discovers the barbecue or, more to the point, the full-on charcoal grill. Huge portions of meat and fish are served up in this amiable villa-cum-paladar, so go easy on the starters, which include quails' eggs, fried chickpeas, and crab mixed with eggplant. La Fontana specializes in just about everything you'll never see elsewhere in Cuba, from lasagna to huge steaks. Big-shot reviews from *Cigar Aficionado* and the *Chicago Tribune* testify to the burgeoning legend.

PALADAR LOS CACTUS DE 33

Map pp228-9   Cuban $$$

☎ 203-5139; Av 33 No 3405 btwn Calles 34 & 36, Playa; ⌚ noon-midnight
Reviewed in international lifestyle magazines and used as a setting for TV specials, this place has impeccable service, elegant surroundings, well-prepared food and (in a Cuban context) outrageous prices. A full pork meal with all the trimmings is pushing CUC$20; the house special, chicken breast with mushrooms, olives and cheese, costs even more. Situated on a quiet street a block from Miramar's arterial Calle 31, the house is characterized by a lone cactus that stands guard in the front yard.

PALADAR VISTAMAR

Map pp228-9   Seafood $$$

☎ 203-8328; Av 1 btwn Calles 22 & 24; ⌚ noon-midnight
The Paladar Vistamar is in the 2nd-floor family-room-turned-restaurant of a private residence in Miramar that faces the sea. The oceanside ambience is embellished by a beautiful swimming pool that spills its water into the sea. If enjoying delicious seafood dishes overlooking the crashing ocean sounds enticing, this could be your bag. Most mains run from CUC$8 to CUC$15 with salad.

EASTERN HABANA

Eastern Habana's eating options are centered on the two large historic forts that border the harbor channel. Outside of this, the larger neighborhoods of Regla and Guanabacoa have very few palatable restaurants, although the fishing village of Cojímar boasts the ever popular La Terraza, a former Hemingway favorite.

BAR EL POLVORÍN Map p227   Café $

☎ 860-9990; Castillo de los Tres Santos Reyes Magnos del Morro, Parque Histórico Militar Morro-Cabaña; ⌚ 10am-4am
This bar is just beyond Restaurante Los Doce Apóstoles, and offers drinks and light snacks on a patio overlooking the bay. There's zero shade here, but it's perfect for those famous Habana sunsets. Watch out for the energetic dancing that goes on into the small hours at weekends.

CINCO ESQUINAS Map p230   Cafe $

cnr Calixto García & 24 de Febrero, Regla; ⌚ 9am-10pm
Looking for somewhere to eat in Regla is like looking for the Niagara Falls in the Sahara. Bring a packed lunch! If desperation sets in, there are drinks and a few edible tidbits available at this Palmares place situated on 'Five Corners' in between the Parque Guaicanamar and the Colina Lenin. There's a vastly unhealthy **chicken booth** nearby.

RESTAURANTE LAS ORISHAS

Map p231   International $

cnr Martí & Lamas, Guanabacoa; ⌚ 10am-midnight
This Santería-themed place in Guanabacoa has a very pleasant garden bar in a courtyard with colorful Afro-Cuban sculptures. The menu is reasonable and varied, with everything from a CUC$1 microwaved cheese pizza to a CUC$20-plus lobster. There's good **rumba music** (p139) here at weekends.

PALADAR DOÑA CARMELA

Map p227   Cuban $$

☎ 863-6048; Calle B No 10, Parque Histórico Militar Morro-Cabaña; ⌚ 7-11pm
A good private dining option when it's open, this paladar offers quality chicken, pork and seafood in a very pleasant alfresco setting. It makes a good dinner before or

after the *cañonazo* (shooting of the cannons) at Fortaleza de San Carlos de la Cabaña, but check ahead as opening times can be irregular.

RESTAURANTE LA DIVINA PASTORA

Map p227   Cuban $$

☎ 860-8341; Fortaleza de San Carlos de la Cabaña, Parque Histórico Militar Morro-Cabaña; ☽ noon-11pm

Just beyond the Dársena de los Franceses is a battery of huge 18th-century cannons. Located behind the guns, the upscale but approachable La Divina Pastora offers well-prepared seafood, including lobster and fish. You can also just sit and soak in the views with an icy Cristal and some crisp *tostones*.

RESTAURANTE LA TERRAZA

Map p231   Seafood $$

☎ 93-92-32; Calle 152 No 161, Cojímar; ☽ restaurant noon-11pm, bar 10.30am-11pm

Another shrine to the ghost of Ernest Hemingway, La Terraza specializes in seafood such as stuffed squid (CUC$7) and paella (CUC$7 to CUC$15), and does a roaring trade with the hordes of Papa fans who drop by daily. The terrace dining room overlooking the bay is pleasant. More atmospheric, however, is the old bar out front, where mojitos still only cost a couple of convertibles. Check out the classic wooden refrigerators and don't miss the black-and-white photos of Hemingway in the terrace dining room.

RESTAURANTE LOS DOCE APÓSTOLES

Map p227   Cuban $$

☎ 863-8285; Castillo de los Tres Santos Reyes Magnos del Morro, Parque Histórico Militar Morro-Cabaña; ☽ noon-11pm

Set in the shadow of El Morro, this restaurant is named for the battery of 12 cannons atop its ramparts. It serves *comida criolla*, and is a better-than-average government-run kitchen. Prices are fair.

OUTER HABANA

Outer Habana has scant fare for travelers unless they're happy surviving on peso pizza and cheese-and-ham sandwiches. There are, however, two restaurants of note in and around Parque Lenin.

LAS RUINAS Map p232   International $$$

☎ 57-82-86; Cortina de la Presa; ☽ 11am-midnight Tue-Sun

On the southeast side of Parque Lenin, Las Ruinas is one of Habana's most celebrated restaurants – at least in an architectural sense. It's a striking combination of an old ruined sugar mill juxtaposed with offbeat modern architecture that includes some eye-catching stained-glass windows designed by Cuban artist René Portocarrero. Antique furnishings enhance the elegant atmosphere inside, but the food – which is grossly overpriced – doesn't quite live up to the lavish setting. The menu includes lobster, plus a selection of Cuban and Italian dishes, and you'll be lucky to get much change out of CUC$30. Overrated.

RESTAURANTE EL BAMBÚ

Map p232   Vegetarian $$$

☎ 54-72-78; Jardín Botánico Nacional; ☽ noon-5pm Tue-Sun

This is the first and finest in vegetarian dining in Habana and has led the way in government efforts to educate *habaneros* (inhabitants of Habana) in the benefits of a meatless diet. The all-you-can-eat lunch buffet is served alfresco deep in the botanical gardens (p96), with the natural setting paralleling the wholesome tastiness of the food. For CUC$15 you can help yourself to unlimited amounts of soup, salad, root vegetables, tamales and eggplant caviar; herbs grown on the premises figure prominently in the dishes. Juices, desserts and coffee are on offer too. it makes an excellent trip when coupled with a visit to the gardens.

Ententainment ◼

Entertainment

In Habana singing and dancing are a way of life – as natural to the average *habanero* (inhabitant of Habana) as walking or breathing. Take a stroll around the atmospheric streets of Habana Vieja of an evening and you'll hear music pouring seductively out of every corner: the tap-tap-tap of a dancer's heel from behind a closed door in Calle Mercaderes, a piano melody drifting softly across dreamy Plaza Vieja, two guitarists slumped down in Calle Obispo belting out a romantic ode to Che. Follow the soundtrack and take your pick. Nearly every restaurant and bar in Habana's engaging old town has a resident band or roving salsa quintet, and listening privileges are almost always free.

But it's not all trumpet-stabbing *son* (Cuba's basic form of popular music) and starry-eyed troubadours. An obligatory night out in Habana is a rip-roaring cabaret show, closely followed by a stand-up comedy show or an evening at the opera. And the talent doesn't stop there. A central ethos of the Cuban revolution was that entertainment should be a right of the masses; by slashing entry prices and setting up organizations to promote music and theater, Castro and his cronies have been encouraging art and culture ever since.

PERFORMING ARTS

The Cubans pursue the arts like they pursue their sport: passionately, dexterously and with a heartfelt desire to achieve great results from limited resources. It's an ethos that has ensured that the country is consistently rubbing shoulders with the world's cultural giants. However downbeat your theater/bar/venue, you can pretty much assume that the performance will be high quality.

CLASSICAL MUSIC & OPERA

Boasting at least one internationally recognized homegrown composer in the shape of Amadeo Roldán, Habana's classical musical legacy is stronger than many give it credit for. The Teatro Amadeo Roldán is the place to go for the best-quality performances, and the Iglesia de San Francisco de Paula (p72) and the Basílica Menor de San Francisco de Asís also host regular chamber

---

WHAT'S HAPPENING?

Plays, concerts, book launches, ballets, poetry readings, rap *peñas* (performances or get-togethers) – there's always something happening in Habana. The problem is finding out when and where. Here are some tips to get plugged in to what's on.

- The TV program *Hurón Azul* is a select schedule of the week's biggest cultural events, and is broadcast every Thursday night at 10:25pm on Cubavisión (Channel 6).
- *Cartelera de la Habana* has broader listings (in Spanish) of things happening all over town, and is published biweekly by the Ministry of Culture. This is one of your best resources; it's sold at newspaper kiosks for 20 centavos. Look for it on alternate Thursdays.
- The English-Spanish *Cartelera* is aimed at the tourist population. It comes out every Thursday but it lists what the ministry thinks you want to see; still, it's good for non-Spanish speakers. Look for it in big hotels.
- The daily newspaper *Juventud Rebelde* has decent cultural listings.
- Concert flyers usually appear around Calle 23 (La Rampa) from Calle L up to Parque de los Rockeros (Rocker's Park) at Calle G (Av de los Presidentes).
- Radio stations are constantly promoting upcoming cultural events; tune in to Radio Taino (93.3 FM) or Radio Habana (94.9FM).
- Check out www.cubarte.cult.cu and www.afrocubaweb.com for concerts, dance and fine-art listings.
- There's nothing better than word of mouth. Because the state publishes *Cartelera* and produces *Hurón Azul,* you have no chance of learning of anything underground through these resources; also, by talking to people, you'll learn about spontaneous happenings.
- Every cinema posts its schedule for the upcoming week at every other city cinema, and theaters post a schedule at their box office.

music. Quality opera can be seen weekly at the Gran Teatro de la Habana in Centro Habana (right).

BASILICA MENOR DE SAN FRANCISCO DE ASÍS Map p220
Plaza de San Francisco de Asís, Habana Vieja; tickets CUC$3-8; ⏰ **from 6pm Thu-Sat**
Plaza de San Francisco de Asís' glorious church (p73), which dates from 1737, has been reincarnated as a 21st-century museum and concert hall. The old nave hosts choral and chamber music two to three times a week (check the schedule at the door), and the acoustics inside are excellent. It's best to bag your ticket at least a day in advance.

TEATRO AMADEO ROLDÁN Map pp224-5
☎ **832-1168; cnr Calzada & Calle D, Vedado; tickets CUC$10**
Constructed in 1922 and burnt down by an arsonist in 1977, this wonderfully decorative neoclassical theater was rebuilt in 1999 in the exact style of the original. Named after Amadeo Roldán, the Cuban composer who was responsible for bringing Afro-Cuban influences into modern classical music, the theater is one of Habana's grandest, boasting two different auditoriums. The Orquesta Sinfónica Nacional play in the 886-seat Sala Amadeo Roldán, while soloists and small groups are showcased in the 276-seat Sala García Caturla.

DANCE
Thanks to dance diva Alicia Alonso (p28), the Cuban National Ballet is world famous, but Cubans also excel at plenty of other dancing styles, most notably flamenco.

CENTRO ANDALUZ Map p222
☎ **863-6745; Paseo de Martí No 104 btwn Genios & Refugio, Centro Habana;** ⏰ **6-11pm Tue-Sun**
A major Habana flamenco venue, the spit-and-sawdust Centro Andaluz on Paseo de Martí (Prado) regularly hosts blinding performances of what Spanish playwright Federico Lorca once poetically referred to as 'the music of hope and despair.' The dancing embodies much the same essence. The venue serves food (p117), and you can inquire about guitar lessons (p191).

GRAN TEATRO DE LA HABANA
Map p222
☎ **861-3096; cnr Paseo de Martí & San Rafael, Centro Habana; tickets CUC$20**
The amazing neobaroque Gran Teatro, located in the Centro Gallego (p80), is the seat of the acclaimed Ballet Nacional de Cuba, founded in 1948 by Alicia Alonso (p28). It is also the home of the Cuban National Opera. A theater since 1838, it contains the grandiose Teatro García Lorca, along with two smaller concert halls: the Sala Alejo Carpentier and the Sala Ernesto Lecuono, where art films are sometimes shown. For upcoming events check out the handwritten notices posted under the colonnades on the sidewalk outside, or inquire at the ticket office (⏰ 9am-6pm Tue-Sat, 9am-3pm Sun).

MESÓN DE LA FLOTA Map p220
☎ **863-3838; Mercaderes No 257 btwn Amargura & Brasil; admission free;** ⏰ **shows from 9pm**
The Mesón de la Flota is Cuba's take on an earthy Andalucian flamenco club – although it's also an excellent restaurant (p114) and hotel (p158). As they have done with other foreign cultural genres, the Cubans have taken to this traditionally Spanish musical art with gusto and stamped their own authority on such classic flamenco *toques* (forms) as *seguiriyas* (a deep, expressive style) and *soleares* (a solemn yet melodic form). Warming up at 9pm nightly, the in-house band and dancers raise the stakes gradually as they search for the indefinable and elusive spirit that aficionados know as *duende*.

THEATER
With a well-entrenched and influential arts movement, Habana boasts a theater scene that is unmatched elsewhere in the Caribbean (and possibly Latin America), even if the auditoriums themselves may sometimes look a little run-down. Offerings run the whole gamut, ranging from plays by Lorca to rumba with the Conjunto Folklórico Nacional to close-to-the-bone comedy sketches to performances by internationally renowned ballet troupes. While the skill and professionalism of these performances easily matches European and North American standards, ticket prices rarely exceed CUC$10.

SALA TEATRO EL SÓTANO

Map pp224-5

☎ 832-0630; Calle K btwn Calles 25 & 27, Vedado
If you understand Spanish, it's well worth attending a performance of the Grupo Teatro Rita Montaner in the Sala Teatro El Sótano, not far from the Hotel Habana Libre. The best shows are on Friday and Saturday at 8:30pm, and Sunday at 5pm. This is cutting-edge contemporary Cuban theater at its best.

SALA TEATRO HUBERT DE BLANCK

Map pp224-5

☎ 830-1011; Calzada No 657 btwn Calles A & B, Vedado; tickets CUC$5
This theater, named for the founder of Habana's first conservatory of music, is home to Cuba's leading theater company, Teatro Estudio. You can usually see plays in Spanish on Saturday at 8:30pm and Sunday at 7pm; tickets are sold just prior to the performance.

TEATRO AMÉRICA Map p222

☎ 862-5695; Av de Italia No 253 btwn Concordia & Neptuno, Centro Habana
Housed in a classic art deco *rascacielo* (skyscraper) on Av de Italia (Galiano), Teatro América seems to have changed little since its theatrical heyday in the 1930s and '40s. It plays host to vaudeville, comedy, dance, jazz and salsa, and shows are normally staged on Saturday at 8:30pm and Sunday at 5pm. You can also inquire about **dance lessons** (p146).

TEATRO BRECHT Map pp224-5

cnr Calles 13 & I, Vedado; ☾ shows 8:30pm Sat, 5pm Sun
The Brecht has varied performances on Saturday at 8:30pm and Sunday at 5pm. Tickets go on sale one hour before the performance.

TEATRO FAUSTO Map p222

☎ 863-1173; Paseo de Martí No 201, Centro Habana
Another art deco eye-catcher on Paseo de Martí, the Teatro Fausto is renowned for its sidesplitting comedy shows on Friday, Saturday and Sunday. There's an open-sided **theater bar** across the street on the corner of Colón.

TEATRO KARL MARX Map pp228-9

☎ 203-0801, 209-1991; cnr Av 1 & Calle 10, Miramar
An ugly building but a great venue – size-wise the Karl Marx puts other Habana theaters in the shade, with a seating capacity of 5500 in a single auditorium. The very biggest events in Habana happen here, such as the closing galas for the jazz and film festivals and rare concerts by *trovadores* (singers of traditional poetic songs) such as Carlos Varela and Silvio Rodríguez. It also hosted Welsh rockers the Manic Street Preachers in 2001, the first Western rock band to play live on the island (Fidel Castro was in the audience).

TEATRO MELLA Map pp224-5

☎ 833-5651; Línea No 657 btwn Calles A & B, Vedado
Occupying the site of the old Rodi Cinema on Línea, the Teatro Mella is named after the famous communist and revolutionary hero Julio Antonio Mella. The program here is one of Habana's most comprehensive, offering an international ballet festival (p14), comedy shows, theater, dance and intermittent performances from the famous Conjunto Folklórico Nacional. If you have kids, come to the children's show on Sunday at 11am. The theater has a seating capacity of 1475.

TEATRO NACIONAL DE CUBA

Map pp224-5

☎ 879-6011; cnr Paseo & Calle 39, Vedado; tickets CUC$10
One of the twin pillars of Cuban cultural life in Habana, the Teatro Nacional de Cuba on the Plaza de la Revolución is the modern rival to the old-world Gran Teatro in Parque Central. Built in the 1950s as part of Jean Forestier's grand city expansion, the complex hosts landmark concerts, foreign theater troupes, La Colmenita children's company and the Ballet Nacional de Cuba. The main hall, the Sala Avellaneda, stages big events such as musical concerts or plays by Shakespeare, while the smaller Sala Covarrubias puts on a more daring program (the seating capacity of the two theaters combined is 3300). The 9th floor is a rehearsal and performance space where the newest, most experimental stuff happens. The **ticket office** (☾ 9am-5pm) is at the

far end of a separate single-story building beside the main theater. Also on the premises are the **Café Cantante Mi Habana** (p140) and the **Piano Bar Delirio Habanero** (p139).

TEATRO NACIONAL DE GUIÑOL
Map pp224-5
☎ 832-6262; Calle M btwn Calles 17 & 19
The Teatro Nacional de Guiñol, underneath the Focsa building, presents puppet shows for children on Saturday at 5pm and Sunday at 10:30am and 5pm.

DRINKING

Most bars in Habana have at least one resident band that serenades customers enthusiastically from dusk till dawn. The music is nearly always traditional and the musicians themselves are – almost without exception – enviably talented.

Barhopping is easiest in Habana Vieja, where Habaguanex has done a great job in restructuring some of the city's venerable old drinking houses into atmospheric bars and taverns. Here, in the heart of the old town, you'll find the city's only microbrewery, a couple of overhyped 'Hemingway-once-got-drunk-in-here' bars and the perennially lively Calle Obispo.

Centro Habana's bars are edgier and a little more down-at-heel than their Habana Vieja counterparts, while Vedado and Playa are the domain of cabaret shows and smoky nightclubs.

BAR DOS HERMANOS Map p220
☎ 861-3436; San Pedro No 304, Habana Vieja;
☼ 24hr
Out of the way and a little seedy, Bar Dos Hermanos was a favorite Habana hangout of Spanish poet Federico García Lorca during his three months in Cuba in 1930. With its long wooden bar and salty seafaring atmosphere, it can't have changed much since.

BAR LA MARINA Map p220
cnr Oficios & Brasil, Habana Vieja; ☼ 10am-11pm
This pleasant outdoor courtyard with a 'ceiling' made out of twisted vines is as an agreeable old-town nook as any. You can grab a bite to eat, feast on popcorn, or just sip quietly on a mojito while the resident Cuban combo strums along.

TOP FIVE HOTEL BARS
- Courtyard bar-café – Hotel Telégrafo (p164)
- Galería Bar – Hotel Nacional (p167)
- El Pórtico – Hotel NH Parque Central (p164)
- La Marina Bar – Hotel Armadores de Santander (p161)
- Roof terrace bar – Hotel Ambos Mundos (p160)

BAR-CLUB IMÁGENES Map pp224-5
☎ 33-36-06; Calzada No 602, Vedado; drink minimum CUC$5; ☼ 9pm-5am
This upscale piano bar attracts something of an older crowd with its regular diet of *boleros* (romantic love songs) and *trova* (traditional poetic songs), but sometimes there are surprise concerts by big-name musicians; check the schedule posted outside. Meals are available (and affordable).

BOSQUE BOLOGNA Map p220
Obispo No 460, Habana Vieja; ☼ 10am-midnight
A fern-filled terrace that fills the space of a demolished building on Calle Obispo, the Bologna is always busy with drinkers and diners drawn in by a combination of its effervescent music and highly persuasive waiters. It's a perfect warm-up for an extended Habana Vieja bar crawl.

CAFÉ FRESA Y CHOCOLATE
Map pp224-5
Calle 23 btwn Calles 10 & 12, Vedado;
☼ 9am-11pm
A small patio bar at the Centro Cultural Cinematográfico, this place is the nerve center of Habana's cinema community, with a young, hip clientele of actors, writers and film lovers. Named after Tomás Gutierrez Alea's Oscar-nominated movie, it hosts a number of regular happenings, both here and in the adjoining building, including the once-monthly El Último Jueves del Mes (p134) debate night.

CAFÉ PARÍS Map p220
Obispo No 202, Habana Vieja; ☼ 24hr
Jump into the mix by grabbing one of the rough-hewn tables at this Habana Vieja standby known for its live music and gregarious atmosphere. On good nights, the rum flows, talented musicians jam, and spontaneous dancing and singing erupt in the crowd.

EL ÚLTIMO JUEVES DE CADA MES

Habana is a city of many secrets, and few are more revealing than the topical and upfront discussion nights that convene once a month at the **Centro Cultural Cinematográfico** (Map pp224–5; Calle 23 btwn 10 & 12; admission free; 🕙 4–6pm) under the banner of El Último Jueves de Cada Mes.

Held – as the Spanish title implies – on the last Thursday of every month, these interactive debate nights are hosted by a small panel of academics, intellectuals and experts from the arts magazine *Temas* in front of a respectful but enthusiastic public audience. While subjects are invariably film or TV orientated, debates can be forthright and feisty, covering such potentially divisive issues as public morals or the validity of a recent Cuban soap opera entitled *La Cara Oculta de la Luna* (The Dark Side of the Moon), which highlights homosexuality and the contraction of the AIDS virus. Audience participation is encouraged and the forum is not only highly informative, it also provides a fascinating insight into the parameters of public debate in a supposedly totalitarian society.

El Último Jueves de Cada Mes is open to anyone wishing to attend and entrance is free. The topics for upcoming debates are usually posted up on a board in the adjacent Café Fresa y Chocolate a few days in advance. Foreign visitors should note that all debates take place in Spanish.

CAFÉ TABERNA Map p220

☎ 861-1637; cnr Mercaderes & Brasil, Habana Vieja; 🕙 noon–midnight

A rocking bar-restaurant that pays both pictorial and musical homage to Cuba's *Bárbaro del Ritmo* (Barbarian of Rhythm), Benny Moré, the Café Taberna is where you can witness some of Habana's biggest and brassiest salsa sounds. Characterized by its long, well-stocked bar, and evocative images of Moré and other assorted mambo kings, the building fills a pale blue 18th-century house on the corner of Plaza Vieja and is always busy.

EL BATURRO Map p220

cnr Av de Bélgica & Merced, Habana Vieja; 🕙 11am–11pm

Part of a long tradition of drinking houses situated next to train stations, El Baturro is a rough-and-ready Spanish bistro with a long wooden bar and an all-male – aggressively so – clientele.

EL FLORIDITA Map p220

☎ 867-1300; Obispo No 557, Habana Vieja; 🕙 11am–midnight

Promoting itself as the 'cradle of the daiquirí,' El Floridita was a favorite of expat Americans long before Ernest Hemingway dropped by in the 1930s (hence the name, which means 'little Florida'). Indeed its fame began soon after WWI when a bartender named Constante Ribalaigua began using shaved ice to make frozen daiquirís. Hemingway developed a penchant for the refreshing cocktail and ultimately they christened a drink in

his honor: the Papa Hemingway special (basically, a daiquirí made with grapefruit juice). His record – legend has it – was 13 doubles in one sitting. Any attempt to equal it at the current prices (CUC$6 a single shot) will cost you a small fortune – and a huge hangover.

FUNDACIÓN HAVANA CLUB

Map p220

Museo del Ron, San Pedro No 262, Habana Vieja; 🕙 9am–midnight

The bar in the famous Museo del Ron (p75) is one of the best places to get acquainted with Cuba's potent national drink. Try taking it like the Cubans do: straight up with no ice.

LA BODEGUITA DEL MEDIO Map p220

☎ 867-1374; Empedrado No 207, Habana Vieja; 🕙 11am–midnight

Made famous thanks to the rum-swilling exploits of Ernest Hemingway, a visit to Habana's most celebrated bar has become de rigueur for literary sycophants and Walt Whitman wannabes. Notables including Salvador Allende, Fidel Castro, Nicolás Guillén, Harry Belafonte and Nat King Cole have all left their autographs on La Bodeguita's wall. These days the clientele is less luminous, with package tourists bussed in from Varadero delighting in the bottled bohemian atmosphere and the CUC$4 mojitos, which – though good – have lost their Hemingway-esque shine. The B del M has proved to be so popular that it has been successfully exported; branches now exist in Puerto Vallarta (Mexico) and Palo Alto (California).

LA DICHOSA Map p220

cnr Obispo & Compostela, Habana Vieja;
🕙 10am-midnight

It's hard to miss the rowdy La Dichosa on busy Calle Obispo, despite the fact that it doesn't display its name outside. Small and cramped, with at least half the space given over to the resident band, this is a good place for a quick drink before heading off down the road.

LA LLUVIA DE ORO Map p220

☎ 862-9870; Obispo No 316, Habana Vieja;
🕙 24hr

It's on Obispo and there's always live music belting through the doorway – so it's always crowded. But with a higher-than-average hustler-to-tourist ratio, it might not be your most intimate introduction to Habana. Small snacks are available and the musicians' 'hat' comes round every three to four songs. Bring plenty of small change.

LA TABERNA DE LA MURALLA

Map p220

☎ 866-4453; cnr San Ignacio & Muralla, Habana Vieja; 🕙 11am-midnight

Habana's best (and only) homebrew pub is situated on Plaza Vieja. Set up by an Austrian company in 2004, this no-nonsense drinking establishment serves smooth, cold homemade beer at sturdy wooden benches set up outside on the cobbles or indoors in an atmospheric beer hall. Get a group together and the staff will serve the amber nectar in a tall plastic tube; you draw the beer out of a tap at the bottom. There's also an outside grill where you can order good helpings of chorizo, fish and kebabs.

MONSERRATE BAR Map p220

☎ 860-9751; Obrapía No 410, Habana Vieja;
🕙 10am-midnight

Traveler's tip: the Monserrate Bar daiquirís are half the price of those sold at the El Floridita one block down the road, thanks to the fact that a certain Ernest Hemingway never drank here. Skip the cheap food (it's cheap for a reason) and concentrate on cramming in the cocktails.

OPUS BAR Map pp224-5

cnr Calzada & Calle D, Vedado; 🕙 3pm-3am

With individual candlelit tables, overstuffed chairs and Sly and the Family Stone on the airways, this is Habana's (good) approximation of a lounge. The wall of windows make it a great sunset spot and performances in the Teatro Amadeo Roldán downstairs are broadcast via closed-circuit TV – a good alternative if the show is sold out.

PRADO NO 12 Map p222

Paseo de Martí No 12, Centro Habana;
🕙 noon-11pm

This slim flat-iron building on the corner of Paseo de Martí and San Lázaro serves drinks and simple snacks. Despite a major renovation five years ago, Prado No 12 still seems to be in a 1950s time warp. Soak up the atmosphere of this amazing city here after a sunset stroll along the Malecón (Av de Maceo).

LIVE MUSIC

Cabarets and nightclubs mean dancing and, not surprisingly, Habana has plenty of stellar options. Venues to look out for are La Zorra y El Cuervo in Vedado for jazz, the hip Havana Café in the Hotel Meliá Cohiba for hot contemporary sounds, and the legendary Casa de la Música in Miramar for scorching salsa. At all these places you can see Cuba's top musical acts performing for less than CUC$20.

CABARET

Habana is famous for its glitzy cabaret shows with big bands, skillful dancers, stylish singers and lots of glamorous pizzazz. The most celebrated cabaret of all is held outdoors at the flamboyant Tropicana nightclub in Marianao, which has been running continuously since 1939. Many cabarets become nightclubs after their shows have finished for the night.

CABARET NACIONAL Map p222

☎ 863-2361; cnr Paseo de Martí & San Rafael, Centro Habana; admission CUC$10; 🕙 10pm-3am

The Cabaret Nacional, below the Gran Teatro de la Habana, has a show nightly at 11:30pm if enough patrons are present. It's a little camper than other Habana cabarets and the noise sometimes filters through into the Lorca auditorium next door. Its couples-only here and there's a minimum dress policy – no shorts or T-shirts. The

Nacional also has a CUC$5 matinee known to locals as the *disco temba*. These popular afternoon get-togethers feature taped music from the 1970s and '80s, and are all the rage in Habana at the moment with the 35-plus set.

CABARET PARISIÉN Map pp224-5
Hotel Nacional, cnr Calles O & 21, Vedado; admission CUC$35; ☉ from 9:10pm
Cabaret Parisién, in the Hotel Nacional, is one rung down from the Tropicana in both price and quality. Nonetheless, this longstanding nightly cabaret show is well worth a look, especially if you're staying in or around Vedado. Typically, the doors open at 9:10pm, with dinner at 9:30pm (an extra CUC$20) and then the show. It's the usual mix of frills, feathers and seminaked women, but the choreography is first class and the whole spectacle has excellent kitsch value. As with most cabarets, after midnight the Parisién becomes a disco.

CABARET SALÓN ROJO Map pp224-5
☎ 33-37-47; Calle 21 btwn Calles N & O, Vedado; admission CUC$10; ☉ from 10pm Tue-Sun
Although George Raft's opulent Hotel Capri closed a couple of years back, it's once notorious cabaret show, the Salón Rojo (Red Room), seems to have been given an indefinite reprieve. While the cabaret is no longer the Mob-infested gambling den of yesteryear, the acts and music in the trussed up and revamped Salón Rojo are still hot, pulsating and ever popular with affluent Cubans. For heated music and no-holds-barred dancing, this is the place to come.

CABARET TURQUINO Map pp224-5
25th fl, Hotel Habana Libre, cnr Calles 23 & L, Vedado; admission CUC$10; ☉ 10:30pm-4:30am
If you want a classy but affordable cabaret show, look no further than the Turquino on the 25th floor in the Hotel Habana Libre. Popular bands (including Los Van Van) play here regularly, and the views are spectacular. Locals swear by this place.

COPA ROOM Map pp224-5
☎ 33-40-51; Hotel Riviera, cnr Paseo & Malecón, Vedado; admission CUC$20; ☉ 10pm-4am
Doormen in tuxes and an atmosphere that's pure 1950s kitsch make the refurbished Copa Room a nostalgic draw.

Built as part of Mafia boss Meyer Lansky's Hotel Riviera in 1957, the nightclub was requisitioned by Castro's rebel army two years later (Fidel actually held a press conference in the Copa Room on January 21, 1959) as the glitter was quickly taken out of Lansky's hedonistic honeymoon. But the Copa Room lived to fight another day. Reopened in the early 2000s as a cabaret-nightclub, the Copa Room has nightly shows that are sharp, professional and highly entertaining, and with only a CUC$20 entry fee (including one cocktail), it's more economical than either the Parisién or the Tropicana.

HAVANA CAFÉ Map pp224-5
☎ 833-3636; Hotel Meliá Cohiba, Paseo btwn Calles 1 & 3, Vedado; admission CUC$10; ☉ from 9:30pm
The Havana Café is a fancy nightclub-cum-cabaret at the Hotel Meliá Cohiba that is open nightly from 9:30pm. The decor is 1950s American retro, with old cars, motorcycles, gas pumps, and even an airplane hanging from the ceiling. It's hip and trendy (this, after all, is the Meliá), and most people come here to have dinner and dance. After 1am the tables are cleared and the place rocks to 'international music' until the cock crows.

TROPICANA Map pp228-9
☎ 267-1871; Calle 72 No 4504, Marianao; admission CUC$70; ☉ from 8:30pm Tue-Sun
A city institution since it opened in 1939, the world-famous Tropicana was one of the few examples of Habana's Las Vegas–style nightlife to survive the clampdowns of the Castro revolution. Immortalized in Graham Greene's 1958 classic *Our Man in Havana*, this open-air cabaret show is where the book's protagonist, Jim Wormold, takes his overindulged daughter Milly to celebrate her 17th birthday. 'Chorus girls paraded 20 feet up among the great palm trees, while pink and mauve searchlights swept the floor,' wrote Greene of the gaudy proceedings. He may as well have been filing a modern-day entertainment review. The Tropicana still features a bevy of scantily clad señoritas who climb down from the palm trees to salsa dance amid colorful flashing lights on stage. The only difference is that these days the tickets sell for a slightly less-than-socialist CUC$70.

FOLK, SALSA & TRADITIONAL

Cuba's traditional *son* and salsa music can be heard for free almost anywhere but if you just can't get enough of the real deal, check out any of the places below.

CASA DE LA AMISTAD Map pp224-5
☎ 830-3114; Paseo No 406, Vedado; admission free; ☒ Tue-Sun

Housed in a lovely rose-colored mansion on leafy Paseo, the Casa de la Amistad hosts *son* and salsa music every night except Monday in an Italian Renaissance–style garden. Buena Vista Social Club luminary Compay Segundo was a regular before his death in 2003, and a number of Cuban TV shows have been made at the site. Other perks include a reasonably priced restaurant, a bar, a cigar shop and the house itself, which is a real Cuban beauty.

CASA DE LA TROVA Map pp224-5
☎ 879-3373; San Lázaro No 661, Vedado; admission free; ☒ 6pm-midnight Tue-Sun

Strangely, Habana's Casa de la Trova is a bit of a damp squib compared to other famous Casas de la Trova in Santiago de Cuba and Camagüey. It's traditionally a haven for *son* music of the type popularized by Ry Cooder's Buena Vista Social Club, but the schedule here is sporadic. Check the upcoming program before turning up.

CASA DE LAS AMÉRICAS Map pp224-5
☎ 55-27-06; cnr Calles G & 3, Vedado

This cultural institution founded by the Cuban government in April 1959 hosts talks, workshops, expositions and an annual literature prize, as well as sporadic music concerts in its 1st-floor function room. Call by or check the latest *Cartelera* for upcoming events.

EL GATO TUERTO Map pp224-5
☎ 66-22-24; Calle O No 14 btwn Calles 17 & 19, Vedado; drink minimum CUC$5; ☒ noon-6am

Once the headquarters of Habana's alternative artistic and sexual scene, this chic bar with live music still packs in the baby boomers in its role as a well-known shrine to the Cuban *bolero*. Hidden in a quirky two-story house with turtles swimming in a pond out front, the 'One-Eyed Cat' (as 'Gato Tuerto' translates into English) boasts an upstairs restaurant, Café Concerto El Gato Tuerto (p119), along with a downstairs bar and performance space. Come here at weekends to witness scores of 40-somethings belting out *boleros* word for word with the band, shouting requests and cramming the dance floor.

EL HURÓN AZUL Map pp224-5
☎ 832-4551; cnr Calles 17 & H, Vedado; admission CUC$1-5

El Hurón Azul is the social club of the Unión Nacional des Escritores y Artistas de Cuba (Uneac; National Union of Cuban Writers & Artists), Cuba's leading cultural institution. Frequented by a number of famous writers and intellectuals, this charming mansion hosts musical performances outside in its garden. Wednesday is the Afro-Cuban Peña del Ambia (admission CUC$5) and Saturday it's authentic Cuban boleros (admission CUC$1; ☒ 10pm to 2am); there's jazz (admission CUC$1; ☒ 5pm) and trova (admission CUC$1; ☒ 5pm) on alternate Thursdays. It doesn't get much better than this.

LA CASA DE LA MÚSICA CENTRO HABANA Map p222
☎ 878-4727; Av de Italia btwn Concordia & Neptuno, Centro Habana; admission CUC$5-25; ☒ shows 4pm & 10pm

Imagine seeing U2 play live for $5. One of the understated successes of the Cuban revolution is that you can witness top musical performers playing in person for next to nothing. This Casa de la Música is edgier than its counterpart in Miramar (below) – some have complained it's too edgy – and there are big salsa bands and plenty of 'name' acts thrown in for good measure. There are two daily shows, and both are popular with locals. Check the upcoming weekly schedule on the door outside.

LA CASA DE LA MÚSICA MIRAMAR Map pp228-9
☎ 202-6147; Calle 20 No 3308, Miramar; admission CUC$10-20; ☒ 10pm Tue-Sat

The Casa de la Música in Miramar is one of Habana's top music venues, launched with a concert by renowned jazz pianist Chucho Valdés in 1994. It's run by national Cuban recording company Egrem, and the programs are generally a lot more authentic than the cabaret entertainment you see at the hotels.

GAY & LESBIAN HABANA

The acceptance of homosexuality, transvestism and transsexualism in Cuba has grown considerably since the 1980s, thanks primarily to the work of Mariela Castro, daughter of Cuban vice president Raúl Castro and niece of Fidel. As director of the Cuban National Center for Sex Education, based in Habana, Mariela has long been an important activist for gay and lesbian rights on the island, and her voice and persistence on issues such as bisexuality and AIDS has often been highly influential. Recent developments include a proposal for free sex-reassignment surgery and the emergence of a popular new Cuban soap opera called La Oculta de la Luna (The Dark Side of the Moon), which has tackled such formerly prickly topics as homosexual love and the contraction of the AIDS virus.

For gay travelers in search of an active alternative Habana nightlife, opportunities are slowly opening up. Same-sex couples should have few problems shooting the breeze with the weekend crowds on the Malecón (Av de Maceo) or mingling with the masses at the Tropicana. While there still aren't any gay venues per se in the city, a burgeoning colorful nighttime scene offers plenty of safe cruising opportunities in Vedado, plus the chance to attend some stomping unofficial parties in the suburbs. Longtime gay meeting places in Vedado (Map pp224-5) include outside Cine Yara on the intersection of Calles 23 and L, and in the streets and spaces surrounding the Coppelia.

Head to any of these spots on a Friday and Saturday night and you'll soon get wind of the private fiestas – spontaneous parties that are mostly gay, with a healthy dose of bisexuals and friends thrown in for good measure. Habana's scene is renowned for its talented drag shows, although you'll rarely see transvestites flaunting it in public. A popular venue for bigger shindigs is Parque Lenin (p96) – it's a little removed from the center but, by all accounts, it's an excursion that is well worth making.

As with other foreign-Cuban couplings, non-Cubans will often be expected to pick up the bill for drinks, taxis etc when escorting Cuban partners to these places.

As well as Valdés, platinum players such as NG la Banda, Los Van Van, Aldaberto Alvarez and Su Son play here regularly, and you'll rarely pay more than CUC$20. Many travelers have said that this Casa de la Música has a more relaxed atmosphere than its namesake in **Centro Habana** (p137).

LA MAISON Map pp228-9
☎ 204-1543; Calle 16 No 701, Miramar; admission CUC$30; ☽ from 6pm
Located in a beautiful eclectic mansion, La Maison (p155) hosts a nightly fashion show with an accompanying program of music. Entry includes a meal in the complex's fancy **restaurant** (p125).

SALÓN ROSADO BENNY MORÉ
Map pp228-9
El Tropical; ☎ 206-1281; cnr Av 41 & Calle 46, Miramar; admission CUC$10; ☽ 9pm-late
For something completely different, check out the very caliente (hot) action at this outdoor venue. The Rosado packs in hot, sexy Cuban youths dancing madly to Los Van Van, Pupi y Su Son Son or Habana Abierta; it's a fierce scene and female travelers should expect aggressive come-ons. Some travelers pay pesos, others dollars – more of that Cuban randomness for you. Friday to Sunday is best.

JAZZ

Cuban jazz is synonymous with Chucho Valdés and – this being Habana – seeing the great Grammy-winning improviser in person is by no means out of the question. Should Chucho be taking a night off, however, don't worry; Señor Valdés has left a great trio of quirky jazz venues rocking in his wake.

JAZZ CAFÉ Map pp224-5
☎ 55-33-02; top fl, Galerías de Paseo, cnr Calle 1 & Paseo, Vedado; drink minimum CUC$10; ☽ noon-late
This upscale joint overlooking the Malecón is like a jazz supper club, with tables and a decent menu; come here for cocktails at sunset. Locals will tell you it is one of Habana's best jazz venues – at night, the club swings into action with jazz, timba (modern salsa mixed with funk, rap and rock) and occasionally straight-up salsa. Pity the dance floor is just a strip between the tables.

JAZZ CLUB LA ZORRA Y EL CUERVO
Map pp224-5
☎ 66-24-02; cnr Calles 23 & O, Vedado; admission CUC$5; ☽ from 10pm
Vedado's most famous jazz club is La Zorra y El Cuervo (the Vixen and the Crow), which

attracts long lines of committed jazz fiends. The subterranean performance space is smoky and a little cramped (the official capacity is 130), but the freestyle jazz showcased here is second to none. In the past, this club has hosted such big names as Chucho Valdés and George Benson.

PIANO BAR DELIRIO HABANERO
Map pp224-5

☎ 873-5713; cnr Paseo & Calle 39; admission CUC$5; ⊗ 3-7pm & 10pm-3am Tue-Sun
This suave and sophisticated lounge upstairs in the Teatro Nacional hosts everything from young *trovadores* to smooth, improvised jazz. The deep-red couches abut a wall of glass overlooking the Plaza de la Revolución and it's stunning at night with the Martí memorial alluringly backlit. This is where to escape when the action at the adjoining Café Cantante Mi Habana (p140) nightclub gets too hot. There's a daily *peña* at 3pm.

RUMBA
The music of Black slaves, rumba (p37) is one of Habana's most spontaneous musical genres. To be sure of catching some of the city's earthiest contemporary rhythms head to one of the following venues.

CALLEJÓN DE HAMEL Map pp224-5
Vedado; ⊗ from noon Sun
Aside from its funky street murals and psychedelic art shops, the main reason to come to Habana's high temple of Afro-Cuban culture is for the frenetic rumba music that kicks off every Sunday at around noon. For aficionados, this is about as raw and hypnotic as it gets, with interlocking drum patterns and lengthy rhythmic chants powerful enough to summon up the spirit of the *orishas* (Santería deities). Due to a liberal sprinkling of tourists these days, some argue that the Callejón de Hamel has lost much of its basic charm. Don't believe them. This place can still deliver.

CONJUNTO FOLKLÓRICO NACIONAL
Map pp224-5

El Gran Palenque, Calle 4 No 103 btwn Calzada & Calle 5, Vedado; admission CUC$5; ⊗ 3pm alternate Sat
The Conjunto Folklórico Nacional, founded in 1962, specializes in Afro-Cuban dancing

(all of the drummers are Santería high priests) and offers some of the best rumba in the city. It has toured the world – everywhere from New York to Angola – and is internationally famous. You can see the group perform at the Sábado de Rumba on every other Saturday at El Gran Palenque, or to get in on the action you can organize dance lessons (p191).

LAS ORISHAS Map p231
cnr Martí & Lamas, Guanabacoa; admission CUC$3; ⊗ from 10pm
Situated in the heart of Habana's Santería community, Las Orishas is a funky restaurant (p126) that on the weekend hosts live rumba music, including regular visits from the Conjunto Folklórico Nacional. The pleasant garden bar is surrounded by colorful Afro-Cuban sculptures that depict various Santería deities, such as Babalou Aye, Yemaya and Changó. Well off the beaten track and hard to get to at night, this quirky music venue is usually visited by foreigners in groups. Few leave unhappy. Indeed, if you want to see rumba dancing at its gritty best, this is the place to be.

ROCK, RAP & REGGAE
In the modern kaleidoscope of Cuban music, there's room for almost anything, including myriad North American and European influences. Rock's resurgence was given the official nod of approval in 2000 with the unveiling of a statue of John Lennon (p87) at a park in Vedado by Fidel Castro. One year later, the Cuban leader was a surprise attendee at a concert given in the Karl Marx Theater by Welsh rockers the Manic Street Preachers. The acceptance of rap and *reggaeton* (Cuban hip-hop) goes back even further to the emergence of the annual Alamar hip-hop festival in 1995; these days it's all over town.

ANFITEATRO PARQUE ALMENDARES
Map pp224-5

Calle 23, Vedado; admission 2 pesos
This riverside amphitheater hosts regular musical events and special concerts by the likes of Frank Delgado and Interactivo. It's an intimate place to catch some terrific music. Regular *peñas* include reggae (⊗ 8pm Friday) and rap (⊗ 8pm Sat).

LA MADRIGUERA Map pp224-5

☎ 879-8175; Quinta de los Molinos, cnr Calzada de Infanta & Salvador Allende, Vedado; admission 20 pesos; ◷ 9am-7pm Mon-Wed, Fri & Sat, 9am-midnight Thu

Locals bill it as a 'hidden place for open ideas,' while outsiders are bowled over by the musical originality and artistic innovation on display here. Welcome to La Madriguera, home to the Asociación Hermanos Saíz, the youth wing of Uneac. Located in Quinta de los Molinos, this is where the pulse of Cuba's young musical innovators beats the strongest. Come here for arts, crafts, spontaneity and, most of all, music. The program is varied but there is a strong bias towards the Cuban three Rs: *reggaeton*, rap and rumba.

PATIO DE MARÍA Map pp224-5

☎ 81-07-22; Calle 37 No 262 btwn Paseo & Calle 2, Vedado

Unique in Cuba for a number of reasons, the Patio de María is a nexus point for Habana's burgeoning counterculture, hosting everything from rock music to poetry readings. Run by María Gattorno, the venue has received heavy media coverage in Cuba and abroad, partly due to Gattorno's AIDS and drug-prevention educational work. You can catch all kinds of entertainment here, from videos and debates to workshops and theater, but the real deal is the rock nights (to canned music) that take off most weekends. Check the schedule posted at the door or head to Parque de los Rockeros on the corner of Calles 23 and G to find out what's happening.

DANCE CLUBS

Habana's dance clubs range from the suave Café Cantante Mi Habana in the Teatro Nacional de Cuba to wall-vibratingly loud hotel discos such as Pico Blanco, which continue playing pop music, techno and salsa well into the small hours of the morning, washed down with plenty of Cuban rum. Alternatively you can visit an infinitely more *caliente* venue such as the Karachi Club in Vedado or the Palmero in Centro Habana, where you can mingle congenially with local Cubans as they dance energetically to *timba*, salsa-jazz, *reggaeton* and rap.

CABARET LAS VEGAS Map pp224-5

☎ 870-7939; Calzada de Infanta No 104 btwn Calles 25 & 27, Vedado; admission CUC$5; ◷ 10pm-4am

Don't get duped into thinking this is another Tropicana. On the contrary, Cabaret Las Vegas is a rough and seedy local music dive where a little rum and a lot of *No moleste, por favors* will help you withstand the overzealous entreaties of the hordes of haranguing prostitutes. There is, however, a midnight show.

CAFÉ CANTANTE MI HABANA

Map pp224-5

☎ 879-0710; cnr Paseo & Calle 39; admission CUC$10; ◷ 4pm-5am Tue-Sat

The Café Cantante Mi Habana, below the Teatro Nacional de Cuba (use the side entrance), is a hip disco that offers live salsa music and dancing as well as bar snacks and food. With a clientele consisting mainly of 'yummies' (young urban Marxist managers) and aging sugar-daddy tourists with their youthful Cuban girlfriends in tow, this place tends to get more feisty than the adjacent Piano Bar Delirio Habanero (p139). The music, however, is quality, and the disco has regular appearances from name performers such as Haila María Mompie. There's a dress code (no shorts, T-shirts or hats may be worn inside), there's no entry for those under 18 and no photos are allowed. Café Cantante has 4pm matinees for the older folks, including a rap matinee on Saturday.

CLUB LA RED Map pp224-5

☎ 832-5415; cnr Calles 19 & L, Vedado; admission CUC$3-5; ◷ 10pm-5am

Club La Red is a Vedado disco-club that rarely gets animated before 11:30pm on a Friday or Saturday. Expect piped Western dance music with the odd revved-up *reggaeton* number thrown in for good measure.

CLUB TROPICAL Map pp224-5

☎ 832-7361; cnr Línea & Calle F, Vedado; admission CUC$5; ◷ 9pm-2am

Cheap but a little out of the way, this Vedado nightspot is where you come when your budget's blown but you still want to dance the night away to a variety of salsa, pop and rap.

VOICES OF HABANA: TONY TELLA

Taxi driver, Miramar

Sum up Habana in one sentence. Habana is incredible! It has such a great mix of architecture and people – and here everyone is the same, there is no class. **What defines a habanero?** *Habaneros* [inhabitants of Habana] are great talkers. They talk louder and live faster than other Cubans. They like to think that the best of everything is in Habana. **What is the best Cuban rum and why?** Caney rum *añejo* [aged] 12 years is my favorite. It is still made in the old Bacardí factory in Santiago de Cuba. I always drink it straight up

with no ice. **What's the best thing about your neighborhood?** The cleanliness and the tranquillity. **Is the food here so terrible?** No. It depends on where you eat. For government places you've got El Palenque, El Aljibe and La Cecilia; for private places try La Cocina de Lilliam, Paladar Vistamar or Los Nardos. **What is your favorite Habana night out?** The Macumba Habana in Playa; it's got food, drink, dancing, the lot, all in one place. **How can the inquisitive traveler find the 'real' Cuba?** Check out Barrio Chino [Chinatown], stroll down El Bulevar [Calle San Rafael] or wander along Galiano [Av de la Italia]. Or you can visit a *disco temba*, a place where people go after work [from 3pm onwards] to listen to American and Cuban music from the '70s and '80s. There's a good one in the Casa de la Música in Centro Habana.

As related to Brendan Sainsbury

DISCOTECA AMANECER
Map pp224-5

☎ 832-9075; Calle 15 btwn Calles N & O, Vedado; admission CUC$3-5; ☻ 10pm-4am
Discoteca Amanecer (Dawn Disco) is another cheap Vedado nightspot that mixes pop and rap. Whether you'll want to stay here until dawn is another matter.

EL CHEVERE Map pp224-5

☎ 204-5162; Parque Almendares, cnr Calles 49A & 28A, Vedado; admission CUC$6-10; ☻ from 10pm
One of Habana's most popular discos, this alfresco place in a lush park gets local tongues wagging, and hosts a good mix of Cubans and tourists.

KARACHI CLUB Map pp224-5

☎ 832-5415; cnr Calles 17 & K, Vedado; admission CUC$3-5; ☻ 10pm-5am
The Karachi is a ferociously *caliente* disco situated on a leafy Vedado street corner. Rumba dancing has been reported here, but you're far more likely to encounter Euro-disco, techno and rap.

MACUMBA HABANA

☎ 33-05-68/9; cnr Calle 222 & Av 37, La Lisa; admission CUC$10-20; ☻ from 10pm
Cocooned in a residential neighborhood southwest of Cubanacán is Macumba, one of Habana's biggest venues for live salsa.

The outdoor setting is refreshing and the sets are long, so you'll get a lot of dancing in. You can also dine at **La Giradilla** (from ☻ 6pm) in the same complex. This is a great place to catch jazz-salsa combos and *timba* music; NG La Banda performs regularly. Hotels and **Infotur** (p197) sell excursions here, but you're better off organizing the trip yourself (a taxi should cost around CUC$8 to CUC$10).

PALERMO Map p222

☎ 861-9745; cnr San Miguel & Amistad, Centro Habana; admission CUC$2; ☻ from 11pm Thu-Sun
Don't tell the respectable owners of your *casa particular* (private house that lets out rooms to foreigners) you're heading here – they'll run a mile. Palermo is a dance club with a heavy rap scene. Fun but *fuerte* (tough).

PICO BLANCO Map pp224-5

☎ 833-4187; 14th fl, Hotel St John's, Calle O No 216 btwn Calles 23 & 25, Vedado; admission CUC$5; ☻ from 9pm
An average hotel with a surprisingly less-than-average nightclub, the Pico Blanco is situated on the 14th floor of the Hotel St John's in Vedado. The program can be hit or miss: one night it's karaoke and cheesy *boleros,* another it's jamming with some rather famous Cuban musicians. Check the schedule posted in the hotel window. The **rooftop bar** has terrific views.

CINEMAS

As the host of the annual Festival Internacional del Nuevo Cine Latinoamericano (p14), movie-loving Habana has a plethora of popular cinemas and movie houses – over 200, in fact – and maintains the cutting-edge Instituto Cubano del Arte e Industria Cinematográphicos (Icaic; Cuban Film Institute). Most foreign films are shown here in their original language with Spanish subtitles, although Hollywood blockbusters are more common than many visitors imagine. Fortunately, there are plenty of thought-provoking Cuban and Latin American movies to balance out the banality.

Film-showing times tend to vary, although most cinemas will have a matinee and a couple of evening shows. There is always a daily schedule posted outside every cinema that highlights what films are showing at other cinemas all over Habana, plus session times.

Tickets generally cost CUC$2.

CINE ACTUALIDADES Map p222
☎ 861-5193; Av de Bélgica No 262, Centro Habana
The Actualidades is a timeworn cinema in a central location behind the Hotel Plaza in Centro Habana. Check out the handwritten schedule posted on the window to find out what's on.

CINE CHARLES CHAPLIN Map pp224-5
☎ 831-1101; Calle 23 No 1157 btwn Calles 10 & 12, Vedado
The Chaplin is an art-house cinema that shows quality Cuban movies and other rare cinematic gems.

CINE LA RAMPA Map pp224-5
☎ 878-6146; Calle 23 No 111, Vedado
La Rampa hosts film festivals and houses the country's extensive film archive. You can catch specialist movie seasons here dedicated to contemporary film icons such as Robert de Niro.

CINE PAYRET Map p222
☎ 863-3163; Paseo de Martí No 505, Centro Habana
Habana's largest and most popular cinema is situated opposite the Capitolio Nacional, and presents a good variety of both Spanish-speaking and Hollywood movies. The Payret has been in operation since 1878.

CINE RIVIERA Map pp224-5
☎ 830-9564; Calle 23 No 507, Vedado
Another classic movie house that shows a good selection of North American, Cuban, Latin American and European films.

CINE YARA Map pp224-5
☎ 832-9430; cnr Calles 23 & L, Vedado;
⏰ 12:30pm
The city's most prestigious cinema, Cine Yara was put up in the 1950s as part of the Habana's Radiocentro development. The second-largest cinema in Habana, it has three auditoriums and opens at 12:30pm daily.

CINECITO Map p222
☎ 863-8051; cnr San Rafael & Consulado, Centro Habana
Tucked behind the Hotel Inglaterra on pedestrianized San Rafael, Cinecito shows films for children.

MULTICINE INFANTA Map pp224-5
☎ 878-9323; Calzada de Infanta No 357, Vedado
Habana's fanciest cinema was refurbished for the prestigious 2006 Festival Internacional del Nuevo Cine Latinoamericano, and its four auditoriums sparkle afresh.

CIRCUSES

CIRCO TROMPOLOCO Map pp228-9
cnr Av 5 & Calle 112, Playa; admission CUC$10
Habana's permanent big top has performances at 7pm Thursday to Sunday plus a weekend matinee. It's great for the kids.

Activities

Activities

While history and culture are its obvious strong points, Habana can also offer museum-weary travelers plenty of exciting land- and water-based activities with which to while away a spare afternoon. Fishing á la Hemingway is top of the list for many, closely followed by scuba diving and boat trips, but don't rule out tennis, golf, baseball and – as a spectator sport, at least – boxing.

WATER-BASED ACTIVITIES

Cuba's main boating and diving center is at Marina Hemingway (p185) in Barlovento, 20km west of central Habana. There are a number of water-based activities available here, including boat trips, snorkeling, deep-sea fishing and scuba diving. Habana's other marina (Map pp218-19; Villa Blanca Km 18, Playa Tarará), 18km east of the city, was closed at the time of research due to storm damage. It should have reopened by the time of publication.

BOAT TRIPS

A five-hour 'seafari' costs CUC$40 per person and includes a boat trip along the Habana littoral, with some snorkeling and fishing thrown in. The trip leaves from the Marina Hemingway, but can be booked at the major Habana hotels.

DEEP-SEA FISHING

Situated on the fast-flowing Gulf Stream, the Habana area offers some great opportunities for deep-sea fishing; the Marina Hemingway even holds its own international fishing tournaments every June, September and November. Never one to rest on his laurels, it was Hemingway himself who pioneered fishing as a sport in Cuban waters, and with some good tackle and a little beginner's luck you can follow nautically in his famous footsteps.

MARLIN NAÚTICA Map pp228-9
☎ 204-6848; Marina Hemingway, cnr Av 5 & Calle 248, Barlovento; ☻ 8:30am-4:30pm
The Marlin Naútica office is situated in a complex at the end of the second harbor channel in the Marina Hemingway. The cheapest fishing trips offered here cost from CUC$150 for four anglers for four hours; a captain, sailor, open bar and tackle are included in the price. More comprehensive packages cost CUC$280/390/480 for four/six/eight hours. Marlin season is June to October.

DIVING & SNORKELING

Although it is possible to organize diving excursions from Habana, the reefs and water clarity aren't on a par with the more extensive dive sites that are found elsewhere on the island, most notably on the Isla de la Juventud. Due to the temporary closure of the Marina Tarará in the Playas del Este, at the time of research the only place to organize diving near Habana was the Marina Hemingway.

Instead of just turning up at the marina to organize some diving, it is far easier to book your diving excursion through a hotel-based tourist agency in the city. The travel agents at the Hotels Habana Libre (p167), NH Parque Central (p164), Inglaterra (p164) and Nacional (p167) are particularly helpful.

LA AGUJA MARLIN DIVING CENTER
Map pp228-9
☎ 204-5088; Marina Hemingway, cnr Av 5 & Calle 248, Barlovento; ☻ 8:30am-4:30pm
This small diving center between the Marlin port and the shopping center in Marina Hemingway offers scuba diving for CUC$30/CUC$50 for one/two immersions, plus CUC$5 for gear. It generally has one morning and one afternoon departure. Diving excursions to Varadero or Playa Girón can also be arranged; the latter has some great drop-offs. Reader reviews have been favorable.

LAND-BASED ACTIVITIES

While Habana might have scant fare for aspiring golfers, horseback riders and tennis players, the possibilities for dance lessons are limitless.

CYCLING

Back in the early 1990s, when cars were as rare as capitalists, Habana was a well-known cyclist's paradise. Indeed, at one point, there were an estimated 500,000 bikes in operation in the city.

Over the past few years, however, thanks to cheaper gas prices, and closer political and economic ties with oil-rich Venezuela, the volume of traffic on Habana's streets has increased exponentially while provisions such as bike lanes and pedestrian crossings have failed to keep apace. Although bike trips around Cuba are still popular with foreigners, tackling Habana alone on two wheels is an entirely different proposition.

If you *do* decide to take the plunge (and with a new bicycle-hire shop in in the Manzana de Gómez shopping center in Centro Habana, it's a realistic possibility), be sure to pedal carefully, wear a helmet, and avoid cycling during the morning and evening rush hours, when car fumes are particularly pungent. For a recommended cycling tour around Habana's statues, see p104.

EL ORBE Map p222

☎ 860-2617; Manzana de Gómez, Monserrate & Agramonte, Centro Habana; hire 1 hr/1 day/7 days/10 days CUC$2/12/60/75; ⏰ 9:30am-4:45pm Mon-Sat

El Orbe is the only place in the city that hires out quality bikes to foreigners. The machines are mainly Raleighs imported from Canada, with 21 gears and Shimano brakes, and on Habana's uneven streets they do a commendable and reliable job. The shop also has a supply of helmets and bike locks, as well as an on-site mechanic who'll fix up your bike for free.

DANCE LESSONS

As so many Cubans are born dancers, your chances of getting a spontaneous lesson with a local teacher are pretty good. If you're staying in a casa particular (private house that lets out rooms to foreigners), ask there. If you're not, don't fret – many hotels also offer dance instruction. For something more organized, try one of the following options. See p191 for longer courses.

MUSEO DEL RON Map p220

☎ 861-8051; San Pedro No 262, Habana Vieja; 2hr class CUC$10; ⏰ 9am Mon-Fri

The quickest and easiest way to get into a dance class in Habana is to turn up for an

---

VOICES OF HABANA: VILMA HITCHMAN MIRANDA

Sports coordinator, Diez de Octubre

Sum up Habana in one sentence. Habana is *mi amor* [my love]. **What defines a habanero?** *Habaneros* [inhabitants of Habana] are sociable people. They are also highly traditional. Family life is very important and everyone knows their neighbors. **How has Habana changed in the last 10 years?** The economic conditions were harder in the late 1990s, but things have got better. **What are future prospects for cricket in Cuba?** Here in Cuba all sport has a great future and we are working hard to develop cricket. So in the future, why not? **How do you get about the city?** I use the *camello* [metro bus] or I drive. I have a 1993 Peugeot 205. **How do you rate Habana's baseball chances this season?** For me the Industriales will triumph, but ask a person from Santiago de Cuba and you'll get a different answer. **How can the inquisitive traveler find the 'real' Cuba?** Walk around the city streets and you will see the real Cuba everywhere. **What is the best thing about your neighborhood?** The people; they are like a family. I can go anywhere without any problems. **What do people talk about on the Malecón?** The Malecón [Av de Maceo] is a place to fall in love; it is a traditional place to meet friends, usually after 10pm. The location is ideal as *habaneros* love to be close to the sea.

As related to Brendan Sainsbury

on-the-spot lesson at the Museo de Ron. The price is CUC$10 for two hours and you don't even need to bring a partner. This place gets good reports from foreigners and Cubans alike.

TEATRO AMÉRICA Map p222
☎ 862-5416; Av de Italia No 253 btwn Concordia & Neptuno, Centro Habana; 1hr class CUC$8
Housed in Centro Habana, this place can fix you up with both a class and a partner for CUC$8 per hour under the watchful eye of artistic director Jorge Samá.

GOLF

Boasting just two golf courses in the entire country, Cuba isn't a place to come for a golfing vacation. Should you get the spontaneous urge to swing a nine iron, however, you can always make your way to Habana's solitary golf course in Boyeros, or – better still – venture 140km east to the tourist haven of Varadero, where you'll find an international-standard 18-hole course.

CLUB DE GOLF LA HABANA Map p232
☎ 45-45-78; Carretera de Venta Km 8, Reparto Capdevila, Boyeros; 9/18 holes CUC$20/30; ☎ 8am-8pm
Habana's golf club lies between Vedado and the airport, but poor signposting makes it difficult to find: ask locals for directions to the *golfito* or Diplo Golf Club. Originally titled the Rover's Athletic Club, it was established by a group of British diplomats in 1948, and the clientele today is still largely made up of the diplomatic corps. There are nine holes (par 35), with 18 tees to allow 18-hole rounds. As well as green fees, there are extra fees for clubs, cart and caddie. In addition, the club has five **tennis courts** and a **bowling alley** (☎ noon-11pm) for members. Nonmembers can use the club's **swimming pool** for a small fee.

HORSEBACK RIDING

The only facilities for horseback riding in Habana are in Parque Lenin (p96), 20km south of the city center. More often than not young men will accost you with offers of horse rental as you enter the park, but there have been reports from travelers that some of these animals are poorly treated. It is

better to head to the Motel Herradura, about 2km west of the Av San Francisco entrance, and inquire there.

TENNIS

Good tennis facilities are scant in Habana. As with gyms, your best bet is to head to the top-end hotels. The Hotel Nacional (p167) in Vedado and the Occidental Miramar (p170) in Playa both have good tennis courts. There are also decent courts at Club Habana (p91) in Flores.

HEALTH & FITNESS

There's no need to let your personal exercise regime slip while you're in Habana, although you might have to shop around a bit to find the kind of tip-top gym facilities you're used to at home. Jogging along the Malecón (Av de Maceo) first thing in the morning is a rare pleasure.

GYMS

There are no fitness chains or private health clubs in Habana, although a handful of the better hotels have their own in-house gym facilities. Habana's best hotel gym is situated in the Hotel Meliá Cohiba (p168) in Vedado, and boasts weight machines, cardiovascular equipment, hot showers, a punch bag and a sauna. Nonguests can use the facilities for CUC$10. Other hotels with gyms include the Hotel Nacional (p167), the Hotel Sevilla (p164), the Hotel Meliá Habana (p170) and the Hotel Vedado (p166). All of the gyms charge similar fees.

Another excellent gym is located in Club Habana (p91), 18km to the west of the city on the road to the Marina Hemingway. With an air-conditioned weights room, fancy massage parlor, carpeted floors and state-of-the-art interior, this place is frequented mainly by government officials and foreign diplomats. Guests pay CUC$15.

JOGGING & RUNNING

Before you 'forget' to pack your running shoes, remember that Habana, with its spectacular Malecón (p86), boasts one of the world's most scenic municipal jogging routes. The sidewalk from the Castillo San Salvador de la Punta to the outer borders of Miramar measures 8km, though you can add on a few extra meters for veering around holes in the pavement, splashing waves, *jineteros* (touts) and old men with fishing lines.

Due to the dramatic upsurge in traffic in recent years, the air along the Malecón has become increasingly polluted. As a result, this run is best tackled first thing in the morning or just before sunset.

Visitors staying out in Miramar (Map pp228-9) can jog safely along Av 5, which has proper pedestrian crosswalks and a long tree-lined footpath running down the middle of the street. This is where you'll see the foreign diplomats' wives (and husbands) out training with their sun visors and iPods. Another fine running option is in Parque Lenin (p96), though sketchy transportation schedules mean this place is a little more difficult to get to.

YOGA

Yoga classes are offered intermittently in the peaceful garden of the Museo de Artes Decorativas (p86). Check the notice board outside the museum for the next session.

You may also be able to drop in on classes held at the Teatro Nacional (p88) on the Plaza de la Revolución. The class schedule is normally posted at the box office.

WATCHING SPORTS

Access to sports matches is considered a national right in Cuba, and you'll rarely pay more than a couple of convertibles to attend a game.

BASEBALL

Baseball in Cuba isn't just a sport – it's a national obsession, as visitors to the famous *esquina caliente* (literally 'hot corner') in Parque Central (p82) will testify. Habana's own exalted baseball team are the Industriales, or 'Los Azules,' as it is sometimes known. Its main rivals are the boys from Santiago de Cuba although, closer to home, it also has to contend regularly with the Metropolitanos, Habana's nominal second team (for diehards, there's no contest: the Metropolitanos are to the Industriales as the Mets are to the New York Yankees). For those with even a passing interest in the sport, a visit to a game is highly recommended. Getting under the skin of Cuban baseball is both revealing and fun.

ESTADIO LATINOAMERICANO
Map pp224-5
☎ 870-6526; Zequiera No 312, Cerro; admission 3 pesos; ☾ games 7.30pm Tue, Wed & Thu, 1.30pm Sat & Sun

From October to April (and into May if one of Habana's teams makes it into the play-offs), baseball games take place at this 58,000-seat stadium in Cerro, just south of Centro Habana. Entry costs three pesos (but staff like to charge foreigners CUC$1). The benches are cement – painful after nine innings. Unfortunately, getting here by public transportation is difficult.

BASKETBALL

Basketball is second only to baseball as a spectator sport in Habana, though the games are a little harder to find. Habana's local team, the Capitalinos, compete during the winter months.

CIUDAD DEPORTIVA Map pp218-19
☎ 54-50-00; Av de la Independencia at Vía Blanca, Cerro; admission 5 pesos

'Sport City' is Cuba's premier sports training center, and big basketball, volleyball, boxing and track contests happen at the coliseum here. The M-2 *camello* (metro bus) from Av Bolívar in Centro Habana stops across the street.

SALA POLIVALENTE RAMÓN FONST
Map pp224-5
☎ 881-4196; Av de la Independencia, Vedado; admission 1 peso

Raucous basketball and volleyball games are held at this tatty Soviet-era stadium opposite the main bus station.

BOXING

Cuba is one of the world's most formidable boxing powers and two of its world-class heavyweights – Teófilo Stevenson and Felix Savón – have each brought home three Olympic gold medals. Travelers keen to cast an eye over the current crop of young hopefuls should drop by one of the city's leading boxing clubs and check out what's on offer.

ANYONE FOR CRICKET?

Cricket first made its entry into Cuban society in the early 20th century when members of the local aristocracy teamed up with traveling diplomats from Britain and Australia for impromptu games in Habana. The sport got a further impetus in the 1920s when immigrants from the cricket-playing countries of Jamaica and Barbados arrived to work on the island's booming sugar plantations and formed their own teams. Before long, players were competing in prestigious local tournaments such as the annual cricket festival in Baraguá, held on Slave Emancipation Day every August 1. In 1952, Cuba even staged its first international against an all-star team from Jamaica.

But, in the 1960s and '70s, under the leadership of one-time baseball-player Fidel Castro, Cuban cricket almost died out. The revival came in 1998 after Leona Ford, the daughter of a cricket-playing Barbadian immigrant, proposed a six-week cricket-coaching course with representatives from the Caribbean nation of Trinidad and Tobago. Interest quickly spread and, within a couple of years, cricket had gained the support of the Cuban government which, since the collapse of the Soviet Union in 1991, has been determined to re-emphasize the country's intrinsic Caribbean heritage against the all-pervading American influence of baseball.

Today there are almost 4000 practicing cricket players in Cuba spread across nine different provinces, as well as a factory in Pinar del Río province that manufactures very basic cricket bats and stumps. Furthermore, after Cuba's acceptance as an affiliate member of the International Cricket Council (ICC) in 2002, the island was invited to form its own national team, which competed for the first time in February 2007 against guest teams from England, Jamaica and India.

Since this is Cuba, you can even don a pair of gloves yourself and train alongside some of the champions of tomorrow.

GIMNASIO DE BOXEO RAFAEL TREJO

Map p220

☎ 862-0266; Cuba No 815 btwn Merced & Leonor Pérez, Habana Vieja; ⏱ training from 4pm, matches 7pm Fri

The Trejo is a small and intimate boxing-club-cum-arena in the heart of Habana Vieja's less touristy southern quarter. Here you can see matches (CUC$1) or drop by to watch training. Travelers (including women) interested in boxing can find a trainer here.

KID CHOCOLATE Map p222

☎ 861-1546; Paseo de Martí, Centro Habana; ⏱ matches 7pm Fri

Named after Eligio 'Kid Chocolate' Sardiñas, Cuba's first professional world boxing champion, this large sports complex directly opposite the Capitolio usually hosts matches on Fridays at 7pm; admission is approximately CUC$0.50.

SOCCER

Soccer (football) is a fringe sport in baseball-mad Cuba and doesn't inspire anywhere near the devotion that can be seen in most other Latin American countries. That said, you'll probably see plenty of kids chasing a ball around in the dilapidated parks and squares of urban Habana. Visitors up for a spontaneous kick about will always be welcomed enthusiastically into the fray.

Cuba's interest in soccer was reignited briefly by the arrival of former Argentine soccer icon Diego Maradona on the island in 2000 to receive treatment for a life-threatening heart condition caused by years of drug addiction. The soccer star became personal friends with Fidel Castro and had a tattoo of the Cuban leader's face inked reverently onto his left shin.

Cuba has only qualified for the soccer World Cup finals once, way back in 1938, when the country reached the quarter finals of the competition before losing 8-0 to Sweden.

ESTADIO PEDRO MARRERO

Map pp228-9

Av 41 No 4409 btwn Calles 44 & 50, Miramar

Built in 1929 and capable of holding 28,000 spectators, the Pedro Marrero stadium is Cuba's soccer temple. Head here to see both interprovincial and international games, with Cuba taking on such regional soccer giants as Costa Rica and the USA in the Concacaf Gold Cup (played in odd-numbered years). Games are usually played at the weekends, starting at 3pm. Admission to the games is approximately CUC$0.50.

Shopping

Shopping

If shopping is one of your favorite vacation pastimes, don't make a special trip to Habana. To the relief of many and the disappointment of a few, Western-style consumerism hasn't yet reached the time-warp streets of Cuba's austere capital. That's not to say you have to walk away empty-handed. Cuba's tourist industry has upped the ante considerably in recent years and specialist shops are spreading fast.

The holy grail for most foreign souvenir hunters is a box of Cuban cigars, closely followed by a bottle of Cuban rum, both of which are significantly cheaper than in stores overseas. Another often overlooked bargain is a bag of Cuban coffee, a potent and aromatic brew made from organically grown beans and best served espresso style with a dash of sugar.

Elsewhere memorabilia is thin on the ground. Aimed strictly at the tourist market, there are cheap dolls, flimsy trinkets, mediocre wood carvings and low-quality leather goods, but Cuba is a world leader in none of these things. Far better as long-lasting souvenirs are salsa CDs, arty movie posters, musical instruments or strings of Santería beads.

In the realm of books you'll find plenty of erudite exposés of Che, Fidel and José Martí in a number of different languages plus a plethora of glossy coffee-table books. Look out in particular for cheap books at the famous secondhand book market (p152) in Plaza de Armas.

Painting is another of Cuba's fortes, and local artists are both numerous and talented. If you buy an original painting, print or sculpture, be sure to ask for a receipt to prove you bought it at an official sales outlet; otherwise, it could be confiscated by customs upon departure (see Exporting Artwork, below).

In a country where clothes were – until recently – rationed, and lycra is still considered to be the height of cool, finding the latest pair of Tommy Hilfiger jeans could prove a little difficult. Incurable fashion junkies can spend their convertibles on *guayaberas* (pleated, buttoned men's shirts) or a yawningly predictable Che Guevara T-shirt. Take your pick.

Opening Hours

Cuba is different to other Latin American countries in that there is no afternoon siesta; however, some stores do close for lunch. In general, opening times are 9am to 5pm Monday to Saturday, with some of the more tourist-orientated stores opening on Sunday from 9am to noon.

Consumer Taxes

Most stores list their prices with the tax included. The price you see displayed is thus the price you pay at the till.

Bargaining

Although bargaining is almost nonexistent in shops in Habana, you can try out your haggling skills at open-air markets that sell souvenirs to tourists. If it's your first time in the city, don't expect Moroccan-style deals and discounts; after nearly 50 years of state-sponsored socialism, bartering isn't really part of Cuban culture.

EXPORTING ARTWORK

When buying art at an official outlet, always ask for a receipt to show Cuban customs, especially if the object won't fit in your suitcase.

To discourage private trading of works of art, officials often confiscate undocumented artwork at the airport. If you've purchased a work of art at a state-run gallery and have the receipts, you shouldn't have a problem, but it's always better to have a certificate to export artwork anyway (and you'll definitely need one if you've purchased directly from the artist).

Certificates to export artwork are issued by the **Registro Nacional de Bienes Culturales** (Map pp224-5; Calle 17 No 1009 btwn Calles 10 & 12, Vedado; ⏰ 9am-noon Mon-Fri). To obtain an export certificate, you must bring the objects here for inspection, fill in a form, queue for two hours, pay a fee of between CUC$10 and CUC$30 (which covers from one to five pieces of artwork), and return 24 hours later to pick up the certificate.

It makes sense not to leave this bit of business until your last day.

HABANA VIEJA

Habana Vieja is as good as it gets shopping-wise in Cuba, with plenty of stores and galleries aimed directly at the tourist market.

CASA DEL ABANICO

Map p220   Handicrafts

☎ 863-4452; Obrapía No 107 btwn Mercaderes & Oficios; ⏰ 9am-5pm Mon-Fri, 9am-noon Sat
The Abanico is a small specialist store that sells fine-quality hand-painted fans. It is primarily aimed at the tourist market.

ESTUDIO GALERÍA LOS OFICIOS

Map p220   Art

☎ 863-0497; Oficios No 166; ⏰ 10am-5:30pm Mon-Sat
Situated next door to the Galería de Carmen Montilla, this gallery is worth seeing for the large, hectic but intriguing canvases by Nelson Domínguez, whose workshop is upstairs.

FERIA DE LA ARTESANÍA

Map p220   Handicrafts

Tacón btwn Tejadillo & Chacón; ⏰ Wed-Sat
Habana's best open-air handicraft market is on Calle Tacón, and sells all kinds of interesting souvenirs. Paintings, *guayaberas*, woodwork, Che everything, leather items and jewelry are all on display and, if you thought communism had put an end to the fine art of business negotiation, try your haggling skills with the amiable stall holders here. If you buy paintings, make sure you arrange an export license (it's easy – see Exporting Artwork, opposite), or you risk losing your loot at customs upon leaving Cuba; if they're deemed 'national treasures' they'll be confiscated. Smaller artworks can be tucked safely in luggage.

GALERÍA DE CARMEN MONTILLA

Map p220   Art

☎ 866-8768; Oficios No 162; ⏰ 9:30am-5pm Mon-Sat
This important art gallery is named for Carmen Montilla, a celebrated Venezuelan painter who maintained a studio here until her death in 2004. Spread across three floors, the house exhibits the work of Montilla, plus paintings by other popular Cuban and Venezuelan artists. The rear courtyard features a huge ceramic mural by Alfredo Sosabravo – it's worth a peep.

TOP 10 SOUVENIRS

- Bottle of rum
- Box of cigars
- Movie poster
- Musical instrument
- CD of Cuban music
- *Guayabera* (pleated, buttoned men's shirt)
- Handicraft
- Painting or print
- Secondhand book
- Humidor

GALERÍA MANOS Map p220   Handicrafts

Obispo No 411 btwn Aguacate & Compostela; ⏰ 10am-6pm Mon-Fri, 10am-5pm Sat
This gallery is effectively a small craft outlet, with dolls, masks and other handmade souvenirs supplied by local people. Many of the objects are inspired by the city's vibrant Afro-Cuban community.

GALERÍA VICTOR MANUEL

Map p220   Antiques, Art

Plaza de la Catedral; ⏰ 9am-9pm
Taking pride of place in Plaza de la Catedral, this expensive gallery is about as high-end as Habana shopping gets. Displayed in a beautiful baroque building you'll find wonderful humidors, captivating paintings, Tiffany-style glass lamps, fantastic wooden figurines and lots of fine silver jewelry.

HABANA 1791 Map p220   Perfume

☎ 861-3525; Mercaderes No 156; ⏰ 9:30am-6pm
A specialist shop that sells perfume made from tropical flowers, Habana 1791 has the air of a working museum. Floral fragrances are mixed by hand and you can see the petals drying in a laboratory out the back.

LA CASA DEL HABANO

Map p220   Cigars

☎ 862-9293; Hostal Conde de Villanueva, Mercaderes No 202; ⏰ 9am-6pm
Cigar aficionados flock to this smoky cigar shop situated inside the beautiful Hostal Conde de Villanueva, popularly considered to be the expert's choice. Dodge the rogue cigar sellers on Calle Obispo, and come and join them.

LA CASONA CENTRO DE ARTE

Map p220   Art

☎ 861-8544; Muralla No 107; ☺ 10am-5pm
Mon-Fri, 10am-2pm Sat

This state-owned foundation on Plaza Vieja
is located in the baroque **Casa de los Condes de
Jaruco** (p69) and sells some fantastic original
handicrafts and works of art (with receipts
that should allow their export). It also hosts
great solo and group shows by up-and-
coming Cuban artists.

LA MODERNA POESIA

Map p220   Books, Music

☎ 861-6640; Obispo No 527; ☺ 10am-6pm
Mon-Sat

One of Habana Vieja's most comprehensive
bookstores, La Modern Poesia also sells CDs
and posters. The store, which fills a bulky
art deco building, also has a considerable
English-language section.

LONGINA MÚSICA

Map p220   Instruments, Music

☎ 862-8371; Obispo No 362; ☺ 10am-7pm Mon-
Sat, 10am-1pm Sun

One of Habana Vieja's top-quality music
shops, this place has a good selection of CDs,
plus musical instruments such as bongos,
guitars, maracas, guiros and congas. It often
places music speakers in the street outside to
grab the attention of passing tourists.

MARCO POLO Map p220   Spices

Mercaderes No 111 btwn Obispo & Obrapía;
☺ 9am-7:30pm

This is a popular spice and herb store that
is always busy with both foreigners and
locals. Run by Habaguanex, its large range
of varied products can be used for both
gastronomic and medicinal purposes.

MERCADO DEL ORIENTE

Map p220   Souvenirs

☎ Mercaderes No 109 btwn Obispo & Obrapía;
☺ 9am-6pm

Calle Mercaderes (Merchant St) is chocka-
block with eclectic shops such as this one.
Revamped by the City Historian's Office a
few years back, the Mercado del Oriente
has a Far Eastern theme – the **Casa de Asia**
(p69) is next door – and sells furniture,
textiles, porcelain, glass and silver objects
from places such as China.

PALACIO DE LA ARTESANÍA

Map p220   Shopping Mall

Cuba No 64; ☺ 9am-7pm

For one-stop shopping for souvenirs, cigars,
crafts, CDs, clothing and jewelry at fixed
prices, join the gaggle of tour-bus escapees
here. This building is the former Palacio de
Pedroso, erected by Habana mayor Mateo
Pedroso in 1780; in the mid-19th century it
was Habana's high court, and later it became a police headquarters. Today's small
stores are gathered around a beautifully
shaded central patio replete with verdant
plants; it's something akin to an 18th-
century version of an American shopping
mall, but with oodles of charm.

PUBLICACIONES DE LA OFICINA
DEL HISTORIADOR Map p220   Books

Mercaderes No 111 btwn Obispo & Obrapía;
☺ 9am-6pm Mon-Fri, 9am-1pm Sat

The definitive word on Habana Vieja's colonial history can be uncovered here in large,
photo-friendly coffee-table books that
showcase the development and restoration
of Old Habana. The small store sells mainly
books, postcards and back copies of the
cultural magazine *Opus* (which prints part
of its text in English).

SECONDHAND BOOK MARKET

Map p220   Books

Plaza de Armas; ☺ 9am-5pm Mon-Sat

This is a popular book market held in Habana's oldest square. Amid the Che polemics
and the ubiquitous translations of Castro's
'History Will Absolve Me' speech, you can
find a few literary gems.

TALLER DE SERIGRAFÍA RENÉ
PORTOCARRERO Map p220   Art

Cuba No 513 btwn Brasil & Muralla; ☺ 9am-4pm
Mon-Fri

The Taller de Serigrafía René Portocarrero
has paintings and prints by young Cuban
artists in the CUC$30 to CUC$150 range.
You can see the artists at work here.

TALLER EXPERIMENTAL DE GRÁFICA

Map p220   Art

☎ 862-0979; Callejón del Chorro No 6;
☺ 10am-4pm Mon-Fri

Habana's funkiest art gallery sells engrav-
ings and prints (CUC$15 to CUC$800) that

you can see being made on the premises. Edgy and experimental, the painters here offer darker, bolder and more provocative work than found elsewhere in the city.

CENTRO HABANA

Centro Habana is a great place to get acquainted with how the Cubans go shopping – you might even find the odd hidden bargain yourself.

AREA DE VENDEDORES POR CUENTA PROPIA Map p222   Market

Máximo Gómez No 259; ☽ 9am-5pm Mon-Sat, 9am-1pm Sun

The Area de Vendedores por Cuenta Propia is a permanent flea market just beyond the Parque de Fraternidad that is Cuban to the core. Hidden in a hive of buyers and sellers are Santería beads, books, leather belts…the list goes on. Nothing is expensive.

GALERÍA LA ACACIA

Map p222   Antiques, Art

☎ 861-3533; San Martín No 114 btwn Industria & Consulado; ☽ 10am-3:30pm Mon-Fri, 10am-noon Sat

This important gallery has paintings by leading artists such as Zaida del Rio, plus antiques. Export permits are arranged.

LA MANZANA DE GÓMEZ

Map p222   Shopping Mall

cnr Agramonte & San Rafael

An elegant European-style covered mall built in 1910 and named after then Cuban president José Miguel Gómez, the Manzana is a long way from the resplendent shopping extravaganza of yore. Nonetheless, this huge chunk of mildewed neoclassical real estate is both central and convenient – and hence normally very busy. Hidden away inside the murky and rather cavernous interior you'll find shoe stores, clothing boutiques, an art gallery, a shabby restaurant and El Orbe (p145) bike rentals.

VARIADADES GALIANO

Map p222   Clothing, Accessories

cnr San Rafael & Av de Italia; ☽ 10am-6pm Mon-Sat, 9am-1pm Sun

The main shopping streets for Cubans are San Rafael and Av de Italia (Galiano). At the

CLOTHING SIZES

Measurements approximate only, try before you buy

Women's Clothing					
Aus/UK	8	10	12	14	16	18
Europe	36	38	40	42	44	46
Japan	5	7	9	11	13	15
USA	6	8	10	12	14	16
Women's Shoes					
Aus/USA	5	6	7	8	9	10
Europe	35	36	37	38	39	40
France only	35	36	38	39	40	42
Japan	22	23	24	25	26	27
UK	3½	4½	5½	6½	7½	8½
Men's Clothing					
Aus	92	96	100	104	108	112
Europe	46	48	50	52	54	56
Japan	S		M	M		L
UK/USA	35	36	37	38	39	40
Men's Shirts (Collar Sizes)					
Aus/Japan	38	39	40	41	42	43
Europe	38	39	40	41	42	43
UK/USA	15	15½	16	16½	17	17½
Men's Shoes					
Aus/UK	7	8	9	10	11	12
Europe	41	42	43	44½	46	47
Japan	26	27	27½	28	29	30
USA	7½	8½	9½	10½	11½	12½

point where the thoroughfares meet stands Variadades Galiano, the Bloomingdales of Cuban department stores (and a former Woolworths), which sells everything from mesh tank tops to old records. With its strangely evocative interior that mixes aspiring 1950s New York with dingy 1970s Moscow, this place offers an authentic glimpse into how Cubans go shopping.

VEDADO

Vedado is home to two of Habana's best shopping malls and a couple of decent art galleries.

GALERÍAS DE PASEO

Map pp224-5   Shopping Mall

Calle 1 & Paseo; ☽ 9am-6pm Mon-Sat, 9am-1pm Sun

Galerías de Paseo is a surprisingly upscale shopping center, with even a car dealership. It sells Adidas and Chanel clothes, and other consumer items to tourists and affluent Cubans. There's a **Bim Bom** (p118) ice-cream parlor here too.

LA HABANA SÍ Map pp224-5 — Music
cnr Calles L & 23; ⊙ 10am-10pm Mon-Sat, 10am-7pm Sun

With an enviable location on Habana's busiest traffic intersection, La Habana Sí is a classic music store run by government arts agency Artex. Stacked up inside is a good selection of CDs, books, postcards, crafts, videos and DVDs (of mainly Cuban movies). It's an excellent stop for Cuban-music addicts.

LIBRERÍA ALMA MATER
Map pp224-5 — Books
☎ 870-2060; cnr San Lázaro & Calle L; ⊙ 9am-9pm Mon-Fri, 9am-7pm Sat

The Librería Alma Mater contains one of the largest offerings of books in Spanish and English in Cuba.

PLAZA CARLOS III
Map pp224-5 — Shopping Mall
Av Salvador Allende btwn Arbol Seco & Retiro; ⊙ 10am-6pm Mon-Sat

After Plaza de las Américas in Varadero, this is probably Cuba's flashiest shopping mall – and there's barely a foreigner in sight. Dresses, radios and bicycles – they're all on sale here. Step in to see the double economy working at a feverish pitch.

SERVANDO GALERÍA DEL ARTE
Map pp224-5 — Art
cnr Calles 23 & 10; ⊙ 9am-6pm Tue-Sat

This cool gallery next to the Cine Charles Chaplín and opposite the Centro Cultural Cinematográfico is in an arty part of town and displays some interesting modern paintings and prints.

STUDIO OF SALVADOR GONZÁLEZ ESCALONA Map pp224-5 — Art
Callejón de Hamel No 1054; ⊙ 10am-6pm

Since 1990 a local painter named Salvador González Escalona has converted Callejón de Hamel into an open-air art center with vivid murals and funky street sculpture. Salvador has a studio at No 1054, where his paintings may be viewed (and purchased), and the studio organizes free cultural activities in the street outside.

PLAYA & MARIANAO

Playa and Marianao boast a couple of music outlets, a leading cigar store and Habana's only true 'boutique.'

CASA DE LA MÚSICA MIRAMAR
Map pp228-9 — Music
☎ 204-0447; cnr Av 35 & Calle 20; ⊙ 10am-10pm

An outlet of Egrem, Cuba's national music recording and publishing company, at

THE CUBAN CIGAR

Groucho Marx, Che Guevara, George Burns, Arnold Schwarzenegger...you don't need to be a subscriber to *Cigar Aficionado* magazine to understand the popularity of the aromatic Cuban cigar. Sigmund Freud allegedly puffed his way through a box a day, Winston Churchill had a size named in his honor, while John F Kennedy reportedly told his press secretary Pierre Salinger to order in a thousand of his favorite Petit Upmanns the night before signing into law the US trade embargo on Cuba.

The unsurpassed quality of Cuban cigars stems from an accidental combination of geography, terrain and skill. Tobacco is grown primarily in the rust red fields of Pinar del Río province in the island's verdant west, and all genuine Cuban cigars are hand rolled by trained 'experts' before being packed in tightly sealed cedar boxes and classified into 42 different types and sizes.

Cuba's flagship brand is Cohiba, created in 1966 for diplomatic use and popularized by Fidel Castro, who used to puff on Cohiba Espléndidos before he gave up smoking for health reasons in 1985. Other international favorites include the Partagás brand, rolled in Habana since 1845; the superstrong Bolívar, named after South America's formidable liberator; the classic Montecristo No 2, another *fuerte* (strong) smoke much admired by Cubans; and the milder Romeo y Julieta brand, invented in 1903 by a Cuban who had traveled widely in Europe.

In terms of purchasing, always avoid buying cigars on the street. These substandard smokes are nearly always of dubious quality, with air pockets and hard wrappings containing protuberances; indeed, some are outright fakes. Good places to wise up on cigars include the Casa del Habano in the Hostal Conde de Villanueva (p151) in Habana Vieja, the Real Fábrica de Tabacos Partagás (p83) in Centro Habana, and the Casa del Habano (opposite) in Miramar. You can only export 23 single cigars duty free.

Miramar's **Casa de la Música** (p137), this place has an excellent selection of CDs.

EGREM TIENDA DE MÚSICA

Map pp228-9   Instruments, Music

☎ 202-7922; Calle 18 No 103; ☽ 9am-6pm Mon-Sat

Of the various Egrem stores spread across the capital, this is one of the best. It specializes in CDs, musical instruments and accessories.

LA CASA DEL HABANO

Map pp228-9   Cigars

☎ 206 9509; cnr Av 5 & Calle 16; ☽ 10am-6pm Mon-Sat, 10am-1pm Sun

Along with the **Casa del Habano** (p151) located in the Hostal Conde de Villanueva in Habana Vieja, this is, arguably, the city's best cigar shop. Features include an upscale cigar salesroom, a smoking room where you can purchase individual cigars, and a celebrated bar-restaurant, **La Casa de Quinta y 16** (p125).

LA MAISON

Map pp228-9   Clothing, Accessories

☎ 204-1541; Calle 16 No 701; ☽ 9am-5pm

Housed in an eclectic Miramar mansion with an Italian Renaissance–style garden, La Maison is Habana's center of haute couture, with a large boutique selling designer clothing, shoes, handbags, jewelry, cosmetics and souvenirs. Models strut the catwalk here in outlandish costumes at a nightly fashion show that includes **dinner** (p125) and a **music performance** (p138).

Sleeping

Sleeping

Habana offers foreign visitors two distinctly different accommodation options. Firstly there are government-run hotels, which vary in standard and price from the basic to the resplendent. Secondly there are privately operated casas particulares (p160), family homes where the owners are permitted to let out up to two rooms a night to foreigners. Casa prices in Habana start at around CUC$20 a night and rarely exceed CUC$35.

Compared to other Latin American cities, Habana suffers from a dearth of good budget hotels, though in most cases the similarly priced casas provide a perfectly adequate substitute. At the opposite end of the scale, the city has some truly amazing colonial hotels, most of them housed in meticulously restored historic buildings in Habana Vieja and run by the government agency Habaguanex.

The best city hotel base is undoubtedly Habana Vieja, where the bulk of the cafés, bars, museums and tourist sights are located. Another excellent option is the adjacent district of Centro Habana. Vedado has its own sights and nightlife, but these are rather spread out and detached from the historical core, while Playa and Marianao are well over 8km from the main action.

PRICE GUIDE

The price symbols in this chapter indicate the price for a double room in the low season.

$$$	over CUC$130 a night
$$	CUC$60-130 a night
$	under CUC$60 a night

HABANA VIEJA

Habana Vieja's specialty is restored period hotels and staying in one of these magnificent establishments can be a memorable, if expensive, treat.

There are, however, a few considerations worth taking into account before booking a room in this area. Firstly Habana Vieja is a highly condensed urban neighborhood that squeezes over 70,000 people into an area of just 4.5 sq km. While parts of the quarter might resemble a living museum, noise, grime and dilapidated tenements are all part of the neighborhood's colorful package. Don't expect desertlike tranquility and don't be surprised if the local salsa band carries on playing until well after midnight.

Secondly this is Cuba, a country that is emerging tentatively from a lengthy and austere *período especial* (special period), and goods are rationed and shortages are still a part of everyday life. However plush your fancy colonial hotel might appear on the outside, you can pretty much assume that it's unlikely to have the water pressure of Cancún or the food quality of New York. What it *will* have, though, is bags of atmosphere and a tangible sense of living history.

RESIDENCIA ACADÉMICA CONVENTO DE SANTA CLARA

Map p220   Hostel $

☎ 866-9327; Cuba btwn Sol & Luz; r per person CUC$25

An unbelievable bargain situated right in the heart of Habana Vieja, this unique place offering just nine rooms in a former convent (p73) fills up quickly. Renowned among backpackers as an alternative casa particular, the quirky and central old-town building is both spacious and safe, and retains bags of original atmosphere. Some of the rooms are dorm style, holding up to six beds.

MESÓN DE LA FLOTA

Map p220   Period Hotel $

Habaguanex; ☎ 863-3838; Mercaderes No 257 btwn Amargura & Brasil; s/d CUC$45/65; 🖳

Habana Vieja's smallest and most reasonably priced period hotel is an old Spanish tavern decked out in maritime motifs and located within spitting distance of gracious Plaza Vieja. Five individually crafted rooms contain all of the modern comforts and amenities, while downstairs a busy restaurant (p114) serves up delicious tapas and scrumptiously prepared *platos principales* (main dishes). For music lovers the real draw card, however, is the nightly **flamenco** (p131), the quality of which could rival anything in Andalucía. Sit back and soak up the intangible spirit of the dance.

HOSTAL BELTRÁN DE LA SANTA CRUZ Map p220   Period Hotel $$

Habaguanex; ☎ 860-8330; San Ignacio No 411 btwn Muralla & Sol; s/d low season CUC$70/110, high season CUC$80/130; 🔀 🖳
Excellent location, friendly staff and plenty of old-world authenticity make this compact inn a winning option. Housed in an 18th-century building and offering just 11 spacious rooms, this place is highly intimate, and its service has been lauded by both travelers and reviewers.

HOSTAL DEL TEJADILLO

Map p220   Period Hotel $$

Habaguanex; ☎ 863-7283; Tejadillo No 12; s/d low season CUC$70/110, high season CUC$80/130; 🔀 🖳
You can't get much closer to luscious Plaza de Catedral than the Tejadillo. Restored in 2000, this hotel-cum-inn situated in an old colonial house just one block north of Habana's most atmospheric square is a great base from which to explore the secret nooks and crannies of dreamy Habana Vieja. It's slightly cheaper than its Habaguanex competitors, and 17 of the 32 rooms have kitchenettes, though some rooms facing away from the street are windowless. However, nothing can take away from the peaceful ambience of the hotel's two inner patios and fantastic location.

HOSTAL VALENCIA

Map p220   Period Hotel $$

Habaguanex; ☎ 867-1037; Oficios No 53; s/d low season CUC$70/110, high season CUC$80/130; 🖳
The Valencia resembles a 17th-century Spanish coach house with its hanging

---

BOOK ACCOMMODATION ONLINE

For more accommodation reviews and recommendations by Lonely Planet authors, check out the online booking service at www.lonelyplanet.com. You'll find the true, insider lowdown on the best places to stay. Reviews are thorough and independent. Best of all, you can book online.

TOP FIVE SLEEPS

- Hostal Conde de Villanueva (below)
- Hotel Raquel (p161)
- Hotel Sevilla (p164)
- Hotel Nacional (p167)
- Hotel Meliá Habana (p170)

---

vines, huge doorways (and rooms) and a renowned **paella restaurant** (p115); one half expects Don Quixote and Sancho Panza to come wandering down the staircase. Slap bang in the middle of the historical core and with a price that makes it one of the cheaper offerings in the current Habaguanex stable, the Valencia is an excellent choice, with good service and plenty of atmosphere. Next door is the similarly historic **Hotel El Comendador** (Habaguanex; ☎ 867-1037; Obrapía No 55; s/d low season CUC$70/110, high season CUC$80/130).

HOTEL LOS FRAILES

Map p220   Period Hotel $$

Habaguanex; ☎ 862-9383; Brasil No 8 btwn Oficios & Mercaderes; s/d low season CUC$70/110, high season CUC$80/130; 🔀 🖳
This engaging 22-room hotel just off Plaza Vieja sports a tranquil inner courtyard where staff bustle to and fro dressed as monks. Stained-glass windows and rough-hewn furniture add an extra monastic feel. Upstairs, away from the solemnity, comfortable rooms are distinguished by good art, tasteful furniture and bright modern fittings; the four rooms with balconies are the best. An added perk is the resident woodwind quartet in the lobby; the musicians are so good that they regularly lure in bevies of passing tour groups for impromptu concerts.

HOSTAL CONDE DE VILLANUEVA

Map p220   Period Hotel $$

Habaguanex; ☎ 862-9293; Mercaderes No 202; s/d low season CUC$80/130, high season CUC$95/160; 🔀 🖳
If you're going to splash out on one night of luxury in Habana, you'd do well to check out this highly lauded colonial gem. Restored under the watchful eye of city historian Eusebio Leal a few years back, the Hostal Conde de Villanueva has converted a grandiose city mansion into an intimate

CASAS PARTICULARES

Want to get the local take on baseball? Need some help with your faltering Spanish? Dying to fathom out the subtleties of Habana's effervescent nightlife? It's simple: look no further than your trusty casa particular, Cuba's unique variation on the family-run guesthouse and the best – some would say the *only* – way of getting underneath the skin of this complex yet seductive city.

Legalized in 1996 as part of the economic reforms ushered in by the *período especial* (special period), casas particulares are private houses that let out rooms to foreigners at refreshingly affordable rates. In order to qualify, casa owners must first pay a set monthly tax to the Cuban government and conform to a certain set of rules and regulations (only two rooms are allowed per house and only two adults are allowed per room).

Thanks to regular inspections by government officials, legal casas particulares are – almost without exception – clean, homely and remarkably well run. Other advantages are their prices (rarely more than CUC$35 a night), their ubiquity (there are literally thousands in Habana alone) and the fact that, by staying in one, you are putting money directly into the pockets of hard-working and often hard-up Cubans.

Not surprisingly, casas come in all shapes and sizes, from resplendent colonial villas to modest downtown apartments with shared bathrooms. Sometimes you'll have to step over the family dog to get to your bedroom, while at others you'll enjoy your own private entrance and a room full of antique furniture.

If you're stumped for choice, it's easy to shop around for a casa in Habana by looking for the small blue-and-white sign that all legal houses display on their front door. Alternatively you can try prebooking using www.cubacasas.net or www.casaparticular.org.

See opposite for casas particulares in Habana Vieja, p163 for casas in Centro Habana, p166 for casas in Vedado, and p169 for casas in Playa and Marianao.

and thoughtfully decorated hotel, with nine bedrooms spread spaciously around an attractive inner courtyard (complete with resident peacock). Opening onto the cobbled streets below, the upstairs rooms contain stained-glass windows, chandeliers, arty sculptures, huge bathrooms and – best of all – a fully working whirlpool bath. After a few weeks in the Cuban outback, it could be just what the doctor ordered.

HOSTAL PALACIO O'FARRILL

Map p220   Period Hotel $$

Habaguanex; ☎ 860-5080; Cuba No 102-108 btwn Chacón & Tejadillo; s/d low season CUC$80/130, high season CUC$95/160; 😶 ▢

One of Habaguanex' – and Habana's – most impressive hotels, the Palacio O'Farrill is a staggeringly beautiful neoclassical palace that once belonged to Don Ricardo O'Farrill, a Cuban sugar entrepreneur who was descended from a family of Irish nobility. Taking the verdant Emerald Isle as its theme, much of the interior decor has been painted green, giving the plant-filled courtyard and reception areas a soothingly shady feel. Rooms are large, with satellite TV and air-con, and – if not quite in the luxury bracket – are furnished in an authentic Spanish colonial style. The hotel's communal areas are equally attractive, with a patio, a fountain, antique furnishings

and a well-positioned terrace; there's even 24-hour internet and up-to-date business facilities.

HOSTAL SAN MIGUEL

Map p220   Period Hotel $$

Habaguanex; ☎ 862-7656; cnr Cuba & Peña Pobre; s/d low season CUC$80/130, high season CUC$95/160; 😶 ▢

Located close to the harbor with tremendous views out across the water to Fortaleza de San Carlos de la Cabaña, the elegant San Miguel was once owned by Cuban newspaper magnate Antonio San Miguel y Segalá, whose periodical *La Lucha* played an important role in the 1895 War of Independence. Characterized by high ceilings, Carrera marble floors and a plethora of faded prerevolution photos, the San Miguel's 10 individually decorated rooms retain a rather fetching old-world feel that blends in perfectly with the building's neoclassical belle epoque decor. A very pleasant old-town retreat.

HOTEL AMBOS MUNDOS

Map p220   Hotel $$

Habaguanex; ☎ 860-9529; Obispo No 153; s/d low season CUC$80/130, high season CUC$95/160; 😶 ▢

Hemingway's Habana hideout and the place where he is said to have penned his guerrilla classic *For Whom the Bell Tolls* (Castro's bedtime reading during the war in the mountains), the pastel pink **Ambos Mundos** (p71) is a Habana institution and a obligatory stop for anyone on a tour of 'Hemingway-once-fell-over-here' bars. Small, sometimes windowless, rooms suggest overpricing, but the lobby bar is classic enough (follow the sound of the romantic piano melody) and a drink on the rooftop terrace is one of the city's finest treats.

HOTEL ARMADORES DE SANTANDER
Map p220   Period Hotel $$
Habaguanex; ☎ 862-8080; San Pedro No 4; s/d low season CUC$80/130, high season CUC$95/160; ⚅ ▯
This charming maritime-themed hotel situated next to Habana's famous port once housed the offices of a Spanish shipbuilding company (the name means 'Ship Owners from Santander'). The initials JC carved above the door pay homage to the building's original proprietor, José Cabrero Mier, who oversaw fleets of ships that transported goods and troops between Habana and Spain. The modern-day hotel has been renovated with plenty of architectural flourishes (check out the ornate ceiling in the lobby), and a number of the 39 rooms are split-level with an interconnecting spiral staircase. Other bonuses include a terrace bar, harbor-facing balconies and an

atmospheric lobby furnished with a clutch of old-fashioned leather couches. The location by the docks isn't Habana's prettiest, but it doesn't lack authenticity.

HOTEL FLORIDA Map p220   Period Hotel $$
Habaguanex; ☎ 862-4127; Obispo No 252; s/d low season CUC$80/130, high season CUC$95/160; ⚅ ▯
They don't make them like this anymore. Built in 1836, the Florida is an architectural extravaganza built in the purest colonial style, with arches and pillars clustered around a central courtyard loaded with atmosphere. Habaguanex has restored the building with loving attention to detail, and the amply furnished rooms have retained their original high ceilings and wonderfully luxurious finishes. Complemented by an elegant café and an amiable **bar-nightspot** (⚇ from 8pm), this colonial jewel should be checked out by anyone with even a passing interest in Cuba's architectural heritage.

HOTEL RAQUEL
Map p220   Period Hotel $$$
Habaguanex; ☎ 860-8280; cnr Amargura & San Ignacio; s/d low season CUC$105/180, high season CUC$115/200; ⚅ ▯
Encased in a dazzling 1908 palace (that was once a bank), the painstakingly restored Hotel Raquel takes your breath away with

HABANA VIEJA CASAS PARTICULARES

Noemi Moreno (Map p220; ☎ 862-3809; Apt 2, Cuba No 611 btwn Luz & Santa Clara; r CUC$25) A simple, clean room in great location behind convent; there are also rooms in Apartment 1.

Ramón & Maritza (Map p220; ☎ 862-3303; Luz No 115 btwn San Ignacio & Inquisidor; r CUC$25) Two big interconnecting rooms in colonial house; friendly owners.

Migdalia Carraballe (Map p220; ☎ /fax 861-7352; Santa Clara No 164 btwn Cuba & San Ignacio; r CUC$25-35) Two rooms with balconies overlooking the Iglesia y Convento de Santa Clara.

Casa de Pepe & Rafaela (Map p220; ☎ 862-9877; San Ignacio No 454 btwn Sol & Santa Clara; r CUC$30) One of Habana's best casas particulares – there are antiques and Moorish tiles throughout, three rooms with balconies and gorgeous new bathrooms, and an excellent location. The owners' son also rents rooms in a charming colonial house at San Ignacio No 656 (r CUC$25).

Eliberto Barrios Suárez (Map p220; ☎ 863-3782; eliberto62@webcorreosdecuba.cu; Apt 3A, San Juan Díos No 112 btwn Aguacate & Compostela; apt US$30) A nice two-bedroom duplex apartment with kitchen.

Pablo Rodríguez (Map p220; ☎ 861-2111; pablo@sercomar.telemar.cu; Compostela No 532 btwn Brasil & Muralla; r CUC$30) An old colonial house with original frescoes. Pablo rents two rooms with bathroom, fan and fridge.

Juan & Margarita (Map p220; ☎ 867-9592; Apt 8, Obispo No 522 btwn Bernaza & Villegas; apt CUC$60) A super-central two-bedroom apartment with flexible and friendly hosts. Juan speaks excellent English and has a lot of local knowledge.

its grandiose columns, sleek marble statues and intricate stained-glass ceiling. Replete with intricate art nouveau flourishes, the reception area in this marvelous eclectic building is a tourist sight in its own right. Architecture aside, the rooms here are well presented, if a little noisy, and the rooftop bar (with an adjacent cupola) is a great place to sink a cold beer while overlooking the urban bustle of Habana Vieja. Other pluses include a small gym-sauna, friendly staff and a great central location.

HOTEL SANTA ISABEL

Map p220   Period Hotel $$$

Habaguanex; ☎ 860-8201; Baratillo No 9; s/d CUC$190/240; ⊠ ▣

Considered to be one of Habana's finest hotels – as well as being one of its oldest (it first began operations in 1867) – the Hotel Santa Isabel, on the east side of the Plaza de Armas, is housed in the **Palacio de los Condes de Santovenia** (p76), the former palace of a decadent Spanish count. In 1998 this three-story baroque beauty was upgraded to five-star status but, unlike other posh Cuban hotels, it actually comes close to justifying the billing. The 17 regular rooms have oodles of historic charm, and are all kitted out with attractive Spanish colonial furniture and paintings by contemporary Cuban artists. No wonder ex–US president Jimmy Carter stayed here during his landmark visit in 2002.

CENTRO HABANA

Centro Habana contains a convenient mix of historic hotels and cheap reliable staples, plus a couple of international-class gems thrown in for good measure. Geographically speaking, many of the better options are clustered in or around Parque Central, including the Inglaterra (the city's oldest hotel), the NH Parque Central (one of its swankiest) and the Saratoga (one of its newest). West of Paseo de Martí (Prado) you'll find a handful of more basic options, such as the Lido, the Caribbean, the Deauville and the Lincoln.

Centro Habana has a plethora of casas particulares (opposite), offering far more variety and choice than Habana Vieja. Be careful when searching the streets west of Paseo de Martí with a suitcase or rucksack in tow; daylight robbery (in the form of bag snatching) is not unheard of in this area.

CASA DEL CIENTÍFICO

Map p222   Hotel $

☎ 862-1607, 862-1608; Paseo de Martí No 212; s/d with shared bathroom CUC$25/31, with private bathroom CUC$45/55; ⊠ ▣

Eclectic meets eccentric in this eye-catching palace that was once the residence of Cuba's second president. These days the hotel's grand stairways, hidden courtyards and withered terraces maintain a slightly more abandoned air (expect the odd cobweb and a good coating of dust) but, with its central location and time-warp prerevolutionary atmosphere, it makes an evocative introduction to Habana. The rooms are ordinary but adequate, and there's a rather becoming **restaurant** (✕ 6pm-midnight) on the 1st floor. This is also a great place to catch vivid snippets of local Habana life; check out the kids who play baseball against the side wall on Trocadero.

HOTEL LIDO Map p222   Hotel $

Islazul; ☎ 867-1102; Consulado No 210; s/d low season CUC$25/36, high season CUC$36/40; ⊠

Squeezed into scruffy Calle Consulado, the easy-on-the-wallet Lido is a budget travelers' mecca. The secret lies in a strangely unexotic mix of location, price and friendly, no-nonsense service offered up by the staff behind reception. Unlike other cheap establishments in Habana, the Lido – rather refreshingly – has no pretensions. The rooms might be a little cell-like and the showers intermittently cold, but for CUC$25 a night in the low season you're getting good security, a prime location and basic but clean rooms (all have satellite TV and air-con) for less than the price of an average casa particular. It's about the closest thing Habana gets to a backpackers hostel.

HOTEL LINCOLN Map p222   Hotel $

Islazul; ☎ 862-8261; Virtudes No 164; s/d low season CUC$30/40, high season CUC$39/46; ⊠

A peeling nine-story giant on a corner of busy Av de Italia (Galiano), the Hotel Lincoln was the second-tallest building in Habana when it was built in 1926. Overshadowed by taller opposition these days, the hotel still offers 135 air-con rooms with TV in an atmosphere that is more 1950s than 2000s. Notoriety hit this hotel in 1958 when the M-26-7 (26th of July Movement; Fidel Castro's revolutionary organiza-

CENTRO HABANA CASAS PARTICULARES

Juan Carlos (Map p222; ☎ 863-6301, 861-8003; Crespo No 107 btwn Colón & Trocadero; r CUC$15-20) A big, spotless house with natural light throughout. The cheapest room has a shared bathroom. Good value.

Julio & Elsa Roque (Map p222; ☎ 861-8027; julloroq@yahoo.com; Apt 2, Consulado No 162 btwn Colón & Trocadero; r CUC$15-25) Julio and Elsa rent two rooms with different amenities; the cheaper room has shared bathroom, fan only and cold water. Both Julio and Elsa are superhelpful and mines of information. English spoken.

Dulce Hostal (Map p222; ☎ 863-2506; Amistad No 220 btwn Neptuno & San Miguel; r CUC$20) A beautiful colonial house with tile floors and soaring ceilings; Dulce María González is a quiet, friendly hostess.

Martha Obregón (Map p222; ☎ 870-2095; marthaobregon@yahoo.com; upper apt, Gervasio No 308 btwn Neptuno & San Miguel; r CUC$20-25) The little balconies at this nice home have small street views. It's popular and often full.

Niurka O Rey (Map p222; ☎ 863-0278; Aguila No 206 btwn Animas & Virtudes; r CUC$20-25) A sparkling blue house with a slightly less sparkling but adequate interior. There's one room with a bathroom, and parking is close by.

Alejandro Osés (Map p222; ☎ 863-7359; 1st fl, Malecón No 163; r CUC$25) This popular place has two rooms and sea views. English spoken.

Amada Pérez Güelmes & Antonio Clavero (Map p222; ☎ 862-3924; upper apt, Lealtad No 262 btwn Neptuno & Concordia; r CUC$25) Two rooms are available in this pleasant colonial house.

Carlos Luis Valerrama Moré (Map p222; ☎ 867-9842; 2nd fl, Neptuno No 404 btwn San Nicolás & Manrique; r CUC$25) A big space with living-cum-dining-room and balcony.

Elicio Fernández (Map p222; ☎ 861-7447; Apt 405, Aguila No 314 btwn Neptune & Concordia; r UC$25) Breezy rooms with fan, shared bathroom and lots of natural light. The building has a doorman and elevator, and rooftop views.

Esther Cardoso (Map p222; ☎ 862-0401; esthercv2551@cubarte.cult.cu; Aguila No 367 btwn Neptuno & San Miguel; r CUC$25) This artist's palace is like an oasis in the desert with tasteful decor, funky posters, spick-and-span bathrooms and a spectacular roof terrace. Book early.

La Casona Colonial (Map p222; ☎ 870-0489; cubarooms2000@yahoo.com; Gervasio No 209 btwn Concordia & Virtudes; r CUC$25) Jorge Díaz has several rooms around nice courtyard; one has three beds with a shared bathroom. It's good for longer stays.

Rufino Añel Martín & Pilar Rodríguez Santos (Map p222; ☎ 862-4149; Neptuno No 556 btwn Lealtad & Escobar; r CUC$25) Located in a lively, edgy area. The helpful hosts can cook and do laundry.

Paraiso Vista al Mar (Map p222; ☎ 861-8112; 14th fl, Malecón No 51 btwn Carcel & Genios; r CUC$30) If it's a view you're after and you don't mind traveling up 14 floors in an antiquated elevator, check out this spacious option right run by Tamara Valdés.

Triny Vital (Map p222; ☎ 867-9132; lower apt, Calle Aguila No 118 btwn Colón & Trocadero; apt CUC$50) A two-bedroom independent apartment with kitchen that sleeps four to five.

tion) kidnapped five-time motor-racing world champion Carlos Fangio from the downstairs lobby on the eve of the Cuban Grand Prix. A small '**museum**' on the 8th floor records the event for posterity. Otherwise the hotel is friendly but timeworn.

HOTEL CARIBBEAN Map p222　　Hotel $
Islazul; ☎ 860-8233; Paseo de Martí No 164 btwn Colón & Refugio; s/d low season CUC$36/48, high season CUC$41/54; ❄
Cheap but not always so cheerful, the Caribbean – which was the recipient of a long-awaited 2006 makeover – offers aspiring

Cuban renovators a lesson in how *not* to decorate. Dark, poky rooms contain basic facilities such as shower, TV and air-con, but it's all a bit rough around the edges and the price – while competitive – isn't justified by the facilities. Budget travelers should try the Lido around the corner first.

HOTEL PARK VIEW Map p222　　Hotel $
Habaguanex; ☎ 861-3293; cnr Colón & Morro; s/d low season CUC$52/76, high season CUC$52/86; ❄ ▯
Built in 1928 with American money, the Park View's reputation as the poor man's

Sevilla isn't entirely justified. Its location alone (within baseball-pitching distance of the Museo de la Revolution) is enough to consider this mint green city charmer a viable option. Chuck in clean rooms, modern furnishings (the hotel was renovated in 2002 by Habaguanex) and a small but perfectly poised 7th-floor **restaurant** (🕑 breakfast, lunch & dinner) and you've got yourself a veritable bargain. Other bonuses include cable TV, friendly doormen and a 24-hour downstairs bar.

HOTEL DEAUVILLE Map p222   Hotel $$
Hotetur; ☎ 866-8812; cnr Av de Italia & Malecón; s/d/tr CUC$61/88/99; 🛇 🖭
The Deauville is housed in a kitschy seafront high-rise that sharp-eyed Habana-watchers will recognize from picturesque Malecón-at-sunset postcards. But while the location might be picture-perfect, the facilities inside this former Mafia gambling den don't quite match up to the stellar views. Currently reborn in peach and red, and already showing the effects of the corrosive sea water, the Deauville has handy facilities and a reasonably priced restaurant that is popular with the mid-priced tour-circuit crowd. It's great for an early-morning Malecón (Av de Maceo) stroll.

HOTEL PLAZA Map p222   Hotel $$
Gran Caribe; ☎ 860-8592; Agramonte No 267; s/d CUC$80/120; 🛇 🖭
The Plaza has the potential to be an illustrious frontrunner on the hotel scene, but rather like the photogenic Buicks that chug asthmatically around the streets outside, its elegant facade is only half the story. Erected in 1908, this hotel sports the restaurant **Los Portales** (p116), tiled marble floors and a rather fancy lobby. But step upstairs to one of the 188 rooms and, more often than not, you'll find damp bedding, windows that don't open properly and curtains hanging off the railings. A cheaper hotel could get away with it, but this place has delusions of grandeur.

HOTEL TELÉGRAFO Map p222   Hotel $$
Habaguanex; ☎ 861-1010, 861-4741; Paseo de Martí No 408; s/d low season CUC$80/130, high season CUC$95/160; 🛇 🖭
A bold royal-blue charmer, this Habaguanex beauty juxtaposes old-style archi-

tectural features (the original building hails from 1888) with futuristic design flourishes that include silver sofas, a huge winding central staircase and an awesome tile mosaic emblazoned on the wall of the downstairs café. The rooms are equally spiffy.

HOTEL INGLATERRA
Map p222   Hotel $$
Gran Caribe; ☎ 860-8595; Paseo de Martí No 416; s/d/tr CUC$84/120/168; 🛇 🖭
Back in the 1890s, this was José Martí's Habana hotel of choice and it's still playing on the fact – which says something about the current state of affairs. The **Inglaterra** (p80) is a better place to hang out than actually book a room, with its exquisite Moorish lobby and crusty colonial interior easily outshining the lackluster and often viewless rooms. The rooftop bar is a popular watering hole and the downstairs foyer is a hive of bustling activity; there's also a downstairs alfresco bar, **El Louvre** (🕑 11am-midnight). Beware of the streets outside, which are full of overzealous hustlers.

HOTEL SEVILLA Map p222   Hotel $$$
Gran Caribe; ☎ 860-8560; Trocadero No 55 btwn Paseo de Martí & Agramonte; s/d CUC$151/206; 🛇 🖭 🖭
Al Capone once hired out the whole 6th floor, Graham Greene used it as a setting for his novel *Our Man in Havana* and the Mafia used it as an operations centre for its narcotics racket; refurbished by the French Sofitel group in 2002, the Hotel Sevilla now sparkles like the colonial jewel of old, with spacious rooms, comfortable beds and a rather surreally located ground-floor swimming pool (bathers are overlooked by a crumbling tenement, complete with lines of drying washing). The hotel's high point (in more ways than one) has to be the superb 9th-floor **restaurant** (🕑 from 7pm), where you can enjoy dinner overlooking the muggy streets of Habana Vieja. A violinist serenades diners with a wonderfully melancholic rendition of 'As Time Goes By.'

HOTEL NH PARQUE CENTRAL
Map p222   International Hotel $$$
Cubanacán; ☎ 860-6627; Neptuno btwn Paseo de Martí & Agramonte; s/d CUC$205/270; 🛇 🖭 🖭
If you have a penchant for hanging out in expensive five-star hotel lobbies sipping end-

less cups of coffee, the Parque Central could be just the place for you. Outside of the two Meliás, this is without a doubt Habana's best international-standard hotel, with professional service and stellar business facilities on a par with top-ranking five-star hotels elsewhere in the Caribbean. Although the sumptuous lobby and well-furnished rooms may lack the historical riches of the old town's venerable Habaguanex establishments, the ambience here is far from antiseptic. Bonus facilities include a full-service business center, a rooftop pool-fitness-center-Jacuzzi, an elegant lobby bar, a celebrated restaurant, and excellent international telephone and internet links. Two of the bedrooms are wheelchair accessible. At the time of writing, the Parque Central was in the process of constructing a large new wing on Calle Virtudes directly behind the existing building.

HOTEL SARATOGA Map p222 Hotel $$$
Habaguanex; ☎ 868-1000; Paseo de Martí No 603; r patio/street view CUC$240/290; ⊠ 🖥 🖭
One of Habana's newest, ritziest and most dramatic hotels, the glittering Saratoga is an architectural work of art that sits pretty on the intersection of Paseo de Martí and Dragones, with fantastic views over toward the Capitolio. Sharp, if officious, service predominates here, and highlights include the extracomfortable beds, power showers and a truly decadent rooftop swimming pool. But not surprisingly, there's a price for all this luxury. The Saratoga is Habana's most expensive hotel and, while its facilities impress, its service can't quite match up to that of the marginally cheaper Meliás.

VEDADO

Most of Vedado's grandiose hotels were built with Mafia money in the 1930s, '40s and '50s, when Habana rocked to the all-night parties of influential American mobsters such as Meyer Lansky and Salvatore 'Lucky' Luciano. But, while the casinos might have long since shut up shop and the Mob beat a hasty retreat back to Miami and New York, Vedado's once opulent accommodation options still offer guests a hint or two of their former prerevolutionary greatness.

An expansive selection of casas particulares also punctuates the leafy avenues and quiet side streets of Habana's most salubrious neighborhood.

HOTEL BRUZÓN Map pp224-5 Hotel $
Islazul; ☎ 877-5684; Bruzón No 217 btwn Pozos Dulces & Av de la Independencia; s/d CUC$22/28
Closed for renovations at the time of writing, the jaded Bruzón has long been overdue for a facelift. Formerly the one and only reason to stay at this tatty Islazul establishment was its proximity to the Astro bus station; it'll need to do something drastic in order to attract anyone other than rock-bottom budget hunters in the future.

HOTEL COLINA Map pp224-5 Hotel $
Islazul; ☎ 33-40-71; fax 33-41-04; cnr Calles L & 27; s/d low season CUC$40/50, high season CUC$46/60; ⊠
The coziest and friendliest of Vedado's cheaper accommodation options, the Colina has 80 basic rooms with air-con, satellite TV and intermittent hot water, plus there's a good people-watching sidewalk café just off the reception. Though not exactly luxurious, it's cheaper and better value than the Vedado or St John's hotels nearby.

HOTEL EL BOSQUE
Map pp224-5 Hotel $$
Gaviota; ☎ 204-9232; Parque Almendares, Calle 28A btwn Avs 49A & 49B; s/d CUC$45/60; ⊠ 🖥
Cheap and grossly underrated, the Hotel El Bosque is the better and less costly arm of the Gaviota-run Kohly-Bosque complejo (complex). Clean, friendly and genteel, the hotel lies on the banks of the Río Almendares, and is a good (and rare) midrange choice in this neck of the woods. The 54 rooms are small but functional, there's 24-hour internet, and a pleasant terrace out back overlooks the wooded slopes of the nearby river. The Gaviota shuttle bus whisks guests into central Habana four times a day for CUC$5.

HOTEL ST JOHN'S
Map pp224-5 Hotel $$
Gran Caribe; ☎ 33-37-40; Calle O No 216 btwn Calles 23 & 25; s/d low season CUC$50/67, high season CUC$56/80; ⊠ 🖭
A fair to middling Vedado option, Hotel St John's has a rooftop pool, clean bathrooms, reasonable beds and the ever popular nightclub Pico Blanco (p141), if wall vibrating Cuban discos are your thing. On the negative side,

VEDADO CASAS PARTICULARES

Angela Muñiz Rubio (Map pp224–5; ☎ 879-6851; San Miguel No 1116 btwn Mazón & Basarrate; r CUC$25) Rents rooms near Museo Napoleónico; two have private bathrooms.

Basilia Pérez Castro (Map pp224–5; ☎ 832-3953; bpcdt@hotmail.com; Apt 7, lower fl, Calle 25 No 361 btwn Calles K & L; r CUC$25) Two rooms with independent entrances, fridge, phone and TV. A mellow, good-value place.

Guillermina & Roberto Abreu (Map pp224–5; ☎ 833-6401; Apt 13A, Paseo No 126 btwn 5 & Calzada; r CUC$25) Two spacious rooms with views. Elevator.

Maribel & Luis Garcé (Map pp224–5; ☎ 832-1619; Calle 19 No 356 upstairs btwn Calles G & H; r CUC$25) This nice young couple rent a smallish room with a little balcony.

Natalia Rodes (Map pp224–5; ☎ 832-8909; Apt 11B, 11th fl, Calle 19 No 376 btwn Calles G & H; r CUC$25) Shared bathroom, nice bed, expansive views.

Nelsy Alemán Machado (Map pp224–5; ☎ 832-8467; Apt 1, Calle 25 No 361 btwn Calles K & L; r CUC$25) An independent, laidback place with fridge.

Pilar Palma (Map pp224–5; ☎ 831-8918; Apt 9, Calle O No 202 btwn Calles 23 & 25; r CUC$25) Prime location near Calle 23 (La Rampa); friendly owner.

Armando Gutiérrez (Map pp224–5; ☎ /fax 832-1876; Apt 7, Calle 21 No 62 btwn Calles M & N; r CUC$25-30) This friendly place has a nice room with balcony and fridge. English spoken. Elevator.

Beatriz & Julio (Map pp224–5; ☎ 832-5778; Calle 25 No 367 btwn Calles K & L; r CUC$25-30; 🞕) Close to university and central hotels. It has a separate entrance.

Melba Piñeda Bermudez (Map pp224–5; ☎ 832-5929; lienafp@yahoo.com; Calle 11 No 802 btwn Calles 2 & 4; r CUC$25-30) A sweet room with nice furnishings and a private terrace in a beautiful colonial home on a quiet street. Helpful owners.

Eddy Gutiérrez Bouza (Map pp224–5; ☎ 832-5207; Calle 21 No 408 btwn Calles F & G; r CUC$30; 🞕) A huge colonial house with fantastic host who is an excellent source of information about Habana.

Julio Padilla Martín (Map pp224–5; ☎ 832-5709; juliop_martin@hotmail.com; Apt 7B, Calle K No 210 btwn Línea & 15; r CUC$30-35) Good for groups. English is spoken.

Manuel Martínez (Map pp224–5; ☎ 832-6713; Apt 22, Calle 21 No 4 btwn Calles N & O; r CUC$30-35) There are 10 to 12 casas particulares in this magnificent art deco building constructed in 1945. This one overlooks the gardens of the Hotel Nacional; it's a classic view.

Marta Vitorte (Map pp224–5; ☎ 885-7792; martavitorte@hotmail.com; Apt 14, Calle G No 301 btwn 13 & 15; r CUC$35-40) Two rooms in a deluxe apartment with phenomenal views, great beds and a wraparound terrace. English spoken.

the staff here are sometimes unresponsive, the breakfast is mediocre and there's none of the exotic colonial atmosphere that you get in Habana Vieja. Ask for a west-facing room for a killer view over the Malecón.

HOTEL VEDADO Map pp224–5   Hotel $$
Gran Caribe; ☎ 836-4072; Calle O No 244 btwn Calles 23 & 25; s/d low season CUC$50/67, high season CUC$56/80; 🞕 🖳 🖭

The eight-story Hotel Vedado is sprawled across two buildings in tatty Calle O and falls into the midrange price bracket. However, despite the presence of a swimming pool, a gym and a nightly cabaret show, something about this place doesn't quite hit the spot.

Maybe it's the stroppy, uninterested staff behind reception (you don't feel so much a guest here as a number), or the rather uninspiring rooms, or the disorganized and overcrowded lobby – all of which would be semiacceptable in a cheaper place but here just seem, well, substandard. At this price you're better off treating yourself to a night in Habana Vieja.

HOTEL VICTORIA Map pp224–5   Hotel $$
Gran Caribe; ☎ 833-3510; cnr Calles M & 19; s/d low season CUC$55/70, high season CUC$65/90; 🞕 🖭

A well-heeled and oft overlooked option, the Victoria is a diminutive five-story hotel situated within spitting distance of the more expensive Nacional. Deluxe and compact, though (due to its size) invariably full, this venerable Gran Caribe establishment is housed in an attractive neoclassical building dating from 1928, and contains a swimming pool, a bar and a small shop. A sturdy midrange accommodation option.

HOTEL RIVIERA Map pp224-5 Hotel $$
Gran Caribe; ☎ 836-4051; cnr Paseo & Malecón; s/d low season CUC$74/106, high season CUC$91/130; 🗙 🖳 🖭

A riot of '50s kitsch, the Riviera was built in 1957 by Mafia boss Meyer Lansky as a Vegas-style gambling haven. At the time it was considered to be the last word in opulence and luxury in Habana, and celebrities flocked from far and wide to enjoy its lavish facilities. The hotel was requisitioned by the new revolutionary government in 1959, with Castro promptly shutting down the casino and seeing that Lanksy and his assorted henchmen beat a hasty retreat back to Florida. But the Riviera remained to fight another day. Or did it? As with much of Habana, time seems to have stood still in this faded '50s classic, with the 354 beleaguered rooms looking like they haven't seen a decent makeover since Lansky last checked out. Nevertheless there are a lot of facilities here, including a fantastically retro lobby, a holiday-camp-style swimming pool, a buffet restaurant, a slightly iffy coffee shop (near the pool), and the famous Copa Room (p136) cabaret show. Despite its choice location right on the Malecón, you'll need a taxi or a good pair of legs to get to most places.

HOTEL PRESIDENTE
Map pp224-5 Hotel $$$
Gran Caribe; ☎ 33-37-53; cnr Calzada & Calle G; s/d CUC$90/140; 🗙 🖳 🖭

Built in 1928 with an art deco influence, the 10-story Hotel Presidente wouldn't be out of place in New York. There are 160 rooms here, plus a swimming pool and a 10th-floor bar. The lobby, meanwhile, sports an eye-catching black-and-white marble floor and is awash with antiques. Renovated six years ago, the hotel has relatively good decor throughout, although – in common with most Cuban hotels – ongoing maintenance (or lack of it) is always an issue. The main problem with the Presidente, however, is its rather out-of-the-way location.

HOTEL NACIONAL
Map pp224-5 Hotel $$$
Gran Caribe; ☎ 873-3564; cnr Calles O & 21; s/d low season CUC$120/170, high season CUC$150/200, ste CUC$1000; 🗙 🖳 🖭

The cream of the hotel crop and the flagship of the government-run Gran Caribe chain, the neoclassical-neocolonial–art deco Hotel Nacional (p85) is as much a city monument as it is an international accommodation option. Even if you haven't got the money to stay here, chances are you'll find yourself sipping at least one icy mojito in the hotel's exquisite oceanside bar. Steeped in history (p56) and containing rooms that enthusiastically advertise the details of illustrious occupants past, this towering Habana landmark sports two swimming pools, a sweeping manicured lawn and its own top-class nighttime cabaret show, the Cabaret Parisién (p136); one of its lavish restaurants, El Rincón de Cine (🕒 24hr), has the best burgers and milk shakes in Cuba. While the rooms might lack some of the fancy gadgets of deluxe Varadero, the ostentatious communal areas and the ghosts of Winston Churchill, Frank Sinatra, Lucky Luciano and Errol Flynn, which seem to hover in the luxurious lobby, all add up to a fascinating and unforgettable experience.

HOTEL TRYP HABANA LIBRE
Map pp224-5 International Hotel $$$
Gran Caribe; ☎ 834-6100; cnr Calles L & 23; r from CUC$200; 🗙 🖳 🖭

Habana's biggest and boldest hotel opened in March 1958 on the eve of Batista's last waltz. Once part of the Hilton chain, in January 1959 the Hotel Habana Libre (p85) was commandeered by Castro's rebels, who put their boots over all the plush furnishings and turned it into a temporary HQ (Castro effectively ran the country from a suite on one of the upper floors). Now efficiently managed by Spain's Meliá chain as an urban Tryp Hotel, this skyline-hogging modernist giant has 574 rooms, all kitted out to international standard with small balconies and up-to-date fittings that could do with an imaginative makeover. The tour desks in the lobby are helpful for out-of-town excursions and the 25th-floor Cabaret Turquino (p136) is a city institution.

VOICES OF HABANA: EDDY GUTIÉRREZ

Casa particular owner, Vedado

Sum up Habana in one sentence. Habana is a living museum. **What defines a habanero?** *Habaneros* [inhabitants of Habana] are jovial, musical and very hospitable people. They are the kind of people with whom you can quickly become friends. **How has Habana changed in the last 10 years?** The social life has changed with the influence of tourism. It has become more cosmopolitan. Cubans now study more languages by using books and by watching language programs on Cuban TV. **What, in your opinion, is the finest Cuban cigar and why?** The best cigars are made from tobacco grown in the Vuelta Abajo region [in Pinar del Río Province], which has the ideal climate and soil. Hoyo de Monterrey José Gener 1860 are excellent, as are Robainas. **What's the best thing about your neighborhood?** The security and the people; Vedado is a very secure area. It also has plenty of parks, good access to the Malecón [Av de Maceo] and a vibrant student population. **Why are Cubans such skillful dancers?** It's in the culture, in the blood. **How can the inquisitive traveler find the 'real' Cuba?** You must come independently rather than as part of a group, and visit the cheaper places – for example, Los Nardos restaurant in Centro Habana, or the Hanoi restaurant in Habana Vieja. **What are the hottest sounds in Habana right now? Where can you hear them?** Jazz, which you can hear at the Jazz Café and the La Zorra y El Cuervo in Vedado; also salsa and *reggaeton* [Cuban hip-hop], which you can hear just about anywhere.

As related to Brendan Sainsbury

HOTEL MELIÁ COHIBA

Map pp224-5   International Hotel $$$
Cubanacán; ☎ 833-3636; Paseo btwn Calles 1 & 3; r CUC$225; ❄ 💻 🏊
Effortlessly professional, the more central of Habana's two Meliá hotel options hits the spot with knowledgeable staff and modern, well-polished facilities. After a few weeks in the Cuban outback, you'll be impressed by the responsiveness of the service at this oceanside concrete giant, although the ambience is probably more international than Cuban. For workaholics there are rooms especially kitted out for business travelers, and 59 units have Jacuzzis. On the lower levels there's a shopping arcade, one of Habana's plushest **gyms** (p146) and the ever popular **Havana Café** (p136).

PLAYA & MARIANAO

While Playa's and Marianao's plush hotels offer travelers plenty of four-star gimmicks and resort-style creature comforts, the location – 8km to 12km west of the city center – is too far removed from Habana's signature sights to be convenient.

There are also four top-notch casas particulares in this area (opposite).

HOSTAL COSTA SOL

Map pp228-9   Hotel $
☎ 209-0828; cnr Av 3A & Calle 60; s/d CUC$25/36
Operated by the Ministerio de Educación Superior, this is an intimate place with only 12 rooms (nine of which have en suite bathrooms). The staff are friendly enough and there's a cheap **restaurant** (breakfast CUC$3, lunch or dinner CUC$7). The main problem is its location: far from anywhere.

HOTEL MIRAZUL Map pp228-9   Hotel $
☎ 204-0088/45; Av 5 No 3603 btwn Calles 36 & 40; r CUC$50
The Hotel Mirazul is an elegant old mansion now operated as a hotel by the Ministerio de Educación Superior. There are eight air-conditioned rooms with TV, a restaurant-bar, and students receive a discount. It's excellent value and usually full.

HOTEL EL VIEJO Y EL MAR

Map pp228-9   Hotel $$
Cubanacán; ☎ 204-6336; Marina Hemingway, cnr Av 1 & Calle 248
Don't be fooled by the Hemingway legend. The Hotel El Viejo y El Mar (the Old Man and the Sea) at the Marina Hemingway is a rather dull six-story concrete pile

situated – a little inconveniently – 20km west of colonial Habana. At the time of writing the hotel was temporarily closed to foreign tourists due to Misión Milagros (p189). You're not missing much.

HOTEL KOHLY
Map pp228-9   Hotel $$

Gaviota; ☎ 204-0240; cnr Av 49A & Calle 36; s/d CUC$50/65; ⊠ ▣ ▧

Despite its plethora of facilities (gym, bars, massage, beauty salon, tennis court, swimming pool and excellent pizza restaurant) and reputation as an 'upscale' hotel, the Kohly's 136 air-conditioned rooms and concrete-carpeted communal areas have a rather utilitarian feel. Nonetheless, this amiable Gaviota establishment is efficiently run, with four daily shuttle buses (CUC$5) whisking guests into central Habana (a good 10km away). If you're in the area, the cheaper and cozier Bosque (p165) just down the road is also worth checking out.

APARTHOTEL MONTEHABANA
Map pp228-9   Aparthotel $$

Gaviota; ☎ 206-9595; Calle 70 btwn Avs 5A & 7; s/d CUC$60/80, apt from CUC$100; ⊠ ▣ ▧

This modern Gaviota giant opened in December 2005 with the promise of something a little different. One hundred and one of the rooms here are apartments with living rooms and fully equipped kitchens – a great opportunity to hit the Habana markets and find out how the Cubans cook. To help you in the kitchen there are microwaves, refrigerators, toasters and coffee machines – even your own cutlery. If you're not up to cooking, there's a restaurant (breakfast CUC$8, dinner buffet CUC$15). Elsewhere the facilities are shiny and new, with 24-hour internet, car rental and an on-site minimarket. Guests can use the pool at the Occidental Miramar next door.

HOTEL EL COMODORO
Map pp228-9   Resort Hotel $$

Cubanacán; ☎ 204-5551; cnr Av 1 & Calle 84; s/d low season CUC$68/90, high season CUC$70/101, 1-/2-/3-bedroom units low season CUC$68/128/158, high season CUC$76/155/195; ⊠ ▧

Next door to the Meliá Habana, but not in the same league, the Hotel El Comodoro is a huge complex of rooms and bungalows

that sprawls like a minivillage next to the ocean about 15km west of La Habana Vieja. The place certainly has potential, but all of the rooms (including 134 in the main four-story building, 10 in a two-story block facing the ocean and 328 bungalow units spread around their own swimming pool) are tired, worn and in urgent need of a coat of paint or two. The bungalow units, which are substantially newer, come with sitting room, TV, kitchenette, fridge and one to three bedrooms. Elsewhere the hotel has a small – make that tiny – sandy beach protected from the waves by a large iron seawall, a run-down tennis court and a drab looking shopping mall. Service at this hotel has been described as *Fawlty Towers*–like.

HOTEL PALCO
Map pp228-9   Hotel $$

Cubanacán; ☎ 204-7235; Calle 146, btwn Avs 11 & 13; s/d low season CUC$74/94, high season CUC$91/111; ⊠ ▣ ▧

Attached to the Palacio de las Convenciones, Hotel Palco is a top business hotel with 180 rooms, a business center, a pool, two restaurants, two bars and a cigar shop. It's unlikely you'll stay here unless you're coming to Habana to attend a conference/symposium/product launch. The place is normally block booked and the staff are notorious for not answering the phone.

PLAYA & MARIANAO CASAS PARTICULARES

Rina & Geraldo (Map pp228-9; ☎ 202-4112; Av 3A No 8610 btwn Calles 86 & 88; r CUC$25-30) This casa has two clean rooms, one with sun terrace. Flexible hosts.

Mayda Bellón Trueba (Map pp228-9; ☎ 203-4490; Av 33 No 3404 btwn Calles 34 & 36; r CUC$30) A palatial, private spot. Nine houses rent in this tranquil block, allowing big groups to arrange casa accommodation together. English spoken.

Suites Olimpia Jorge Pérez (Map pp228-9; ☎ /fax 202 4126; Calle 96 No 535 btwn Avs 5F & 7, Miramar; r CUC$30-35) This casa has a fridge.

Marta Rodríguez (Map pp228-9; ☎ 203-8596; Calle 42 No 914; r CUC$40) Rents two rooms outfitted with TV, VCR, stereo and fridge.

HOTEL BELLO CARIBE

Map pp228-9   Hotel $$

Cubanacán; ☎ 33-05-67; Calle 158 btwn Calles 29 & 31; s/d CUC$75/95

Situated near the Palacio de las Convenciones and Cuba's biotech facilities, the Bello Caribe is the closest Habana hotel to José Martí International Airport. It is currently being used by Misión Milagros (p189) and is closed to foreign tourists.

HOTEL COPACABANA

Map pp228-9   Hotel $$

Gran Caribe; ☎ 204-1037; cnr Av 1 & Calle 44; s/d CUC$85/130; ▣

The five-story Hotel Copacabana is a 168-room hotel complex right on the coast, and although there's no beach, a seawall creates a protected pool. At the time of writing it was undergoing renovation after a spell with Misión Milagros (p189) but when it reopens it should be a viable midrange option.

HOTEL CHATEAU MIRAMAR

Map pp228-9   Hotel $$

Cubanacán; ☎ 204-1951; Av 1 btwn Calles 62 & 64; s/d CUC$95/120; ▣ ▣ ▣

The Hotel Chateau Miramar is a medium-sized five-story hotel used primarily by businesspeople. The 50 rooms with mini-fridges are functional, though they struggle to justify the four-star billing. There's a post office at the reception and a swimming pool next to the sea. This small hotel has a more intimate feel than its neighbors, and many feel the service here is superior.

PANORAMA HOTEL HAVANA

Map pp228-9   Resort Hotel $$

Gaviota; ☎ 204-0100; cnr Av 3 & Calle 70; s/d/tr CUC$95/120/145; ▣ ▣ ▣

Gaviota's flashy new 'glass cathedral' opened in 2003, making it one of Habana's newest hotels. The strange aesthetics – acres of blue-tinted glass – improve once you step inside the monumental lobby, where elevators whisk you promptly up to one of 317 airy rooms that offer great views over Miramar and beyond. Extra facilities include a business center, a photo shop, numerous restaurants, and a spacious and shapely swimming pool. The Panorama is almost too big, however, giving the place a rather deserted and antiseptic feel.

OCCIDENTAL MIRAMAR

Map pp228-9   Resort Hotel $$$

Gaviota; ☎ 204-3584; cnr Av 5 & Calle 74; s/d CUC$100/135; ▣ ▣ ▣

Formerly the Novotel, this 427-room colossus was taken over by Gaviota a few years back and has benefited as a result. Professional staff, great business facilities and high standards of service are par for the course here. There are also plenty of sporty extras if the isolated location starts to grate, including tennis courts, swimming pool, sauna, gym and games room. A regular shuttle bus whizzes guests into central Habana for CUC$5.

HOTEL MELIÁ HABANA

Map pp228-9   International Hotel $$$

Cubanacán; ☎ 204-8500; Av 3 btwn Calles 76 & 80; s/d from CUC$225; ▣ ▣ ▣

Ugly outside but beautiful within, Miramar's gorgeous Hotel Meliá Habana is one of the city's best-run and best-equipped accommodation options. Inside, the 409 rooms (four of which are wheelchair accessible) are positioned around a salubrious lobby abundant in ferns, hanging vines, marble statues and gushing water features; outside, Cuba's largest and most beautiful swimming pool stands next to a desolate, rocky shore. But the area in which the Meliá trumps all opposition is its service, which is polite, punchy and professional. The **buffet restaurant** (☽ breakfast, lunch & dinner) is equally memorable. Despite the high room rates, the Meliá often has special offers, with rooms going for as little as CUC$165.

EASTERN HABANA

HOTEL PANAMERICANO

Map p231   Hotel $

Islazul; ☎ 95-10-00/10; cnr Av Central & Paseo Panamericano, Cojímar; s/d low season CUC$49/54; ▣ ▣

At the entrance to Cojímar, 2km from the Hemingway bust, this architectural aberration was built to house athletes attending the 11th Pan-American Games in 1991 – though you could be forgiven for thinking it was 1961. Inconveniently located and rough around the edges, the establishment was undergoing a renovation at the time of research after a spell as a Misión Milagros (p189) convalescent home.

Excursions

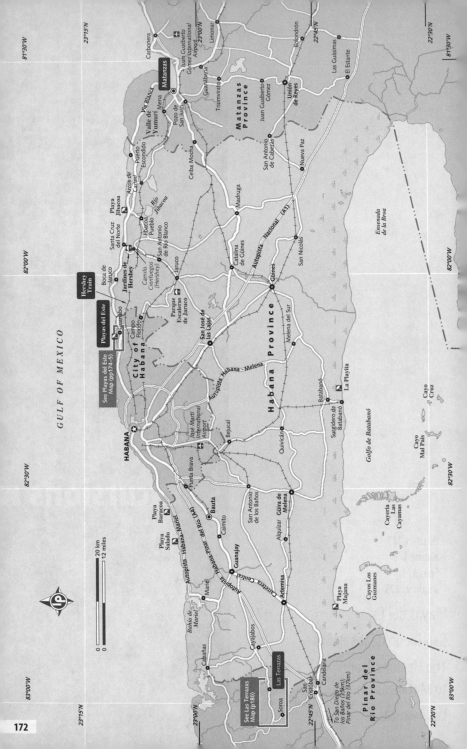

Excursions

Habana lies at the epicenter of a verdant and agriculturally rich rural region, much of which is well worth exploring in its own right. Bereft of the ugly urban sprawl of other Latin American cities, the capital is surrounded on three sides by Habana province, a vast swathe of well-tilled patchwork fields and palm-dotted colonial towns that is frequently ignored by travelers breezing through from Varadero or Pinar del Río. One of the reasons for this is the lack of decent transportation in the area, meaning that travel without a car is often challenging, though by no means impossible. Indeed one of the region's highlights is a journey in itself – the legendary *Hershey Train*, a stop-at-all-stations electric locomotive that rattles its way sedately from Casablanca to Matanzas in much the same way that it did almost 100 years ago.

Habana's magnificent coastline splays out on both sides of the capital, holding a plethora of bays and beaches. To the west lie the rocky shores of Playa Salado and Playa Baracoa, while to the east you'll find Playa Jibacoa and a 9km ribbon of golden sand known as Playas del Este. While not quite worthy of the resort status of Varadero, this is Habana's down-at-heel Coney Island and, not surprisingly, the place is packed on summer weekends.

While the area around Habana is mainly flat, the terrain to the west rises precipitously as you reach the border with Pinar del Río province. Encased here in beautiful pine-filled forests lie two of the capital's most popular back-to-nature getaways: Las Terrazas, a friendly ecovillage, and the spa town of San Diego de los Baños, where people have been lapping up the medicinal waters since the early 17th century. If the verve of crowded Habana gets too hot for you to handle, these two rural havens are excellent escapes.

BEACHES
The Cuban archipelago boasts over 300 beaches and the vast majority of them can be found on the country's north coast. Habana's own idyllic tropical paradise lies 20km to the east of the city at **Playas del Este** (p174), a colorful collection of popular beaches that stretch from Bacuranao to Guanabo.

NATURE
Recently heralded by the WWF as the world's most sustainable country, Cuba is never short of rustic environmental surprises. Nature enthusiasts will love **Las Terrazas** (p179), a model ecovillage nestled picturesquely in the midst of a Unesco-protected nature reserve that is rich in birdlife, indigenous plants and forward-thinking agricultural practices.

SPAS
Cuba has a surprising number of health spas and thermal baths thanks to a relative abundance of underground natural springs. One of the most celebrated bathhouses is the Balneario at **San Diego de los Baños** (p176), a rural spa complex that has been popular with Cubans for over a century but has only recently been discovered by a growing trickle of foreign visitors.

JOURNEYS
'The road is life,' wrote Jack Kerouac, and seldom have four words had such a compelling effect on adventure-seeking travelers. Should you be the sort who gets ants in your pants after five days walking around the monuments of the Cuban capital, consider taking a journey east into the hinterland of Habana province, where you can poke your nose around some of the areas that the tour agencies never intended you to see. Considered to be the city's best backdoor escape, the rattling **Hershey Train** (p177) leaves Casablanca five times a day for Matanzas, stopping at over 40 eccentrically named stations along the way. Don't miss it.

PLAYAS DEL ESTE

In Cuba you're never far from an idyllic diamond-dust beach, and Habana is no exception. Indeed, the city's very own pine-fringed Riviera, Playas del Este, begins just 18km to the east of the capital at the small resort of Bacuranao, before continuing east through Tarará, El Mégano, Santa María del Mar and Boca Ciega to the town of Guanabo, 27km from Habana. Although none of these places has so far witnessed the kind of megadevelopment reminiscent of Cancún or Varadero, Playas del Este is still a popular tourist draw card and, during the summer months of July and August, this is where all of Habana comes to play and relax on the soft white sands and in the clear aquamarine waters of the beautiful Atlantic coastline.

But while the beaches might be postcard perfect, Playas del Este can't yet boast the all-round tourist facilities of other Cuban resorts such as Varadero and Cayo Coco, much less the all-out luxury of celebrated Caribbean getaways. Come here in the winter and the place often has a timeworn and slightly abandoned air and, even in the summer, seasoned beach bums might find the tatty restaurants and ugly Soviet-style hotel piles more than a little incongruous.

But for those who dislike modern tourist development or are keen to see how the Cubans get out and enjoy themselves at weekends, Playas del Este is a breath of fresh air.

Interestingly, each of the six beaches that dot this 9km stretch of attractive coastline has its own distinct flavor allowing travelers to shop around until they find something to suit their individual tastes. **Tarará** is a yacht and diving haven, **Santa María del Mar** is where the largest concentration of resorts (and foreigners) can be found, while at the rustic Cuban end of the strip, **Guanabo** has its own vibrant local community, complete with shops, a nightclub and plenty of cheap casas particulares (private houses that let out rooms to foreigners).

The hotel area of Santa María has seen an elevated security presence in recent years that – while keeping prostitution at bay – has eliminated much of the area's local color, and at

PLAYAS DEL ESTE

INFORMATION
Banco Popular de Ahorro...............1 G2
Clínica Internacional Habana del Este.2 B1
Infotur Guanabo.........................3 G2
Infotur Santa María.....................4 B1

SIGHTS & ACTIVITIES
Club Nautica............................5 C1

SLEEPING
Aparthotel Las Terrazas.................6 B1
Hotel Blau Arenal.......................7 D2
Villa Los Pinos.........................8 A1
Villa Playa Hermosa.....................9 G2

EATING
Bim Bom................................10 F2

El Cubano...............................11 F2
El Piccolo..............................12 H1
Pizzería Mi Rinconcito..................13 A1

TRANSPORT
Bus 400................................14 E2
Bus 400................................15 H2
Bus 400................................16 F2

times Santa María can be like a graveyard. You'll find Cuban families on the beach at Guanabo, Cuban holidaymakers and gay couples at **Boca Ciega**, foreign tourists and their friends at Santa María, and men and women in search of each other at the western end of **El Mégano**. A very pretty part of Santa María is accessible from the parking area on Calle 13.

There are no 'sights' to speak of in Playas del Este. Rather, people come here either to relax or to play on the beach. There are a number of **Club Nautica** points spaced along the beaches east of Club Mégano, where you can rent equipment such as pedal boats, kayaks, snorkeling gear, banana boats and catamarans; a paddle around the coast exploring the mangrove-choked canals is a pleasure. Other beach toys like windsurfers, water bikes and badminton gear may also be available; many people rent this sort equipment all along the beach to Guanabo, but check gear carefully as we've received complaints about faulty equipment.

At the time of research, the yachting and diving facilities at Marina Tarará had been temporarily relocated to the Marina Hemingway (p185) in the west. A number of Playas del Este's hotels were also taking part in the Misión Milagros project (p189) and as a consequence were closed to tourists.

Information & Sights

Banco Popular de Ahorro (Av 5 No 47810 btwn Calles 478 & 480) You can change money here.

Clinica Internacional Habana del Este (Av de las Terrazas, Santa María; ☾ 24hr) This clinic also has a pharmacy on site.

Club Nautica (Playa Santa María del Mar; ☾ 10am-4pm) Club Nauticas are located along the coast, but the most central is outside Club Atlántico in the middle of Playa

Santa María del Mar. You can rent pedal boats (CUC$6 per hour), banana boats (CUC$5 per 5 minutes), kayaks (one-/two-person CUC$2/4 per hour), snorkeling gear (CUC$4) and catamarans (CUC$12 per hour).

Infotur Guanabo (☎ 7-96-68-68; Av 5 btwn Calles 468 & 470; ☾ 8.30am-5.30pm) Tourist information office.

Infotur Santa María (☎ 7-96-11-11; Av de las Terrazas btwn Calles 10 & 11; ☾ 8:30am-5:30pm) Another tourist information office facing a popular strip of tourist beach.

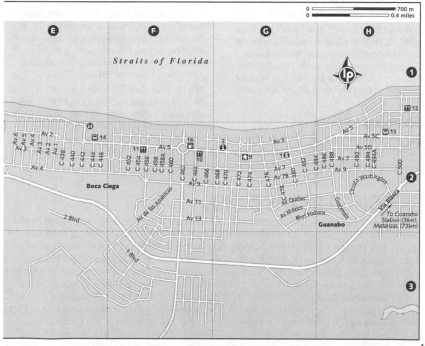

175

Eating

Bim Bom (cnr Av 5 & Calle 464; ice creams CUC$1-3; ☼ 11am-1am) Need a break from the beach? Get your ice creams here.

Pizzería Mi Rinconcito (Av de las Terrazas & Calle 4; mains CUC$2-3.50; ☼ noon-9:45pm) This place has pizza, pasta and salads. It's regularly recommended for its pizza.

El Cubano (Av 5 btwn Calles 456 & 458; meals CUC$6-8; ☼ 11am-midnight) A spick-and-span place with a full wine rack, checkered tablecloths and good chicken cordon bleu.

El Piccolo (☎ 7-96-43-00; cnr Av 5 & Calle 502; meals CUC$7-10; ☼ 11am-midnight) This place is considered by many *habaneros* (inhabitants of Habana) to be the best pizza restaurant in Cuba, and they're not far wrong. Although it's out of the way and a little more expensive the Playas del Este's other pizza joints, it's well worth it.

Sleeping

Villa Playa Hermosa (Islazul; ☎ 7-96-27-74; Av 5D btwn Calles 472 & 474; s/d low season CUC$16/18, high season CUC$20/35; ⊠ ⊠) This villa has 47 rooms in small single-story bungalows with shared bathrooms and TV. It's a popular spot with vacationing Cubans, so expect music, dancing and drinking to all hours.

Aparthotel Las Terrazas (Islazul; ☎ 7-97-13-44; Av del Sur btwn Calles 9 & 10; 1/2/3-bedroom apt low season CUC$36/54/63, high season CUC$50/75/88; ⊠ ⊠) This place has relatively comfortable apartments with cooking facilities, fridges and TVs. The split-level pool is inviting and the disco, set away from the hotel, is a popular nightspot.

Hotel Blau Arenal (☎ 7-97-15-20; s/d incl full board low season CUC$70/100, high season CUC$95/150; ⊠ ⊠) Playas del Este's most stylish option, this modern hotel is on the Laguna Itabo. It has 166 rooms set around a translucent pool; ground-floor rooms have patios, but suites are much larger and cost about 20% more.

Villa Los Pinos (Gran Caribe; ☎ 7-97-13061; fax 97-15-24; Av de las Terrazas No 21 btwn Calles 5 & 7; 2-bedroom house low/high season CUC$120/160; ⊠ ⊠ ⊠) A terrific option if you're after private accommodation with style. The collection of houses here have kitchens, TVs and a personal feel; the majority also have swimming pools.

SAN DIEGO DE LOS BAÑOS

San Diego de los Baños, 130km southwest of Habana, is a tiny resort town nestled between two mountain ranges that is considered to be Cuba's best spa. It is also one of its oldest, dating back to the early 1600s, when a leprous slave stumbling upon its medicinal waters took a revitalizing bath and was miraculously cured. Thanks to the area's proximity to Habana, a small settlement grew up on the site of San Diego's natural mineral springs in the ensuing years and in 1891 the Spanish established the first spa under medical supervision here.

The **Balneario San Diego** is a slightly decrepit bathing complex where thermal waters of 30°C to 40°C are used to treat muscular and skin afflictions. It's a perfectly reasonable place to visit as long as you don't turn up expecting five-star spa facilities or the Cuban version of Banff Springs. Mud from the mouth of the Río San Diego is used here for mud baths, but the sulfurous waters of the natural mineral springs are potent and immersions of only 20 minutes per day are allowed. Massage is also available, along with other health services including 15 day courses of acupuncture. These facilities are among the finest in the country and many Cubans are prescribed treatment here by their family doctors.

If you're looking for cold water, you can swim at the **Hotel Mirador pool**.

Five kilometers directly west of San Diego de los Baños is **Parque La Güira**, which holds the former Hacienda Cortina, a large sculpture park built during the 1920s and '30s. Entered via a huge crenellated gateway, the artificial ruins include a Chinese pavilion and attractive clusters of bamboo. It's worth a quick stop if you're passing through – though more for its slightly surreal atmosphere than for the sights themselves. A huge state-operated restaurant is situated just above the park, but the cabins here are reserved for vacationing military personnel. The park is a nature reserve, and is a favorite spot for **bird-watching**.

During the October 1962 Cuban Missile Crisis, Ernesto 'Che' Guevara transferred headquarters of the Western Army to **Cueva de los Portales**, 11km west of Parque La Güira. The *cueva* (cave) is in a pretty area 1km off the main road, and was declared a national monument in the 1980s. A small museum contains a few of Che's rough belongings. Three other caves called **El Espejo**, **El Salvador** and **Cueva Oscura** are up on the hillside. Together these sites make a cool side trip not just for Che aficionados, but for nature lovers as well.

Sights & Activities

Balneario San Diego (☎ 8-3-7812; ✆ 8am-4pm) Offers mud baths (CUC$20) and 20-minute mineral baths (shared/private pools CUC$4/6). Massages (CUC$25) are also available, as are 15-day courses of acupuncture.

Hotel Mirador pool (admission CUC$1; ✆ 9am-6pm)

Eating

Restaurante La Güira (Parque La Güira; meals CUC$5) A notoriously ugly place with undependable opening hours; don't bank on much more than a quick drink here.

Hotel Mirador Parrillada (☎ 8-7-8338; meals CUC$7) The hotel has an open-air *parrillada* (grill restaurant). There is also a proper restaurant inside the hotel itself serving Cuban cuisine.

Sleeping

Carlos Alberto González (Calle 21A No 3003 btwn Calles 30 & 32; r CUC$20) Carlos runs a local casa particular that has been enthusiastically recommended by readers. If this place is full, the owners can point you in the direction of a few others.

TRANSPORTATION

Distance from Habana 130km

Direction West

Travel Time 2½ hours

Car It's a fairly straightforward drive down the Autopista Habana–Pinar del Río to the San Diego de los Baños exit (Km 102). From here the town is 21km to the northwest along a narrower country road.

Taxi As there is no regular bus service to San Diego de los Baños, getting there without a car can be problematic (although it's a popular trip with long-distance cyclists). A taxi from Habana will cost approximately CUC$80 to CUC$90. A better option is to travel by bus to Las Terrazas (p181), stop overnight, and then pick up a taxi the next morning to take you the last 60km to San Diego de los Baños.

Hotel Mirador (Islazul; ☎ 8-7-8338; s/d low season CUC$30/37, high season CUC$34/41; ❄ ➁) A pleasant hotel situated adjacent to the hot springs, the Mirador has comfortable rooms with fridge (some with views) and a pleasant swimming pool. Service is helpful and friendly.

THE HERSHEY TRAIN TO MATANZAS

To catch a colorful and vivid glimpse of bucolic Cuba just outside the city limits, there's no better method of transportation than the *Hershey Train*, an antiquated electric locomotive that plies its lazy route from Casablanca station to Matanzas five times a day, stopping at just about every house, hut, horse stable and hillock in between.

Built in 1921 by US chocolate czar Milton S Hershey (1857–1945), the line was originally designed to link the giant sugar mill in the town of Hershey with Habana and Matanzas. But running along an isolated rural route, the railway quickly became a lifeline to local communities in the area and an indispensable part of the provincial transportation network.

In 1959 the Hershey factory was nationalized and renamed **Camilo Cienfuegos** after Cuba's celebrated rebel commander, but the train continued to operate, still – unofficially – keeping hold of its old chocolate-inspired nickname. In true postrevolutionary 'waste not, want not' fashion, it also continued using the same tracks, locomotives, carriages, signals and stations, and became – quite literally – a chugging antique box on wheels.

An excursion on the *Hershey Train* to Matanzas isn't a luxury outing. Leaving five times a day from Casablanca station on the east side of Habana harbor, the train is famous for its slowness; travelers should be aware that many of the route's 40-plus stations are situated in the middle of nowhere, a good 5km hike from the nearest settlement. Furthermore, time-tables are sketchy and erratic, and are regularly interrupted by such spontaneous calamities as 'cow on the line' or 'train shut for cleaning.' But for adventurous travelers, therein lays the beauty. This is Cuba as the Cubans see it – the journey is a microcosm of rural life, with all its daily frustrations, foibles and, um, fun.

Once you're on the train, it's really up to you where you get off. Beach bums can disembark at **Guanabo** and wander 2km to the north for a taste of Habana's rustic eastern resorts (p174) and plenty of welcoming casas particulares. History buffs can get off at **Camilo Cienfuegos** and stroll around the ruins of the old Hershey sugar mill or wander a kilometer or so to the north for lunch in the rural ambience of the **Jardines de Hershey**. Other attractions include **Playa Jibacoa**, the small settlement of **Arcos de Canasí** and the beautiful **Valle de Yumurí**.

If you want to make the excursion into a two-day trip, continue on to Matanzas where you can stay overnight in a casa particular and come back the next day on a more comfort-able and rapid Víazul bus.

WHEN SUGAR WAS KING

Sugarcane was first introduced into Cuba by the Spanish in the 16th century. With its flat rolling plains and fertile limestone soil, the island provided ideal growing conditions for the new crop, and within decades sugar had become Cuba's biggest export. During the 17th and 18th centuries, the island played second fiddle to the French colony of Haiti as a world sugar producer but, following Toussaint L'Ouverture's bloody slave rebellion in 1791, thousands of French planters fled west to Cuba, bringing with them their business know-how and modern sugar-production techniques.

In the two centuries that followed, Cuba grew from a nascent sugar economy into the world's biggest exporter, with a huge influx of African slave labor pushing production through the roof and creating vast fortunes for the country's new class of land owners. Soot-stained sugar mills dotted the Cuban countryside, fields of cane swayed like giant grass in the tropical breeze and strapping armies of muscular *macheteros* (sugarcane cutters) hit the fields from November to June to take part in the backbreaking *zafra* (sugar harvest). But the boom wasn't to last. Devastated by the two independence wars in the late 19th century, when huge areas of cane fields were razed, the industry faced ruin and production fell into a seemingly terminal decline.

Fatefully, it was only a temporary blip. Pulled out of the mire in the early 1900s by profit-hungry American busi-nessmen who brought up struggling Cuban mills and land on the cheap, sugar made an unlikely comeback that was as dramatic as it was sweet. Cuba's second big sugar high took place between 1915 and 1920, when the world sugar price hit $0.22 per pound and production peaked out at over four million tons annually. Huge amounts of money were made almost overnight in an era that became known as the 'dance of the millions,' and Habana reaped the economic benefits with a lavish public-works program that saw the construction of such landmark buildings as the Presidential Palace (now the Museo de la Revolución; p81), the Estación Central de Ferrocarriles (p71) and the US$17 million Capitolio Nacional (p79). But Cuba's overreliance on its sweet-tasting mono crop would come back to haunt it.

Following the 1959 revolution, one of the first belligerent acts of the US government was to cancel Cuba's preferential sugar quota in retaliation for Castro's ongoing nationalization campaign. However, the 'punishment' soon backfired. The very next day the Soviet Union stepped in and bought up the same hefty quota lock, stock and barrel, and a new 30-year Soviet-Cuban alliance was sealed right under Washington's nose.

Sugar production in Cuba peaked in 1970 when a bumper harvest hit nearly 10 million tons but, thanks to foreign competition, antiquated production techniques and the massive growth of the tourist economy, it's been declining ever since. In 2002 the government shut down 70 of its 150 sugar mills in a drastic restructuring campaign. One notable casualty was the Camilo Cienfuegos (Hershey) mill (p177). Here, as in other sugar towns, all laid-off workers have been offered graduate study programs and continue to draw their full salaries (around 400 pesos a month). The aim is to raise the basic level of schooling among ex–sugar workers from ninth to 12th grade, although it's still too early to measure the program's success. By 2004 annual sugar production in Cuba had leveled out at 2.5 million tons.

Eating

Cremería Atenas (Plaza de Vigía; ⊙ 9am-9pm) A tasty ice-cream joint next to the Café Atenas in the Plaza de Vigía in Matanzas.

Jardines de Hershey (☎ 692-20-26-85; Camilo Cienfuegos) If you're disembarking at Camilo Cienfuegos (Hershey), these unkempt yet beautiful gardens 1km to the north have an attractive but basic eating option in an open-sided thatched-roof restaurant in the grounds.

Café Atenas (☎ 45-25-34-93; Plaza de la Vigía, Matanzas; ⊙ 10am-11pm) Matanzas' best eating place is opposite the Teatro Sauto on Plaza de la Vigía. It offers pizza, spaghetti, sandwiches, beer, coffee and stupendous chicken-and-shrimp bruschettas, and has friendly service.

Sleeping

There are currently no hotels that accept foreigners in central Matanzas. If you decide to overnight in the city, you can try one of the following congenial casas particulares.

Hostal Alma (☎ 45-24-78-10; Calle 83 No 29008 btwn Calles 290 & 292; r CUC$20-25; 🍽) Alberto Hernández rents two rooms in a colonial house with a roof terrace, sun lounges and a pleasant central courtyard. Meals are available. Alberto is an excellent host and an expert on Matanzas' history.

Hostal Azul (☎ 45-24-78-10; Calle 83 No 29012 btwn Calles 290 & 292; r CUC$20-25; 🍽) A huge colonial room in quiet house; Yoel Báez and Aylín Hernández are very attentive hosts. Hostal Azul shares a phone with Hostal Alma.

Anita & Luis Alberto Valdés (☎ 45-24-33-97; 2nd fl, Calle 79 No 28205 btwn Calles 282 & 288; r CUC$25; 🍽) This place has two bedrooms with separate bathrooms. Top hosts and huge, delicious meals.

TRANSPORTATION

Distance from Habana 98km

Direction East

Travel Time Three to four hours

Bus Víazul runs three times a day from Matanzas to Habana at 9am, 12:15pm and 7pm. The journey takes two hours and costs CUC$7.

Ferry To get to Casablanca train station for the start of this excursion, take the ferry across Habana harbor from the Muelle Luz in Habana Vieja. Ferries run every 10 to 15 minutes and cost CUC$1. The crossing takes 10 minutes and delivers you right next to the station.

Train The *Hershey Train* runs five times a day, leaving Casablanca station (☎ 862-4888) at 4:43am, 8:35am, 12:39pm, 5:21pm and 9:17pm. Ideally the journey takes three hours to reach Matanzas (CUC$2.80), but it's nearly always late. See p188 for further details.

LAS TERRAZAS

The lush, ecofriendly community of Las Terrazas, 60km to the west of the capital, is one of Cuba's most innovative and inspiring environmental projects. During the early 20th century, the mountains in the area had been denuded by a combination of fire and short-sighted agricultural techniques, and their inhabitants lived in poor and difficult conditions. To counter the problem, a reservoir was created in 1971, and a model settlement was built beside it, taking its name from the hillside terraces that had been planted with pines to prevent erosion. The experiment was so successful that in 1985, 25,000 hectares around Las Terrazas were declared the Reserva Sierra del Rosario, Cuba's first Unesco-sanctioned biosphere reserve.

In 1990, the then minister of tourism Osmani Cienfuegos (brother of the revolutionary hero Camilo Cienfuegos) approved plans for an upmarket ecotourism resort in Las Terrazas as a means of providing employment for the village's 890 inhabitants. Between 1992 and 1994, a 'green' hotel was built with workers drawn from Las Terrazas and it quickly became a model for hotels of its kind. A vibrant arts community with open studios and woodwork and pottery workshops took hold in the village to service the new ecotourists, and the settlement prospered, even producing its own national celebrity in the shape of Polo Montañez, a local lumberjack and singer who managed to knock out two best-selling albums before his death in a car crash in 2002. Cienfuegos (now in his eighties) is still heavily involved in Las Terrazas, and is regarded as the motivating force behind its success.

LAS TERRAZAS

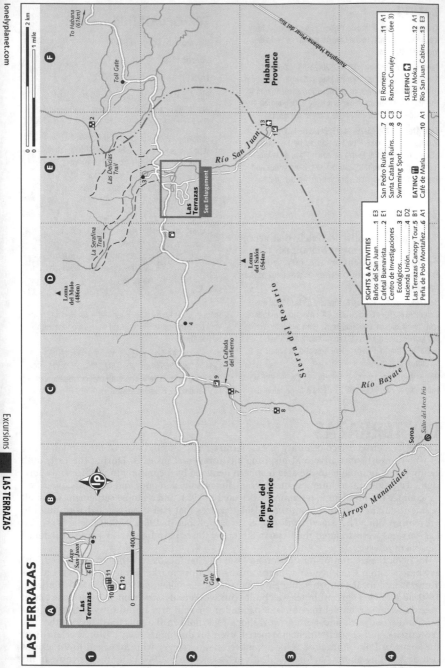

0   1 mile
0   2 km

SIGHTS & ACTIVITIES

Baños del San Juan................1	E3
Cafetal Buenavista...............2	E1
Centro de Investigaciones	
Ecológicos.........................3	E2
Hacienda Unión..................4	D2
Las Terrazas Canopy Tour....5	B1
Peña de Polo Montañez......6	A1
San Pedro Ruins.................7	C2
Santa Catalina Ruins...........8	C3
Swimming Spot..................9	C2

EATING 🍴
Café de María...................10	A1
El Romero.........................11	A1
Rancho Curujey...............(see 3)	

SLEEPING 🛏
Hotel Moka.......................12	A1
Río San Juan Cabins.........13	E3

To Habana (61km)

Toll Gate

Habana Province

Las Delicias Trail

La Serafina Trail

Las Terrazas
See Enlargement

Río San Juan

Loma del Mulo (486m)

Loma del Salón (564m)

Sierra del Rosario

La Cañada del Infierno

Pinar del Río Province

Río Bayate

Arroyo Manantiales

Soroa

Salto del Arco Iris

Toll Gate

Autopista Habana–Pinar del Río

Las Terrazas

Lago San Juan

0   400 m

With 117 species of birds and 800 different types of plants, Las Terrazas is a popular place for hiking. Due to poor signage and the area's protected status, guides are generally necessary; they can be arranged at Hotel Moka or the Centro de Investigaciones Ecológicas. The two most popular hikes are the two- to three-hour **La Serafina** and **Las Delicias** trails. More-adventurous travelers will enjoy the 13km **Cascadas del San Claudio** trail, which takes walkers to a 20m-high waterfall with access to a natural swimming pool and offers the possibility of overnight camping. Other outdoor activities include **horseback riding**, **swimming** in the river and **canopy tours**.

About 1.5km up the hill from the eastern toll gate are the ruins of the **Cafetal Buenavista**, a coffee plantation built in 1802 by French refugees from Haiti. During the 19th century there were 54 similar coffee estates around Las Terrazas, although coffee isn't grown commercially here anymore. The huge *tajona* (grindstone) at the back of the property once extracted the coffee beans from their shells before the beans were dried on huge platforms. The ruins of the quarters of some of the 126 slaves held here can be seen alongside the drying platforms. The attic of the master's house (now a restaurant) was used to store the beans until they could be carried down to the port of Mariel by mule. There are decent views from here.

From just below Hotel Moka, a 3km road runs down the Río San Juan to small falls and natural swimming holes called the **Baños del San Juan**. This popular spot has naturally terraced rocks with clean, bracing waters cascading into a series of pools. If it's too crowded for your taste, you can head downriver to more private pools.

Hacienda Unión, 3.5km west of the Hotel Moka access road, features a country-style restaurant and a set of old coffee-estate ruins.

On La Cañada del Infierno (the Trail to Hell), midway between the Hotel Moka access road and the western toll gate, a road follows the Río Bayate down to the 19th-century **San Pedro** and **Santa Catalina** coffee-estate ruins. A kilometer off the main road, a bar overlooks a popular **swimming spot**.

The lakeside house of Polo Montañez is now a small museum called **Peña de Polo Montañez**, which contains various gold discs and assorted memorabilia. It's right in the village.

Sights & Activities

Baños del San Juan (admission CUC$3) This is a series of small falls and natural swimming holes. There's a simple restaurant here serving palatable plates of fried chicken, rice and salad for a few convertibles.

Centro de Investigaciones Ecológicas (☎ 82-77-29-21) Arranges horseback riding (CUC$6 per hour) and two- to three-hour guided hikes (CUC$20 for one or two persons). The trails are poorly marked, so you really do need a guide.

Las Terrazas Canopy Tour (☎ 82-77-85-55; tour CUC$25) The only canopy tour in Cuba can be arranged down by Lago San Juan. It is very popular.

Eating

Café de María (coffee CUC$1-2; ◷ 9am-9pm) This tiny café right next to El Romero makes what is, without a doubt, the best coffee in Cuba. The aromatic brew is grown locally (ie on the other side of the patio) and is organic. It's so delicious, it's almost worth making the trip out from Habana just for this.

Rancho Curujey (meals CUC$4-8; ◷ 9am-9pm) This is a rustic thatched-roof bar-restaurant situated next to the Centro Investigaciones Ecológicas and overlooking a

beautifully picturesque lake. The food is standard *comida criolla* (rice, beans and pork).

El Romero (◷ 9am-9pm) A full-blown ecorestaurant that specializes in vegetarian fare. This place uses homegrown

---

TRANSPORTATION

Distance from Habana 60km

Direction West

Travel Time 45 minutes

Bus There are no direct buses from the capital to Las Terrazas, but a daily transfer bus from Habana to Viñales via Soroa can drop you near the Hotel Moka. Inquire at Havanatur (p67) in Habana for times and schedules.

Taxi A return taxi, stopping off for three to four hours in the village, should cost about CUC$65.

Tour All of the Habana tour agencies (p66) offer day trips to Las Terrazas. The excursion includes transportation, a hike, a tour of the local community, a visit to the Cafetal Buenavista, a swim in the Río San Juan and lunch. The tour's cost is approximately CUC$39.

organic vegetables and herbs, and solar energy, and keeps its own bees. Browsing the menu – replete with hummus, bean pancakes, pumpkin-and-onion soup and extra-virgin olive oil – may make you think you've woken up in San Francisco.

Sleeping

Río San Juan Cabins (s/d CUC$13/22) These five riverside cabins are 3km south of Lago San Juan. Book at Hotel Moka.

Hotel Moka (☎ 82-77-86-00; s/d low season CUC$60/80, high CUC$75/110; 🐾) Melting into the surrounding woods and containing a tree growing through the airy lobby, the Hotel Moka is one of Cuba's most interesting and well-maintained places to stay. The 26 bright, spacious rooms have fridge and satellite TV, and activities ranging from horseback riding to guided hikes can be arranged on site.

Directory ▮

Directory

TRANSPORTATION

Flights, tours and rail tickets can be booked online at www.lonelyplanet.com/travel_services.

AIR

The only realistic way of reaching Habana from an outside country is by air.

All travelers leaving Cuba are expected to pay a CUC$25 departure tax at José Martí International Airport. The tax is paid at a cashier's window just after you've checked your luggage and received a boarding card. Departure-tax payments are accepted in cash only.

Airlines

Most of the popular airlines have offices in the Airlines Building on Calle 23 (La Rampa) in Vedado, close to the intersection with the Malecón (Av de Maceo). There is additional representation at Terminal 3 of José Martí International Airport.

Despite a dubious safety record, Cuban national carrier Cubana de Aviación serves 11 Cuban cities, as well as numerous destinations in Europe, Canada, Latin America and the Caribbean. Aerocaribbean also provides scheduled flights to destinations within Cuba.

Aerocaribbean (code 7L; Map pp224–5; ☎ 879-7524, 870-4965; www.aero-caribbean.com; Airlines Bldg, Calle 23 No 64, Vedado)

Air Canada (code ACA; Map pp224–5; ☎ 836-3226/27; www.aircanada.com; Airlines Bldg, Calle 23 No 64, Vedado)

Air Europa (code AEA; Map pp228–9; ☎ 204-6905/6/7/8; www.air-europa.com; Miramar Trade Center, cnr Av 3 & Calle 80, Playa)

Air France (code AFR; Map pp224–5; ☎ 833-2642; www.airfrance.com; Airlines Bldg, Calle 23 No 64, Vedado)

Air Jamaica (code AJM; Map pp224–5; ☎ 833-3636; www.airjamaica.com; Hotel Meliá Cohiba, Paseo btwn Calles 1 & 3, Vedado)

Air Transat (code TSC; www.airtransat.com)

Cubana de Aviación (code CU; Map pp224–5; ☎ 834-4446, 649-5666; www.cubana.cu; Airlines Bldg, Calle 23 No 64, Vedado)

Iberia (code IBE; Map pp228–9; ☎ 204-3444; www.iberia.com; Miramar Trade Center, cnr Av 3 & Calle 80, Playa)

Lacsa (code LRC; Map pp224–5; ☎ 833-3114; www.grupotaca.com; Hotel Habana Libre, cnr Calles L & 23, Vedado)

CLIMATE CHANGE & TRAVEL

Climate change is a serious threat to the ecosystems that humans rely upon, and air travel is the fastest-growing contributor to the problem. Lonely Planet regards travel, overall, as a global benefit, but believes we all have a responsibility to limit our personal impact on global warming.

Flying & Climate Change

Pretty much every form of motorized travel generates CO_2 (the main cause of human-induced climate change) but planes are far and away the worst offenders, not just because of the sheer distances they allow us to travel, but because they release greenhouse gases high into the atmosphere. The statistics are frightening: two people taking a return flight between Europe and the US will contribute as much to climate change as an average household's gas and electricity consumption over a whole year.

Carbon Offset Schemes

Climatecare.org and other websites use 'carbon calculators' that allow travelers to offset the level of greenhouse gases they are responsible for with financial contributions to sustainable travel schemes that reduce global warming – including projects in India, Honduras, Kazakhstan and Uganda.

Lonely Planet, together with Rough Guides and other concerned partners in the travel industry, support the carbon offset scheme run by climatecare.org. Lonely Planet offsets all of its staff and author travel.

For more information check out our website: www.lonelyplanet.com.

LAN (code LAN; Map pp224-5; ☎ 831-6186; www.lan
.com; Airlines Bldg, Calle 23 No 64, Vedado)

LTU International Airways (code LTU; Map pp224-5;
☎ 833-3524; www.ltu.com; Airlines Bldg, Calle 23 No
64, Vedado)

Martinair (code MPH; Map pp224-5; ☎ 833-3729; www
.martinair.com; cnr Calles 23 & E, Vedado)

Mexicana de Aviación (code MXA; Map pp224-5; ☎ 833-
3532; www.mexicana.com.mx; Airlines Bldg, Calle 23 No
64, Vedado)

Virgin Atlantic (code VIR; Map pp228-9; ☎ 204-0747;
www.virginatlantic.com; Miramar Trade Center, cnr Av 3 &
Calle 80, Playa)

Airport

Twenty-five kilometers southwest of
Habana via Av de la Independencia (Av de
Rancho Boyeros), José Martí International Airport
(code HAV; Map p232; ☎ 33-56-66) serves
the international and domestic needs of air
travelers arriving in and leaving the Cuban
capital. On a clear run it takes 30 minutes
to get into central Habana by taxi.

There are a number of terminals here.
Terminal 1, on the southeast side of the
runway, handles only domestic Cubana de
Aviación flights. Opposite, on the north
side of the runway, but 3km away via Av
de la Independencia, is Terminal 2, which
receives Corsair flights and charters from
Miami. All other international flights use
Terminal 3, an ultramodern facility that
opened in 1998 at Wajay, 2.5km west of
Terminal 2. Charter flights by Aerocaribbean, Aerogaviota and Aerotaxi to Cayo
Largo del Sur and elsewhere use the Caribbean Terminal (also known as Terminal 5),
at the northwest end of the runway, 2.5km
west of Terminal 3. (Terminal 4 hasn't been
built yet.)

BICYCLE

While rural Cuba might be a cyclist's paradise, negotiating the increasingly clogged
streets of urban Habana is an entirely different matter. If you *do* elect to use two wheels
rather than four, be sure to wear a helmet,
cycle at an off-peak time (Saturday or Sunday mornings are quietest), and take extra
care when weaving in and out of the traffic.

Habana has just one official bike-hire
outlet; it's called El Orbe (p145) and is located in Centro Habana.

BOAT

Cruise Ships & Yachts

Cruise ships that include Habana on their
itineraries are few and far between due to
the ongoing US trade embargo, which pro-
hibits vessels calling at Cuban ports from
visiting the US for six months.

Access by private yacht or cruiser is a little easier. Habana is served by one port authority in the Marina Hemingway (Map pp228-9;
☎ 209-7270; cnr Av 5 & Calle 248, Santa Fe),
situated 20km west of Habana. The marina
has four identical docking channels, which
are 1km long by 15m deep by 6m wide. No
prior visas or reservations are required for
those traveling by yacht, but you'll have to
purchase CUC$25 tourist cards upon arrival
if you plan to stay longer than 72 hours.
Private yachts bound for Cuba should try
to make radio contact with the Cuban port
authorities over channel 16 or 7462 SSB before crossing the 12-mile limit. Say *llamando
seguridad marítima* (calling maritime security) and quote the name of the port.

Required documents include the passports
of everyone on board; the ownership papers,
title and registration certificate of the vessel;
and the clearance document from your last
port, with Cuba listed as your destination.

Ferries

Ferries shuttle from Habana Vieja to Regla
and Casablanca, leaving every 10 or 15
minutes from Muelle Luz (Map p220; cnr
San Pedro & Santa Clara, Habana Vieja).
Thanks to an attempted hijacking in 2003,
expect to be searched before boarding. Foreigners are usually charged CUC$1, and the
crossings take 10 minutes.

BUS

Local Buses

Bus travel in Habana is not for the faint-hearted. Queues, crowds, belching fumes and the kind of claustrophobia that even Houdini would have struggled with are all part of the unrelenting package. Regular city buses are called *guaguas* (*wah*-wahs), while the much larger metro buses are termed *camellos* (camels) for their two elevated metallic humps that allow room for more passengers. Within the city the fare is a flat 25 centavos in an extended bus with an accordion connection in the middle or 50 centavos in a regular bus, which you must toss into a box near the driver or pay to a conductor.

You will find queues at most *paradas* (bus stops), even though they may be difficult to spot at first glance. To mark your place ask for *el último* (the last in line), and when the bus arrives get behind that person. At the originating stops, there are generally two lines, one for *sentados* (people who want a seat) and another for *parados* (people willing to stand). The second line moves faster and is best if you're going only a short distance and have no luggage.

Gas-guzzling *camellos* run along the routes of Habana's projected Moscow-style subway system, which was never built due to lack of money. The buses can squeeze in up to 300 passengers (uncomfortably) into their two humps and are hauled by fume-belching heavy-duty trucks. All have the prefix M before their number and run on well-established routes:

M-1	Alamar–Vedado via Parque de la Fraternidad
M-2	Parque de la Fraternidad–Santiago de las Vegas
M-3	Alamar–Ciudad Deportiva
M-4	Parque de la Fraternidad–San Agustín via Marianao
M-5	Vedado–San Agustín
M-6	Calvario–Vedado (corner of Calles 21 and L)
M-7	Parque de la Fraternidad–Alberro via Cotorro

Long-Distance Buses

Buses depart from Habana to every corner of Cuba. Of the two main bus companies, **Víazul** (www.viazul.com) is undoubtedly the best option with punctual, air-conditioned coaches to destinations of interest to travelers. Víazul is a convertible service for tourists and well-heeled Cubans, and you can be confident you'll get where you want to on these buses. Its buses cost slightly more than those of its competitor Astro, but the difference is marginal and gets even more negligible the further you travel. It's also a good way to meet other foreigners.

Víazul buses leave from the **Víazul Bus Terminal** (Map pp218-19; ☎ 881-1413, 881-5652; cnr Calle 26 & Zoológico, Nuevo Vedado), which is inconveniently situated 3km southwest of Plaza de la Revolución. It'll cost you CUC$5 in a taxi to get here from Parque Central.

Tickets for Víazul services are sold immediately prior to the departure in the Venta de Boletines office. You can get full schedules on the website or at Infotur (p197), which also sells tickets. Bookings via the Víazul website are unreliable and best avoided. Reservations with Víazul are advisable during peak travel periods (June to August, Christmas and Easter) and on popular routes. Destinations include Cienfuegos (CUC$20, five hours, two daily), Pinar del Río (CUC$11, four hours, two daily) and Varadero (CUC$10, three hours, three daily).

The other option is Astro, whose new fleet of modern Chinese-made buses venture to slightly more off-the-beaten track places. Astro sells passages to Cubans in pesos and tourists in convertibles, so you'll meet lots of locals this way. Foreign students with a Cuban *carnet* (identification document) can pay in pesos. If you plan on taking Astro buses, check ahead of time as there's never any printed schedule and only two tickets per bus are available for foreigners on each departure (although if there's space left 30 minutes before departure, staff will sell the seats to anyone). Many services only run on alternate days.

Astro buses depart from the **Terminal de Ómnibus** (Map pp224-5; ☎ 870-9401; cnr Av de la Independencia & Calle 19 de Mayo, Vedado), near the Plaza de la Revolución. Tickets sold in Cuban convertibles are readily available at the office marked **Venta de Boletines** (☎ 870-3397; ⏰ 24hr), down the hall to the right of the main entrance.

There's also a new daily Havanatur transfer bus that runs Habana–Soroa–Viñales, with further connections from Viñales. Inquire at Havanatur (p67) in Miramar.

CAR

With a plethora of inexpensive taxis and walking options, there's little reason to rent a car in Habana unless you intend to drive well beyond the city's limits. If you do decide to take the plunge, bear in mind that Habana's road rules are sketchy, signage is conspicuous by its absence and traffic is getting more congested by the day.

Fuel & Spare Parts

Gas is widely available in Servi-Cupet and Oro Negro stations all over Habana. The stores are often open 24 hours and may have a small spare-parts store on site. Gas is sold by the liter and comes in regular (CUC$0.75/L) and *especial* (CUC$0.95/L) varieties. Rental cars are advised to use especial. All gas stations have efficient pump attendants, usually in the form of *trabajadores sociales* (students in the process of studying for a degree).

While you cannot count on spare parts to be available per se, Cubans have decades of experience in keeping old wrecks on the road without factory parts, and you'll see them do amazing things with cardboard, string, rubber tubes and clothes hangers to keep a car mobile.

Petty theft of mirrors, antennas, taillights etc is common, so it's worth paying someone a convertible or two to watch your car for the night.

If you need air in your tires or you've got a puncture, use a gas station or visit the local *ponchero* (fixer of flat tires). There often aren't measurers, so make sure they don't overfill the tires.

Rental

Renting a car in Habana is very straightforward and you can usually be signed up and fitted out in well under an hour. You'll need your passport, driver's license and refundable CUC$200 deposit (in cash or non-US credit card). Note that there are very few rental cars with automatic transmission.

If you want to rent a car for three days or fewer, it will come with limited kilometers, while with contracts for three days or more, you'll get unlimited kilometers. In Cuba you pay for the first tank of gas when you rent a car (CUC$0.95/L) and return it empty – a suicidal policy that sees many tight-fisted tourists running out of gas a kilometer or so from the drop-off point. Just to make it worse, you will not be refunded for any gas left in the tank.

If you lose your rental contract or keys, you'll pay a CUC$50 penalty. Drivers under 25 pay a CUC$5 fee, while additional drivers on the same contract pay a CUC$15 surcharge.

Check over the car carefully with the rental agent before driving into the sunset as you'll be responsible for any damage or missing parts. Make sure there is a spare tire of the correct size, a jack and a lug wrench. Check also that there are seat belts and that all the doors lock properly.

We have received many letters about poor/nonexistent customer service, bogus spare tires, forgotten reservations and other car-rental problems. Reservations are only accepted 15 days in advance and are still not guaranteed. While agents are usually accommodating, you might end up paying more than you planned or have to wait hours until someone returns a car. The more Spanish you speak and the friendlier you are, the more likely problems will be resolved to everyone's satisfaction (tips to the agent might help). As with most Cuban travel, always be ready to go to plan B.

There's no shortage of car-rental offices in Habana. The fanciest cars are provided by Rex Rent a Car, and the most economical by Micar. Somewhere in between lie Havanautos, Cubacar, and Vía Rent a Car. Bank on paying CUC$60 a day for the cheapest small car and well over CUC$100 for something fancier. All of the car agencies have a info desk at the airport.

Cubacar Hotel Deauville (Map p222; cnr Av de Italia & Malecón, Centro Habana); Hotel Inglaterra (Map p222; Paseo de Martí No 416, Centro Habana); Hotel Meliá Cohiba (Map pp224–5; ☎ 833-3636; Paseo btwn Calles 1 & 3, Vedado); Hotel Meliá Habana (Map pp228-9; Av 3 btwn Calles 76 & 80, Playa); Hotel NH Parque Central (Map p222; Neptuno btwn Paseo de Martí & Agramonte, Centro Habana)

Havanautos Hotel Nacional (Map pp224–5; cnr Calles O & 21, Vedado); Hotel Riviera (Map pp224–5; cnr Paseo & Malecón, Vedado); Hotel Sevilla (Map p222; ☎ 866-8956; Trocadero No 55 btwn Paseo de Martí & Agramonte, Centro Habana)

Micar Calle 21 (Map pp224–5; cnr Calles 21 & M, Vedado); Calle 23 (Map pp224–5; cnr Calles 23 & H, Vedado); Hotel Nacional (Map pp224–5; ☎ 873-3891; cnr Calles O & 21, Vedado); Malecón (Map pp224–5; cnr Malecón & Calle 23, Vedado)

Rex Rent a Car (Map pp224-5; ☎ 33-77-88; cnr Línea & Malecón, Vedado)

Vía Rent a Car Aparthotel Montehabana (Map pp228-9; Calle 70 btwn Avs 5A & 7, Playa); Hotel Kohly (Map pp228-9; ☎ 204-2606; cnr Av 49A & Calle 36, Kohly); Occidental Miramar (Map pp228-9; cnr Av 5 & Calle 74, Playa); Panorama Hotel Havana (Map pp228-9; cnr Av 3 & Calle 70, Playa)

Road Rules

Cubans drive how they want, where they want. It seems chaotic at first, but it has its rhythm. Seat belts are supposedly required and maximum speed limits are technically 50km/h in the city, 90km/h on highways and 100km/h on the Autopista (the national highway), but some cars can't even go that fast – and those that can go faster still.

While the rest of Cuba is refreshingly traffic free, Habana is fast becoming a congested city, with cheap Venezuelan oil adding more vehicles to the road by the day.

A major problem is lack of signage: road junctions and turnoffs are often not indicated at all. Not only is this distracting, it's also incredibly time-consuming. The dearth of signage also extends to road instructions. Often a one-way street is not clearly indicated or a speed limit not highlighted, which can cause problems with the police (who won't understand your inability to telepathically absorb the rules).

TAXI

Metered tourist taxis are readily available at all of the upscale hotels, with the air-conditioned Nissan taxis charging higher tariffs than the non-air-conditioned Ladas. The cheapest official taxis are operated by Panataxi (☎ 55-55-55) and cost CUC$1 flagfall, then CUC$0.50 a kilometer. Tourist taxis charge CUC$1 a kilometer and can be ordered from Taxi OK (Map pp228-9; ☎ 204-9518; Calle 8 btwn Avs 1 & 3, Miramar). Almost all hotel receptions will be able to book you a taxi relatively quickly.

The cheapest taxis are the older yellow-and-black Ladas, which are state-owned but rented out to private operators. They won't wish to use their meters, as these are set at an unrealistically low rate, but you can bargain over the fare. They're not supposed to pick up passengers within 100m of a tourist hotel.

Bici-taxis

If you bargain hard, two-seater bici-taxis (bicycle taxis) will take you anywhere around Centro Habana for CUC$2. It's a lot more than a Cuban would pay, but cheaper and more fun than a tourist taxi. Bici-taxis are licensed to carry only Cubans, and drivers may wish to go via a roundabout route through the backstreets to avoid police controls (if the drivers get caught breaking the rules, it's their problem not yours).

Colectivos

Colectivos are old prerevolution American cars that act as collective taxis for Cubans. They're not supposed to take foreigners but, if you're stuck somewhere out of the way – Guanabacoa, for instance – you can bargain for a ride.

TRAIN

Trains to most parts of Cuba depart from Estación Central de Ferrocarriles (Map p220; ☎ 862-4971, 861-8540; Av de Bélgica & Arsenal, Habana Vieja). Foreigners must buy tickets for dollars at La Coubre Train Station (☎ Map p220; 862-1006; cnr Av del Puerto & Desamparados, Habana Vieja; ☉ 9am-3pm Mon-Fri). If it's closed, try the Lista de Espera office adjacent, which sells tickets for trains leaving immediately. Kids under 12 travel half-price. Rail services include Holguín (CUC$27, one daily), Mantanzas (CUC$4, eight daily) and Pinar del Río (CUC$6.50, one daily). Services are routinely delayed or canceled; always double-check scheduling and the terminal from which your train will leave.

Cristina Station (Map pp224-5; cnr Av de México & Arroyo, Cuatro Caminos) lies about a kilometer southwest of the Estación Central de Ferrocarriles. It handles local trains within the city limits but is notoriously unreliable. The once convenient train to Boyeros (for Parque Lenin) and ExpoCuba was not working at the time of writing.

The Casablanca Train Station (Map p230; ☎ 862-4888), next to the ferry wharf on the east side of the harbor, is the western terminus of the only electric railway in Cuba. In 1917 the Hershey Chocolate Company of the US state of Pennsylvania built this line to Matanzas, and trains still depart for

Matanzas five times a day (currently at 4:43am, 8:35am, 12:39pm, 5:21pm and 9:17pm). The 8:35am service is an 'express.' You'll travel via Guanabo (CUC$0.80, 25km), Camilo Cienfuegos (Hershey; CUC$1.45, 46km), Jibacoa (CUC$1.65, 54km) and Canasí (CUC$1.95, 65km) to Matanzas (CUC$2.80, 90km). The train usually leaves Casablanca on time but often arrives an hour late. It's a scenic four- to five-hour trip, and tickets are easily obtainable at the station (except on weekends and holidays when it could be crowded). For more information, see p177.

PRACTICALITIES

ACCOMMODATIONS

Accommodations in Habana run the whole gamut, ranging from the CUC$25 a night Hotel Lido to the CUC$290 a night Hotel Saratoga, with plenty of variety and quality in between.

For the purposes of this book, budget means anything under CUC$60 for two people in the low season. In this range, casas particulares (private houses that let out rooms to foreigners) compete with rough-and-ready government hotels in dire need of a renovation (with a couple of notable exceptions). As a result, private rooms are usually the best deal, though bear in mind that in cheaper casas particulares (around CUC$20), you may have to share a bathroom, and the room will have a fan instead of air-con. Only the most deluxe casas particulares in Vedado and Miramar

will cost anything over CUC$35; in these places you'll be assured of quality amenities and attention.

The midrange category is a lottery, with some stylish colonial hotels for CUC$60 to CUC$130 a double in the low season, and some less distinguished places. In midrange hotels, you can expect air-con, hot-water bathrooms, clean sheets, satellite TV, a restaurant and a swimming pool – although the architecture is often uninspiring and the food not exactly gourmet.

Unsurprisingly, the most comfortable hotels cost CUC$130 and up for two people. These are usually partly foreign- or Habaguanex-owned and maintain international standards, although service can sometimes be a bit lax. Rooms have quality beds and linens, a minibar, international phone service and perhaps a terrace or view. In this category, Habana has some real gems.

Factors influencing rates are the time of year, the location and the hotel chain. Low season is usually mid-September to early December, and February to May (except for Easter week), though different hotels post slightly different schedules. Check before you book.

Casas Particulares

Private rooms are the best option for independent travelers in Habana, and a great way of meeting locals on their home turf. Staying in these family-run establishments will show you the city with its guard down, and your understanding (and appreciation) of Habana will be far richer as a result. Casa owners also often make excellent tour guides.

MISIÓN MILAGROS

Misión Milagros (Miracle Mission) is the unofficial name given to a pioneering medical program hatched between Cuba and Venezuela in 2004 that offers free eye treatment for impoverished Venezuelans in Cuban hospitals. By the beginning of 2006, over 150,000 Venezuelans had been successfully treated for eye ailments caused by cataracts, glaucoma, diabetes and other diseases under the scheme and, as a result, the program had been extended to at least 10 other Latin American and Caribbean countries, including Guyana and Bolivia.

In order to participate in Misión Milagros, foreign patients are first diagnosed and selected in their home country before being flown free of charge to Habana for treatment. Here advanced laser technology is able to correct easily rectified eye disorders and restore obscured or diminished vision within a matter of hours. Newly sighted patients are given complimentary accommodation in a variety of Cuban hotels and are bused around for free on a special fleet of Chinese-made Astro buses.

At the time of writing, a number of tourist hotels in Habana were temporarily out of action due to the Misión Milagros program. These included the Copacabana and Bello Caribe in Playa, El Viejo y El Mar in Marina Hemingway, the Panamericano in Cojímar and a number of hotels in Playas del Este.

Owners of casas particulares must keep a register of all guests and report each new arrival within 24 hours. For these reasons, you will find it hard to bargain for rooms. You will also be requested to produce your passport. For more information, see p160.

Hotels

All tourist hotels and resorts are at least 51% owned by the Cuban government and are administered by one of five main organizations.

Islazul has the cheapest hotels, and is the only accommodation option that rents to both Cubans and foreigners (although at different prices). While the facilities can be variable and the architecture a tad Soviet-esque, Islazul hotels are invariably clean, cheap, friendly and, above all, Cuban. One downside is the blaring on-site bars and discos that often keep guests awake until the small hours.

Cubanacán is a step up and offers a mix of midrange options ranging from the scruffy Hotel El Viejo y El Mar in the Marina Hemingway to the boutique Hotel Chateau Miramar in Miramar.

Gaviota manages higher-end Cuban resorts ranging from the value-for-money Hotel Bosque to the ubermodern Hotel Panorama.

Gran Caribe does midrange to top-end hotels, including the three-star Hotel Vedado, the four-star Hotel Inglaterra and, the jewel in its crown, the five-star Hotel Nacional.

Lastly, Habaguanex is based solely in Habana and manages most of the fastidiously restored historic hotels in Habana Vieja. The profits from these ventures go directly toward restoring the old town (see p42).

Because each group has its own niche, throughout this book we mention the chain to which a hotel belongs to give you some idea of what to expect on the ground.

BUSINESS HOURS

Some offices are open from 8:30am to 5:30pm Monday to Saturday with a lunch break from 12:30pm to 1:30pm, although most stay open continuously from 9am to 5pm. Offices remain closed every other Saturday. Post offices are generally open 8am to 6pm Monday to Saturday; banks only open 9am to 3pm weekdays and close at noon on the last working day of each month.

Shopping hours are generally from 9am to 5pm Monday to Saturday and 9am to 2pm Sunday. Pharmacies are open from 8am to 8pm daily, while museums maintain hours from 9am to 5pm Tuesday to Saturday and 8am to noon Sunday. Make a note that a lot of touristy stuff is closed in Habana on Monday. Churches are often open only for Mass, although you'll sometimes be let in the back door if you ask around.

Most restaurants are open 10:30am to 11pm daily; paladares (privately run restaurants) usually open at noon and stay open a little later.

CHILDREN

There are many travelers with kids in Cuba, especially Cuban-Americans visiting family with their children; these will be your best sources for on-the-ground information. One aspect of the culture that parents may find foreign (aside from the material shortages) is the physical contact and human warmth that is so typically Cuban: waitresses will mind your baby, strangers will ruffle your kids' hair and Cuban babysitters will quickly introduce your children to the whole neighborhood. Diapers are available in Habana, but can be expensive – best bring your own. Basic kid-specific medicines are also sometimes hard to get. See p66 for sightseeing ideas. For more general advice, check out Lonely Planet's *Travel with Children*.

CLIMATE

Habana has a warm, tropical climate, although the heat is moderated by trade winds. See p26 for further details.

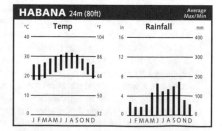

COURSES

Art

The **Taller Experimental de Gráfica** (Map p220; ☎ 7-862-0979; Callejón del Chorro No 6, Habana Vieja) offers classes in the art of engraving. Individualized instruction lasts one month, during which time the student creates an engraving with 15 copies; longer classes can be arranged. The cost is around CUC$250.

Language

The first port of call for aspiring foreign-language students is the **Universidad de la Habana** (Map pp224-5; ☎ 832-4245, 831-3751; dpg@uh.cu; 2nd fl, Edificio Varona, Calle J No 556, Vedado), which offers Spanish courses throughout the year, beginning on the first Monday of each month. Costs start at CUC$100 for 20 hours (one week) – including textbooks – and cover all levels from beginners to advanced. You must first sit a placement test to determine your level. Aspiring candidates can sign up in person at the university or reserve beforehand via email or phone.

Other places to inquire about Spanish courses include **Unión Nacional de Escritores y Artistas de Cuba** (Uneac; Map pp224-5; ☎ 832-4551; cnr Calles 17 & H, Vedado) and **Paradiso** (Map pp224-5; ☎ 832-9538; Calle 19 No 560, Vedado)

Private lessons can be arranged by asking around locally; try your casa particular.

Music & Dance

Courses for foreigners can be arranged throughout the year by the Oficina de Relaciones Internacionales of the **Instituto Superior de Arte** (ISA; Map pp228-9; ☎ 7-208-8075; Calle 120 No 1110, Cubanacán). Courses in percussion and dance are available almost anytime, but other subjects (such as visual arts, music, theater and aesthetics) are offered when teachers are available.

Courses usually involve four hours of classes a week, costing between CUC$10 and CUC$15 per hour. Prospective students must apply in the last week of August for the fall semester, or in the last three weeks of January for spring. The school is closed for holidays from the start of July until the third week in August. The institute also accepts graduate students for its regular winter courses, and an entire year of study here (beginning in September) as part of a regular five year program costs approximately CUC$2500. Accommodations in student dormitories can be arranged.

The **Conjunto Folklórico Nacional** (Map pp224-5; El Gran Palenque, Calle 4 No 103, btwn Calzada and Calle 5, Vedado) teaches highly recommended classes in *son* (Cuba's basic form of popular music), salsa, rumba, mambo and more. The classes start on the first Mondays in January and July, and cost in the vicinity of CUC$400 to CUC$500 for a 15-day course. An admission test places students in classes of four different levels. It also offers 15-day courses in percussion starting on the third Monday in January and the first Monday in July.

Travelers might be able to organize flamenco guitar lessons by inquiring at the **Centro Andaluz** (Map p222; ☎ 863-6745; Paseo de Martí No 104 btwn Genios & Refugio, Centro Habana).

See p145 for one-off dance classes.

CUSTOMS

Cuban customs regulations are complicated. For the full scoop, see www.aduana .islagrande.cu.

Travelers are allowed to bring in personal belongings (including photography equipment, binoculars, musical instrument, tape recorder, radio, personal computer, tent, fishing rod, bicycle, canoe and other sporting gear), gifts up to a value of US$250 and 10kg of medicine in its original packaging. Those over the age of 18 may import 2L of liquor and one carton of cigarettes.

Items that do not fit into the categories mentioned above are subject to a 100% customs duty to a maximum of US$1000.

Items prohibited entry into Cuba include narcotics, explosives, pornography, electrical appliances (which are broadly defined), GPS, prerecorded video cassettes and 'any item attempting against the security and internal order of the country,' including some books. Canned, processed and dried foods are no problem, nor are pets.

Exporting art and items of cultural patrimony is restricted and involves fees, paperwork and forethought. See Exporting Artwork (p150) for details. You are allowed to export 23 single cigars duty free.

DISCOUNT CARDS

There are no youth hostels in Habana, so a HI card won't prove useful. It is also unlikely that a student or seniors' card will get you reduced entry into museums. Students with a Cuban *carnet* (identification document) can pay for museums, bus and train tickets, and theater performances in pesos.

ELECTRICITY

The most common voltage is 110 volts, 60 cycles, but you'll also find 220 volts. Side-by-side sockets that have different voltage are usually labeled, but always ask. The sockets are suited to North American–style plugs with two flat prongs.

EMBASSIES

Most embassies are open from 8am to noon on weekdays.

Austria (Map pp228-9; ☎ 7-204-2825; fax 7-204-1235; Calle 4 No 101, Miramar)

Belgium (Map pp228-9; ☎ 7-204-2410; fax 7-204-1318; Av 5 No 7406, Miramar)

Canada (Map pp228-9; ☎ 7-204-2516; www.dfait -maeci.gc.ca/cuba; Calle 30 No 518, Playa) Also represents Australia.

Denmark (Map p222; ☎ 7-33-81-28; dancons@enet.cu; 4th fl, Paseo de Martí No 20, Centro Habana)

France (Map pp228-9; ☎ 7-204-2308; http://www.am bafrance-cu.org; Calle 14 No 312 btwn Avs 3 & 5, Miramar)

Germany (Map pp224-5; ☎ 7-33-25-69; alemania@enet .cu; Calle 13 No 652, Vedado)

Japan (Map pp228-9; ☎ 7-204-3508; fax 7-204-8902; Miramar Trade Center, cnr Av 3 & Calle 80, Playa)

Mexico (Map pp228-9; ☎ 7-204-7722; fax 7-204-2666; Calle 12 No 518, Miramar)

Netherlands (Map pp228-9; ☎ 7-204-2511; hav@minbuza.nl; Calle 8 No 307, btwn Avs 3 & 5, Miramar)

Spain (Map p222; ☎ 7-33-80-25; embespcu@correo.mae .es; Capdevila No 51, Centro Habana)

Sweden (Map pp228-9; ☎ 7-204-2831; http://www .swedenabroad.com/havanna; Calle 34 No 510, Miramar)

Switzerland (Map pp228-9; ☎ 7-204-2611; fax 7-204-2729; Av 5 No 2005 btwn Avs 20 & 22, Miramar)

UK (Map pp228-9; ☎ 7-204-1771; www.britishembassy .gov.uk/cuba; Calle 34 No 708, Miramar) Also represents New Zealand.

US (Map pp224-5; ☎ 7-833-3546; http://havana .usinterestsection.gov; Interests Section, Calzada btwn Calles L & M, Vedado)

EMERGENCY

The English-speaking staff at **Asistur** (Map p222; ☎ 866-4121, 866-4499; Paseo de Martí No 208, Centro Habana; ⏰ 8:30am-5:30pm Mon-Fri, 8am-2pm Sat) can help with most emergencies, including getting money sent from abroad (except the US), expediting insurance claims, arranging rental cars and booking hotel rooms. This is a place to go if you are a victim of crime or need legal advice. The staff may also be able to help if your credit cards aren't accepted in Cuba.

If you get robbed you will need to obtain a police statement as quickly as possible. Contact the **Policía Nacional Revolucionaria** (Map p220; ☎ 882-0116; Picota btwn Leonor Pérez & San Isidro, Habana Vieja; ⏰ 24hr), located near the Estación Central de Ferrocarriles.

Always carry a copy of your passport in Habana. If you lose the original, report it to your embassy first of all.

GAY & LESBIAN TRAVELERS

While Habana can't be called a queer destination (yet), it's more tolerant than many other Latin American cities. The hit movie *Fresa y Chocolate* (Strawberry and Chocolate) sparked a national dialogue about homosexuality, and Habana is pretty tolerant, all things considered. People from more accepting societies may find this tolerance token (everyone has a gay friend/relative/coworker, whom they'll mention when the topic arises), but what the hell, you have to start somewhere, and both Habana and Cuba are moving in the right direction.

A few gay and lesbian gathering spots have been established, although gay bars and clubs don't really exist on a permanent basis. To connect with private parties, called *fiestas de diez pesos* (10 peso parties; so called for the cost of admission), see p138.

HOLIDAYS

Cuba's public holidays are as follows:

Liberation Day January 1

Labor Day May 1

Commemoration of the Assault of the Moncada Garrison July 26

Independence Day October 10

Christmas Day December 25

Directory PRACTICALITIES

On these days, most shops, offices and museums are closed.

July and August are the main holiday months for *habaneros* (inhabitants of Habana), when most families flock to the beaches of Playas del Este.

See p12 for festivals and events throughout the year in Habana.

INTERNET ACCESS

Cuba's internet service provider is national phone company Etecsa. Etecsa runs two *telepuntos* (internet-cafés-cum-call-centers) in Habana, one in **Habana Vieja** (Map p220; Habana 406; ☺ 8am-9:30pm) and one in **Centro Habana** (Map p222; Águilar No 565; ☺ 8am-9:30pm). The drill is to buy a one-hour user card (CUC$6) with a scratch-off user code and *contraseña* (password), and help yourself to a free computer. These cards are interchangeable in either *telepunto,* so you don't have to use up your whole hour in one go.

The downside of the Etecsa monopoly on the internet is that there are few, if any, independent internet cafés outside of the two *telepuntos* and many of the cheaper hotels – unable to afford the service fee – have had to dispose of their computers. Your best bet is to use the internet facilities at one of Habana's four- or five-star hotels. While the fees here are often higher than at an internet café, the hotels can at least guarantee quick service, fast access and fully functioning computers. Habaguanex have recently installed computers in all of their city-center hotels, which all take the same one-hour interchangeable card (which can purchased for CUC$6).

As internet access for Cubans is restricted, you may be asked to show your passport when using an internet-linked computer.

LIBRARIES

The main city library is the **Biblioteca Pública Provincial Rubén M Villena** (Map p220; Obispo No 59, Habana Vieja; ☺ 8am-9pm Mon-Fri, 9am-4pm Sat).

The **Biblioteca Nacional José Martí** (Map pp224-5; Av de la Independencia, Vedado; ☺ 8am-5:45pm Mon-Sat), on the Plaza de la Revolución in Vedado, is also open to the general public, but you must leave your bags in a cloakroom.

MAPS

Free maps can be procured from Infotur (p197). Cubacar (p187) also produces a good free city map, which highlights its sales offices, but also plenty of other city sights. Most of the Habaguanex hotels offer a decent tear-off map of Habana Vieja that clearly marks all Habaguanex-run properties.

Otherwise your best guide to the old city is *La Habana Vieja Guía Turística,* published by the Instituto Cubano de Geodesia y Cartografía (GeoCuba). It contains 35 maps of the old town, along with 222 pages of references and helpful descriptions in Spanish, English, French and German. It is available at some hotel shops.

GeoCuba also publishes *Ciudad de la Habana Mapa Turístico,* which covers all 15 municipalities in detail, including good scale street maps of the city center and Playas del Este. The fold-out *Guía de Carreteras,* with countrywide and Habana city maps, is very useful if you'll also be exploring other provinces. Highway signs around Habana are poor to nonexistent, and these maps are almost essential for drivers.

MEDICAL SERVICES

Most medical problems can be addressed at the **Hospital Nacional Hermanos Ameijeiras** (Map pp224-5; ☎ 877-6053; San Lázaro No 701, Vedado), just off the Malecón. Foreigners pay in hard currency. Entry is via the lower level below the parking lot off Padre Varela (Belascoaín); ask for 'CEDA' in Section N.

Another decent international clinic is **Clínica Central Cira García** (Map pp228-9; ☎ 204-2811; fax 24-16-33; Calle 18A No 4101, Playa). Consultations at both places cost in the vicinity of CUC$30.

MONEY

Two currencies circulate in Cuba: convertible pesos (CUC$) and Cuban pesos (also called *moneda nacional,* abbreviated to MN). Most things tourists buy are in convertibles (eg accommodations, rental cars, bus tickets, museum admission and internet access). At the time of writing, Cuban pesos were selling at 29 to one convertible, and while there are many things you can't buy with *moneda nacional,* using them on certain occasions means you'll see a bigger slice of authentic Cuba.

As far as money transactions go, cash is king and you should arrive in Cuba with enough to last for the duration of your trip. Changing currency will incur a 10% commission. The best currencies to carry are euros, Canadian dollars or pound sterling; the worst is US dollars and – despite the prices you might see posted up in bank windows – the commission you'll get charged is a whopping 20% (the normal 10% commission plus an extra 10% penalty).

Cadecas (change booths) in every city and town sell Cuban pesos, and travelers are perfectly within their rights to buy them; you won't need more than CUC$10 worth of pesos a week. In addition to the *cadecas* listed in this book, there is almost always a *cadeca* at the local agropecuario (free-enterprise vegetable market). However, most peso shops, restaurants, and buses will also accept the equivalent convertible payment.

You can't take more than CUC$200 out of Cuba. Travelers attempting to smuggle out more are liable to have the money confiscated by customs with no compensation.

See p23 for information about costs, and inside front cover for exchange rates.

ATMs

Although there are numerous ATMs springing up around Habana, at the time of research, none of them were accepting foreign debit cards. Unless you want to risk losing your card, don't attempt to use the machines.

Changing Money

The following is a list of useful banks and kiosks for changing money.

Banco de Crédito y Comercio (Map pp224-5; Línea No 705, Vedado)

Banco de Crédito y Comercio (Map pp224-5; Airlines Bldg, Calle 23 No 64, Vedado)

Banco de Crédito y Comercio (Map pp224-5; Av Independencia No 101, Vedado)

Banco Financiero Internacional (Map p220; cnr Oficios & Brasil, Habana Vieja)

Banco Financiero Internacional (Map pp228-9; cnr Av 5 & Calle 92, Playa)

Banco Metropolitano (Map p222; cnr Av de Italia & San Martin, Centro Habana)

Banco Metropolitano (Map pp224-5; cnr Línea & Calle M, Vedado)

Cadeca (Map p220; cnr Oficios & Lamparilla, Habana Vieja)

Cadeca (Map pp224-5; Calle 23 btwn Calles K & L, Vedado)

Cadeca (Map pp224-5; cnr Calles 19 & A, Vedado)

Cadeca (Map p231; cnr Paseo Panamericano & 5D, Cojímar)

Cambio (Map p220; Obispo No 257; Habana Vieja; ☽ 8am-10pm)

Money-changing kiosk (Map pp224-5; Hotel Habana Libre, cnr Calles L & 23, Vedado)

Money-changing kiosk (Map pp224-5; Hotel Nacional, cnr Calles O & 21, Vedado)

Money-changing kiosk (Map p222; Hotel NH Parque Central, Neptuno btwn Paseo de Martí & Agramonte, Centro Habana)

Money-changing kiosk (Map p222; Hotel Sevilla, Trocadero No 55 btwn Paseo de Martí & Agramonte, Centro Habana)

Credit Cards

Credit cards are liable for an 11.25% commission and thus are normally demoted to the emergencies-only bracket. Some of the better hotels will accept credit cards, and you can draw money on them from most banks, but the commission's always the same.

Traveler's Checks

Traveler's checks in currencies other than US dollars can be exchanged in some banks, but it's a hassle and the commission runs between 4% and 6%.

NEWSPAPERS & MAGAZINES
Foreign Publications

CubaNews (www.cubanews.com) puts out a surprisingly evenhanded monthly business report on the Cuban economy that was formerly published by the *Miami Herald*. Subscription rates are listed on its website, though it's mainly aimed at top executives.

Perhaps the most comprehensive and unbiased news source is the *Havana Journal* (www.havanajournal.com), which is based in the US. News reports are interesting, well written and up-to-the-minute. Of the international heavyweights, the BBC (www.bbc.co.uk) has a good mixture of both quirky and news-breaking stories.

Government Publications

Cuba's two national dailies, the insipid *Granma* (www.granma.cu) and the slightly edgier *Juventud Rebelde*, won't take you more than 10 minutes to read cover to cover, primarily because neither is more than eight pages long. Packed with a mix of politics, politics and – um – politics, *Granma* is the official organ of the Communist Party of Cuba, and was founded in 1963 through the merger of *Revolución* and *Hoy*. It ain't exactly the *New York Times*.

Granma Internacional, a weekly summary of the Cuban press, is published in Spanish, English, French, Portuguese and German. Old men will come up to you on the streets of Habana Vieja and attempt to peddle you a copy for CUC$1.

Other Habana newspapers include *Trabajadores*, the organ of the Central de Trabajadores de Cuba (published Monday), and *El Habanero* (Tuesday and Friday).

The tourism magazine *Prisma* is published every other month in English and Spanish. The best cultural periodical is the beautifully presented *Opus Habana*, which you should be able to browse for free in any Habaguanex hotel. Alternatively, you can pick up back copies at the Publicaciones de la Oficina del Historiador (p152).

PHARMACIES

Cuba has a good selection of international pharmacies catering to foreigners.

Centro Oftalmológico Camilo Cienfuegos (Map pp224-5; Calle L No 151, Vedado)

Cira García Pharmacy (Map pp228-9; ☎ 204-2880; Calle 18A No 4104, Playa; ◷ 24hr)

Farmacia Homopática (Map pp224-5; cnr Calles 23 & M, Vedado; ◷ 8am-8pm Mon-Fri, 8am-4pm Sat)

Farmacia Internacional (Map pp228-9; Hotel El Comodoro, cnr Av 1 & Calle 84, Playa)

Farmacia Taquechel (Map p220; ☎ 862-9286; Obispo No 155, Habana Vieja; ◷ 9am-6pm)

Hospital Nacional Hermanos Ameijeiras (Map pp224-5; ☎ 877-6053; San Lázaro No 701, Vedado)

Pharmacy (Map pp224-5; Hotel Habana Libre, cnr Calles L & 23, Vedado)

Pharmacy (Map p222; Hotel Sevilla, Trocadero No 55 btwn Paseo de Martí & Agramonte, Centro Habana)

Pharmacy (Map pp228-9; cnr Calle 20 & Av 41, Playa; ◷ 9am-8:45pm)

POST

Habana has numerous post offices sprinkled all around the city. Letters and postcards sent to Europe and the US take about a month to arrive. If you're sending stuff to a Cuban from abroad, it'll probably take even longer. Postcards and letters are cheap to send and you don't have to pay more than CUC$1 to send them anywhere in the world. Prepaid postcards, including international postage, are available at most hotel shops and post offices and are the surest bet for successful delivery. For important mail, you're better off using DHL, located in **Miramar** (Map pp228-9; ☎ 204-1578; cnr Av 1 & Calle 26; ◷ 8am-8pm) and at the **Hotel Nacional** (Map pp224-5; cnr Calles O & 21, Vedado; ◷ 8am-8pm); it costs approximately CUC$55 for a 2lb letter pack to Australia, or CUC$50 to Europe. Post offices can be found at the following locations:

Centro Habana (Map p222; cnr San Martín & Paseo de Martí)

Habana Vieja (Map p220; Oficios No 102)

Miramar (Map pp228-9; Calle 42 No 112 btwn Avs 1 & 3)

Vedado (Map pp224-5; cnr Línea & Paseo)

Vedado (Map pp224-5; cnr Calles 23 & C; ◷ 8am-6pm Mon-Fri)

Vedado (Map pp224-5; Av de la Independencia btwn Plaza de la Revolución & Calle 19 de Mayo)

SAFETY

Habana is ostensibly a safe city, and violent crime is rare. A heavy police presence on the streets and stiff prison sentences for crimes such as robbery and assault have acted as a major deterrent to potential thieves and kept the dirty tentacles of organized crime firmly at bay.

That's not to say that incidents don't occur. Indeed petty crime against tourists is on the rise, with bag snatching by youths mounted on bicycles a particular worry.

Keep your money belt on you at all times, making sure that you wear it concealed – and tightly secured – around your waist.

In hotels always use a safety-deposit box and never leave money/passports/credit cards lying around during the day. Theft from hotel rooms is rife in Habana at the moment, with the temptation of earning three times their monthly salary in one fell swoop often too hard to resist for some people.

In bars and restaurants it is wise to always check your change. Intentional overcharging, especially when a customer is mildly inebriated, is tediously common.

Visitors from the well-ordered countries of Europe or litigation-obsessed North America should be subconsciously aware of crumbling sidewalks, manholes with no covers, overenthusiastic drivers, veering cyclists, carelessly lobbed front-door keys (in Habana Centro) and badly pitched baseballs (almost everywhere). Waves cascading over the Malecón sea wall might look romantic, but the resulting slime-fest has been known to throw Lonely Planet–wielding tourists unceremoniously onto their asses.

TELEPHONE

The Cuban phone system is still undergoing some upgrading, so beware of phone-number changes. Normally a recorded message will inform you of any recent upgrades. Habana's two main Etecsa *telepuntos* (p193) have recently been refurbished and the phones generally work pretty well, even if the internet doesn't.

Cell Phones

Cuba's two cell-phone companies are c.com and Cubacel. While you may be able to use your own equipment, you have to pre-buy their services. Cubacel has offices at José Martí International Airport and in the **Miramar Trade Center** (cnr Av 3 & Calle 80, Playa). Its plan costs approximately CUC$3 per day and each local call costs from CUC$0.52 to CUC$0.70. Note that you pay for incoming as well as outgoing calls. International rates are CUC$2.70 per minute to the US and CUC$5.85 per minute to Europe.

Phonecards

Etecsa *telepuntos* (p193) are where you buy phonecards, send and receive faxes, use the internet and make international calls. Blue Etecsa public phones accepting magnetized or computer-chip cards are everywhere. The cards are sold in convertibles (CUC$5, CUC$10 and CUC$20) and pesos (3, 5 and 7 pesos). You can call nationally with either, but you can only call internationally with cards in convertibles. If you are mostly going to be making national and local calls, buy a peso card as it's much more economical.

International calls made with a card cost from CUC$2.50 per minute to the US and Canada, and CUC$5 to Europe and Oceania. Calls placed through an operator or from a hotel cost slightly more.

TIME

Habana is five hours behind GMT/UTC, the equivalent of Eastern Standard Time in the US and Canada. If it's noon in Habana, it will be 9am in California , 11am in Mexico City, 5pm in Britain, 6pm in Western Europe and 5am the next day in New Zealand.

Habana is on daylight saving time from April to September, when the city is only four hours behind GMT/UTC. In other words, clocks are turned an hour back at the beginning of October and an hour forward in late March.

TIPPING

If you're not in the habit of tipping, you'll learn fast in Cuba. Wandering *son* septets, parking guards, ladies at bathroom entrances, restaurant wait staff, tour guides – they're all working for hard-currency tips. Musicians who besiege tourists while they dine, converse or flirt will want a convertible peso, but only give what you feel the music is worth. Washroom attendants expect five or 10 cents, while *parqueadores* (parking attendants) should get CUC$0.25 for a short watch and CUC$1 for 12 hours. For a day tour, CUC$2 per person is appropriate for a tour guide. Taxi drivers will appreciate 10% of the meter fare, but if you've negotiated a ride without the meter, don't tip as the whole fare is going straight into their wallets.

Tipping can quickly *resuelvan las cosas* (fix things up). If you want to stay beyond the hotel check-out time or enter a site after hours, for instance, small tips (CUC$1 to CUC$5) bend rules, open doors and send people looking the other way. For tipping in restaurants and other advice, see p110.

TOURIST INFORMATION

Nearly every hotel in Habana has a tour office and/or travel agency representing one of the five main companies. Anyone off the street can effectively pop in and use them. As there's no real sense of business competition in socialist Habana, all the agencies are much the same in terms of prices, although San Cristóbal Agencia de Viajes has the best tours and guides. See p66 for travel agencies.

Habana's only official tourist information service is Infotur (Map p220; ☎ 33-33-33; www .infotur.cu; Obispo No 358, Habana Vieja; ☼ 8:30am-5:30pm), which sells locally published maps and guidebooks, and can book a variety of excursions and activities at competitive rates (including Víazul bus tickets). The staff speak English and are usually good about answering questions. Aside from its Habana Vieja HQ, Infotur has other offices in Habana Vieja (Map p220; ☎ 862-4586; cnr Obispo & San Ignacio; ☼ 8:30am-5:30pm), Playa (Map pp228-9; ☎ 204-7036; cnr Av 5 & Calle 112; ☼ 8:30am-5pm) and José Martí International Airport (☎ 66-61-01; Terminal 3; ☼ 8:30am-5pm).

TRAVELERS WITH DISABILITIES

Cuba's inclusive culture translates to travelers with disabilities, and while facilities may be lacking, the generous nature of Cubans generally compensates.

Travelers in wheelchairs will find the few ramps ridiculously steep and will have trouble in colonial parts of town, where sidewalks are narrow and streets are cobblestone; elevators are also often out of order.

However, sight-impaired travelers will be helped across streets and (like travelers in wheelchairs) given priority in lines. Etecsa phone centers have telephone equipment for the hearing impaired, and TV programs are broadcast with closed captioning. The Hotels NH Parque Central (p164), Meliá Cohiba (p168) and Meliá Habana (p170) all have specific facilities for travelers with disabilities.

VISAS

Regular tourists who plan to spend up to two months in Cuba do not need visas. Instead, you get a *tarjeta de turista* (tourist card) valid for 30 days (Canadians get 90 days), which can be easily extended for another 30 days once you're in Cuba. Those going 'air only' usually buy the tourist card from the travel agency or airline office that sold them their plane ticket; you'll receive the card on the plane before landing. Package tourists receive their card with their other travel documents.

Unlicensed tourists originating in the US buy their tourist card at the airline desk in the country through which they're traveling en route to Cuba (equivalent of US$25). You are usually not allowed to board a plane to Cuba without this card, but if by some chance you find yourself cardless, you should be able to buy one at the José Martí International Airport in Habana – although this is a hassle (and a risk) that's best avoided. Once in Habana, tourist-card extensions or replacements cost another CUC$25. You cannot leave Cuba without presenting your tourist card, so don't lose it. You are not permitted entry to Cuba without an onward ticket.

The 'address in Cuba' line should be filled in with the name of hotel or a legal *casa particular*, if only to avoid unnecessary questioning. Take care to fill the card out properly and clearly as Cuban customs officials are meticulous.

Extensions

For most travelers, obtaining an extension once in Cuba is easy: you just go to an immigration office and present your documents and CUC$25 worth of stamps. You should obtain these stamps from a branch of Bandec or Banco Financiero Internacional (p194) beforehand. You'll only receive an additional 30 days after your original 30 days; after this expires you must re-enter the country on a separate card and start over again. Attend to extensions at least a few business days before your visa is due to expire and never attempt to travel around Cuba with an expired visa.

Habana's Immigration Office (☎ 203-0307; cnr Factor & Santa Ana, Nuevo Vedado; ☼ 8:30am-noon & 2pm-4pm Mon, Tue, Thu & Fri) is inconveniently located way out in the sticks and you'll need a taxi to get there. It gets crowded so get there early and be prepared to queue. Staff don't generally speak English and aren't over helpful, so make sure you have all your documentation on hand.

Restrictions on US Visitors

In 1961 the US government imposed an order limiting the freedom of its citizens to visit Cuba, and forbidding airline offices and travel agencies in the US from booking tourist travel to Cuba via third countries.

However, the Cuban government has never banned Americans from visiting Cuba, and it continues to welcome US passport holders under exactly the same terms as any other visitor.

Americans traditionally go to Cuba via Canada, Mexico, the Bahamas, Jamaica or any other third country. Most Americans book their trips with a foreign travel agency, which will arrange Cuban tourist cards, flight reservations and accommodation packages.

The immigration officials in Cuba know very well that a Cuban stamp in a US passport can create problems and as result no passports are stamped; instead the Cubans stamp your tourist card.

The US government has an Interests Section in Habana, but American visitors are advised to go there only if something goes terribly wrong. Therefore, unofficial US visitors should be especially careful not to lose their passports while in Cuba, as this would put them in a very difficult position. Many Cuban hotels rent security boxes (CUC$2 per day) to guests and nonguests alike, and you can carry a photocopy of your passport for identification on the street.

There are two types of licenses issued by the US government to visit Cuba: general licenses (typically for family members, artists and academics) and special licenses (for journalists on assignment, foreign officials based in the US, and occasionally for other people on humanitarian grounds). In 1995 the list of permissible travel was expanded to include educational and cultural exchanges, but George W Bush discontinued this license category in 2003, cutting off 70% of the travel that had been deemed 'legal.' Cuban-Americans may visit relatives in Cuba once every three years with a general license. Such permits are never issued for the purpose of business travel or tourism.

For more information, contact the Licensing Division (☎ 202-622-2480; www.treas .gov/ofac; Office of Foreign Assets Control, US Department of the Treasury, 2nd fl, Annex Bldg, 1500 Pennsylvania Ave NW, Washington, DC, 20220).

Under the Trading with the Enemy Act, goods originating in Cuba are prohibited from being brought into the US by anyone but licensed travelers. Cuban cigars, rum, coffee etc will be confiscated by US customs, and officials can create additional problems if they feel so inclined. Possession of Cuban goods inside the US or bringing them in from a third country is also banned.

American travelers who choose to go to Cuba generally get rid of anything related to their trip to Cuba, including used airline tickets, baggage tags, travel documents, receipts and souvenirs, before returning to the US. If Cuban officials don't stamp their passport, there will be no official record of their trip. They also use a prepaid Cuban telephone card to make calls to the US in order to avoid there being records of collect or operator-assisted telephone calls.

Since September 11, 2001, all international travel issues have taken on a new importance, and there has been a crackdown on travel to Cuba. Though it has nothing to do with terrorism, some Americans returning from Cuba have had 'transit to Cuba' written in their passports by Jamaican customs officials. Customs officials at major US entry points (eg New York, Houston, Miami) are onto backpacker types coming off Cancún and Montego Bay flights with throngs of honeymoon couples, or tanned gentlemen arriving from Toronto in January. They're starting to ask questions, reminding travelers that it's a felony to lie to a customs agent as they do so.

The maximum penalty for unauthorized Americans traveling to Cuba is US$250,000 and 10 years in prison. In practice, people are usually fined US$7500. Since George W Bush came into the White House, the number of people threatened with legal action has more than tripled and it's likely to go higher still. Over 100,000 US citizens a year travel to Cuba with no consequences; however, as long as these regulations remain in place, visiting Cuba certainly qualifies as soft adventure travel for Americans.

There are many organizations, including a group of congress people on Capitol Hill, working to lift the travel ban; see www.cu bacentral.com for more information.

WOMEN TRAVELERS

In terms of personal safety, Cuba is a dream destination for women travelers. Most streets can be walked alone at night, violent crime is rare and the chivalrous aspect of machismo means you'll never step into oncoming traffic. But machismo cuts both ways, with protection on one side and pursuit on the other. Cuban women are used

Directory PRACTICALITIES

to *piropos,* the whistles, kissing sounds and compliments that constantly ring in their ears, and might even reply with their own if they're feeling frisky. For foreign women, however, it can feel like an invasion. Like any cross-cultural situation, you'll have to come to terms with it somehow.

Ignoring *piropos* is the first step. But sometimes ignoring them isn't enough. Learn some rejoinders in Spanish so you can shut men up who can't seem to themselves. *No me moleste* (don't bother me), *esta bueno yá* (all right already) and *que falta respeto* (how disrespectful) are good ones, as is the withering 'don't you dare' stare that is part of the Cuban woman's arsenal. Wearing plain, modest clothes might help lessen unwanted attention; topless sunbathing is out. An absent husband, invented or not, seldom has any effect. If you go to a disco, be very clear with Cuban dance partners what you are and are not interested in. Dancing is a kind of foreplay in Cuba and may be viewed as an invitation for something more. Cubans appreciate directness and as long as you set the boundaries, you'll have a fabulous time. Being in the company of a Cuban man is the best way to prevent *piropos,* but if all else fails, retire to the pool for a day out of the line of fire.

Traveling alone can be seen as an invitation for all kinds of come-ons, and solo women travelers will not have an easy time of it. Traveling with a male traveler (or another woman – at least you'll share the barrage) can do wonders. Marriage proposals will come fast and from all corners, as matrimony is an easy way to immigrate for Cubans who want out.

WORK

There are a number of bodies offering volunteer work in Cuba, though it is always best to organize things in your home country first. Just turning up in Habana and volunteering can be difficult, even impossible. Take a look at the following websites:

Canada-Cuba Farmer to Farmer Project (www.farmer tofarmer.ca) A Vancouver-based sustainable agriculture organization.

Canada World Youth (☎ 1-514-931-3526; www.cwy -jcm.org) The head office is in Montreal, Canada.

Cuban Solidarity Campaign (☎ 44-20-72-63-64-52; www.cuba-solidarity.org) The head office is in London, UK.

National Network on Cuba (www.cubasolidarity.com) US-based solidarity group.

Pastors for Peace (☎ 1-212-926-5757; www.ifconews .org) Collects donations across US to take to Cuba.

Witness for Peace (☎ 1-202-588-1471; www.witness forpeace.org) The organization is looking for Spanish speakers for a two-year commitment.

Language

Language

It's true – anyone can speak another language. Don't worry if you haven't studied languages before or if you studied a language at school for years and can't remember any of it. It doesn't even matter if you failed English grammar. After all, that's never affected your ability to speak English! And this is the key to picking up a language in another country. You just need to start speaking.

Learn a few key phrases before you go. Write them on pieces of paper and stick them on the fridge, by the bed or even on the computer – anywhere that you'll see them often.

You'll find that locals appreciate travelers trying their language, no matter how muddled you may think you sound. So don't just stand there, say something! If you want to learn more Spanish than we've included here, pick up a copy of Lonely Planet's comprehensive but user-friendly *Latin American Spanish Phrasebook*.

SOCIAL
Meeting People
Hi!
¡Hola!
Bye!
¡Chau!
Please.
Por favor.
Thank you (very much).
(Muchas) Gracias.
Yes.
Sí.
No.
No.
Excuse me. (to get past)
Permiso.
Sorry!
¡Perdón!
Pardon? (as in 'What did you say?')
¿Cómo?/¿Qué?
Do you speak English?
¿Hablá inglés?
Does anyone speak English?
¿Hay alguien que hable inglés?
Do you understand? (informal)
¿Me entendés?
Yes, I understand.
Sí, entiendo.
No, I don't understand.
No, no entiendo.

Could you please ...? (polite)
¿Puede ... por favor?

speak more slowly	hablar más despacio
repeat that	repetirlo
write it down	escribirlo

Going Out
What's there to do in the evenings?
¿Qué se puede hacer a las noches?

What's on ...?
¿Qué pasa ...?

around here	para acá
this weekend	este fin de semana
today	hoy
tonight	esta noche

Where are the ...?
¿Dónde hay ...?

places to eat	lugares para comer
clubs/pubs	boliches/pubs
gay venues	lugares para gays

Is there a local entertainment guide?
¿Hay una guía de entretenimiento de la zona?

PRACTICAL
Question Words

Who?	¿Quién/Quiénes? (singular/plural)
Who is it?	¿Quién es?
What?	¿Qué?
Which?	¿Cuál/Cuáles? (singular/plural)
When?	¿Cuándo?
Where?	¿Dónde?
How?	¿Cómo?
How much is it?	¿Cuánto cuesta?
Why?	¿Por qué?

Numbers & Amounts

0	cero
1	uno
2	dos
3	tres
4	cuatro
5	cinco
6	seis
7	siete
8	ocho
9	nueve
10	diez
11	once
12	doce
13	trece
14	catorce
15	quince
16	dieciséis
17	diecisiete
18	dieciocho
19	diecinueve
20	veinte
21	veintiuno
22	veintidós
30	treinta
31	treinta y uno
32	treinta y dos
40	cuarenta
50	cincuenta
60	sesenta
70	setenta
80	ochenta
90	noventa
100	cien
1000	mil
2000	dos mil

Days

Monday	lunes
Tuesday	martes
Wednesday	miércoles
Thursday	jueves
Friday	viernes
Saturday	sábado
Sunday	domingo

Banking

I'd like to change ...	Quisiera cambiar ...
cash	dinero en efectivo
money	dinero
a traveler's check	un cheque de viajero

Where's the nearest ATM?
¿Dónde está el cajero automático más cercano?

Where's the nearest foreign exchange office?
¿Dónde está la oficina de cambio más cercana?

Do you accept ... ?	¿Aceptan ... acá?
credit cards	tarjetas de crédito
debit cards	tarjetas de débito
traveler's checks	cheques de viajero

Post

Where's the post office?
¿Dónde está el correo?
I want to buy a stamp/an envelope.
Quiero comprar un estampilla/sobre.

I want to send a ...	
Quiero enviar ...	
fax	un fax
parcel	un paquete
postcard	una postal

Phone & Cell Phones

I want to buy a phonecard.
Quiero comprar una tarjeta telefónica.

I want to make a ...	
Quiero hacer una ...	
call (to ...)	llamada (a ...)
collect call	llamada con cobro revertido

Where can I find a/an ...?
¿Dónde puedo encontrar ...?
I'd like a/an ...
Quiero ...

adaptor plug	un adaptador
charger for my cell phone	un cargador para mi celular
cell phone for hire	un celular para alquilar
prepaid cell phone	un celular pagado por adelantado
SIM card for your network	una tarjeta SIM para su red

Internet

Where's the local internet café?
¿Dónde hay un cibercafé por acá?

I'd like to ...	
Quiero ...	
get online	usar internet
check my email	revisar mi correo electrónico

Transportation

What time does the ... leave?
¿A qué hora sale el ...?

| boat | barco |
| bus | guagua |

What time's the ... (bus)?
¿A qué hora es el ... (colectivo)?

first	primer
last	último
next	próximo

Is this taxi available?
¿Está disponible este taxi?
Please put the meter on.
Por favor, ponga el taxímetro.
How much is it to ...?
¿Cuánto cuesta ir a ...?
Please take me (to this address).
Por favor, lléveme (a esta dirección).

FOOD

breakfast	desayuno
lunch	almuerzo
dinner	cena
snack	snack
to eat	comer
to drink	tomar

Can you recommend a ...?
¿Puede recomendar ...?

bar	un bar
café	un café
restaurant	un restaurante

Is the service charge included in the bill?
¿El precio en el menu incluye el servicio de cubierto?

For more detailed information on food and dining out, see p17.

EMERGENCIES

It's an emergency!
¡Es una emergencia!
Could you help me, please?
¿Me puede ayudar, por favor?
Where's the police station?
¿Dónde está la comisaría?

Call ...!
¡Llame a ...!

the police	la policía
a doctor	un médico
an ambulance!	una ambulancia

HEALTH

Where's the nearest ...?
¿Dónde está ... más cercano?

dentist	el dentista
doctor	el médico
hospital	el hospital

Where's the nearest (night) chemist?
¿Dónde está la farmacia (de turno) más cercana?
I need a doctor (who speaks English).
Necesito un médico (que hable inglés).

Symptoms

I have (a/an) ...
Tengo ...

diarrhoea	diarrea
fever	fiebre
headache	dolor de cabeza
pain (here)	dolor (acá)

I'm allergic to ...
Soy alérgica a ... (for a woman)
Soy alérgico a ... (for a man)

antibiotics	los antibióticos
peanuts	los maníes
penicillin	la penicilina

GLOSSARY

See also p22 for Cuban slang.

agropecuario – free-enterprise vegetable market; also sells rice, beans and fruit

altos – upstairs apartment, when following an address

americano – citizen of any western hemisphere country; a citizen of the US is called a *norteamericano* or an *estadounidense*

Autopista – national highway that runs west to Pinar del Río and east toward Santa Clara

babalawo – *Santería* priest; also spelled *babalao*

bajos – lower apartment, when following an address

balseros – rafter; used to describe the emigrants who escaped to the US in the 1990s on homemade rafts

batá – conical two-headed drum

batanga – subgenre of mambo, popularized by Benny Moré

bici-taxi – bicycle taxi

bloqueo – Cuban term for the US embargo

bohío – thatched hut

bolero – romantic love song

cabildo – town council during the colonial era; also an association of tribes in Cuban religions of African origin

cadeca – change booth

camello – literally 'camel;' metro buses in Habana named for their two humps

campesino – person who lives in the country

caliente – hot

canoñazo – shooting of the cannons; a nightly ceremony performed at the Fortaleza de San Carlos de la Cabaña

casa particular – private house that lets out rooms to foreigners (and sometimes Cubans); all legal casas must display a blue-and-white symbol on their door

chachachá – dance derived from the mambo and *rumba,* invented in 1951

charanga – *son*-influenced music from 1940s and '50s played with violin and flute

chekere – gourd covered with beads to form a rattle

coco taxi – yellow egg-shaped taxi that holds two or three people and runs on batteries

cola – line, queue

colectivo – collective taxi (usually a classic American car) that operates for Cubans

comida criollo – traditional Cuban food; normally rice, beans and pork

conseguir – to get, obtain

convertibles – convertible pesos

criollo – Creole; Spaniard born in the Americas

dalquirí – rum cocktail made with crushed ice and other ingredients; named for the Río Daiquirí, near Santiago de Cuba, where it was invented in 1899

danzón traditional Cuban ballroom dance colored with African influences

El Líder Maximo – Maximum Leader; term often used to describe Fidel Castro

el último – the last; used to ascertain who is last when you join a Cuban queue

Elegguá – god of destiny in *Santería*

encomienda – land with an indigenous workforce; entrusted to an individual by the Spanish Crown during the early colonial era

esquina caliente – literally 'hot corner'; where baseball fanatics debate stars, teams and form in the most animated fashion

Granma – yacht that carried Fidel and his companions from Mexico to Cuba in 1956 to launch the revolution

guayabera – pleated, buttoned men's shirt

habanero/a – inhabitant of Habana

Habaguanex – City Historian's Office; responsible for restoring Habana Vieja

Icaic – Instituto Cubano del Arte e Industria Cinematográficos; Cuban Film Institute

jinetera – woman who attaches herself to male foreigners for monetary or material gain; the exchange may or may not involve sex

jinetero – male tout who hustles tourists

M-26-7 – 26th of July Movement; Fidel Castro's revolutionary organization, was named for his abortive assault on the Moncada army barracks in Santiago de Cuba on July 26, 1953

machetero – one who cuts sugarcane using a machete

Misión Milagros – unofficial name given to a pioneering medical program hatched between Cuba and Venezuela in 2004 that offers free eye treatment for Venezuelans in Cuban hospitals

mojito – stirred drink made from rum, lime juice, sugar, soda, mint leaves and ice

moneda nacional – Cuban pesos; abbreviated to MN

nueva trova – philosophical folk music popularized in the 1960s and '70s

orisha – *Santería* deity

organopónico – urban vegetable garden run by community groups; sells produce from small on-site kiosk

paladar – privately owned restaurant

parada – bus stop

PCC – Partido Comunista de Cuba; Cuba's only political party

pelota – baseball

peninsular – a Spaniard born in Spain but living in the Americas

peña – musical performance or get-together

período especial – special period; Cuba's post-1991 economic reality

piropo – flirtatious remark or commentary

reggaeton – Cuban hip-hop; mix of reggae and hip-hop

Regla de Ocha – see *Santería*

resolver – to resolve or fix a problematic situation

rumba – dance form that originated among plantation slaves during the 19th century; in Cuba today, to rumba simply means 'to party'

salsa – catchall designation used for Cuban music based on *son*

Santería – literally 'saint worship'; Afro-Cuban religion that amalgamates West African *Yoruba* beliefs with Roman Catholicism

santero – priest of *Santería*

son – Cuba's basic form of popular music that jelled from African and Spanish elements in the late 19th century

Taíno – settled, Arawak-speaking tribe that inhabited much of Cuba prior to the Spanish conquest

tambores – *Santería* drumming ritual

telenovela – TV soap opera

timba – modern salsa music mixed with funk, rap and rock

trova – traditional poetic singing

Uneac – Unión Nacional de Escritores y Artistas de Cuba; National Union of Cuban Writers and Artists

Yoruba – Afro-Cuban religion originating in Nigeria

Behind the Scenes

THIS BOOK

This 2nd edition of *Havana* was researched and written by Brendan Sainsbury. Scott Doggett wrote the 1st edition with help from David Stanley, who authored the first two editions of Lonely Planet's *Cuba*. This guidebook was commissioned in Lonely Planet's Oakland office, and produced by the following:

Commissioning Editors Kathleen Munnelly, David Zingarelli

Coordinating Editor Laura Stansfeld

Coordinating Cartographer Marion Byass

Coordinating Layout Designer Pablo Gastar

Managing Editor Barbara Delissen

Managing Cartographers David Connolly, Alison Lyall, Adrian Persoglia

Assisting Editor Kristin Odijk

Assisting Cartographer Jacqueline Nguyen

Cover Designer Marika Kozak

Project Managers Craig Kilburn, Kate McLeod

Language Content Coordinator Quentin Frayne

Thanks to Sally Darmody, Adriana Mammarella, Malcolm O'Brien, Vivek Wagle, Celia Wood, Wendy Wright

Cover photographs Cars traveling through Habana, Mark Lewis/Getty Images (top); Musician on the streets of Habana, Joe Malone/Jon Arnold Images/Alamy (bottom); Playas del Este, Bertrand Gardel/Hemis/Alamy (back)

Internal photographs p6 Christopher P Baker/Lonely Planet Images; p6 Jennifer Dunlop/Alamy; p5 Rick Gerharter/Lonely Planet Images; p4, p7 Richard I'Anson/Lonely Planet Images; p8 Bob Krist/CORBIS; p2 Doug McKinlay/Lonely Planet Images; p5 José Fuste Raga/CORBIS; p88, p141, p145, p168 Brendan Sainsbury.

All images are copyright of the photographer unless otherwise indicated. Many of the images in this guide are available for licensing from Lonely Planet Images: www .lonelyplanetimages.com.

LONELY PLANET: TRAVEL WIDELY, TREAD LIGHTLY, GIVE SUSTAINABLY

The Lonely Planet Story

The story begins with a classic travel adventure: Tony and Maureen Wheeler's 1972 journey across Europe and Asia to Australia. There was no useful information about the overland trail then, so Tony and Maureen published the first Lonely Planet guidebook to meet a growing need.

From a kitchen table, Lonely Planet has grown to become the largest independent travel publisher in the world, with offices in Melbourne (Australia), Oakland (USA) and London (UK). Today Lonely Planet guidebooks cover the globe. There is an ever-growing list of books and information in a variety of media. Some things haven't changed. The main aim is still to make it possible for adventurous individuals to get out there – to explore and better understand the world.

The Lonely Planet Foundation

The Lonely Planet Foundation proudly supports nimble nonprofit institutions working for change in the world. Each year the foundation donates 5% of Lonely Planet company profits to projects selected by staff and authors. Our partners range from Kabissa, which provides small nonprofits across Africa with access to technology, to the Foundation for Developing Cambodian Orphans, which supports girls at risk of falling victim to sex traffickers.

Our nonprofit partners are linked by a grass-roots approach to the areas of health, education or sustainable tourism. Many – such as Louis Sarno who works with BaAka (Pygmy) children in the forested areas of Central African Republic – choose to focus on women and children as one of the most effective ways to support the whole community. Louis is determined to give options to children who are discriminated against by the majority Bantu population.

Sometimes foundation assistance is as simple as restoring a local ruin like the Minaret of Jam in Afghanistan; this incredible monument now draws intrepid tourists to the area and its restoration has greatly improved options for local people.

Just as travel is often about learning to see with new eyes, so many of the groups we work with aim to change the way people see themselves and the future for their children and communities.

THANKS

BRENDAN SAINSBURY

I would like to extend thanks to all of the people who aided me in the production of this book. In Habana, a special thanks to Jorge Puñales, Vilma Hitchman, Stephen Gibbs, Tony Tella, Regla Hernández, Enrique Nuñez del Valle, Eddy Gutiérrez, and Julio and Elsa Roque. Back at the office, thanks to David Zingarelli, my commissioning editor; Kathleen Munnelly for her help in preparing the brief; and Laura Stansfeld for getting this book in tip-top shape for publication. Once again, a special *gracias* to my wife Elizabeth and my son Kieran for accompanying me to Habana, and providing numerous moments of light relief during the write-up.

OUR READERS

Many thanks to the travelers who used the last edition and wrote to us with helpful hints, useful advice and interesting anecdotes:

Ashok Agarwal, Kerri Amos, D Andrew, Felix Bassoon, Kimberley Carpenter, Alex Danilov, Jolanda de Boer, Courtney Elliott, Liliana Gervais, John Grant, Marie-France Guimond, Rafael Inigo Ilarde, Anton Gabriel Jusayan, Mika Länsisalmi, Andre Meyer, Grant O'Neill, Hans Philipsen, Catherine Rolfsen, Conchita Sangrador, Ariella Schiff, Kat Smith, Varouj Symonette, Cathryn Tattersall, Rasmus Thorsen, Frank Tyler, Chris Vatcher

SEND US YOUR FEEDBACK

We love to hear from travelers – your comments keep us on our toes and help make our books better. Our well-traveled team reads every word on what you loved or loathed about this book. Although we cannot reply individually to postal submissions, we always guarantee that your feedback goes straight to the appropriate authors, in time for the next edition. Each person who sends us information is thanked in the next edition – and the most useful submissions are rewarded with a free book.

To send us your updates – and find out about Lonely Planet events, newsletters and travel news – visit our award-winning website: www.lonelyplanet.com /contact.

Note: We may edit, reproduce and incorporate your comments in Lonely Planet products such as guidebooks, websites and digital products, so let us know if you don't want your comments reproduced or your name acknowledged. For a copy of our privacy policy visit www.lonelyplanet.com/privacy.

Notes

Dominique dominique.blanchet7@
wanadoo.fr

Banboko-TANIA
Jaila

Index

See also separate indexes for Eating (p214), Drinking (p215), Entertainment (p215), Shopping (p216) and Sleeping (p216).

Index

Index

000 map pages
000 photographs

Index

MAP LEGEND

ROUTES

Freeway	One-Way Street
Primary Road	Mall/Steps
Secondary Road	Tunnel
Tertiary Road	Walking Tour
Lane	Walking Tour Detour
Under Construction	Walking Trail
Track	Walking Path
Unsealed Road	Pedestrian Overpass

TRANSPORT

Ferry	Rail

HYDROGRAPHY

River, Creek	Lake, Water
Swamp	

BOUNDARIES

Provincial	Cliff
Ancient Wall	

AREA FEATURES

Airport	Cemetery, Christian
Area of Interest	Land
Building, Featured	Zoo, Botanical
Building, Other	Park
Building, Transport	

POPULATION

✪ CAPITAL (NATIONAL)	● Medium City
◉ CAPITAL (STATE)	● Town, Village

SYMBOLS

Sights/Activities
- Beach
- Castle, Fortress
- Christian
- Diving, Snorkeling
- Jewish
- Monument
- Museum, Gallery
- Other Site
- Ruin
- Snorkeling

Eating
- Eating

Drinking
- Drinking
- Café

Entertainment
- Entertainment

Shopping
- Shopping

Sleeping
- Sleeping
- Camping

Transport
- Airport, Airfield
- Bus Station
- Parking Area
- Gas Station
- Other Transport
- Taxi Rank

Information
- Bank, ATM
- Embassy/Consulate
- Hospital, Medical
- Information
- Internet Facilities
- Police Station
- Post Office, GPO
- Telephone
- Toilets
- Other Information

Geographic
- Lighthouse
- Lookout
- Mountain, Volcano
- National Park
- Waterfall

Maps

Straits of Florida

See Eastern Forts Map (p227)

See Centro Habana Map (p222)

See Regla & Casablanca Map (p230)

See Vedado Map (pp224–5)

Casablanca

See Playa & Marianao Map (pp228–9)

Vedado

Centro Habana

Habana Vieja

Bahía de la Habana

Regla

See Habana Vieja Map (p220)

Víazul Bus Terminal

Ciudad Deportiva

Río

San Franc de Pa

Playa

Marianao

Río Quibú

See Parque Lenin Area Map (p232)

Río Jaimanitas

Autopista Habana-Pinar del Río

Embalse Niña Bonita

Parque Zoológico Nacional

Parque Lenin

Embalse Ejército Rebelde

Carretera Central

Punta Brava

Río Almendares

Embalse Paso Sequito

Río Pancho Simón

To Pinar del Río (121km)

Autopista del Mediodía

José Martí International Airport

Santiago de las Vegas

Jardín Botánico Nacional

Santuario de San Lázaro

El Rincón

Bejucal

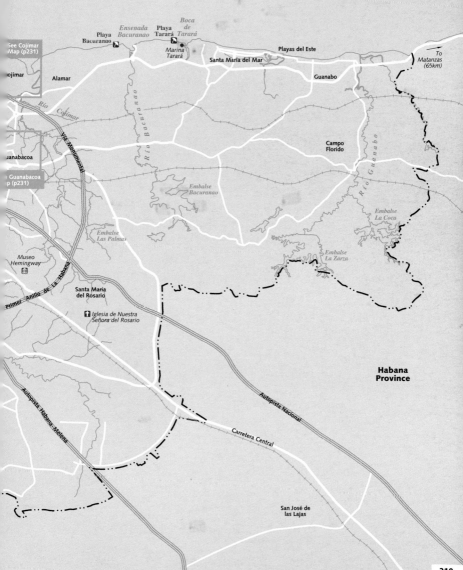

0 ⊏━━━━━━━━ 5 km
0 ■■■■■━━━━ 3 miles

Playa
Bacuranao

*Ensenada
Bacuranao*

Playa
Tarará

*Boca
de
Tarará*

See Cojímar
Map (p231)

*Marina
Tarará*

Playas del Este

Santa María del Mar

To
Matanzas
(65km)

ojímar

Alamar

Guanabo

*Río
Cojimar*

Vía Monumental

Campo
Florido

*Río
Guanabo*

uanabacoa

e Guanabacoa
p (p231)

Río Bacuranao

*Embalse
Bacuranao*

*Embalse
La Coca*

*Embalse
Las Palmas*

*Embalse
La Zarza*

Museo
Hemingway

Primer Anillo de La Habana

Santa María
del Rosario

Iglesia de Nuestra
Señora del Rosario

**Habana
Province**

Autopista Habana-Melena

Autopista Nacional

Carretera Central

San José de
las Lajas

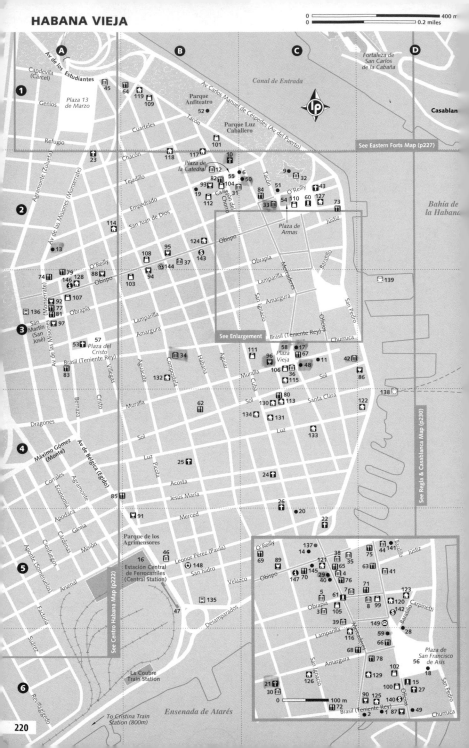

HABANA VIEJA

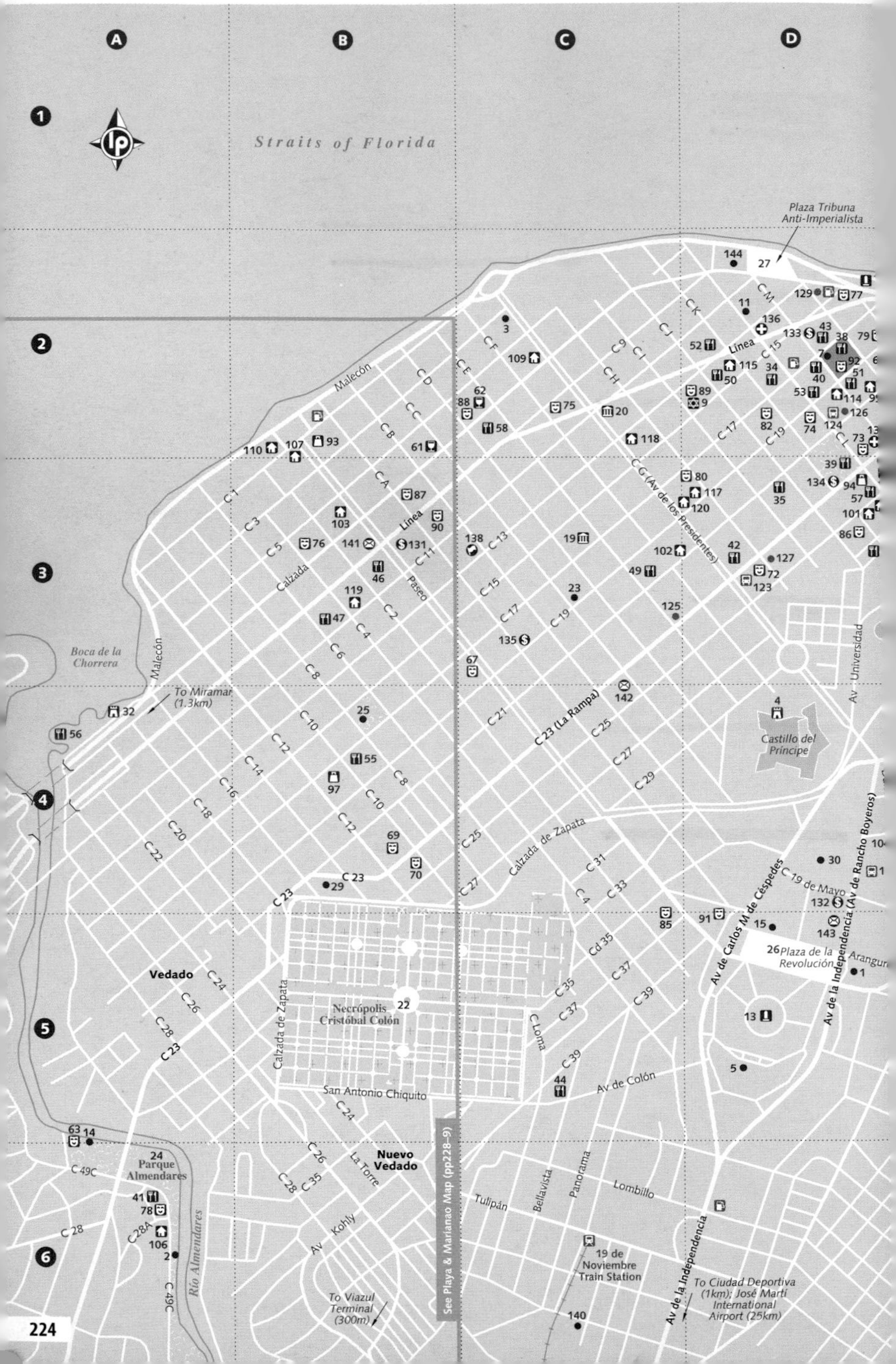

Straits of Florida

A **B** **C** **D**

1

2

Plaza Tribuna Anti-Imperialista

Malecón

3

Boca de la Chorrera

To Miramar (1.3km)

4

Castillo del Príncipe

5

Vedado

Necrópolis Cristóbal Colón 22

San Antonio Chiquito

Parque Almendares 24

Nuevo Vedado

La Torre

Plaza de la Revolución 26

6

To Viazul Terminal (300m)

19 de Noviembre Train Station

To Ciudad Deportiva (1km); José Martí International Airport (25km)

See Playa & Marianao Map (pp228–9)

0
0

See Eastern Forts Map (p227)

Castillo de
los Tres Santos
Reyes del Morro

Via (Monumental)

1

Tunnel

Dársena
de los
Franceses

Bahía de
la Habana

2

108
128
122
37
Malecón (Av Maceo)
Caleta de
San Lázaro

Humboldt
71   54
121
48
1   59
11   60
113   64
31
Parque
Maceo

Príncipe
Vapor

San Lázaro
139   68

Malecón

San Lázaro

Paseo de Martí (Prado)

Agramonte (Zulueta)

Av de las Misiones (Monserrate)

Blanco
Aguila
Crespo

Av de Italia (Galiano)

Lagunas
Ánimas

Callejón
de Hamel

Joyellar
San Lázaro
66
Virtudes
Concordia
Neptuno

Espada
Hospital
Aramburu

Padre Varela (Belascoaín)

Marqués González
Lucena
Oquendo
Soledad

San Miguel
San Rafael
San Martín (San José)

Amistad

Barcelona

Capitolio
Nacional

Habana
Vieja

3

12
16
36
98
84

Calzada de Infanta

San Francisco
San Lázaro

3
21

Zanja
Salud

Zanja

Av Simón Bolívar (Reina)

Escobar
Lealtad
Perseverancia
Campanario
Manrique
San Nicolás

Factoría

Agramonte

Av de Bélgica (Egido)

83
28
Pocito
Av Salvador Allende (Carlos III)
96
Enrique Barnet (Estrella)
Maloja
Sitio
Peñalver
Desagüe
Benjumeda
Santo Tómas
Clavel
Santa Marta

San Carlos

Padre Varela (Belascoaín)

Figuras
Carmen
Rastro

Indio

San Nicolás
Recio

Estación
Central de
Ferrocarriles
(Central Station)

4

See Habana Vieja Map (p220)

La Coubre
Train Station

Calzada de Infanta

Calzada de Ayestarán

Llinás   Bruzón

Av 20 de Mayo

Manglar
Arroyo (Av Manglar)

Av de España (Vives)
Puerta Cerrada
Diaria

Desamparados

Ensenada de Atarés

5

Máximo Gómez (Monte)

Av de México (Cristina)

Cristina
Train
Station

Fabrica

Estadio
Latinoamericano
B

Calzada del Cerro

Cerro

To San Francisco
de Paula (14km)

Via Blanca

6

EASTERN FORTS

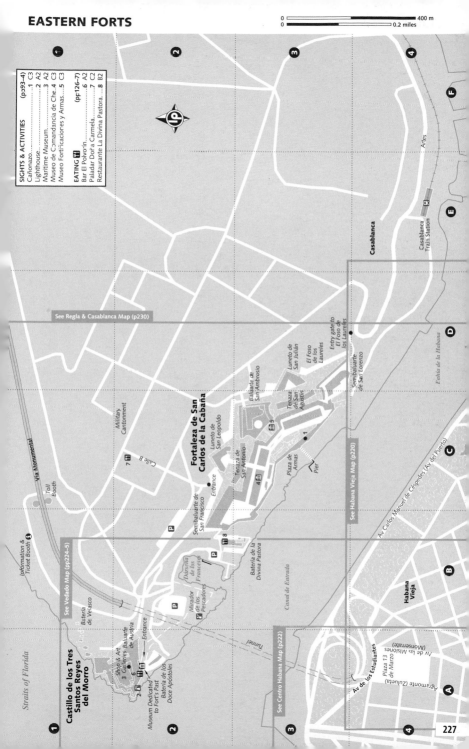

0 ——— 400 m
0 ——— 0.2 miles

See Regla & Casablanca Map (p230)

Casablanca

Casablanca
Train Station

Castillo de los Tres
Santos Reyes
del Morro

Straits of Florida

Información &
Ticket Booth

Batería
de Velasco

Shop & Art
Galleries
Baluarte
de Austria
Entrance

Museum Dedicated
to Fort's Past
Batería de los
Doce Apóstoles

Mirador de los
Pescadores

Dársena
de los
Franceses

Batería de la
Divina Pastora

Semibaluarte de
San Francisco

Entrance

Fortaleza de San
Carlos de la Cabaña

Military
Cantonment

Via Monumental

Toll
Booth

Tenaza de
San Antonio

Luneto de
San Leopoldo

Baluarte de
San Ambrosio

Tenaza de
San Agustín

Luneto de
San Julián

El Foso
de los
Laureles

Entry gate to
El Foso de
los Laureles

Semibaluarte
de San Lorenzo

Plaza de
Armas

Pier

Canal de Entrada

Calle B

Ensenada de la Habana

See Vedado Map (pp224–5)

See Centro Habana Map (p222)

See Habana Vieja Map (p220)

Tunnel

Habana
Vieja

Av Carlos Manuel de Céspedes (Av del Puerto)

Av de las Misiones (Monserrate)
Agramonte (Zulueta)
Av de los Estudiantes
Plaza 13
de Marzo

Artes

A · **B** · **C** · **D**

1

2 · **3**

C   F   G   H

Straits of Florida

Malecón (Av de Maceo)

To Habana
Vieja
(6.5km)

Paseo
Calzada
Linea

1

Boca
de la
Chorrera

Vedado

7

72 Av 3

46

20 Av 1 Av 10

34

48

38 31

78 80

15 25

Parque
Miramar

87

29 21 22

76 39

55 85

Miramar

86

60 75

54 1

19 52 35

18

65 42

69

59 68

74

82 64

66 8

Playa

73

26

81 67

43

9

Av 9

61

Río Quibú

24 C 140

Cubanacán

3

53

2

41

Zamora

Marianao

Ciudad
Libertad

13

12

28 La Paz

Pogolotti

49 83

50

Av 41

77

44 84

Parque
Almendares

C 49C

C 28

C 47

58 Kohly

5

45

Buena Vista

47

Necrópolis
Cristóbal
Colón

2

Nuevo
Vedado

C 23 (La Rampa)

Calzada de Zapata

Av Kohly

Río Almendares

C 49C

3

4

5

6

See Vedado Map (pp224–5)

See Parque Lenin Area Map (p232)

Autopista Habana-Pinar del Río

To Parque
Lenin (14km)

To Pinar
del Río (158km)

229

0 ——————— 500 m
0 ——————— 0.3 mile

A   **B**   **C**   **D**

1

Via Monumental

Carretera al Dique

2   Casablanca

See Eastern Forts Map (p227)

Carretera   Casablanca

3   3   6
Casablanca
Train Station   Artes
9

Bahía de la Habana

See Guanabacoa Map (p231)

4

Ferry

Ensenada de
Marimelena

See Habana Vieja Map (p220)

5   10   Santuario   4

La Piedra

5

Regla

27 de Noviembre   Parque
Guaicanamar

Camilo Cienfuegos

Via Blanca

SIGHTS & ACTIVITIES   (pp93–5 &
     pp144–8)
Colina Lenin.............................1 C6
Estadio Panamericano..............2 D1
Estatua de Cristo.....................3 A3
Iglesia de Nuestra Señora de
   Regla....................................4 B5
Museo Municipal de Regla........5 B5
Museo Municipal de Regla........(see 4)
Observatorio Nacional..............6 A3

EATING   (p126)
Cinco Esquinas.........................7 B5

TRANSPORT   (p93, pp184–9)
Bus M-3...................................8 D6
Ferry Wharf.............................9 A3
Ferry Wharf...........................10 B5

7   Albuquerque   24 de Febrero

Presno   Lenin

Carr Vieja de Regla

Martí

1   Independencia   Oeste

8   Independencia   Oeste

Habana Nueva

Calzada de Regla

**Altura de
Vía Blanca**

COJÍMAR

Boca de Cojímar

Alamar

Cojímar

To Estadio
Panamericano
(250m)

Av Central

Vía Monumental

Río Cojímar

Martí

Doble Vía

GUANABACOA

Regla

Eduardo
Chibás

Guanabacoa
Train Station

Río Cojímar

Rosalina

Soledad

Guanabacoa

La Lima

Parque
Martí

Independencia Oeste

Independencia Este

Calzada de Guanabacoa

Villa
Elena

PARQUE LENIN AREA

0		1 km
0		0.5 miles

See Playa & Marianao
Map (pp228–9)

To Plaza
de la
Revolución
(10.5km)

Av Verona

To Marianao
(5km)

To Guanabacoa
(26km)

Güinera

Arroyo
Naranjo

Av San Francisco

Av San Francisco

Primer Anillo de La Habana

Av San Francisco

Parque Zoológico
Nacional

Av Verona

Av Soto

Parque
Lenin

Carretera de Vento

Calzada de Bejucal

Fontanar

Av Zoo - Lenin

Cortina de La Presa

Embalse
Ejército
Rebelde

Río Almendares

Galápago
de Oro
Train Station

C 243

C 136

C 279

Embalse Paso
Sequito

C 152

Callejón del Jíbaro

Calabazar

(Av de Rancho Boyeros)

C 104

El Globo

C 277

C 289 (Calzada de Bejucal)

Río Pancho Simón

Carretera de Las Guásimas

To Caribbean Terminal
(Terminal 5,
1km)

Carretera de

Mulgas

Rancho Boyeros

Río Almendares

Carretera del Rocío

José Martí
International
Airport

Av Van Troi

Doble Vía

Jardín
Botánico
Nacional

To Terminal 3
(500m)

ExpoCuba
Train Station

Santiago de las Vegas

C 275

SIGHTS & ACTIVITIES	(pp96–7 & pp144–8)
Amusement Park	1 C3
Aquarium	2 C4
Club de Golf La Habana	3 A2
ExpoCuba	4 D5
Galería de Arte Amelia Peláez	5 D3
Horse Hire	6 C3
Japanese Garden	7 D5
Jardín Botánico Nacional	8 D5
Monument to Celia Sánchez	9 C4
Monument to Lenin	10 D4
Pabellones de Exposición	11 D5
Parque Lenin	12 C3
Parque Zoológico Nacional	13 A2
Rodeo Nacional	14 D3

EATING	(p127)
Las Ruinas	15 D4
Restaurante El Bambú	16 D5

TRANSPORT	(p96, pp184–9)
Bus M-2	17 A4
Terminal 1	18 A5
Terminal 2	19 A5